CENSORED 2019

FIGHTING THE FAKE NEWS INVASION

The Top Censored Stories and Media Analysis of 2017–18

Mickey Huff and Andy Lee Roth
with Project Censored

Foreword by
Abby Martin
Cartoons by
Khalil Bendib

Seven Stories Press

New York • Oakland • London

Seven Stories Press
140 Watts Street
New York, NY 10013
www.sevenstories.com

ISBN 978-1-60980-869-3 (paperback)

ISBN 978-1-60980-870-9 (electronic)

ISSN 1074-5998

9 8 7 6 5 4 3 2 1

Book design by Jon Gilbert

Printed in the USA

"The year 2018 marks a new chapter in the story of how the oligarchs try to kill the alternative press and adversarial reporting. Media titans and politicians are finding new ways to censor independent journalism on virtually every web platform under the banner of combating 'fake news' and 'foreign propaganda.' For truth-tellers and researchers facing this new assault, Project Censored and its annual book represent a vitally important tool for highlighting the crucial issues to know and struggles to follow, an essential guide for truth in a 'post-truth' society." —Abby Martin, *The Empire Files*, from the foreword to *Censored 2019*

"Today's fake news becomes tomorrow's fake history. Since 1976, Project Censored has been both calling out media propaganda and censorship as well as highlighting the best of the independent press. If journalism is the rough draft of history, this book goes a long way to getting the record right the first time, stopping fake news in its tracks and ensuring that we have fewer Untold Histories in the future." —Peter Kuznick and Oliver Stone, co-authors of *The Untold History of the United States* book and documentary series

PRAISE FOR PREVIOUS *CENSORED* VOLUMES

"A crucial contribution to the hope for a more just and democratic society."
—Noam Chomsky

"Project Censored is a national treasure in American life, serving to remind us of how crucial it is to be vigilant about making the truth heard in the public sphere . . . *Censored* gives new meaning to the notion that critical citizens are at the core of a strong democracy and that informed resistance is not an option but a necessity."
—Henry A. Giroux, author of *American Nightmare: Facing the Challenge of Fascism*

"Project Censored brings to light some of the most important stories of the year that you never saw or heard about. This is your chance to find out what got buried." —Diane Ravitch, author of *The Death and Life of the Great American School System*

"As trivia, celebrity gossip, blow-by-blow descriptions of the latest foibles of the political elites, entertainment, and corporate-approved stories replace journalism, real news happens increasingly on the fringes, where it is more easily marginalized and ignored. Project Censored rescues the most important stories you should have read but probably never saw from oblivion."
—Chris Hedges, bestselling author of *War is a Force That Gives Us Meaning* and *Empire of Illusion: The End of Literacy and the Triumph of Spectacle*

"The systematic exposure of censored stories by Project Censored has been an important contribution." —Howard Zinn, author of *A People's History of the United States*

"Project Censored is a lifeline to the world's most urgent and significant stories. The Project's list of the top stories that get very little mainstream media traction should in fact drive the reporting agendas of every major news outlet." —Naomi Wolf, author of the bestselling books *The Beauty Myth*; *The End of America*; and *Give Me Liberty*

"[Project Censored] is a clarion call for truth telling." —Daniel Ellsberg, *The Pentagon Papers*

"Project Censored . . . has evolved into a deep, wide, and utterly engrossing exercise to unmask censorship, self-censorship, and propaganda in the mass media." —Ralph Nader, consumer advocate, lawyer, and author

"[Project Censored's] efforts to continue globalizing their reporting network could not be more timely or necessary." —Kristina Borjesson, award-winning freelance journalist

"Most journalists in the United States believe the press here is free. That grand illusion only helps obscure the fact that, by and large, the US corporate press does not report what's really going on, while tuning out, or laughing off, all those who try to do just that. Americans—now more than ever—need those outlets that do labor to report some truth. Project Censored is not just among the bravest, smartest, and most rigorous of those outlets, but the only one that's wholly focused on those stories that the corporate press ignores, downplays, and/or distorts."—Mark Crispin Miller, author, professor of media ecology, New York University

"Project Censored continues to do the work they've been persistently pursuing since 1976: Exposing the secrets that those in power would prefer to keep hidden and the corruption that should be scandalous, but isn't, because the corporate media won't cover it." —David Rovics, musician and activist

"As Project Censored's publisher, I've been amazed at the resilience and joyfulness this organization has shown, year after year. Forever young, and ever more important, Project Censored makes us all better-informed and more empowered as citizens." —Dan Simon, Seven Stories Press

"Project Censored is one of the organizations that we should listen to, to be assured that our newspapers and our broadcasting outlets are practicing thorough and ethical journalism." —Walter Cronkite, anchor, *CBS Evening News*, 1962–1981

"One of the most significant media research projects in the country." —I.F. Stone, American muckraker

Contents

CHAPTER 2: Blurred Lines and Clickbait: The Sh*thole that is Junk Food News
by Susan Rahman and Isabelle Snow, with Tonatiuh Beltran, Tate Dobbins,
Jacqueline Gibbons, Maria Granados, Christina Hamilton, Whitney Howard,

CHAPTER 3: The Magic Trick of Establishment Media:
News Abuse in 2017–2018

CHAPTER 4: Media Democracy in Action
introduction by Steve Macek, with contributions by Samantha Parsons
(UnKoch My Campus), Hans-Joerg Tiede (American Association of
University Professors), Chenjerai Kumanyika (Uncivil), J. Spagnolo
and Elle Aviv Newton (Poets Reading the News), and

CHAPTER 5: Vetting Free Speech: How the United Kingdom Approaches
Freedom of Expression on Campus

CHAPTER 6: #TimesUp: Breaking the Barriers of Sexual Harassment in
Corporate Media for You and #MeToo

CHAPTER 7: Data Activism through Community Mapping
and Data Visualization

The Post-Truth Dilemma

Abby Martin

Donald Trump's stunning electoral victory sent the entrenched Washington, DC, establishment into a tailspin, blaming everyone and everything for Hillary's historic loss—*including me*.

That's right. The US government's official intelligence report on alleged Russian meddling zeroed in on my show *Breaking the Set* on RT America, which ended two years prior to the election, and accused it of fomenting "radical discontent" that contributed to Clinton's downfall.[1]

The actual content analyzed from the show was not about Vladimir Putin or Russia but about fracking, poverty, racism, and war. What the US intelligence apparatus was really saying is that covering these issues is a dangerous threat to democracy and should be vilified as sinister "Russian propaganda."

My generation woke up to the dangers of corporate media consolidation and obedience to sell the Bush Doctrine. Trust in mass media was already at a new low during the 2016 election.[2] But when Trump exploited the idea that the "liberal media" was out to destroy him, being suspect of the corporate press suddenly became a partisan issue.

Now, mass hallucinations abound. Everything is deemed "fake news" if it doesn't praise our anointed leader—or "Russian propaganda" if it counters the sneering punditry. Support for everything from Bernie Sanders to NFL protests to NRA dissent is cast as doing the bidding of the Kremlin. In this inverted reality, for example, criticisms of US foreign policy by third-party presidential candidate Jill Stein are dismissed as mere "Russian talking points."[3]

The Democratic Party has blamed Russia for everything to absolve their own institutional failures. They've enlisted the very same intelligence community that oversaw illegal torture, surveillance, and endless warfare waged against Muslim-majority countries to fight as the "resistance leaders" in this new era of fascism. Sticking with the strategy of courting Republicans, the Democrats are running a record number of former intelligence officials and members of the military in the upcoming elections.[4]

One DC think tank enlisted to fight the New Cold War is the Alliance for Securing Democracy, with its subproject Hamilton 68 Dashboard dedicated to tracking Russian trolls online. Although the group does not reveal its methodology, its findings are reported without question.[5] Curiously, the Alliance's advisory council is comprised of discredited hucksters cashing in on the Russia panic. Several Iraq War architects—Michael Chertoff, Bush's Department of Homeland Security head and co-author of the USA PATRIOT Act; Mike Morrell, former director of the CIA; and notorious neocon warmonger Bill Kristol—are duping the American public to build up US militarism yet again.[6]

Media giants act as if they oppose Trump, but they are precisely the ones who handed him the election by contributing nearly $5 billion in free advertising.[7] The corporate media act as if Trump's criticism of people like Jake Tapper is an affront to press freedom, but they are silent on Julian Assange's arbitrary detention, Israel's execution of journalists in Gaza, and other forms of state repression of reporters and publishers.

Journalists allege Trump is dangerous and mentally unfit, yet they don't oppose him on anything that significantly challenges power or corruption. In fact, they sing bipartisan praise whenever Trump embarks on yet another reckless bombing campaign, gives even more of our tax dollars to war profiteers, invokes debilitating sanctions, or issues belligerent threats against so-called enemy nations.

Appealing to the morality of the status quo press won't work. Under capitalism, the entire journalism industry has become nothing more than a vehicle for advertising. At a time when the planet is facing several cataclysmic environmental catastrophes, our news media are being subsidized and censored by banking institutions, weapons contractors, and oil companies.

The conflicts of interest are so blatant that, in addition to the rotating cast of defense contractors and military generals advocating war, networks even ran interactive segments for Raytheon's Tomahawk missiles after Trump bombed Syria.

The so-called papers of record, the *Washington Post* and *New York Times*, are among the largest purveyors of "fake news," doing PR for the empire with deadly consequences. But their junior partners, including Vox, Daily Beast, and Vice, are some of the worst offenders when it comes to rebranding imperial propaganda for millennials—same intent, different generation. It is easy to spot when they are all in lockstep over the major foreign policy issues of the day.

As the Western press disdains enemy state–funded media like Russia Today and teleSUR for "echoing the government line," the US corporate media machine directly parrots the Pentagon, acting as a dutiful arm of the state. It serves as a mouthpiece for imperial power by telling us who to regard as a foe: Iran, North Korea, Cuba, Venezuela, Syria, Russia, and China—not-so-coincidentally, all countries independent of US economic and military interests.

Clearly the largest empire in human history, the United States has established more than one thousand military bases across the globe, with military personnel in almost every country.[8] It enforces its economic order through brutal military might, and has intervened in countless countries to usurp their democratic processes. In the years since World War II, the United States has intervened at least 57 times to thwart political self determination around the world and secure access for Western business.[9] It has done the same from Latin America to Asia, Africa, Europe, and beyond.

Although it acts as the moral arbitrator of the earth, the United States supplies weapons and training to more than 70 percent of the world's dictatorships.[10] Its unfathomable military budget dwarfs the combined spending of the next 12 countries—all to the benefit of the ultra-rich, who reap astronomical profits while roughly half of the country lives in poverty. In the richest empire in history, 70 percent of the people have less than $1,000 in savings.[11]

This discussion would never be permitted on corporate media. Only a few narrow positions are heard, despite a wide range of opinions and widespread opposition to war. The parameters of debate perpetuate hierarchies of oppression.

Analyzing every issue in the context of how elites have shaped and colonized the planet shapes the narrative of my show, *The Empire Files*. I've traveled from the occupied West Bank to the deadly protests in Venezuela, from the militarized US–Mexico border to the front lines of the drug war in Colombia, and I've seen firsthand how the US media and government lie about the issues and events occurring all across the globe. The reality on the ground completely contradicts the narratives most Americans see, hear, and read.

All of the corporate media outlets are putting out the same stories—stories that serve the interests of the war machine. The alternative to corporate media hegemony that agitates for profits through global conflict is grassroots modes of information production and distribution that work for the people, on their behalf.

The value of Project Censored is that it staunchly lobbies for the commons, exposing the stories that corporate media want buried— the ones that can enrage, inspire, and lead to change. This year's edition highlights Big Pharma's role in the US opioid epidemic, which kills more than 100 Americans a day; $21 trillion of unaccounted-for spending by the US government even as healthcare-for-all is declared beyond reach; and the inspiring recognition of legal rights to protect nature on behalf of the world's indigenous communities. Debunking the empire's propaganda and exposing the truth can make a great impact to strengthen social movements, stop wars, and bring down the world's most powerful people.

The year 2018 marks a new chapter in the story of how the oligarchs try to kill the alternative press and adversarial reporting. Media titans and politicians are finding new ways to censor independent journalism on virtually every web platform under the banner of combating "fake news" and "foreign propaganda." For truth-tellers and researchers facing this new assault, Project Censored and its annual book represent a vitally important tool for highlighting the crucial issues to know and struggles to follow, an essential guide for truth in a "post-truth" society.

ABBY MARTIN is an anti-imperialist journalist, founder of Media Roots, former member of the board of directors at the Media Freedom Foundation/Project Censored, and creator of *The Empire Files*.

Notes

1. "Background to 'Assessing Russian Activities and Intentions in Recent US Elections': The Analytic Process and Cyber Incident Attribution," Office of the Director of National Intelligence, January 6, 2017, https://www.dni.gov/files/documents/ICA_2017_01.pdf.
2. Art Swift, "Americans' Trust in Mass Media Sinks to New Low," Gallup, September 14, 2016, http://news.gallup.com/poll/195542/americans-trust-mass-media-sinks-new-low.aspx.
3. Chris Cuomo, "Jill Stein: U.S. Interferes in Elections, Too," *New Day*, CNN, May 1, 2018, https://www.cnn.com/videos/politics/2018/05/01/jill-stein-russia-meddling-election-cuomo-sot-newday.cnn.
4. Patrick Martin, "The CIA Democrats, Part One," World Socialist Web Site, March 7, 2018, https://www.wsws.org/en/articles/2018/03/07/dems-m07.html.
5. For example, see Mary Papenfuss, "Russia-Linked Accounts Exploit Parkland Shooting on Twitter, Analysts Say," Huffington Post, February 15, 2018, https://www.huffingtonpost.com/entry/bots-exploit-parkland-tragedy_us_5a860acce4b05c2bcac91afo.
6. Matt Taibbi, "The New Blacklist," *Rolling Stone*, March 5, 2018, https://www.rollingstone.com/politics/taibbi-russiagate-trump-putin-mueller-and-targeting-dissent-w517486.
7. Jason Le Miere, "Did the Media Help Donald Trump Win? $5 Billion in Free Advertising Given to President-Elect," International Business Times, November 9, 2016, http://www.ibtimes.com/did-media-help-donald-trump-win-5-billion-free-advertising-given-president-elect-2444115.
8. David Vine, *Base Nation: How U.S. Military Bases Abroad Harm America and the World* (New York: Henry Holt and Company, 2015), 6, quoted on American Empire Project, undated, http://americanempireproject.com/base-nation/; and Nick Turse, "Empire of Bases 2.0: Does the Pentagon Really Have 1,180 Foreign Bases?" TomDispatch.com, January 11, 2011, http://www.tomdispatch.com/blog/175338/nick_turse_the_pentagon%27s_planet_of_bases.
9. William Blum, "Overthrowing Other People's Governments: The Master List," WilliamBlum.org, undated, https://williamblum.org/essays/read/overthrowing-other-peoples-governments-the-master-list.
10. Whitney Webb, "US Provides Military Aid to More Than 70 Percent of World's Dictatorships," MintPress News, September 27, 2017, https://www.mintpressnews.com/us-provides-military-aid-70-percent-worlds-dictatorships/232478/.
11. Emmie Martin, "Only 39% of Americans Have Enough Savings to Cover a $1,000 Emergency," CNBC, January 18, 2018, https://www.cnbc.com/2018/01/18/few-americans-have-enough-savings-to-cover-a-1000-emergency.html.

Introduction

Andy Lee Roth and Mickey Huff

THE BLACK SMOKE OF FAKE NEWS

"Fake news," "post-truth," "truth decay," "information disorders," and more—events from the past year continue to expand the public's vocabulary, and amplify its concern, over what one study from 2018 described as the "growing disregard for facts, data, and analysis in political and civil discourse in the United States."[1] We introduce this year's *Censored* yearbook—subtitled "Fighting the Fake News Invasion" and featuring cover art that updates H.G. Wells's 1898 novel, *The War of the Worlds*—at a period in US history when distrust in formerly respected sources of factual information is paralleled by a glut of propaganda that threatens to suffocate us, much like the "Black Smoke" employed to deadly effect by the invading Martians in Wells's science fiction classic.[2] To many, the present situation may seem as desolate as the landscape depicted in Anson Stevens-Bollen's cover art for this volume.

But *Censored 2019* is a book about *fighting* fake news. This introduction explains what we mean by that phrase and how we at Project Censored see this book's contributing authors and you, the reader, providing protection from and positive alternatives to the black smoke of fake news.

An effective fight against fake news requires at least two types of countermeasures. First, and most directly, we must expose specific instances of misinformation or disinformation. This begins with identifying and fact-checking dubious claims to truth. It extends to include holding correspondents and news outlets to account when they produce false or misleading reports, as this book's chapters on Junk Food News and News Abuse do, for example.

Though a number of often-cited studies have suggested that efforts to counter false or misleading claims ultimately "backfire"—leading true believers confronted by "inconvenient facts" to double down on their commitments to those beliefs—the validity of those studies' findings has been called into question, as Daniel Engber described in a crucial report published by Slate.[3] Instead of the vaunted "boomerang" effect, a trio of studies conducted by Andrew Guess at New York University and Alexander Coppock at Yale found that, when people were confronted with information that conflicted with their views on divisive topics such as capital punishment, gun control, or the minimum wage, the result was what Coppock described as "gorgeous parallel updating," meaning that subjects on either side of an issue adjusted their beliefs to better fit the facts.[4]

Guess and Coppock's findings and similar studies encourage us to continue writing, publicizing, and engaging in criticism of specific news reports and outlets that misinform or disinform the public. Such criticism constitutes a crucial resource in the fight against fake news.

But any successful fight against fake news must also look beyond specific instances of fake news itself—no matter how perspicuous or outrageous these may be—to identify and counter the larger social and cultural factors that make fake news persuasive. Fake news cannot be understood apart from the social networks that make its circulation possible. Put another way, the *contexts* in which fake news circulate are as important as its *contents*.[5] As a result, combatting fake news effectively also requires thinking critically about "how things are *categorised* and *labelled* as fake news" and "the politics of these practices of classification."[6] That broader project requires historical and comparative perspectives.

We start by traveling back in time 80 years to consider lessons from perhaps the most infamous radio broadcast in US history. The October 30, 1938 "War of the Worlds" program, broadcast by CBS Radio, presents an important case study in the creation, circulation, and long-term effects of fake news, and the issues that it raises—the fear of foreign invasion, the power of media, and the importance, and relative rarity, of critical thinking and fact-checking—remain crucial considerations in the struggle against the fake news invasion.

REVISITING *WAR OF THE WORLDS*

H.G. Wells's 1898 science fiction classic, *The War of the Worlds*, dramatized the invasion of Earth by extraterrestrial creatures whose intellectual and technological powers vastly surpassed the planet's human defenders.[7] Set in "the world of fast news, telegrams, [and] electricity" and grounded in the science of its day, Wells's story of a Martian invasion addressed with "tabloid speed" the themes of imperialism, colonization, and ecological disaster.[8]

As timely as these themes are today, in 1938, when Orson Welles and his colleagues planned a radio broadcast of *War of the Worlds*, many of those involved in the production, including Welles himself, expressed concerns that H.G. Wells's original version was so dated that no one listening to the program would find it compelling.[9] To grip the contemporary audiences' attention, the October 30, 1938 broadcast of CBS's *Mercury Theatre on the Air* used a number of dramatic devices to present the drama as though it were an actual crisis in progress. From the use of real place names, including Grover's Mill, near Princeton in New Jersey; to repeated "interruptions" of supposedly regular programming for "breaking news" bulletins featuring radio actors speaking on air authoritatively as news anchors, scientists, and government officials; to the dramatic use of "dead air," the broadcast innovatively deployed elements designed to convey realism.[10]

The broadcast became legendary for allegedly leading to widespread panic throughout the United States. For example, a 2013 PBS *American Experience* documentary about the renowned production began, "Never before had a radio broadcast provoked such outrage, or such chaos."[11] The *American Experience* narrative reflected decades of popular understanding of the broadcast's enduring significance, as an exemplar of the mass media's mighty influence and its audiences' vulnerability to broadcast-induced hysteria.

However, this popular interpretation of the broadcast is at odds with the facts, as Jefferson Pooley and Michael J. Socolow have documented in a series of articles. "The real story behind 'The War of the Worlds' is a bit more complex," they wrote in 2013. "Just as the size of Welles' audience has been exaggerated, so have reports of audience hysteria."[12] Examining the lesser-known history of the broadcast, Socolow and Pooley identify two key factors that explain the enduring and often-repeated tall tales about the broadcast's impacts.

First, the broadcast took place at a time when radio, a newly-developing medium, had begun to compete successfully with print for audience attention and advertising revenues. As Pooley and Socolow document, newspaper editors promoted stories of radio causing widespread panic and consequent public chaos in an effort to undermine trust in radio as a medium and to encourage government regulation of it. The newspaper industry "sensationalized the panic to prove to advertisers, and regulators, that radio management was irresponsible and not to be trusted."[13]

Second, an influential study of the broadcast, Hadley Cantril's *The Invasion from Mars: A Study in the Psychology of Panic* from 1940, reported that "several million American families all over the country gathered around their radios listening to reports of an invasion from Mars," causing "a panic of national proportions."[14] As one of the earliest attempts to evaluate empirically the effects of mass media on audiences, *The Invasion from Mars* "legitimized the myth of the night of terror as perhaps nothing else could."[15]

Despite Cantril's academic credentials, his analysis of the broadcast's impact willfully ignored evidence and promoted little more than a myth about it, as Socolow and Pooley have documented. Professional conflicts and financial motives led Cantril to overstate the broadcast's actual effects on the public.[16] As Pooley and Socolow wrote in a 2013 Slate article, Cantril "remains the only source with academic legitimacy who claims there was a sizable panic."[17] The book's most dramatic claims about widespread panic were nowhere supported by the data.[18]

The data presented in Cantril's book was collected—and most carefully analyzed—by two of Cantril's research assistants, Hazel Gaudet and Herta Herzog. A tension in *The Invasion from Mars*— between Cantril's dramatic claims about the broadcast's effects on its audience and the actual evidence as gathered and analyzed by Herzog and Gaudet—reflects what Pooley and Socolow described as "gender and class biases of academic culture," which "led to Cantril receiving authorship credit despite not having done the bulk of the work."[19]

In the two months following the original broadcast, Herta Herzog and a team of four other researchers (all female) interviewed 135 listeners, among whom 100 were chosen for the study because they had reported being frightened by the broadcast. The interviews showed that, although listeners found the broadcast "exciting," few actually believed it was real—and many engaged in what Herzog called "checking up" to determine that the Martian invasion was a fiction. Based on her analysis of these interviews, in a November 1938 memo Herta Herzog framed the study's central question: Why did some listeners "check up" on the validity of the broadcast while others did not?[20] As Pooley and Socolow document, Cantril resisted making Herzog's analysis of "checking up" central to the manuscript until a colleague (and rival), Paul Lazarsfeld, insisted on it.[21] Beyond its hyperbole, the most significant finding of Cantril's *Invasion from Mars*—namely that audience members used their "critical ability" in attempting to confirm the veracity of the extraordinary broadcast—originated with the research and insights of Herzog and Gaudet.[22]

In H.G. Wells's 1898 novel, humans were no match for the Martians' superior intelligence and technology. Instead, "after all man's devices had failed," the invading Martians were stopped and humanity was saved by "putrefactive" bacteria "against which their systems were unprepared."[23] In 1938, despite both radio's developing influence as a new mass medium and Orson Welles's canny sense of drama, "critical ability," employed by wary audience members who successfully "checked up" on the broadcast's veracity, saved the day, as it were, preventing the eruption of widespread panic. As a very human "device," critical ability—the sense of when and how to engage in "checking up," as Herta Herzog termed it—remains our best defense against an invasion of fake news.

CONNECTING FAKE NEWS AND CENSORSHIP: THE MAIDEN TRIBUTE SCANDAL OF 1885

Fake news is not new, of course, and CBS's 1938 radio broadcast was far from the first time that (some of) the public was gulled by reports of "news" that were flatly untrue.[24] Thus, for example, in 1835 the *New York Sun* published a series of articles that reported the discovery of life on the moon. At the time these hoax reports were widely accepted as true.[25]

History shows that fake news often engenders censorship and other restrictive measures. The Maiden Tribute scandal of 1885 represents a particularly clear case of news faked for the express purpose of influencing law, a purpose its author, William Thomas Stead, achieved despite ultimately having to serve time in prison for his unlawful investigative methods.[26]

In 1885 the *Pall Mall Gazette*, a London newspaper under the editorship of W.T. Stead, ran a sensationalized series of stories on the sex trafficking of children, which inspired a storm of moral indignation and some of the biggest political demonstrations in British political history.[27] The series published by Stead—titled "The Maiden Tribute of Modern Babylon"—supposedly exposed a "white slave trade" involving the capture of young English virgins and their sale as prostitutes to Belgian brothels.[28] After the series was underway, a crowd of some 300,000 people gathered in Hyde Park to express indignation at the criminal vice reported by the *Gazette*.

However, despite Stead's claim of presenting an "authentic record of unimpeachable facts," there were no real victims or slave traders.[29] Without real scandal, Stead and his confederates had arranged for the abduction of a 13-year-old girl, who was then subjected to a forced gynecological exam.

Stead was ultimately jailed for three months for his role in the episode, but by then the *Gazette*'s sensational coverage had already contributed to a burgeoning social purity movement. Most prominently, the National Vigilance Association (NVA) organized campaigns against indecency and immorality—wherever it imagined them to be in the increasingly broad scope of English public life. In 1890 London police helped the NVA to effectively close an exhibition of illustrations by François Rabelais. In Manchester, they seized 25,000 copies of works by Honoré de Balzac. And as a result of the NVA's efforts, an English publisher, Henry Vizetelly, was prosecuted for obscenity due to publishing translations of works by Émile Zola, Gustave Flaubert, and Guy de Maupassant.

The past year has provided ample evidence that the links between fake news (or the fear of it) and censorship did not end in the Victorian era. From Malaysia to France and beyond, a broad spectrum of news outlets has documented governments' efforts to come to grips with fake news by controlling news content.[30] Even in the United States, President Donald Trump has attempted to prevent publications by making the claim that their contents were false; Michael Wolff's exposé of the Trump White House, titled *Fire and Fury*, received strong government pushback, but Trump's attempted censorship of the book only increased the coverage it received in both corporate and independent media outlets.[31]

FIGHTING THE FAKE NEWS INVASION

Unfortunately, not all those who claim to fight fake news have the best intentions, particularly since the term can have myriad definitions.[32] As we noted in *Censored 2018*, the "weaponization" of the concept of fake news since the 2016 election has allowed it to be used by anyone who finds it convenient to disagree with a particular news story, no matter how factually supported that story may be, as a justification for favoring sources that utilize so-called "alternative facts."[33] This has further spawned Trojan horse efforts by the government and establishment media to confront what a majority of the US public believes is a "very serious threat to democracy," all in the name of the public good.[34]

Many of the organizations and institutions addressing fake news also have demonstrable conflicts of interest, and their agendas don't always align with free press principles or the standards promoted by the Society of Professional Journalists in its Code of Ethics.[35] Questionable efforts to address the fake news phenomenon include everything from state legislatures attempting to ban (i.e., censor) fake news, as *SB-1424* in California proposes to do,[36] to companies like Google and Facebook using proprietary algorithms to spike search results or ban pages and links to the websites of well-established investigative publications, such as *CounterPunch*, that consistently challenge official narratives and the status quo.[37]

These dubious efforts are like dragnets, removing far more than websites that produce *actual* fake stories or satire; they also marginalize outlets that publish fact-based investigative reporting about the very topics a free press ought to address in a democratic republic. The vetting is done in the name of fighting fake news, though it is clearly an attempt to establish a hierarchy of legitimacy among news sources, one in which the government, corporate media, and big tech companies determine what is real news and what is fake. This amounts to simply another form of propaganda and censorship, both of which must be exposed and opposed.

Shadowy organizations like PropOrNot (which the *Washington Post* showcased and lauded without reserve) and private fact-checking sites like Snopes may appear to be well intended measures to counter propaganda or misinformation, but these self-appointed watchdogs have at times crossed the line to produce propaganda and disinformation of their own, as independent journalists like Project Censored Award–winner Dave Lindorff have been pointing out for years. Lindorff was blacklisted by PropOrNot, purportedly as a means of "fighting fake news" and calling out "Russian propaganda."[38] As Abby Martin notes in the Foreword for this volume, she too was accused, by a US government intelligence report, of being a Russian propagandist through her show *Breaking the Set* on RT America, which actually focused on fact-based stories ignored by the corporate media in the United States, not tall tales penned by Putin from the Kremlin. Subsequently, RT America journalists were forced to register as foreign agents with the US Justice Department.[39] These McCarthyite actions run far afield of what we at Project Censored advocate in ensuring the maintenance of a truly diverse, robust, and free press.

One upside to the fervor over fake news is that coverage of it has drawn much-needed public attention to various media biases and issues of journalistic integrity. However, when coupled with the most recent attacks on net neutrality by the Trump administration and Ajit Pai's Federal Communications Commission, the fear of fake news contributes to a structural form of censorship that is legitimized by the establishment press. Thus, the *Washington Post* proclaims that "Democracy Dies in Darkness" while it promotes the blacklisting of non-corporate media sources and publishes fake news of its own; Google instructs "Don't be evil" as it undermines its own principles for an open Internet.[40]

Not all who claim to be fighting fake news are equal in putting the public interest first, or even in taking it into consideration. As Abby Martin notes in her Foreword, the establishment press often peddle half-truths and propaganda, even while simultaneously claiming to fight fake news.

INSIDE *CENSORED 2019*

As a continuation of Project Censored's ongoing campaign against contemporary censorship in its many guises, *Censored 2019* addresses the intertwined issues of fake news and censorship by bringing together a diverse group of authors and topics.

Chapter 1 presents the 25 most important but underreported news stories of 2017–2018 as determined by Project Censored's international judges, faculty evaluators, and student researchers. From a global decline in the rule of law (story #1) to the Federal Bureau of Investigation profiling "Black Identity Extremists" (story #10) and new restrictions on prisoners' First Amendment rights (story #23), this chapter once again highlights what the Project's founder, Carl Jensen, originally called "the news that didn't make the news." Like Ludwig Wittgenstein's famous duck–rabbit image, which appeared as either a rabbit or a duck depending on the viewer's orientation to the image, Project Censored's listing of the Top 25 underreported news stories of 2017–2018 can be read as a critique of the shortcomings of US corporate news media, for their failure to adequately cover these stories, or as a celebration of independent news media, without which we would remain either uninformed or misinformed about these crucial stories and issues.[41]

In Chapter 2, students from the College of Marin working with Susan Rahman document this year's most egregious "Junk Food News" stories. Since Project Censored founder Carl Jensen coined the term more than 35 years ago, sensationalist, titillating, and insignificant stories have increasingly invaded and dominated the daily and weekly news cycles. This chapter illustrates the antithesis of the kinds of stories showcased by the Top 25 in Chapter 1. Junk Food News stories are unfortunately ubiquitous, suggesting how style truly trumps substance and spectacle rules the day in much of what passes as "news" among journalism's corporate giants. This past year, while the major news media were once again infatuated with the ongoing shenanigans of the Kardashians and a porn-star-turned-whistleblower, Rahman and her students remind us that the corporate media could have been covering far more important and substantial stories—such as the more than 75 million acres of federal waters sold to the oil and gas industry, or the growing crisis of human trafficking and important steps we could take to stop it. Unfortunately, the mass media news outlets seemed far more interested in President Trump's "shithole" commentary and fleeting tweets than human rights or the environment.

In "The Magic Trick of Establishment Media," John Collins, Nicole Eigbrett, Jana Morgan, and Steve Peraza of Weave News track the past year's most telling examples of corporate media "News Abuse." Former Project Censored director Peter Phillips developed this analytical framework almost 20 years ago to draw attention to another way that corporate news coverage fails to inform the public. Whereas Junk Food News is sensationalistic and trite by nature, distracting and rarely significant, News Abuse, according to the Weave News team, is an "'abuse' of the public trust by news outlets that offer 'spin,' and sometimes outright propaganda, instead of prioritizing proper investigation." In Chapter 3, they write that "News Abuse perpetually operates like a magician's trick, using distraction to direct our attention away from what we really need to know." From distorted coverage of Trump voters, to the suppression of Palestinian perspectives on the Israeli occupation, to mischaracterizations of Black Lives Matter protests in the NFL, the establishment media mislead the public much as Lucy van Pelt double-crosses Charlie Brown, promising to hold the football for him to kick only to pull it away, thwarting both Charlie Brown's misplaced trust and earnest effort.

If the corporate media's Junk Food News and News Abuse often leave the public—like a hapless Charlie Brown—crying "Aaugh!" in frustration, then what is the alternative? Chapter 4, Media Democracy in Action, compiled by Steve Macek, highlights five exemplary initiatives in service of a better-informed public and more robust democracy. Samantha Parsons reports on the campaign by UnKoch My Campus to expose how the billionaire Koch brothers promote their "free market" ideology on campuses across the United States, while Hans-Joerg Tiede describes how the American Association of University Professors is protecting and defending academic freedom, which is essential if institutions of higher education are to serve the common good. Chenjerai Kumanyika, co-host of *Uncivil*, writes about how that podcast aims to "explode the misconceptions and myths" many Americans have about the Civil War and slavery, in order to create a community of citizens who can "push history forward based on that knowledge." As J. Spagnolo and Elle Aviv Newton report, *Poets Reading the News*, an online newspaper written entirely by poets, employs "journalism in verse" to offer unique, resilient responses to such complex issues as gun violence or family detention. And, as Eleanor Goldfield writes, her program, *Act Out!*, attempts to address two permanently pressing questions, "What can I do?" and "Why bother?" Cogently epitomizing the theme of this chapter, Media Democracy in Action, Goldfield proposes that we reframe those questions, asking instead, "What should we build?" and "Who's with me?"

In 2017–2018, disputes over free speech engulfed the campuses of the University of California, Berkeley, the College of William & Mary, and the University of Virginia (among others) and resulted in protests that one *Washington Post* report likened to "a war zone."[42] Sally Gimson, Layli Foroudi, and Sean Gallagher provide an invaluable comparative perspective on campus free speech issues by examining the history of government policies and legislation on free speech on university campuses in the United Kingdom. Their chapter, "Vetting Free Speech," explores how government directives, university policies, and the role of student unions have combined to impact free speech on UK campuses, including contemporary debates over no-platforming, safe spaces, and trigger warnings.

Julie Frechette writes about the manifestations and achievements of fourth-wave feminism in her timely chapter, "#TimesUp: Breaking the Barriers of Sexual Harassment in Corporate Media for You and #MeToo." Frechette analyzes the rise, breadth, and significance of #TimesUp, #MeToo, and related hashtivism movements that came to prominence in the wake of sexual harassment and assault revelations involving renowned celebrities like producer Harvey Weinstein, journalist Charlie Rose, and senator Al Franken. Looking beyond these high-profile cases to consider how low-wage women workers have been routinely exploited, harassed, and sexually assaulted with near impunity, her chapter argues that the historical landscape of patriarchal and misogynistic oppression may now be rapidly changing in what portends to be a paradigm-shifting social justice moment for women everywhere.

In Chapter 7, Dorothy Kidd shows how, in response to digital surveillance of our communications, financial transactions, and physical movements by corporate and government agencies, activists from around the world are harnessing and redirecting the power of "Big Data" to organize for social, economic, and political justice. From the maps produced by the Detroit Geographic Expedition and Institute from 1968 to 1970, to the contemporary use of GPS technology by the Unist'ot'en of northern British Columbia, Canada, as part of an ongoing "indigenous reoccupation" that opposes Chevron Canada's Pacific Trail Pipeline, to the San Francisco Anti-Eviction Mapping Project, Kidd documents "the value of this growing grassroots transnational data activism movement" as a counter to the might of Big Data, especially for groups that have been historically and systemically marginalized by state or corporate power.

In Chapter 8, Peter Phillips, former director of Project Censored and author of *Giants: The Global Power Elite*, explains why it is misleading to use the term "mainstream" to refer to the corporate media. By tracking the consolidation of media ownership alongside the history of Project Censored's own changing use of the terms "mainstream" and "corporate" in describing the nation's major news outlets, Phillips shows why it is no longer accurate to refer to today's corporate media as "mainstream" media. "Corporate media have become a monolithic power structure that serves the interests of empire, war, and capitalism," he writes. "For those of us interested in opposing the destructive agenda of empires of concentrated wealth, it's clearly time to stop using the term 'mainstream media' when 'corporate media' is both more accurate and revealing."

In Chapter 9, "Campus–Newsroom Collaborations: Building Bridges for Investigative Journalism," Patricia W. Elliott challenges the notion of professional journalists as "lock-step participants in corporate censorship." Her chapter describes how students in her courses at the University of Regina School of Journalism have participated successfully in collaborations with establishment journalists, alternative journalists, nonprofit foundations, and progressive research centers as part of Canada's National Student Investigative Reporting Network (NSIRN). Elliott describes how students in her Investigative Journalism and Intermediate Broadcast Journalism courses "were able to bring local voices—namely, rural and Indigenous people suffering from the health and environmental impacts of Saskatchewan's poorly regulated oil and gas industry—to national attention." The students' work helped to break "a long-held code of silence among rural and Indigenous communities that are economically dependent on the industry," she writes. The campus–newsroom collaborations fostered by the NSIRN provide an award-winning model that university faculty and journalists from other institutions could follow.

Censored 2019 concludes with Susan Maret's chapter on how to respond to fake news, bringing the volume back full circle to the themes highlighted in this introduction. Maret's chapter provides an overview of scholars' varied attempts to define this "unstable" phenomenon, before turning attention to how fake news is produced, proliferated, and even evaluated and filtered by the "invisible hand" of proprietary algorithms, which in turn are shaped by advertising networks, hidden agendas, and the public's own information-seeking behaviors. Maret concludes with an examination of ongoing initiatives and promising approaches to address the "controversial, geopolitical social problem" of fake news.

NEWS SMOKE SCREENS OF THE 21ST CENTURY

Eighty years after the "War of the Worlds" broadcast, as fake news moves beyond radio waves and becomes ever more technologically sophisticated, we have our own "black smoke" with which to contend. In our online world, information of any type or quality is just a click, a like, and a share away from traveling around the globe in seconds.

Aviv Ovadya, the chief technologist at the University of Michigan's Center for Social Media Responsibility, presciently warned of a pending "fake news crisis" in the United States before the 2016 presidential election. Ovadya sounded an alarm on what he called an "Infocalypse" (an information apocalypse). In a February 2018 article titled "Infocalypse Now," senior BuzzFeed writer Charlie Warzel updated Ovadya's warning, observing,

> The web and the information ecosystem that had developed around it was wildly unhealthy . . . Platforms like Facebook, Twitter, and Google prioritized clicks, shares, ads, and money over quality of information . . . Our platformed and algorithmically optimized world is vulnerable—to propaganda, to misinformation, to dark targeted advertising from foreign governments—so much so that it threatens to undermine a cornerstone of human discourse: the credibility of fact.[43]

Though certainly driven by propaganda techniques from the past, the new black smoke of fake news now includes bots, trolls, algorithms, filter bubbles, and something called "automated laser phishing," which uses online social media data to create fake video and audio of individuals doing or saying anything, whether or not it ever really happened. If that's not enough, add "diplomacy manipulation" (creating public belief in a particular event that may not have occurred), and "polity simulation" (digital astroturfing used to manipulate political movements online).[44] These technologies are already a reality, and they challenge us to second-guess almost everything we hear, read, or see. Such tools of digital manipulation have even sparked new scholarship updating the classic Propaganda Model of news established by Edward S. Herman and Noam Chomsky 30 years ago to include not only what Ovadya discussed, but also deep state disinformation (such as Central Intelligence Agency media), filter bubbles, and "sock puppets," to name a few well-developed weapons of mass deception.[45] Technology changes quickly and its impacts are often hidden or difficult to understand, which makes keeping adequately informed even more challenging. Furthermore, as reported by Warzel, the very existence of these technologies of manipulation has prompted one computational propaganda scholar, Renee DiResta, to remark,

> Whether it's AI, peculiar Amazon manipulation hacks, or fake political activism—these technological underpinnings [lead] to the increasing erosion of trust . . . It makes it possible to cast aspersions on whether videos—or advocacy for that matter—are real . . . You don't need to create the fake video for this tech to have a serious impact. You just point to the fact that the tech exists and you can impugn the integrity of the stuff that's real.[46]

This has, in fact, already happened. President Trump claimed that the voice on the infamous *Access Hollywood* tape uttering the now-infamous words "grab 'em by the pussy" was digitally faked, because technology experts simply confirmed that it *could* have been. Ovadya wondered, "What happens when anyone can make it appear as if anything has happened, regardless of whether or not it did?"[47] The public's constant bombardment with potentially questionable information creates something Ovadya calls "reality apathy," which occurs when people become so overwhelmed with trying to distinguish what is fake from what is real that they either trust only the news stories that confirm their previously-held beliefs, or, worse yet, they stop attending to news altogether.[48] The latter outcome insures widespread ignorance in a democratic system of governance that requires an informed public if it is to be functional and claim any legitimacy.

CONCLUSION

What Ovadya described is something similar to what we at Project Censored called a "Truth Emergency" over a decade ago, and now refer to as an epistemological crisis. But both Ovadya and Project Censored also recognize signs that people are waking up to the challenges posed by fake news. We firmly believe that critical media education—rather than censorship, blacklists, privatized fact-checkers, or legislative bans—is the best weapon for fighting the ongoing fake news invasion. It is this kind of critical pedagogy that must be adopted to fend off the "black smoke" of fake news propaganda, whether it be foreign or domestic in origin. In addition, a vibrant, independent free press, with transparently-sourced facts and a broad spectrum of perspectives, is necessary in educating and informing the public on key issues of our times. In the end, we will need to arm the public with the "critical ability" to "check up" on the veracity of news broadcasts and publications themselves, even as we attempt to collectively confront the "War of the Worlds" of our time, manifest in our 21st-century media landscape as a war of *words*.

We offer *Censored 2019* as one small—but, we hope, significant—contribution to fighting the fake news invasion. We hope that readers not only enjoy this year's volume but will use the information and ideas presented here to help create a more informed and engaged, equitable and just society.

Notes

1. Jennifer Kavanagh and Michael D. Rich, *Truth Decay: An Initial Exploration of the Diminishing Role of Facts and Analysis in American Public Life* (Santa Monica, CA: RAND Corporation, 2018), iii.
2. In the novel, an official dispatch reported, "The Martians are able to discharge enormous clouds of a black and poisonous vapour by means of rockets . . . It is impossible to stop them. There is no safety from the Black Smoke but in instant flight." H.G. Wells, *The War of the Worlds* (New York: Penguin, 2007 [first published in book form in London by William Heinemann in 1898]), 90.
3. Daniel Engber, "LOL Something Matters," Slate, January 3, 2018, https://slate.com/health-and-science/2018/01/weve-been-told-were-living-in-a-post-truth-age-dont-believe-it.html.
4. Engber, "LOL Something Matters"; and Andrew Guess and Alexander Coppock, "The Exception, Not the Rule? The Rarely Polarizing Effect of Challenging Information," *Alexander Coppock* blog, August 24, 2016, https://alexandercoppock.files.wordpress.com/2014/11/back-lash_apsa.pdf.
5. Liliana Bounegru, Jonathan Gray, Tommaso Venturini, and Michele Mauri, *A Field Guide to "Fake News" and Other Information Disorders* (Amsterdam: Public Data Lab, 2017), 8, https://fakenews.publicdatalab.org/.

6. Ibid., 9–10.
7. *Pearson's Magazine* in the United Kingdom and *Cosmopolitan* magazine in the United States originally published Wells's story in serial form in 1897.
8. Iain Sinclair, "An Introduction to *The War of the Worlds*," British Library, May 15, 2014, https://www.bl.uk/romantics-and-victorians/articles/an-introduction-to-the-war-of-the-worlds. The Martians devastate Earth by discharging "enormous clouds of a black and poisonous vapour" (Wells, *War of the Worlds*, 90), but, in a rich twist of storytelling, Wells also established that the Martians' invasion of Earth was motivated by the depletion of their own planet's natural resources. In the novel's opening pages, the narrator explains conditions on Mars. With an "attenuated" supply of air and the melting of huge polar snowcaps, the Martians' planet has entered its "last stage of exhaustion" (6). Wells's narrator drives the point home: "Before we judge of them too harshly," he urges, "we must remember what ruthless and utter destruction our own species has wrought" (7).
9. See A. Brad Schwartz, *Broadcast Hysteria: Orson Welles's* War of the Worlds *and the Art of Fake News* (New York: Farrar, Straus and Giroux, 2015), 45ff.
10. For example, in the broadcast a news reporter identified as Carl Phillips narrates in real-time as police officers with a white flag of truce approach one of the extraterrestrials' ships. As Phillips breathlessly describes the Martian vessel opening fire with a jet of flame on the officers and surrounding crowd, the broadcast suddenly cuts off. "In CBS's Studio One, Welles held the pause like a conductor for a full six seconds while his cast and crew waited anxiously to get on with the show" (Schwartz, *Broadcast Hysteria*, 75–76). During that silence, many of the audience believed that "they had just heard Phillips and countless others burned to death live on the air" (76).
11. Transcript, "War of the Worlds," *American Experience*, PBS, October 29, 2013, http://www.pbs.org/wgbh/americanexperience/films/worlds/.
12. Jefferson Pooley and Michael J. Socolow, "The Myth of the *War of the Worlds* Panic," Slate, October 28, 2013, http://www.slate.com/articles/arts/history/2013/10/orson_welles_war_of_the_worlds_panic_myth_the_infamous_radio_broadcast_did.html.
13. Ibid.
14. Hadley Cantril, with the assistance of Hazel Gaudet and Herta Herzog, *The Invasion from Mars: A Study in the Psychology of Panic* (New York: Routledge, 2017 [first published in Princeton, NJ, by Princeton University Press in 1940]), 67, 3.
15. Michael J. Socolow, "The Hyped Panic Over 'War of the Worlds,'" *Chronicle of Higher Education*, October 24, 2008, https://www.chronicle.com/article/The-Hyped-Panic-Over-War-of/19341.
16. Jefferson D. Pooley and Michael J. Socolow, "Checking Up on *The Invasion from Mars*: Hadley Cantril, Paul F. Lazarsfeld, and the Making of a Misremembered Classic," *International Journal of Communication* 7 (2013): 1920–48, 1940. See also Jefferson Pooley and Michael J. Socolow, "War of the Words: *The Invasion from Mars* and Its Legacy for Mass Communication Scholarship," in *War of the Worlds to Social Media: Mediated Communication in Times of Crisis*, eds. Joy Elizabeth Hayes, Kathleen Battles, and Wendy Hilton-Morrow (New York: Peter Lang, 2013), 35–56.
17. Pooley and Socolow, "The Myth of the *War of the Worlds* Panic."
18. "The book, to some extent, mimicked the theatricality that was its ostensible subject." Pooley and Socolow, "Checking Up on *The Invasion from Mars*," 1940.
19. Pooley and Socolow, "War of the Words," 37.
20. Ibid.
21. Ibid., 41.
22. Hazel Gaudet analyzed audience data from CBS, which broadcast the program, to determine links between "critical ability" and listeners' education levels. Ibid., 41.
23. Wells, *War of the Worlds*, 184–85.
24. See also, Mickey Huff and Andy Lee Roth, "Introduction," in *Censored 2018: Press Freedoms in a "Post-Truth" World*, eds. Andy Lee Roth and Mickey Huff with Project Censored (New York: Seven Stories, 2017), 17–30, 19ff. For more background on the history of fake news, see *Lapham's Quarterly* (January 2018, Special Issue: "A History of Fake News").

25. In an afterword to *War of the Worlds*, Isaac Asimov considered the *Sun* series in historical context. See Isaac Asimov, "Afterword," in Wells, *War of the Worlds*, 198–206.

26. The following paragraphs draw on Judith R. Walkowitz, *City of Dreadful Delight: Narratives of Sexual Danger in Late-Victorian London* (Chicago: University of Chicago Press, 1992); and Gretchen Soderlund, *Sex Trafficking, Scandal, and the Transformation of Journalism, 1885–1917* (Chicago: University of Chicago Press, 2013).

27. Incidentally, in *War of the Worlds*, H.G. Wells's narrator referred in passing to the *Pall Mall Budget*, a weekly digest of articles from the *Gazette*. The narrator described an article by a "speculative writer of quasi-scientific repute" (Wells, *War of the Worlds*, 140).

28. Stead hoped that his newspaper's dramatic coverage would bolster a campaign to force Parliament to raise the age of sexual consent. The original texts of the four-part series are archived at the W.T. Stead Resource Site, https://attackingthedevil.co.uk/pmg/tribute/.

29. "Authentic record": W.T. Stead, "Notice to Our Readers: A Frank Warning," *Pall Mall Gazette*, July 4, 1885, online at https://attackingthedevil.co.uk/pmg/tribute/notice.php/.

30. See, for example, Andrew Stuttaford, "Fake News, Real Censorship," *National Review*, January 6, 2018, https://www.nationalreview.com/corner/fake-news-real-censorship/; Jeremy Malcolm, "Malaysia Set to Censor Political Speech as Fake News," Electronic Frontier Foundation, March 27, 2018, https://www.eff.org/deeplinks/2018/03/malaysia-set-censor-political-speech-fake-news; and Jon Henley, "Global Crackdown on Fake News Raises Censorship Concerns," *The Guardian*, April 24, 2018, https://www.theguardian.com/media/2018/apr/24/global-crackdown-on-fake-news-raises-censorship-concerns.

31. A representative sampling of corporate and independent coverage includes Sarah Begley, "'Flagrantly Unconstitutional.' *Fire and Fury* Publisher Attacks Trump's Attempt to Block Book," *Time*, January 8, 2018, http://time.com/5092923/fire-fury-michael-wolff-publisher-trump-unconstitutional/; Brian Stelter, "President Trump Tries to Quash Bombshell Book," CNN, January 4, 2018, http://money.cnn.com/2018/01/04/media/president-trump-legal-threat-michael-wolff/index.html; James West, "'Fire and Fury' is on Track to Beat 'The Art of the Deal,' Trump's Own Bestseller," *Mother Jones*, January 18, 2018, https://www.motherjones.com/media/2018/01/fire-and-fury-is-on-track-to-beat-the-art-of-the-deal-trumps-own-best-seller/; and Reed Richardson, "Wolff's Trump Book Highlights White House Press Corps' Access Trap," Fairness & Accuracy In Reporting (FAIR), January 9, 2018, https://fair.org/home/wolffs-trump-book-highlights-white-house-press-corps-access-trap/.

32. For more on these definitions, see two talks by Project Censored director Mickey Huff delivered at Sonoma State University's Social Justice Week events, "Propaganda and Censorship in a Post-Truth World," April 2017, https://www.youtube.com/watch?v=hFbqmEXxYPI; and "Fake News and the Truth Emergency," March 2018, https://www.youtube.com/watch?v=7D82maqwoEI.

33. Huff and Roth, "Introduction," *Censored 2018*, 18–20. In that same volume, see also Chapter 2, Nolan Higdon and Mickey Huff et al., "Post-Truth Dystopia: Fake News, Alternative Facts, and the Ongoing War on Reality," pp. 107–138.

34. "American Views: Trust, Media and Democracy," Knight Foundation, January 16, 2018, https://knightfoundation.org/reports/american-views-trust-media-and-democracy; see the full report, published by Gallup, online at https://kf-site-production.s3.amazonaws.com/publications/pdfs/000/000/242/original/KnightFoundation_AmericansViews_Client_Report_010917_Final_Updated.pdf.

35. "Code of Ethics," Society of Professional Journalists (SPJ), revised September 6, 2014, https://www.spj.org/ethicscode.asp. SPJ lists the following four main principles that all journalists should follow: Seek Truth and Report It, Minimize Harm, Act Independently, and Be Accountable and Transparent.

36. *SB-1424 Internet: Social Media: Advisory Group*, introduced by Senator Richard Pan, February 16, 2018, amended in the California State Senate, March 22, 2018, published on California Legislative Information on May 25, 2018, https://leginfo.legislature.ca.gov/faces/billTextClient.xhtml?bill_id=201720180SB1424.

37. Dave Lindorff, "The Attack on 'Fake News' is Really an Attack on Alternative Media," Salon, November 6, 2017, https://www.salon.com/2017/11/06/the-attack-on-fake-news-is-really-an-attack-on-alternative-media/; Matthew Sheffield, "'Fake News' or Free Speech: Is Google Cracking Down on Left Media?" Salon, October 18, 2017, https://www.salon.com/2017/10/18/fake-news-or-free-speech-is-google-cracking-down-on-left-media/; and Andre Damon, "Facebook and Google Outline Unprecedented Mass Censorship at US Senate Hearing," World Socialist Web Site, January 18, 2018, https://www.wsws.org/en/articles/2018/01/18/cens-j18.html.

38. Lindorff, "The Attack on 'Fake News.'"

39. Aaron Maté, "RT was Forced to Register as a Foreign Agent," *The Nation*, November 16, 2017, https://www.thenation.com/article/rt-was-forced-to-register-as-a-foreign-agent/.

40. Higdon and Huff et al., "Post-Truth Dystopia"; and Sheffield, "'Fake News' or Free Speech." See also Robert Epstein, "The New Censorship: How Did Google Become the Internet's Censor and Master Manipulator, Blocking Access to Millions of Websites?" *U.S. News & World Report*, June 22, 2016, https://www.usnews.com/opinion/articles/2016-06-22/google-is-the-worlds-biggest-censor-and-its-power-must-be-regulated.

41. Ludwig Wittgenstein, *Philosophical Investigations*, 4th ed., trs. G.E.M. Anscombe, P.M.S. Hacker, and Joachim Schulte (Malden, MA: Wiley-Blackwell, 2009), 204. An English translation of the book was first published in Oxford by Basil Blackwell in 1953; the German original was not published until later, in 1958.

42. Jeffrey J. Selingo, "College Students Support Free Speech—Unless It Offends Them," *Washington Post*, March 12, 2018, https://www.washingtonpost.com/local/college-students-support-free-speech--unless-it-offends-them/2018/03/09/79f21c9e-23e4-11e8-94da-ebf9d112159c_story.html.

43. Charlie Warzel, "Infocalypse Now: He Predicted the 2016 Fake News Crisis. Now He's Worried About an Information Apocalypse," BuzzFeed, February 11, 2018, https://www.buzzfeed.com/charliewarzel/the-terrifying-future-of-fake-news. While technologist Aviv Ovadya's concerns are duly noted in this article, there are serious questions regarding *what to do* about fake news that do not involve censorship, which is why Project Censored continues to advocate for critical media literacy education and an open, free press. For more on these concerns, see Sam Wayne and Genevieve Leigh, "University of Michigan Center for Social Media Responsibility Provides Cover for Internet Censorship Campaign," World Socialist Web Site, June 13, 2018, https://www.wsws.org/en/articles/2018/06/13/csmr-j13.html.

44. Warzel, "Infocalypse Now."

45. On these themes, see, for example, Rob Williams, "*The Post* (Truth) World: Reviving the 'Propaganda Model of News' for Our Digital Age," Project Censored, February 2018, https://projectcensored.org/wp-content/uploads/2018/02/PostTruthPMON_WilliamsFinal-2.pdf. For more on CIA media, see Brian Covert, "Played by the Mighty Wurlitzer: The Press, the CIA, and the Subversion of Truth," in *Censored 2017: Fortieth Anniversary Edition*, eds. Mickey Huff and Andy Lee Roth with Project Censored (New York: Seven Stories Press, 2016), 251–84, also online at http://projectcensored.org/wp-content/uploads/2017/09/C17_06_Covert_Played.pdf.

46. Renee DiResta, quoted in Warzel, "Infocalypse Now."

47. Aviv Ovadya, quoted in Warzel, "Infocalypse Now."

48. Ibid.

CHAPTER 1

THE TOP *CENSORED* STORIES AND MEDIA ANALYSIS OF 2017–18

Compiled and edited by Andy Lee Roth

INTRODUCTION

A 2016 RAND study, "The Russian 'Firehose of Falsehood' Propaganda Model," identified two features of the "remarkable evolution" in Russian propaganda since 2008.[1] According to the study's authors, Christopher Paul and Miriam Matthews, contemporary Russian propaganda is distinguished by "high numbers of channels and messages" and a "shameless willingness to disseminate partial truths or outright fictions."

Paul and Matthews proposed two elementary ways to counter Russian propaganda. First, prime audiences with accurate information. Second, rather than fighting specific manipulations, identify the techniques that propagandists regularly use to manipulate audiences.[2]

Although the RAND Corporation and Project Censored differ in myriad ways, the recommendations drawn from the "Firehose of Falsehood" study could also serve to describe the aims of Project Censored's Validated Independent News program.

First, by highlighting important but underreported independent news stories, the Validated Independent News (VIN) program seeks to inform a broad public about news stories that corporate media have marginalized, distorted, or entirely ignored. This chapter features the 25 most important but underreported independent news stories of 2017–2018, as identified and vetted through a rigorous process originally established in 1976 by Project Censored's founder, Carl Jensen. This vetting process aims to ensure that the independent news stories featured here are not only serious and trustworthy works of journalism, but also that they provide information and perspectives on their subject matter that cannot be found in corporate news media. By expanding the range of topics and perspectives deemed newsworthy by the establishment press, the independent reporters and news outlets featured in the following list prime audiences with accurate information and informed perspectives that might otherwise remain unknown.

The Project's VIN program also addresses the second RAND study recommendation, highlighting *how* news can function as propaganda to manipulate audiences. Since 1976, Project Censored has engaged undergraduate students in the task of identifying and vetting the independent news stories that become candidates for inclusion in each year's Top 25 story list. This year, 351 students under the guidance of 15 faculty mentors from 13 college and university campuses across North America participated in this process. Altogether, they identified, reviewed, and summarized more than 300 independent news stories published since March 2017. The stories that passed this review process were posted on Project Censored's website[3] as part of what can be understood as a *networked news commons*.[4] The 25 stories featured in this chapter represent the very best of these students' efforts.

Regardless of whether or not a given story earned a coveted spot in the Top 25 list, in each case the work of identifying, summarizing, and evaluating the news coverage on a given topic provided students with direct, "hands-on" opportunities to assess how corporate news media might function as purveyors of propaganda. Whether working independently or as a member of a small team, each student participating in the Project's Validated Independent News program employed critical thinking skills (e.g., analysis, interpretation, evaluation) in combination with online databases (e.g., ProQuest's Global Newsstream, LexisNexis Academic, EBSCO's Alternative Press Index) in ways that:

> ▸ strengthen critical thinking skills and media literacy,[5]
> ▸ sharpen alertness to a variety of "information disorders,"[6] and
> ▸ enhance appreciation for the importance of a truly free press.

Students' hands-on engagement makes these lessons more powerful and indelible than if similar points had been conveyed through passive learning (e.g., sitting in a lecture hall listening to a talk on the subject, or "cramming" for an exam).

Linking students and faculty from colleges across North America (and, at times, around the world) is one of the crucial elements that make the Validated Independent News program successful. As students in the courses that we teach begin researching their VINs, faculty inform them that they're part of a project that has been underway since 1976. In our experience, students are hungry to contribute to something meaningful that goes beyond the confines of their classrooms. As they come to develop expertise and passion for their story topics, publishing their findings online and in the Project's yearbook gives them a public voice that they might not otherwise have. They become informed and compelling advocates for issues that the general public may not adequately understand. Thus, students' direct, hands-on development of their critical thinking and media literacy skills contributes to an enduring, collective effort to better inform the public about the importance of a truly free press and the existence of high-quality alternatives to the corporate versions of the news that otherwise set a narrow agenda for what and who counts as "important" and "newsworthy" in the United States.

In the "Firehose of Falsehood" study, Paul and Matthews characterized contemporary Russian propaganda as "high-volume and multichannel," "rapid, continuous, and repetitive," and lacking in commitment to "objective reality" and "consistency."[7] Although RAND identified these features as "distinctive" to contemporary Russian propaganda, with some important caveats and exceptions the same descriptors might equally apply to much of what passes for the "news" provided by US corporate media.[8]

Project Censored's annual story lists document the corporate news media's "blind spots and lacunae, its third rails and 'no go' zones" while highlighting and encouraging public support for exemplary independent news reporting.[9] These aims align with the recommendations of the RAND study discussed here: priming the public with accurate information and exposing how propaganda works to persuade. The Project, however, parts ways with the RAND study's framing of propaganda as exclusively a foreign import. For Project Censored, regardless of whether the source in question is foreign or domestic, the aim is to expose and oppose when "news" functions as propaganda.

There's no single, simple answer to the question of why the corporate media have failed to cover the stories that comprise each year's list of *Censored* stories. But one important cause of censorship in journalism can be found in the news media's corporate ties; indeed, it is important to bear in mind that, although many people refer to the nation's major newspapers, TV networks, and cable news stations as the "mainstream" media, it is more accurate to identify these news organizations as *corporate* media.[10] As Edward S. Herman and Noam Chomsky argued in their classic work, *Manufacturing Consent*, news produced by corporate outlets is "filtered" by the imperative to produce profits in the form of advertising revenues.[11] News that does not serve, or runs contrary to, these corporate interests is either not covered at all or is only covered in a partial (incomplete and/or slanted) way.

As with previous years' *Censored* lists, the story summaries that follow are not intended to replace the original news reports on which they are based. Instead, the synopses highlight the stories' key points, ideally in a form that encourages interested readers to retrieve and read the original reports themselves. We present this year's Top 25 story list in hope of informing you, the reader; encouraging you to engage friends, family, and colleagues in conversations on these topics; and, ideally, galvanizing you to action on some of the public issues documented so vividly by the independent reports and news outlets whose work we celebrate.

ACKNOWLEDGMENTS: Geoff Davidian, April Anderson, and Nicole Weeks provided invaluable assistance and welcome camaraderie in helping to prepare this year's slate of several hundred Validated Independent News stories for the Top 25 vote by our panel of judges. Matthew Aldea, April Anderson, Jessica Irrera, Sierra Kaul, Stephanie Richter, Lewis Joseph Smith, Kelly Van Boekhout, Nicole Weeks, and Ryan Wilson undertook the final vetting of this year's *Censored* stories.

A NOTE ON RESEARCH AND EVALUATION
OF *CENSORED* NEWS STORIES

How do we at Project Censored identify and evaluate independent news stories, and how do we know that the Top 25 stories that we bring forward each year are not only relevant and significant, but also trustworthy? The answer is that each candidate news story undergoes rigorous review, which takes place in multiple stages during each annual cycle. Although adapted to take advantage of both the Project's expanding affiliates program and current technologies, the vetting process is quite similar to the one Project Censored founder Carl Jensen established over forty years ago.

Candidate stories are initially identified by Project Censored professors and students, or are nominated by members of the general public, who bring them to the Project's attention through our website.[11] Together, faculty and students vet each candidate story in terms of its importance, timeliness, quality of sources, and corporate news coverage. If it fails on any one of these criteria, the story is not included.

Once Project Censored receives the candidate story, we undertake a second round of judgment, using the same criteria and updating the review to include any subsequent, competing corporate coverage. Stories that pass this round of review get posted on our website as Validated Independent News stories (VINs).[12]

In early spring, we present all VINs in the current cycle to the faculty and students at all of our affiliate campuses, and to our national and international panel of judges, who cast votes to winnow the candidate stories from several hundred to twenty-five.

Once the Top 25 list has been determined, Project Censored student interns begin another intensive review of each story using LexisNexis and ProQuest databases. Additional faculty and students contribute to this final stage of review.

The Top 25 finalists are then sent to our panel of judges, who vote to rank them in numerical order. At the same time, these experts—including media studies professors, professional journalists, and a former commissioner of the Federal Communications Commission, among others—offer their insights on the stories' strengths and weaknesses.[13]

Thus, by the time a story appears in the pages of *Censored*, it has undergone at least five distinct rounds of review and evaluation.

Although the stories that Project Censored brings forward may be socially and politically controversial—and sometimes even psychologically challenging—we are confident that each is the result of serious journalistic effort, and therefore deserves greater public attention.

THE TOP *CENSORED* STORIES AND MEDIA ANALYSIS OF 2017–18

1

Global Decline in Rule of Law as Basic Human Rights Diminish

Will Bordell and Jon Robins, "'A Crisis for Human Rights': New Index Reveals Global Fall in Basic Justice," *The Guardian*, January 31, 2018, www.theguardian.com/inequality/2018/jan/31/human-rights-new-rule-of-law-index-reveals-global-fall-basic-justice.

Student Researcher: Kyle Zucker (College of Marin)

Faculty Evaluator: Susan Rahman (College of Marin)

A 2018 survey conducted in response to global concerns about rising authoritarianism and nationalism shows a major decrease in nations adhering to basic human rights. As the *Guardian* reported, the World Justice Project (WJP)'s "Rule of Law Index 2017–2018" examined legal systems around the world by documenting the experiences of 110,000 households and 3,000 experts and comparing the data with results from previous years.[15] The WJP's Index tabulated these results to calculate scores in eight different categories, including constraints on government powers, absence of corruption, open government, regulatory enforcement, and civil justice, providing an overview of changes in the rule of law since the previous Index was published in October 2016.

In summarizing the WJP's findings, the *Guardian's* report quoted Samuel Moyn, a professor of law and history at Yale University: "All signs point to a crisis not just for human rights, but for the human rights movement. Within many nations, these fundamental rights are falling prey to the backlash against a globalising economy in which the rich are winning."

Since 2016, when the previous WJP Rule of Law Index was published, overall rule of law scores declined in 38 countries, with the greatest declines occurring in the category of fundamental rights, which measures absence of discrimination, right to life and security, due process, freedom of expression and religion, right to privacy, freedom of association, and labor rights. From 2016 to 2018, 71 countries out of 113 dropped in this category. Constraints on government powers, which measures the extent to which those who govern are

bound by law, saw the second greatest declines (64 countries out of 113 dropped).

The Philippines saw the greatest decline in overall rule of law, falling 18 positions to 88th out of 113 countries overall, based on significant drops in constraints on government powers, fundamental rights, order and security, and criminal justice. As the *Guardian* reported, "President Rodrigo Duterte's administration has put a 'palpable strain upon established countervailing institutions of society,' according to Jose Luis Martin Gascon, chairman of the Philippine Commission on Human Rights." Gascon described a "chilling effect" on the country's opposition after attacks on public figures who had criticized Duterte's policies.

Three countries—Burkina Faso, Kazakhstan, and Sri Lanka—improved in the overall rule of law rankings from 2016 by nine positions, according to the WJP's report.

The *Guardian* noted that the United States ranked just 19th out of the 35 countries classified as "high-income" in the report. In the fundamental rights category, the United States fell five places to 26th overall as a result of "worsening levels of discrimination and due process of law plus decreased guarantees of the right to life."

The WJP's 2017–2018 Rule of Law Index received scant attention from US corporate media. The only coverage of it appears to have been a January 2018 article in *Newsweek*,[16] which drew from Bordell and Robins's *Guardian* article.

2

"Open-Source" Intelligence Secrets Sold to Highest Bidders

George Eliason, "The Private Contractors Using Vault 7 Tools for US Gov: Testimony Shows US Intel Needs a Ground-Up Rebuild Part 1," OpEdNews, March 31, 2017, https://www.opednews.com/articles/The-Private-Contractors-Us-by-George-Eliason-Hackers_Intelligence_Intelligence-Agencies_Websites-170331-791.html.

George Eliason, "How Intel for Hire is Making US Intelligence a Threat to the World Part 2," OpEdNews, February 14, 2018, https://www.opednews.com/articles/1/How-Intel-for-Hire-is-Maki-by-George-Eliason-Agencies_Espionage_Intelligence_Intelligence-Agencies-180214-219.html.

Student Researcher: Harrison Brooks (University of Regina)

Faculty Evaluators: Janelle Blakley and Patricia Elliott (University of Regina)

In March 2017, WikiLeaks released Vault 7, which consisted of some 8,761 leaked confidential Central Intelligence Agency (CIA) documents and files from 2013 to 2016, detailing the agency's vast arsenal of tools for electronic surveillance and cyber warfare.[17] Vault 7, which WikiLeaks described as the "largest ever publication of confidential documents on the agency," drew considerable media attention.[18] However, as George Eliason of OpEdNews reported, while Vault 7 documented the tools at the CIA's disposal, the "most important part" of the disclosure—"the part that needs to frighten you," he wrote— is that "it's not the CIA that's using them." Instead, the malware, viruses, trojans, weaponized "zero-day" exploits, and remote-controlled systems detailed in Vault 7 are "unclassified, open-source, and can be used by anyone." Eliason's OpEdNews series reported how the CIA and other agencies came to rely on private contractors and "open source intelligence," and considered the manifold consequences of these revolutionary changes in intelligence gathering.

As Eliason explained in his first OpEdNews article, the CIA is limited by law in what it can do with these hacking tools—but subcontractors are not similarly restricted. ("If these tools were solely in the hands of a US agency," he wrote, "you would be much safer.") By using private contractors, the CIA and other government intelligence agencies gain access to intelligence gathered by methods that they are prohibited from using.

As Tim Shorrock reported in a 2015 article in the *Nation*, "Over the last 15 years, thousands of former high-ranking intelligence officials and operatives have left their government posts and taken up senior positions at military contractors, consultancies, law firms, and private-equity firms. In their new jobs, they replicate what they did in government—often for the same agencies they left."[19] In a 2016 report, Shorrock estimated that 58,000 private contractors worked in national and military intelligence, and 80 percent of those contractors worked for the five largest corporations in the intelligence-contracting industry.[20] In that report, Shorrock concluded that "not only has intelligence been privatized to an unimaginable degree, but an unprecedented consolidation of corporate power inside US intelligence has left the country dangerously dependent on a handful of companies for its spying and surveillance needs."[21]

Early on, Eliason reported, the private contractors who pioneered open-source intelligence realized that they could circulate (or even sell) the information that they gathered *before* the agency for which they worked had reviewed and classified it.[22] In this way, "no one broke any laws," Eliason wrote, because the information "shifted hands" before it was sent to an agency and classified.

This loophole created what Eliason described as a "private pipeline of information" that intelligence contractors could use to their advantage. Members of Congress, governors, news outlets, and others often wanted the same "Intel" that the CIA had, and, Eliason wrote, open-source intelligence contractors "got paid to deliver Intel for groups looking for specific insights" into creating or influencing government policy.

As a result of these changes, according to Eliason's second article, "People with no security clearances and radical political agendas have state sized cyber tools at their disposal," which they can use "for their own political agendas, private business, and personal vendettas."

Although WikiLeaks's Vault 7 exposé received considerable corporate news coverage (see endnote 18 for examples), these reports failed to address Eliason's analysis of the flaws in open-source intelligence and private contractors. A notable exception to this was a March 2017 *Washington Post* editorial by Tim Shorrock. Noting that WikiLeaks's Julian Assange had said the CIA "lost control of its entire cyberweapons arsenal," Shorrock's editorial reviewed the findings from his previous reports for the *Nation* and concluded that overreliance on private intelligence contractors was "a liability built into our system that intelligence officials have long known about and done nothing to correct."[23]

3
World's Richest One Percent Continue to Become Wealthier

Rupert Neate, "Richest 1% Own Half the World's Wealth, Study Finds," *The Guardian*, November 14, 2017, https://www.theguardian.com/inequality/2017/nov/14/worlds-richest-wealth-credit-suisse.

Student Researchers: Nandita Raghavan and Stephanie Rickher (Diablo Valley College)

Faculty Evaluator: Mickey Huff (Diablo Valley College)

In November 2017, the *Guardian* reported on Credit Suisse's global wealth report, which found that the richest 1 percent of the world now owns more than half of the world's wealth. As the *Guardian* noted, "The world's richest people have seen their share of the globe's total wealth increase from 42.5% at the height of the 2008 financial crisis to 50.1% in 2017." This concentrated wealth amounts to $140 trillion, according to the Credit Suisse report. The number of millionaires in the world—approximately 36 million people—is now nearly three times greater than in 2000.

This staggering concentration of wealth comes at an extreme cost, as the *Guardian* noted: "At the other end of the spectrum, the world's 3.5 billion poorest adults each have assets of less than $10,000 (£7,600). Collectively these people, who account for 70% of the world's working age population, account for just 2.7% of global wealth."

The report contained bad news for millennials as well. As Credit Suisse's chairman, Urs Rohner, noted, "Those with low wealth tend to be disproportionately found among the younger age groups, who have had little chance to accumulate assets . . . [W]e find that millennials face particularly challenging circumstances."

Tremendous concentration of wealth and the extreme poverty that

results from it are problems that affect everyone in the world, but wealth inequalities do not receive nearly as much attention as they should in the establishment press. The few corporate news reports that have addressed this issue—including an August 2017 Bloomberg article and a July 2016 report for CBS's *MoneyWatch*—focused exclusively on wealth inequality within the United States.[24] As Project Censored has previously reported, corporate news consistently covers the world's billionaires while ignoring millions of humans who live in poverty.[25]

4

How Big Wireless Convinced Us Cell Phones and Wi-Fi are Safe

Mark Hertsgaard and Mark Dowie, "How Big Wireless Made Us Think that Cell Phones are Safe: A Special Investigation," *The Nation*, March 29, 2018, https://www.thenation.com/article/how-big-wireless-made-us-think-that-cell-phones-are-safe-a-special-investigation/.

"Phonegate: French Government Data Indicates Cell Phones Expose Consumers to Radiation Levels Higher Than Manufacturers Claim," Environmental Health Trust, June 2, 2017, updated June 2018, https://ehtrust.org/cell-phone-radiation-scandal-french-government-data-indicates-cell-phones-exposeconsumers-radiation-levels-higher-manufacturers-claim.

Marc Arazi, "Cell Phone Radiation Scandal: French Government Data Indicates Cell Phones Expose Consumers to Radiation Levels Higher Than Manufacturers Claim," *Dr. Marc Arazi* blog, June 3, 2017, http://arazi.fr/wp2/2017/06/press-releasecell-phone-radiation-scandal-french-government-data.

Marc Arazi, "Phonegate: New Legal Proceedings against ANFR and Initial Reaction to the Communiqué of Nicolas Hulot," *Dr. Marc Arazi* blog, December 2, 2017, http://arazi.fr/wp2/2017/12/press-release-phonegate-new-legal-proceedings-against-anfr-and-initial-reaction-to-the-communique-of-nicolas-hulot.

Student Researchers: John Michael Dulalas, Bethany Surface, and Kamila Janik (San Francisco State University) and Shannon Cowley (University of Vermont)

Faculty Evaluators: Kenn Burrows (San Francisco State University) and Rob Williams (University of Vermont)

A Kaiser Permanente study (published December 2017 in *Scientific Reports*) conducted controlled research testing on hundreds of pregnant women in the San Francisco Bay area and found that those who had been exposed to magnetic field (MF) non-ionizing radiation associated with cell phones and wireless devices had 2.72 times higher risk of miscarriage than those with lower MF exposure.[26] Furthermore, the study reported that the association was "much stronger" when MF was measured "on a typical day of participants' pregnancies." According to lead investigator De-Kun Li, the possible effects of MF exposure have been controversial because, "from a public health point of view, everybody is exposed. If there is any health effect, the potential impact is huge."[27]

A March 2018 investigation for the *Nation* by Mark Hertsgaard and Mark Dowie showed how the scope of this public health issue has been inadequately reported by the press and underappreciated by the public. Hertsgaard and Dowie reported that the telecom industry has employed public relations tactics, first pioneered by Big Tobacco in the 1960s and developed by fossil-fuel companies in the 1980s, to influence both the public's understanding of wireless technologies and regulatory debates.

The wireless industry has "war-gamed" science by playing offense as well as defense, actively sponsoring studies that result in published findings supportive of the industry while aiming to discredit competing research that raises questions about the safety of cellular devices and other wireless technologies.[28] When studies have linked wireless radiation to cancer or genetic damage, industry spokespeople have pointed out that the findings are disputed by other researchers. This strategy has proven effective, Hertsgaard and Dowie reported, because "the apparent lack of certainty helps to reassure customers, even as it fends off government regulations and lawsuits that might pinch profits." As Hertsgaard and Dowie concluded,

> Lack of definitive proof that a technology is harmful does not mean the technology is safe, yet the wireless industry has succeeded in selling this logical fallacy to the world . . . The upshot is that, over the past 30 years, billions of people around the world have been subjected to a massive public-health experiment: Use a cell phone today, find out later if it causes cancer or genetic damage. Meanwhile, the wireless industry has obstructed a full and fair understanding of the current science, aided by government agencies that have prioritized commercial interests over human health and news organizations that have failed to inform the public about what the scientific community really thinks. In other words, this public-health experiment has been conducted without the informed consent of its subjects, even as the industry keeps its thumb on the scale.

The stakes of this public health experiment continue to rise with the increasing prevalence of Wi-Fi and Bluetooth technologies as well as the development of the "Internet of Things" and anticipated 5G wireless networks.

Multiple studies, including one published in the *American Journal of Epidemiology* in October 2017, have correlated long-term exposure to cell phone radiation with risk for glioma (a type of brain tumor), meningioma, DNA damage, and other serious conditions.[29] In May 2017, the California Department of Public Health released safety guidelines in response to possible health impacts from cell phone radiation. Yet this information was withheld from the public for seven years, and only released after litigation.[30] The American Academy of Pediatrics has clear recommendations to reduce children's exposure to cell phone radiation[31]—yet pregnant women continue to use wireless devices on their abdomens and children are given cell phones as toys.

The wireless industry claims to be in compliance with health and safety regulations and opposes mandatory disclaimers about keeping phones at a safe distance. Yet they also oppose updating cell phone radiation testing methods in ways that would accurately represent real-life use.

As the Environmental Health Trust and Marc Arazi have reported, recent scientific research and court rulings from France underscore these concerns about wireless technology radiation. Under court order, the National Frequency Agency of France (ANFR) recently disclosed that nine out of ten cell phones exceed government radiation safety limits when tested in the way they are actually used, next to the human body. As the Environmental Health Trust reported, French activists coined the term "PhoneGate" because of parallels to the 2015 Volkswagen emissions scandal (referred to informally as "Dieselgate") in which Volkswagen cars "passed" diesel emission tests in the lab, but actually had higher emissions when driven on real roads.[32] In the same way, cell phones "passed" laboratory radiation tests when the "specific absorption rate" (SAR), which indicates how much radiation the body absorbs, was measured at a distance of 15 mm (slightly more than half an inch). However, the way people actually carry and use cell phones (for example, tucked into a jeans pocket or bra, or held in contact with the ear) results in higher levels of absorbed radiation than those found in lab tests.

The French data was also corroborated by a 2017 independent investigation by the Canadian Broadcasting Corporation (CBC) which tested cell phones and found SAR values that surpassed US and Canadian allowable standards when the phones were tested in body contact positions. These findings were replicated by the US Federal Communications Commission, which concluded that radiation levels reach as high as 300 percent of the limit for safe exposure.

As reported by the Environmental Health Trust (EHT), French law ensures that SAR levels are identified prominently on cell phone packaging and that cell phone sales are banned for young children.[33] In 2016, new French policies stated, "*ALL wireless devices, including tablets, cordless phones, remote controlled toys, wireless toys, baby monitors and surveillance bracelets, should be subjected to the same regulatory obligations as cell phones.*"[34] EHT also reported that, according to *Le Monde*, France would attempt to ban cell phones from schools, colleges, and playgrounds as of 2017.[35]

Although local media might announce the findings of a few selected studies, as the *San Francisco Chronicle* did when the Kaiser Permanente study was published,[36] the norm for corporate media is to report the telecom industry line—that is, that evidence linking Wi-Fi and cell phone radiation to health issues, including cancer and other medical problems, is either inconclusive or disputed. Such was the case, for example, when the *Wall Street Journal* published an article in February 2018 titled "Why the Largest Study Ever on Cellphones and Cancer Won't Settle the Debate."[37] Similarly, in May 2016 the *Washington Post* published an article titled "Do Cellphones Cause Cancer? Don't Believe the Hype."[38] As Hertsgaard and Dowie's *Nation* report suggested, corporate coverage of this sort is partly how the telecom industry remains successful in avoiding the consequences of their actions.

5

Washington Post Bans Employees from Using Social Media to Criticize Sponsors

Andrew Beaujon, "The Washington Post's New Social Media Policy Forbids Disparaging Advertisers," *Washingtonian*, June 27, 2017, https://www.washingtonian.com/2017/06/27/the-washington-post-social-media-policy/.

Josh Delk, "Washington Post Prohibits Social Media Criticism of Advertisers," The Hill, June 28, 2017, http://thehill.com/blogs/blog-briefing-room/news/339930-washington-post-prohibits-social-media-criticism-of-advertisers.

Whitney Webb, "Bezos Bans WaPo Staff from Criticizing Corporate Advertisers on Social Media," MintPress News, July 17, 2017, https://www.mintpressnews.com/washington-post-staff-banned-criticizing-advertisers/229821/.

Student Researcher: Bryan Sergel (Indian River State College)

Faculty Researcher: Elliot D. Cohen (Indian River State College)

In June 2017, Andrew Beaujon reported in the *Washingtonian* on a new policy at the *Washington Post* that prohibits the *Post*'s employees from conduct on social media that "adversely affects the *Post*'s customers, advertisers, subscribers, vendors, suppliers or partners." In cases of such conduct, according to the policy, *Post* management reserved the right to take disciplinary action "up to and including termination of employment." According to the report, the *Post*'s policy went into effect on May 1 and applies to the entire company.

In addition to restricting criticism, the *Post*'s new policy encourages employees to snitch on one another: "If you have any reason to believe that an employee may be in violation of the *Post*'s Social Media Policy . . . you should contact the *Post*'s Human Resources Department." The *Post* declined to comment on the policy to the *Washingtonian*.

At the time of the news report, the Washington-Baltimore News Guild, which represents newsroom and commercial employees at the *Post*, was protesting the company-wide action and was seeking to have the controversial parts of the policy removed in a new labor agreement.

As Whitney Webb noted in a report for MintPress News, "This new policy offers a simple loophole to corporations that wish to avoid criticism from the *Post*, as becoming a sponsor of the paper would quickly put an end to any unfavorable coverage."

Webb's report also addressed how the policy might affect the *Post*'s coverage of stories involving the CIA. Four months after Jeff Bezos purchased the *Post*, Amazon Web Services signed a $600 million contract with the CIA for web hosting services that now serve "the entire U.S. intelligence community."[39] (Bezos is the CEO of Amazon.) According to Webb, "long before" the *Post*'s new policy restricting employees' use of social media went into effect, "some had speculated that the connections between the CIA and the *Post* were already affecting its reporting. For example, last year, the *Post* openly called for the prosecution of [Edward] Snowden, despite having previously used the whistleblower's leaks for their Pulitzer Prize–winning report on illegal NSA spying."

Former *Post* reporters suggested that, although criticizing the CIA would not technically be prohibited under the company's new policy, doing so might jeopardize one's career. In 2013, John Hanrahan, a former *Post* reporter, told AlterNet, "*Post* reporters and editors are aware that Bezos, as majority owner of Amazon, has a financial stake in maintaining good relations with the CIA—and this sends a clear message to even the hardest-nosed journalist that making the CIA look bad might not be a good career move."[40]

Corporate news coverage of the *Washington Post*'s social media policy has been extremely limited. In July 2017, Fox Business News caught up with the story in a brief 74-second "Business Alert" during its *Mornings with Maria* program.[41] The segment cited the *Washing-*

tonian as the source of its information, while adding that Jeff Bezos "was not part of the executive team that determined the policy," according to a spokesperson for the *Post*. "This is tricky territory when we get into free speech here," Fox Business News's Tracee Carrasco concluded. *The Wall Street Journal* published an opinion piece by James Freeman, which questioned the policy, speculated that it was "corporate boiler plate accidentally imported from some non-journalistic digital outfit," and called on Bezos to "do what journalists do when they make a mistake. Retract it."[42]

6
Russiagate: Two-Headed Monster of Propaganda and Censorship

Aaron Maté, "MSNBC's Rachel Maddow Sees a 'Russia Connection' Lurking Around Every Corner," The Intercept, April 12, 2017, https://theintercept.com/2017/04/12/msnbcs-rachel-maddow-sees-a-russia-connection-lurking-around-every-corner/.

Norman Solomon, "Is MSNBC Now the Most Dangerous Warmonger Network?" Truthdig, March 1, 2018, https://www.truthdig.com/articles/msnbc-now-dangerous-warmonger-network/.

Robin Andersen, "Backlash Against Russian 'Fake News' is Shutting Down Debate for Real," Fairness & Accuracy In Reporting (FAIR), November 29, 2017, https://fair.org/home/backlash-against-russian-fake-news-is-shutting-down-debate-for-real/.

Matt Taibbi, "The New Blacklist," *Rolling Stone*, March 5, 2018, https://www.rollingstone.com/politics/taibbi-russiagate-trump-putin-mueller-and-targeting-dissent-w517486.

Student Researcher: Moira Feldman (University of Vermont)

Faculty Evaluator: Rob Williams (University of Vermont)

Russiagate, which began as a scandal over Russian efforts to sway the 2016 US election, has since proliferated into a drama of dossiers, investigative councils, Russian adoption cover-ups, and an ever-changing list of alleged scandals. As journalists from the Intercept, Truthdig, Fairness & Accuracy In Reporting, *Rolling Stone*, and other independent outlets documented, corporate media coverage of Russiagate has created a two-headed monster of propaganda and censorship. By saturating news coverage with a sensationalized narrative, Russiagate has superseded other important, newsworthy stories. Furthermore, corporate news coverage that has been reflexively hostile toward Russia also serves to link political protest in the United States with Russian operatives and interests in ways that discredit legitimate domestic activism.

In April 2017, Aaron Maté reported on a quantitative study conducted by the Intercept of MSNBC's *Rachel Maddow Show*, the

second most popular weekday show on cable news. The Intercept's analysis of every episode broadcast between February 20 and March 31, 2017 found that "Russia-focused segments accounted for 53 percent of these broadcasts." As Maté noted, Maddow's Russia coverage "dwarfed the time devoted to other top issues," including Trump's escalating crackdown on undocumented immigrants, the legal battle over Trump's Muslim ban, and other administration scandals and stumbles.

The Intercept was not the only independent voice critical of MSNBC's coverage. In an article published by Truthdig, Norman Solomon observed, "As the cable news network most trusted by Democrats as a liberal beacon, MSNBC plays a special role in fueling rage among progressive-minded viewers toward Russia's 'attack on our democracy' that is somehow deemed more sinister and newsworthy than corporate dominance of American politics (including Democrats), racist voter suppression, gerrymandering and many other U.S. electoral defects all put together."

Beyond MSNBC, other influential US media players have fueled Russiagate fears. In November 2017, Twitter announced policy changes that banned all advertising from two international news outlets owned by Russia, Sputnik and RT. As Robin Andersen of Fairness & Accuracy In Reporting (FAIR) and others revealed, the social media giant based its decision on a single US intelligence report.[43]

The Russiagate narrative that monopolized corporate news cycles throughout 2017 has had real consequences. For example, in February 2018 the Department of Defense's Nuclear Posture Review (last updated in 2010) called for the improvement and readiness of US nuclear capabilities because "Russia's activities and policies have reduced stability and security, increased unpredictability, and introduced new dangers into the security environment."[44]

Russiagate has also been consequential for "'anti-system' movements," from Bernie Sanders's electoral campaign to Black Lives Matter, Brexit, and the Catalan independence movement, as Matt Taibbi reported in *Rolling Stone*. Under the influence of Russiagate rhetoric, according to Taibbi, "We've jumped straight past debating the efficacy of democracy to just reflexively identifying most anti-establishment sentiment as illegitimate, treasonous, and foreign in nature." Russiagate, he wrote, has been used as "a hammer" against all "political outsiders."

Corporate news coverage has continued to fan popular fears that Russia threatens US democracy. For example, in February 2018, for a segment titled "The Unwitting," CNN brought cameras to the door of an elderly Florida woman, who had organized a local event for Trump supporters, to accuse her of working with Russian organizers.[45] That same month, a *New York Times* article reported that Russians had used fake Facebook personas to organize political rallies in the United States, which included, for example, posing as the "United Muslims of America" to promote a July 2016 event called "Support Hillary. Save American Muslims."[46] Many people suffer when lies are reported as facts, but it seems that corporate media are the only ones that profit when they reinforce blind hostility—against not only Russia but also legitimate domestic dissent.

7

Regenerative Agriculture as "Next Stage" of Civilization

Ronnie Cummins, "Regeneration: The Next Stage of Organic Food and Farming—and Civilization," Organic Consumers Association, May 28, 2017, www.organicconsumers.org/essays/regeneration-next-stage-organic-food-and-farming%E2%80%94and-civilization.

Student Researcher: Amber Yang (San Francisco State University)

Faculty Evaluator: Kenn Burrows (San Francisco State University)

Regenerative agriculture represents not only an alternative food production strategy but a fundamental shift in our culture's relationship to nature. As Ronnie Cummins, director of the Organic Consumers Association and a founding member of Regeneration International, wrote, regenerative agriculture offers a "world-changing paradigm" that can help solve many of today's environmental and public health problems. Climate disruption, diminishing supplies of clean water, polluted air and soil, rising obesity, malnutrition and chronic disease, food insecurity, and food waste can all be traced back to modern food production, Cummins noted, and regenerative agriculture is designed to address these problems from the ground up.

The array of techniques that comprise regenerative agriculture rebuilds soils and sequesters carbon.[47] Regenerative farming, Cummins wrote, could potentially draw a critical mass of 200–250 billion tons of carbon from the earth's atmosphere over the next 25 years, mitigating or even reversing key aspects of global warming. Regenerative agricultural techniques allow carbon to be stored in soils and living plants, where it can increase food production and quality while reducing soil erosion and the damaging runoff of pesticides and fertilizers.

In 2012, nearly two dozen governments around the world (including the United States) spent an estimated $486 billion to subsidize 50 million industrial farmers who, Cummins wrote, "routinely over-till, over-graze (or under-graze), monocrop, and pollute the soil and the environment with chemicals and GMOs to produce cheap commodities . . . Meanwhile, 700 million small family farms and herders, comprising the 3 billion people who produce 70 percent of the world's food on just 25 percent of the world's acreage, struggle to make ends meet."[48] Similarly, Cummins reported, "corrupt, out-of-control governments continue to subsidize fossil fuels to the tune of $5.3 trillion a year, while spending more than $3 trillion annually on weapons, mainly to prop up our global fossil fuel system and overseas empires."[49]

Industrial farming systems effectively "mine" soils, decarbonizing them and, in the process, destroying forests and releasing 44–57 percent of all climate-destabilizing greenhouse gases (including carbon dioxide, methane, and nitrous oxide).

"The basic menu for a Regeneration Revolution," Cummins wrote, "is to unite the world's 3 billion rural farmers, ranchers and herders with several billion health, environmental and justice-minded consumers to overturn 'business as usual' and embark on a global campaign of cooperation, solidarity and regeneration." According to food activist Vandana Shiva, who is quoted in Cummins's report, "Regenerative agriculture provides answers to the soil crisis, the food crisis, the health crisis, the climate crisis, and the crisis of democracy."

Regenerative agriculture has received limited attention in the establishment press, highlighted by only two recent, substantive reports in the *New York Times Magazine* and Salon.[50]

8

Congress Passes Intrusive Data Sharing Law under Cover of Spending Bill

Robyn Greene, "Somewhat Improved, the CLOUD Act Still Poses a Threat to Privacy and Human Rights," Just Security, March 23, 2018, https://www.justsecurity.org/54242/improved-cloud-act-poses-threat-privacy-human-rights/.

David Ruiz, "Responsibility Deflected, the CLOUD Act Passes," Electronic Frontier Foundation, March 22, 2018, https://www.eff.org/deeplinks/2018/03/responsibility-deflected-cloud-act-passes.

Student Researcher: L. Joseph Smith (Diablo Valley College)

Faculty Evaluator: Mickey Huff (Diablo Valley College)

Hidden in the massive omnibus spending bill approved by Congress in February 2018 was the Clarifying Lawful Overseas Use of Data (CLOUD) Act of 2018. The CLOUD Act enables the US government to acquire data across international borders regardless of other nations' data privacy laws and without the need for warrants.

The CLOUD Act was subject to almost no deliberation as the Senate was working swiftly to avoid a prolonged government shutdown. Describing how congressional leaders decided, behind closed doors, to attach an "un-vetted, unrelated data bill" to the $1.3 trillion government spending bill, the Electronic Frontier Foundation's David Ruiz wrote that Congress had "a professional responsibility . . . to debate the merits and concerns of this proposal amongst themselves, and this week, they failed." Due to this failure, Ruiz continued, "U.S. laws will be bypassed on U.S. soil." The CLOUD Act gives US and foreign police new mechanisms for seizing data—including private emails, online chats, Facebook posts, and Snapchat videos—from around the world, with few restrictions on how that information is used or shared.

Specifically, the CLOUD Act adds provisions to two existing laws that protect constitutional rights in the digital age. As Robyn Greene reported for Just Security, the CLOUD Act creates an exception to the Stored Communications Act, enabling certified foreign governments to request personal data directly from US companies. Such contracts would partially negate the Mutual Legal Assistance Treaty, which mandates that foreign governments must obtain a warrant through the Department of Justice before requesting data.

While noting that the bill passed in the omnibus spending vote included some improvements on previous versions of the CLOUD Act, Greene wrote that "the new bill failed to incorporate any changes to improve privacy protections for Americans. It still requires only that foreign governments minimize data in a manner similar to what is required under the Foreign Intelligence Surveillance Act, and it still permits foreign governments to share U.S. persons' communications back to the U.S. government with few limitations on how the U.S. government may use that data."

Many other provisions of the CLOUD Act also leave significant room for potential abuse. The act fails to specify which criminal behaviors might warrant a request for personal data. It also fails to specify a time frame for the approval process. This loophole allows nations to request and obtain data before receiving proper approval. By passing the CLOUD Act without critical examination, Congress failed to consider adding safeguards that could make the CLOUD Act "a boon, rather than a threat, to privacy and human rights," Greene concluded.

The little corporate news coverage that the CLOUD Act received tended to put a positive spin on it. *The Washington Post* ran an opinion piece on the topic co-authored by Lisa O. Monaco, the former Homeland Security advisor to President Obama, and John P. Carlin, the former assistant attorney general for the US Department of Justice's National Security Division.[51] Their op-ed sang the praises of the CLOUD Act as a "promising solution" that would allow US law enforcement to access US company data being stored overseas. They made no mention of potential risks to the privacy of citizens' personal data.

Similarly, a March 2018 CNET report also defended the CLOUD Act.[52] The article focused on those in favor of the legislation, including Microsoft president Brad Smith, who claimed it gave "tech companies like Microsoft the ability to stand up for the privacy rights of our customers around the world," and Senator Orrin Hatch, who praised the act for creating "a commonsense framework to encourage international cooperation to resolve conflicts of law." Overall, the CNET report highlighted the liberties that the CLOUD Act would provide corporations by simplifying legal issues concerning overseas servers while only briefly mentioning concerns, such as those voiced by an ACLU spokesperson, Neema Singh Guliani. She expressed reservations about the CLOUD Act, questioning how it would require companies to distinguish between a national government seeking data for legitimate law enforcement purposes and requests intended for crackdowns on journalists or dissidents. The article as a whole sidelined this narrative and stood in favor of the corporations that stand to benefit from the CLOUD Act.

9
Indigenous Communities around World Helping to Win Legal Rights of Nature

Kayla DeVault, "What Legal Personhood for U.S. Rivers Would Do," *YES! Magazine*, September 12, 2017, http://www.yesmagazine.org/issues/just-transition/corporations-have-legal-personhood-but-rivers-dont-that-could-change-20170912.

Eleanor Ainge Roy, "New Zealand River Granted Same Legal Rights as Human Being," *The Guardian*, March 16, 2017, https://www.theguardian.com/world/2017/mar/16/new-zealand-river-granted-same-legal-rights-as-human-being.

Mihnea Tanasescu, "When a River is a Person: From Ecuador to New Zealand, Nature Gets Its Day in Court," The Conversation, June 19, 2017, https://theconversation.com/when-a-river-is-a-person-from-ecuador-to-new-zealand-nature-gets-its-day-in-court-79278.

Student Researcher: Erik Dylan Robledo (Citrus College)

Faculty Advisor: Andy Lee Roth (Citrus College)

In March 2017, the government of New Zealand officially recognized the Whanganui River—which the indigenous Maori consider their ancestor—as a living entity with rights. By protecting the Whanganui against human threats to its health, the New Zealand law established "a critical precedent for acknowledging the Rights of Nature in legal systems around the world," Kayla DeVault reported for *YES! Magazine*. As DeVault wrote, from New Zealand and Australia to Canada and the United States, "we are seeing a revival" of communities seeking to protect natural systems and resources on the basis of "non-Western, often indigenous" worldviews that challenge the values of "colonial" governments.

The *YES! Magazine* story described how, after a legal battle spanning more than 100 years, the Maori Iwi secured protection for the Whanganui by forcing the government to honor Maori "practices, beliefs, and connection" to the river.

As DeVault wrote, if the Maori were able to bridge "the gap in Western and indigenous paradigms in New Zealand, surely a similar effort to protect the Missouri River could be produced for the Standing Rock and Cheyenne River nations by the American government."

In the battle over the Dakota Access pipeline, DeVault reported, the Ho-Chunk Nation of Wisconsin "amended its constitution to include the Rights of Nature."

As DeVault noted, if the US government were to recognize the Missouri River's personhood status, the Dakota Access pipeline would become "a much different battle": Injuries to the river, including the alteration or curtailment of its free-flowing nature, could result in lawsuits. The risk of future chemical spills could then be sufficient to stop the US Army Corps of Engineers from permitting the pipeline, and any negotiations would require "legitimate consultation and consent from the river's representatives."

If more tribes followed the path of the Ho-Chunk Nation in affirming the rights of nature, DeVault concluded, we might finally see "an end to nonconsented infrastructure projects in Indian Country."

In a detailed article published by the Conversation, Mihnea Tanasescu noted that New Zealand's law differed from previous rights of nature laws adopted in Ecuador and Bolivia by designating "specific guardians" for the Whanganui River, including leaders of the indigenous communities that fought for its protection and representatives of the British Commonwealth. As Tanasescu pointed out, the identification of specific representatives is important because without that provision "there is no guarantee that the intended community will be the one that ends up speaking for nature"; "ambiguous language" could permit abuse, as has happened in Ecuador, where all of nature was granted standing and anyone can go to court to protect it.[53] In contrast, Tanasescu concluded, "By granting natural entities personhood one by one and assigning them specific guardians, over time New Zealand could drastically change an ossified legal system."

A few corporate media outlets have covered the New Zealand case and subsequent decisions in India. However, these reports have not provided the depth of coverage found in the independent press or addressed how legal decisions in other countries might provide models for the United States. For example, in July 2016 the *New York Times* reported on New Zealand's 2014 Te Urewera Act, through which the government gave up formal ownership of an 821-square-mile national park to establish the land as a legal entity with "all the rights, powers, duties and liabilities of a legal person."[54] *The Times* report foreshadowed the possibility that New Zealand's third longest river, the Whanganui, might be granted similar, enhanced legal status. Unlike the *YES! Magazine* report, the *Times*'s coverage did not address how the New Zealand decisions might apply to the United States, mentioning only in passing that New Zealand's attorney general "said he had talked the idea over with Canada's new attorney general." In March 2017, the *Washington Post* covered the legal victories by indigenous groups that gave the Whanganui River in New Zealand and the Ganges and Yamuna Rivers in India "the same legal status as humans."[55] *USA Today* ran an Associated Press report on the Indian court's ruling on the Ganges and Yamuna, mentioning the New Zealand decision as precedent.[56]

10

FBI Racially Profiling "Black Identity Extremists"

Jana Winter and Sharon Weinberger, "The FBI's New U.S. Terrorist Threat: 'Black Identity Extremists,'" *Foreign Policy*, October 6, 2017, http://foreignpolicy.com/2017/10/06/the-fbi-has-identified-a-new-domestic-terrorist-threat-and-its-black-identity-extremists/.

Hatewatch Staff, "FBI 'Black Identity Extremists' Report Stirs Controversy," Southern Poverty Law Center, October 25, 2017, https://www.splcenter.org/hatewatch/2017/10/25/fbi-black-identity-extremists-report-stirs-controversy.

Amy Goodman, interview with Christian Picciolini, "Life After Hate: Trump Admin Stops Funding Former Neo-Nazis Who Now Fight White Supremacy," *Democracy Now!*, August 17, 2017, https://www.democracynow.org/2017/8/17/life_after_hate_trump_admin_stops.

Brandon E. Patterson, "Police Spied on New York Black Lives Matter Group, Internal Police Documents Show," *Mother Jones*, October 19, 2017, http://www.motherjones.com/crime-justice/2017/10/police-spied-on-new-york-black-lives-matter-group-internal-police-documents-show/#.

Student Researcher: Hailey Schector (Syracuse University)

Faculty Evaluator: Jeff Simmons (Syracuse University)

In August 2017, the counterterrorism division of the Federal Bureau of Investigation (FBI) issued an intelligence assessment warning law enforcement officers, including the Department of Homeland Security, of the danger of "Black Identity Extremists."[57] Jana Winter and Sharon Weinberger reported for *Foreign Policy* that, as "white supremacists prepared to descend on Charlottesville, Virginia, in August, the FBI warned about a new movement that was violent, growing, and racially motivated. Only it wasn't white supremacists; it was 'black identity extremists.'"

The Southern Poverty Law Center (SPLC)'s Hatewatch staff reported that the FBI's intelligence assessment used the term "BIE" (the Bureau's acronym for "Black Identity Extremists") to describe "a conglomeration of black nationalists, black supremacists, and black separatists, among other disaffiliated racist individuals who are anti-police, anti-white, and/or seeking to rectify perceived social injustices against blacks." According to the SPLC report, the FBI was "taking some heat from historians, academics and former government officials for creating the new 'BIE' term," which categorized a range of activists not by their common ideologies or goals, but by race.

Independent news outlets reported that, in the wake of Charlottesville and at a time when the Trump administration had defunded organizations that encouraged hate-group members to leave those groups, the FBI's increased focus on nonwhite groups seemed like a diversion. Thus, for example, the SPLC suggested that the leaked

THE FBI CELEBRATES BLACK HISTORY MONTH:

Once Upon a Time in the Sixties and Seventies, CoInTelPro pursued, harassed and decimated the leadership of the Black liberation Movement, arresting and framing your Elders on false confessions obtained through torture (opening the way to Abu Ghraib a generation later). The guilty federal agents and torturers thus got away with murder and lived Happily Ever After.

The End.

document "might be a deliberate attempt by the Trump administration to divert attention away from the larger, more serious threat of white supremacists and other far-right extremists." In particular, the FBI assessment made a leap when it defined a wide array of activist groups as "a movement." Referencing the shooting of Michael Brown in Ferguson, Missouri, the FBI report posited that it was "very likely" that subsequent incidents of alleged police abuse of African Americans had "spurred an increase in premediated, retaliatory lethal violence against law enforcement."

The corporate media have covered the FBI report on "black identity extremists" in narrow or misleading ways. In October, an opinion piece in the *New York Times* challenged the FBI's use of the "BIE" label,[58] while Fox News broadcast a 99-second clip, with an ominous soundtrack added, reporting that the FBI had declared "Black Identity Extremists" as a "violent domestic threat."[59] In November, NBC News covered the story, and even acknowledged the FBI's history of going after black groups, but the report also suggested that "lawmakers" were leading the fight against the racial profiling, by "demanding answers."[60] Coverage like this both draws focus away from the active white supremacist movement and feeds the hate and fear on which such a movement thrives.

11

US Air Force Seeks to Control Seventy Percent of Nevada's Desert National Wildlife Refuge

"Thousands Oppose Trump Administration's Attempted Seizure of Nevada's Desert National Wildlife Refuge for Expanded Bombing Range," Center for Biological Diversity, March 8, 2018, https://www.biologicaldiversity.org/news/press_releases/2018/desert-bighorn-sheep-03-08-2018.php.

Tay Wiles, "The Air Force Wants to Expand into Nevada's Wild Desert," *High Country News*, February 14, 2018, https://www.hcn.org/issues/50.4/military-the-air-force-wants-to-expand-into-nevadas-wild-desert.

Student Researcher: Ky Tucker (College of Western Idaho)

Faculty Evaluator: Michelle Mahoney (College of Western Idaho)

"More than 32,000 people have submitted comments opposing a military takeover of most of Nevada's Desert National Wildlife Refuge," the Center for Biological Diversity reported in March 2018. In order to expand its Nevada Test and Training Range, the US Air Force wants to take control of nearly 70 percent of the 1.6-million-acre refuge. That would give more than two-thirds of the refuge to the US military and would strip protections for wildlife and restrict public access.

The Desert National Wildlife Refuge is the largest national wildlife refuge in the lower 48 states. President Franklin D. Roosevelt in 1936 designated the refuge as a site for the protection of desert bighorn sheep. The Mojave desert tortoise—which has long been in danger due to human destruction of its habitat—is among the many species that inhabit the refuge.

As the Center for Biological Diversity reported, the Air Force's plans call for industrializing the largely untouched wildlands with dozens of miles of new roads, more than 100 miles of fencing, two air strips, and radio signal emitters.

In January 2018, more than 200 people attended a public meeting in Las Vegas hosted by the Air Force, and everyone who spoke opposed the land seizure. Many of the attendees joined together to chant, "Don't bomb the bighorn!"

As Tay Wiles reported in a February 2018 *High Country News* article, loss of access to the land is a "major concern" for the Moapa Band of Paiutes, whose reservation is east of the refuge. Their ancestral lands span much of southern Nevada, and today the Moapa rely on access to the Desert National Wildlife Refuge for traditional resources, including medicinal herbs and big game. "People say, 'It's just desert,' but it means a lot to us," Tribal Council Chairman Greg Anderson told *High Country News*.

The Air Force is required to respond to public comments in a final environmental impact statement, which is expected in Fall 2018. Congress will decide the fate of the Desert National Wildlife Refuge when it takes action on the Air Force's final recommendation.

Media coverage of public opposition to the Air Force plan has been almost nonexistent. In December 2017 the *Las Vegas Review-Journal* ran a story on the topic, with a follow-up report in January 2018 that focused on opposition to the plan.[61] The closest thing to a corporate media organization covering the topic was NBC's Las Vegas affiliate, KSNV. Its coverage was brief, though it did provide the dates and locations of the Air Force's public hearings on the proposed plan.[62]

The Air Force's plans for the Desert National Wildlife Refuge in Nevada are part of a broader trend toward military expropriation of public lands. The US Navy is secretly conducting electromagnetic warfare training over the Olympic National Forest in Washington;[63] the Air Force wants to test new high-speed weapons—"hypersonics"—in the air space above more than 700,000 acres of public land in Utah, beyond the boundaries of its current Test and Training Range;[64] and, in May 2018, E&E News reported that House Natural Resources Chairman Rob Bishop (R-UT) had added provisions to the latest version of the National Defense Authorization Act (NDAA) that would "permit indefinite land withdrawals from the Interior Department for military installations with an integrated natural resources management plan."[65] E&E reported that the language of this provision is "nearly identical" to a previous bill (*H.R. 4299*) that passed the Natural Resources Committee in November 2017 before being struck down in conference.

12

ICE Intends to Destroy Records of Inhumane Treatment of Immigrants

Victoria López, "ICE Plans to Start Destroying Records of Immigrant Abuse, Including Sexual Assault and Deaths in Custody," American Civil Liberties Union (ACLU), August 28, 2017, updated May 29, 2018, https://www.aclu.org/blog/immigrants-rights/ice-and-border-patrol-abuses/ice-plans-start-destroying-records-immigrant.

Kali Holloway, "ICE Plans to Start Destroying Records Detailing Immigrant Sexual Abuse and Deaths in Its Custody," AlterNet, August 29, 2017, https://www.alternet.org/immigration/ice-plans-start-destroying-records-detailing-immigrant-sexual-abuse-and-deaths-its.

Student Researchers: Ellisha Huntoon (Sonoma State University), Katherine Epps (California State University, East Bay), and Kelly Van Boekhout (Diablo Valley College)

Faculty Evaluator: Mickey Huff (Sonoma State University/Diablo Valley College)

In recent years, numerous news reports have highlighted illegal or inhumane actions committed by US Immigration and Customs Enforcement (ICE) officials in their attempts to expel illegal immigrants. Despite the severity and frequency of these abuses, any official records documenting them may soon be destroyed. According to the American Civil Liberties Union (ACLU), ICE officers in the past year have been given provisional approval by the National Archives and Records Administration (NARA) to destroy thousands of records that document unlawful ICE actions.

As Kali Holloway reported for AlterNet, these records include information on illegal detainment of immigrants, inhumane holding conditions, sexual abuses by officers, and wrongful deaths of detainees while in ICE custody. As Victoria López of the ACLU wrote, "ICE proposed various timelines for the destruction of these records ranging from 20 years for sexual assault and death records to three years for reports about solitary confinement." Although murder does not have a statute of limitations, apparently documentation of it can, as long as the crime was committed while the victim was in ICE custody.

In detention centers from California and Texas to Alabama and Georgia, detainees systematically endure complete isolation with no provision of time outdoors and little to no communication with family. In January 2018, for example, the San Francisco Chronicle reported on the case of 27 women in a Richmond, California, jail who wrote a collective letter detailing continual abuses they face due to their immigration status.[66] The women reported being unable to use the restroom regularly, as well as enduring restrictions that prevented their access to proper healthcare.

In April 2017, the *New York Times* reported that President Trump intended to curtail current regulations imposed on detention centers to make way for the influx of detainees under his presidency.[67] These plans would benefit the prison–industrial system, of course, but would also likely lead to a tremendous increase in inhumane conditions for detainees. Although news coverage has brought ICE abuses to public attention, no major establishment news outlet is reporting on ICE's efforts to officially destroy documentation that could verify accusations of its mishandling, mistreatment, abuse, and even murder of people in its custody.

13

The Limits of Negative News and Importance of Constructive Media

Christopher Reeve Linares, "News and the Negativity Bias: What the Research Says," The Whole Story (Medium), October 25, 2017, https://thewholestory.solutionsjournalism.org/news-and-the-negativity-bias-what-the-research-says-78a0bca05b11.

Student Researcher: Amber Yang (San Francisco State University)

Faculty Evaluator: Kenn Burrows (San Francisco State University)

Historically, journalism has highlighted social problems in order to expose wrongdoing, inform the public, and spur reform. This "watchdog" role is vital to a democratic society. However, as Christopher Reeve Linares reported for The Whole Story, as a result of a "negativity bias," news reporting often fails to "capture and circulate some of the most essential information that society needs to understand and solve its problems." As Anthony Leiserowitz, director of the Yale Project on Climate Change Communication, observed, "Perceived threat without efficacy of response is usually a recipe for disengagement or fatalism."[68] Reeve Linares's report highlighted recent research on the consequences of negative news overload and how "solutions journalism" can help empower news consumers as engaged actors.[69]

Research shows that negative news overload has led news consumers to feel increasingly depressed, anxious, and helpless. A 2014 study by NPR, the Robert Wood Johnson Foundation, and the Harvard School of Public Health found that 40 percent of the 2,505 respondents polled said that watching, reading, or listening to the news was one of the biggest daily stressors in their lives.[70] Only juggling schedules of family members and hearing about what politicians were doing rated higher as stressors, affecting 48 percent and 44 percent of respondents, respectively.

A study published in *Nature Climate Change* examined how newsrooms in the United States and United Kingdom covered the series of reports released in 2013–14 by the Intergovernmental Panel on Climate Change. The panel's first report, which focused on the impacts of rising sea levels, ocean acidification, and increasing temperatures, received significantly more coverage than the panel's final report, which dealt with climate change adaptations.[71] This leads to what Leiserowitz, the director of the Yale climate change project, calls a "hope gap."[72] The prospect of people disconnecting from news should worry journalists—but the possibility that relentlessly negative news might actually weaken citizenship is even more troubling.

As an alternative to relentlessly negative news coverage, "constructive journalism" aims to produce stories that engage and inspire readers while remaining committed to journalism's core function of informing the public. The Constructive Journalism Project defines constructive journalism as "rigorous, compelling reporting that includes positive and solution-focused elements in order to empower audiences and present a fuller picture of truth, while upholding journalism's core functions and ethics."[73] As Cathrine Gyldensted, a pioneer in the field of contructive journalism, has written, constructive stories orient audiences toward the future and transform conflicts into possibilities by expanding the mind, storming the brain, changing the question, telling the story correctly, and moving the world.[74]

Not only does the establishment press seldom utilize solutions or constructive journalism, it has not even covered these innovations in journalism as newsworthy topics. In reviewing corporate news for relevant coverage, we found just two reports on the effects of "negativity bias." In March 2017, the *Financial Times* published an opinion piece that cited recent research suggesting that financial journalists are "more negative about market falls than positive about market rises."[75] And in May 2017, CNN posted a video report that revealed how the "real" media bias in coverage of the 2016 presidential election and the first 100 days of President Trump's administration was neither liberal nor conservative, but rather a generalized negativity bias that led the press to concentrate solely on the flaws of the two political parties and, subsequently, the Trump administration.[76] However, in both the *Financial Times*'s and CNN's reports, negativity bias was presented as an isolated phenomenon—specific to financial reporting or campaign coverage—rather than identified as pervasive in corporate media framing of most issues.

14
FBI Paid Geek Squad Employees as "Confidential Human Source" Informants

Aaron Mackey, "Geek Squad's Relationship with FBI is Cozier Than We Thought," Electronic Frontier Foundation, March 6, 2018, https://www.eff.org/deeplinks/2018/03/geek-squads-relationship-fbi-cozier-we-thought.

"Sneak Squad: FBI Paid Geek Squad Staff as Informants, New Documents Reveal," RT, March 7, 2018, updated March 8, 2018, https://www.rt.com/usa/420758-geek-squad-fbi-eff.

Student Researcher: Dominique Boccanfuso (University of Vermont)

Faculty Evaluator: Rob Williams (University of Vermont)

New documents released to the Electronic Frontier Foundation (EFF) show that the Federal Bureau of Investigation's Louisville field officers have been paying Best Buy Geek Squad employees as informants for more than a decade. A Geek Squad facility in Kentucky has been violating customers' constitutional rights by secretly handing over data found on customer computers to the FBI whenever employees suspected customers of possessing illegal material, such as child pornography. Evidence indicates that the FBI treated Geek Squad employees as confidential human sources, or "CHS," and that at least four Geek Squad CHS were paid for their "services" to the FBI.

In 2014, a California doctor, Mark Rettenmaier, was prosecuted for child pornography found on his computer after the Geek Squad had worked on it. The EFF filed a Freedom of Information request in May 2017 to gain a better understanding of the Geek Squad's relationship with the FBI, since such a partnership "potentially circumvents computer owners' Fourth Amendment rights." The Fourth Amendment protects citizens' right to privacy, including protection from unreasonable searches and seizures by the government. The searches of customers' computers by the Geek Squad are a clear violation of this right because they constituted warrantless searches at the direction of the FBI.

The judge in Rettenmaier's case dismissed the child pornography charges after throwing out much of the evidence collected by investigators due to "false and misleading statements" made by an FBI agent.[77]

Best Buy argued that the company has a moral obligation to report their findings to the FBI and that their employees do not actively seek out illegal material. However, evidence from the case shows that Geek Squad employees who worked on Rettenmaier's computer found the questionable image in an "unallocated space," meaning that forensic software was likely required to locate it.

For more than a decade, there was no corporate media coverage on the relationship between Best Buy's Geek Squad and the FBI; US citizens remained unaware that entrusting the Geek Squad with their computers made them vulnerable to searches for incriminating materials. Rettenmaier's prosecution drew attention to the relationship between Best Buy's Geek Squad and the FBI, which in turn spurred some coverage from corporate sources, including *Fortune* magazine, with coverage derived from the EFF report, and the *Washington Post*.[78]

15
Digital Justice: Internet Co-ops Resist Net Neutrality Rollbacks

Kaleigh Rogers, "Rural America is Building High-Speed Internet the Same Way It Built Electricity in the 1930s," Motherboard (Vice), December 1, 2017, https://motherboard.vice.com/en_us/article/ywnz37/electric-coops-internet-america-cooperatives-broadband.

Kaleigh Rogers, "Ignored by Big Telecom, Detroit's Marginalized Communities are Building Their Own Internet," Motherboard (Vice), November 16, 2017, https://motherboard.vice.com/en_us/article/kz3xyz/detroit-mesh-network.

Sammi-Jo Lee, "How Internet Co-ops Can Protect Us from Net Neutrality Rollbacks," YES! Magazine, November 22, 2017, http://www.yesmagazine.org/people-power/how-internet-co-ops-can-protect-us-from-net-neutrality-rollbacks-20171122.

J. Gabriel Ware, "When They Couldn't Afford Internet Service, They Built Their Own," YES! Magazine, March 26, 2018, http://www.yesmagazine.org/people-power/when-they-couldnt-afford-internet-service-they-built-their-own-20180326.

Student Researcher: Amber Yang (San Francisco State University)

Faculty Evaluator: Kenn Burrows (San Francisco State University)

More than 300 electric cooperatives across the United States are building their own Internet with high-speed fiber networks. These locally-owned networks are poised to do what federal and state governments and the marketplace have not accomplished. First, they are protecting open Internet access from the Internet service providers (ISPs) that stand to pocket the profits from the rollbacks of net neutrality the Trump administration announced in November 2017. Second, they are making affordable and fast Internet accessible to anyone, narrowing the digital divide that otherwise deepens individual and regional socioeconomic inequalities.

In Detroit, for example, 40 percent of the population has no access of any kind to the Internet. Because of Detroit's economic woes, many big telecom companies have apparently decided that it is not worthwhile to invest in expanding their networks to these communities. Internet connectivity is a crucial economic leveler without which people can fall behind in school, health, and the job market.

In response, a growing cohort of Detroit residents started a grassroots movement called the Equitable Internet Initiative, through which locals have begun to build their own high-speed Internet. The initiative started by enlisting digital stewards—locals who were interested in working for the nonprofit coalition. Many of these stewards began with little or no tech expertise, but after 20 weeks of training they developed the skills necessary to install, troubleshoot, and maintain a network from end to end. They aim to build shared tools, like a forum and a secured emergency communication network—and to educate their communities on digital literacy, so people can truly own the network themselves.

Detroit is not the only city with residents who aim to own their Internet. Just 30 of the more than 300 tribal reservations in the United States have Internet access. Seventeen tribal reservation communities in San Diego County have secured wireless Internet access under the Tribal Digital Village initiative. Another local effort, Co-Mo Electric Cooperative, which was originally established in 1939 to bring electric power to farms in central Missouri, has organized to crowdfund the necessary resources to establish its own network. By 2014, co-op members enjoyed connection speeds in the top 20 percent of the United States, and the fastest in Missouri. By 2016, Co-Mo's entire service area was on the digital grid.

Co-ops looking to expand the Internet can face political setbacks.

In his move to dismantle net neutrality rules, Federal Communications Commission Chairman Ajit Pai made it clear that he does not consider the Internet a utility, though that is how these co-ops are treating it. The biggest dilemma for cities is the erosion of the capacity for communities to solve their own problems. Yet, as success stories travel, they inspire other communities to ask how they can do the same thing. As a result, local Internet service providers are bringing the power back to their people.

There has been no coverage of these success stories by corporate news media, except for an August 2016 *New York Times* report on how the Northeast Oklahoma Electric Cooperative built its own fiber-based Internet.[79]

16
$21 Trillion in Unaccounted-for Government Spending from 1998 to 2015

Greg Hunter, "Missing $21 Trillion Means Federal Government is Lawless—Dr. Mark Skidmore," USAWatchdog, December 3, 2017, https://usawatchdog.com/missing-21-trillion-means-federal-government-is-lawless-dr-mark-skidmore/.

Andy Henion, "MSU Scholars Find $21 Trillion in Unauthorized Government Spending; Defense Department to Conduct First-Ever Audit," MSU Today, December 11, 2017, https://msutoday.msu.edu/news/2017/msu-scholars-find-21-trillion-in-unauthorized-government-spending-defense-department-to-conduct/.

"$21 Trillion of Unauthorized Spending by US Govt Discovered by Economics Professor," RT, December 16, 2017, updated January 17, 2018, https://www.rt.com/usa/413411-trillions-dollars-missing-research/.

Student Researcher: Andrea Fekete (North Central College)

Faculty Evaluator: Steve Macek (North Central College)

Two federal government agencies, the Department of Defense (DoD) and the Department of Housing and Urban Development (HUD), may have accumulated as much as $21 trillion in undocumented expenses between 1998 and 2015. Independent news sources, including RT and USAWatchdog, reported this finding based on an investigation conducted by Mark Skidmore, a professor of economics at Michigan State University. Skidmore began to research the alleged irregularities in DoD and HUD spending after hearing Catherine Austin Fitts, who was assistant secretary of HUD during the George H.W. Bush administration, say that the Department of Defense's Office of Inspector General (OIG) had found $6.5 trillion worth of military spending that the Department of Defense could not account for.[80]

The figure given by Fitts was 54 times the US Army's $122 billion budget as authorized by Congress, leading Skidmore to think that Fitts had meant $6.5 *billion* in undocumented spending, not $6.5 *trillion*. Typically, adjustments in public budgets are only a small fraction of authorized spending. In an article for *Forbes*, co-authored with Laurence Kotlikoff, Skidmore said the "gargantuan nature" of the undocumented federal spending "should be a great concern to all tax payers."[81]

Working with Fitts and two graduate students, Skidmore investigated reports from the websites of the Departments of Defense and Housing and Urban Development as well as the Office of Inspector General. In one of these reports, Skidmore found an appendix that showed a transfer of approximately $800 billion from the US Treasury to the Army. As MSU Today reported, not only did Skidmore's queries to the OIG go unanswered, but the OIG also at one point disabled links to "all key documents showing the unsupported spending." Skidmore and his colleagues were able to continue their research because they had already downloaded and stored the relevant documents.[82]

Shortly after Skidmore's findings went public, the Pentagon announced the first ever audit of the Department of Defense. Although the Pentagon is responsible for $2.4 trillion in assets, including personnel, real estate, and weapons, it has never been audited.[83] The announced audits are set to begin in 2018 and projected to take place annually thereafter. RT's report quoted the DoD's comptroller, David L. Norquist, who explained that the OIG had hired independent public accounting firms to audit the Pentagon's finances because it is "important that the Congress and the American people have confidence in DoD's management of every taxpayer dollar." MSU Today reported that the DoD did not explain what led to the audit, but that Skidmore believed his team's efforts to compile the government documents and make them public "may have made a difference."

Apart from the article in *Forbes* that Skidmore co-authored and an NPR story on the OIG's decision to undertake an audit of the

Pentagon, US corporate media have failed to recount any of the details concerning the significant findings of Mark Skidmore's research.[84]

17

"Model" Mississippi Curriculum Omits Civil Rights Movement from School Textbooks

Sierra Mannie, "Why Students are Ignorant about the Civil Rights Movement," Hechinger Report, October 1, 2017, http://hechingerreport.org/students-ignorant-civil-rights-movement/.

Student Researchers: Zander Manning, Jessica Picard, and Jared Yellin (University of Massachusetts Amherst)

Faculty Evaluator: Allison Butler (University of Massachusetts Amherst)

Inadequate textbooks used in the Mississippi school system are affecting civil rights education, Sierra Mannie reported for the Hechinger Report in October 2017.

In 2011, Mississippi adopted new social studies standards. Before then, public schools in the state were not required to teach the Civil Rights Movement, and the phrase "civil rights" was mentioned only three times in the 305-page document that outlined the previous standards. As Mannie wrote, "The Civil Rights Movement was once a footnote in Mississippi social studies classrooms, if it was covered at all."

With its 2011 adoption of social studies standards establishing an expectation that students learn civil rights in much greater depth, the state was heralded as a model for other states by the Southern Poverty Law Center (SPLC): A March 2012 SPLC report stated, "Mississippi's recent adoption of a Civil Rights/Human Rights strand across all grade levels should be a model for other states."[85] However, even as Mississippi's new standards were intended to be a model system for other states to emulate, an investigation by the Hechinger Report and Reveal from the Center for Investigative Reporting found, according to Mannie, that "all of the state's 148 school districts rely on textbooks published before the model standards appeared as part of their social studies material."

One textbook, titled *Mississippi: The Magnolia State*, was published in 2005 and is commonly used throughout the state. This text entirely omits mentioning the civil rights–era Freedom Riders and the laws that these young activists challenged. By contrast, the textbook refers to Mississippi's governor from 1904 to 1908, James K. Vardaman, more than 60 times. Vardaman, known as "the Great White Chief," staunchly advocated the lynching of African Americans. The 2011 standards did not mention Vardaman once.

Some teachers see these textbooks as a problem for children, especially those in school districts closely tied to historic events that the assigned readings do not cover. Mannie's report quoted a high school teacher, Camille Lesseig, from a county in eastern Mississippi where a third of children live in poverty: "That first year I had maybe one or two white students, so it was overwhelmingly African-American, and here's this book that doesn't really acknowledge them at all." Lesseig concluded, "It would be wrong for me to use that book given the context of where I taught."

Despite the significant budget cuts Mississippi's public education system has faced in the past two decades, which have made implementing the new standards more difficult, some teachers have still managed to participate in a week-long training program to educate themselves about civil rights history. Located at the state's Department of Archives and History, this program helps teachers utilize archived documents and other resources to enhance students' learning experiences.

Although Mannie's report focused on Mississippi, the problem is not confined to that state. Drawing on SPLC data, in 2013 Henry Louis Gates Jr. wrote that, as of 2011–2012, "only 19 states specifically require teaching *Brown v. Board of Education*, while 18 states require coverage of [Martin Luther King]; 12, Rosa Parks; 11, the March on Washington; and six, Jim Crow segregation policies."[86] Gates observed, "the civil rights movement and, more generally, African-American history, are being left out, and it's not only black students who are suffering. You can't have a 'conversation about race' only among black people! This is *American* history, after all."

As of May 2018, major corporate news outlets have not covered this issue at all. Mannie's story was reposted by independent news sources and blogs, most notably Truthout, Reveal, and the *Clarion-Ledger*. It is important to note that, while the Hechinger Report partners with corporate media such as CNN, NBC, and the *Washington*

Post, these outlets did not republish Mannie's story. The lack of coverage despite existing institutional partnerships suggests that this story did not coincide with the values, agendas, and missions of these large media corporations.

18
Adoption Agencies a Gateway for Child Exploitation

Joshua Philipp, "Child Trafficking through International Adoption Continues Despite Regulations," *Epoch Times*, March 15, 2018,
https://www.theepochtimes.com/child-trafficking-through-international-adoption-continues-despite-regulations_2464370.html.

Student Researcher: Erika Banuelos (Indian River State College)

Faculty Evaluator: Elliot D. Cohen (Indian River State College)

As the *Epoch Times* reported in March 2018, "Global adoption is a big business, fraught with loose regulations and profit incentives that have made it a target for kidnappers, human traffickers, and pedophiles." Though some countries have banned all foreign adoptions, and most others attempt to regulate them, "the problem has continued," Joshua Philipp reported.

In 2016, Uganda tightened its foreign adoption laws to restrict "fast-track foreign adoptions" which had previously allowed children with living parents to be "whisked overseas in a matter of days" under the guise of adoption, according to a Reuters report.[87] In 2017, the Firstpost news outlet reported on a "kidnap-for-adoption" racket in India in which an adoption agency was found guilty of "stealing babies from impoverished unwed mothers, rape survivors and marginalised families."[88]

In the United States, the Intercountry Adoption Universal Accreditation Act has required since July 2014 that "all agencies or persons that provide adoption services on behalf of prospective adoptive parents . . . be accredited or approved, or be a supervised or exempted provider, in compliance with the Intercountry Adoption Act and Department of State accreditation regulations."[89] However, as Philipp reported, abuse of adoptions, including trafficking and exploitation, "has continued even in the United States." The United States remains among the top destinations for trafficking, according to UNICEF USA.[90]

As Geoffrey Rogers, CEO of the US Institute Against Human Trafficking, told the *Epoch Times*, "approximately 60 to 70 percent of kids that are trafficked in the United States come out of the foster care system."[91] Often this occurs through a process known as "re-homing," in which people who have adopted children "pass the children to new parents with almost no regulation," Philipp wrote. In these situations, children are more likely to suffer abuse or exploitation. With domestic adoptions, processes and procedures protect the rights of birth mothers, future adoptive parents, and the children themselves. However, as a 2015 study found, "these safeguards are often absent when parents adopt children from overseas."[92]

The establishment press has done virtually nothing to bring global corruption of adoption processes to light, especially in the United States. Extensive searches of three prominent news databases using multiple search terms located no corporate news coverage of any of the connections between international adoptions and child exploitation reported by the *Epoch Times*.

19
People Bussed across US to Cut Cities' Homeless Populations

Outside in America team, "Bussed Out: How America Moves Its Homeless," *The Guardian*, December 20, 2017, www.theguardian.com/us-news/ng-interactive/2017/dec/20/bussed-out-america-moves-homeless-people-country-study.

Alastair Gee, "America's Homeless Population Rises for the First Time Since the Great Recession," *The Guardian*, December 6, 2017, www.theguardian.com/us-news/2017/dec/05/america-homeless-population-2017-official-count-crisis.

Student Researcher: Izzy Snow (College of Marin)

Faculty Evaluator: Susan Rahman (College of Marin)

An investigative report by the *Guardian* studied homeless relocation plans in major cities and counties across the United States. Released in December 2017, the 18-month investigation recorded 34,240 journeys made by homeless people participating in a variety of city and county relocation programs between 2011 and 2017. Relocation programs provide people who are homeless with free one-way bus or plane tickets out of a given city.

"Some of these journeys provide a route out of homelessness," according to the *Guardian*'s in-depth report. The report notes, however,

"That is far from the whole story." Although the programs' stated goals are to help people, the *Guardian* noted how relocation schemes "also serve the interests of cities, which view free bus tickets as a cheap and effective way of cutting their homeless populations."

According to the report, "People are routinely sent thousands of miles away after only a cursory check by authorities to establish they have a suitable place to stay once they get there." Some relocated people told the *Guardian* that they ended up back on the streets, in their new location, "within weeks of their arrival."

Most of the people who participated in relocation programs learned about them through word of mouth or from a caseworker. In most programs, an applicant must provide the contact information for a friend or relative they know in the city to which they intend to travel. However, programs that were investigated did not routinely confirm whether that contact could actually provide shelter assistance to the program participant. Programs were also found to rarely check in with travelers after they had left their original cities.

In Florida, for example, only three cities recorded data on the relationship between the relocated person and his or her contact in the new city. The Southernmost Homeless Assistance League, a relocation program in Key West, Florida, requires that applicants sign a contract stating that their relocation is permanent. The program denies homeless assistance to people who return after taking a free bus from Key West. This program, the *Guardian* noted, did not maintain records on the more than 350 people who had left Key West through its relocation services.

The Guardian analyzed data from 2010 to 2017 that was provided by homeless relocation programs from 16 major cities and counties across the United States. The majority of these programs were in California, based in Humboldt County and in the cities of Chico, San Francisco, Santa Cruz, Santa Monica, and Long Beach. The study included data from four cities in Florida: Fort Lauderdale, West Palm Beach, Sarasota, and Key West. New York, Phoenix, Portland (OR), Denver, Reno, and Salt Lake City also provided data. From these 16 locations, the *Guardian* recorded that more than 20,000 homeless people had traveled around the United States as part of homeless relocation programs during the study period. The majority (88 percent) of bussed homeless people were moved to cities with lower median incomes than their point of origin, to take advantage of a lower cost of living and potentially affordable housing.

Data received from San Francisco revealed the enormous impact of that city's homeless relocation program. In 2005, the city's homeless population was 6,250, with no travelers bussed out of the city. In 2017, the homeless population was just over 7,600, after a total of 10,570 homeless people had been bussed out of the city in the intervening 12 years. *The Guardian* calculated that, without the homeless relocation program, there could have been as many as 18,000 homeless people in San Francisco in 2017.

The Guardian noted that these figures did not include homeless people who traveled to or from the city independently of a relocation program, people who became homeless while living in San Francisco, or homeless people who might have found a home during the 12-year period. From 2010 to 2015, only three travelers from San Francisco's program were contacted after relocation. In 2016, a majority of people were contacted, but city officials refused to provide the *Guardian* with information about those individuals' current housing status. A homeless person is estimated to cost the city of San Francisco an average of $80,000 per year, based on the cost of policing and medical services.

Portland and Santa Monica were in the minority of cities in which housing programs checked in with homeless migrants. According to Portland officials, 70 percent of the city's 416 relocated persons still had housing in their new cities after three months. In Santa Monica, 60 percent were still housed six months after relocating. However, there was no additional data to check if this housing was designed to be permanent or if it lasted longer than three to six months.

Regardless of limited evidence on whether relocation programs actually achieve their long-term goals, cities use data from these programs as a demonstration of aid provided to their homeless populations. In San Francisco, though, the *Guardian* found that approximately half of the 7,000 homeless people the city has claimed to help were given only bus tickets.

Democracy Now! and the *PBS NewsHour* featured interviews with Alistair Gee, who edited the *Guardian* story.[93] The *Guardian* report was also featured in a four-minute segment on *NBC Nightly News* and was mentioned in passing by the *Los Angeles Times* as an "amazing investigation."[94] Major broadcast news outlets, such as Fox News, have mentioned housing relocation, but often without the kind of systemic, critical perspective taken by the *Guardian* in its study.[95] The issue has remained largely ignored by other major outlets, such as the *New York Times, Washington Post,* and *USA Today.*

20

Extravagant Hospital Waste of Unused Medical Supplies

Marshall Allen, "What Hospitals Waste," ProPublica, March 9, 2017, https://www.propublica.org/article/what-hospitals-waste.

Student Researchers: Blane Erwin and Alyssa Hain (North Central College)

Faculty Evaluator: Steve Macek (North Central College)

Hospitals in the United States are wasting millions of dollars' worth of sterile and unused medical supplies, practices that impact the cost of healthcare, as Marshall Allen reported for ProPublica in March 2017. The type of equipment that gets thrown away ranges from simple items like surgical masks that cost just over a dollar each, to more expensive equipment such as $4,000 infant warmers or even $25,000 ultrasound machines. These wasted supplies add up, accounting for a significant amount of a hospital's operating costs which Americans pay for through higher healthcare costs.

Marshall Allen's report cited a University of California, San Francisco (UCSF) study focused on UCSF's own medical center.[96] In its neurosurgery department, the study found almost $1,000 in wasted resources per patient, accounting for nearly $3 million in estimated annual costs. Notably, many doctors in the UCSF study were unaware of the costs of discarded medical supplies. In response to the study's finding, UCSF established incentives to reduce unnecessary waste, resulting in savings of more than $800,000 per year.

All US hospitals follow infection control policies that often leave little choice about what to do with supplies left in operating rooms after surgery or unused items left in patients' rooms after patients are discharged. Due to strict waste management guidelines, the waste will most likely end up in an incinerator rather than a landfill. As ProPublica's report noted, this kind of waste occurs all over the country, despite the existence of nonprofit organizations that accept unused medical supplies as donations and ship them to international medical facilities that are in need.

For example, the organization Partners for World Health has been collecting discarded supplies, filling shipping containers, and sending them to hospitals in desperate need of the supplies, in countries such as Greece and Syria. In 2017, the organization sent seven containers of medical supplies valued at $250,000 each. These supplies included everything from sterile needles to ultrasound machines.

Although facilities that receive donated supplies eventually make use of them, the discarded equipment still accounts for millions out of the donating hospitals' operating budgets, increasing the cost of healthcare. And this is all happening while poorer hospitals in rural areas of the United States are unable to afford the high-quality medical supplies that big hospitals are discarding.

Topical and industry-focused news websites, including Healthcare Finance and FierceHealthcare, covered the story, but these outlets target healthcare professionals instead of the majority of the health-care-purchasing American public.[97] *The Washington Post* published an article, written by the original author of the ProPublica report, Marshall Allen, in its "PostEverything" section.[98] It's important to note how the *Post* presented Allen's article. PostEverything is an online-only opinion section that hosts content from contributors who are not regular *Post* reporters. *The Post* chose not to publish Allen's article in print form, and the outlet framed it as "opinion," despite the factually-based hard-hitting ProPublica report on which his article was based. Although the *Post* version still communicated the scope of the issue, it did not have the impact of the original ProPublica report. In March 2017, *U.S. News & World Report* also published an article based on the ProPublica report.[99]

21
Parkland Shooter's JROTC Connections Spotlight Militarization of Schools

Pat Elder, "JROTC, Military Indoctrination and the Training of Mass Killers," World Beyond War, February 16, 2018, https://worldbeyondwar.org/jrotc-military-indoctrination-training-mass-killers/.
Pat Elder, "The Junior Reserve Officer Training Corps is Not a Substitute for Education," Truthout, February 16, 2017, http://www.truth-out.org/opinion/item/39509-the-junior-reserve-officer-training-corps-is-not-a-substitute-for-education.

Amy Goodman, interview with Pat Elder, "Inside the U.S. Military Recruitment Program that Trained Nikolas Cruz to be 'A Very Good Shot,'" *Democracy Now!*, February 21, 2018, https://www.democracynow.org/2018/2/21/inside_the_us_military_recruitment_program.

Amy Goodman, interview with Pat Elder, "Florida Gunman Nikolas Cruz Knew How to Use a Gun, Thanks to the NRA and the U.S. Army," *Democracy Now!*, February 23, 2018, https://www.democracynow.org/2018/2/23/florida_gunman_nikolas_cruz_knew_how.

Pat Elder, "Cruz, Instagram, and the Civilian Marksmanship Program," World Beyond War, February 27, 2018, http://worldbeyondwar.org/cruz-instagram-cmp/; reposted as "How the Civilian Marksmanship Program Has Become a Premier Arms Dealer," BuzzFlash, March 6, 2018, http://www.buzzflash.com/commentary/cruz-instagram-and-the-cmp-as-the-nation-s-premier-arms-dealer.

Student Researcher: Bethany Surface (San Francisco State University)

Faculty Evaluator: Kenn Burrows (San Francisco State University)

Public officials have offered their thoughts and prayers to the families of some 141 children, educators, and other people who have been killed in the dozens of school shootings in the United States since April 20, 1999, when Eric Harris and Dylan Klebold killed 12 students, a teacher, and then themselves at Columbine High School in Littleton, Colorado.[100] On February 14, 2018, 19-year-old Nikolas Cruz killed 17 students at Marjory Stoneman Douglas High School in Parkland, Florida. As has become the norm, the Parkland shootings were followed by prodigious media and government hand-wringing about the Second Amendment and the influence of the National Rifle Association (NRA).

But one aspect of Cruz's biography that was not given much, if any, critical attention by the establishment press was his membership in his high school's Army Junior Reserve Officers' Training Corps (JROTC) program before he was expelled. A series of reports and interviews by Pat Elder, for World Beyond War, Truthout, and *Democracy Now!*, highlighted Cruz's connections to the Army JROTC program and its connections to other organizations, including the Civilian Marksmanship Program and the NRA.

Examining links between JROTC programs and the militarization of schools, Elder, who directs the National Coalition to Protect Student Privacy, an organization that confronts militarism in schools, wrote, "Few in America have connected the dots between military indoctrination and firearms instruction on the one hand, and the propensity for training mass killers, whether their crimes are committed as enlisted soldiers in atrocities overseas or in American high schools." Cruz not only participated in Marjory Stoneman Douglas High School's

JROTC program, he was also a member of its four-person marksmanship team, which operated under the auspices of the Civilian Marksmanship Program and had received $10,000 in funding from the National Rifle Association "to upgrade and replenish equipment," *Democracy Now!* reported. As Elder told *Democracy Now!*, the NRA "realize that if they can start linking the children with the guns at age 13 in the high schools, it's a win-win proposition for them and for the sellers of weaponry."

Florida is "arguably the most friendly state in terms of the militarization of the schools," Elder said. Its statutes "allow a student who takes four years of JROTC to substitute biology, physical science, physical education and art for this straight-jacketed military indoctrination program." In an article for World Beyond War, he further noted that, in Florida, JROTC is regarded as an Advanced Placement course for which students earn points toward their weighted GPAs, even though many of the courses are taught by retired soldiers with no teaching credentials and little or no college education. Florida, Elder explained, has simply gone further than other states, many of which allow JROTC participation to substitute for requirements in physical education and American government and civics.

As *Democracy Now!* reported, the Army awarded the Medal of Heroism to three JROTC cadets who died in the Parkland, Florida, shooting: 15-year-old Peter Wang and two 14-year-old freshmen, Martin Duque and Alaina Petty. Elder noted that the awarding of Army medals to JROTC cadets was "another example of the militarization of youth." The Army would treat Wang, who was reportedly wearing a full uniform and trying to help other students when he was killed, "as a full-fledged soldier at his burial," Elder said.

Some 1,600 American high schools enroll students in military-run marksmanship programs, teaching children as young as 13 to shoot lethal weapons, Elder told *Democracy Now!*. JROTC programs are regulated by the Civilian Marksmanship Program (CMP). In the *Democracy Now!* interview, Elder described the CMP as the NRA's "proxy." As he explained, the CMP was established by Congress in 1903, after the Spanish–American War, with the goal of ensuring that large numbers of Americans, and especially youth, would know how to shoot weapons in the event of a war. In 1996, the CMP was priva-

WELL REGULATED MILITIA BEING NECESSARY TO THE SAFETY OF A FREE STATE...

SUTHERLAND SPRINGS, TX

LAS VEGAS, NV

ORLANDO, FLA

www.OMEGAPRS.ORG

SANDY HOOK NEWTOWN, CT

COLUMBINE, COLORADO, etc..., etc...

THANK YOU, NRA.

tized after congressional testimony by Paul Simon and Frank Lautenberg, who called the CMP a "boondoggle" and "a gift to the NRA." Since then, Elder told *Democracy Now!*, the CMP "has managed to bankroll $160 million in privately traded securities" by selling "discarded Army weapons," as it was mandated to by Congress.

The Army gifts outdated weaponry to the CMP which, in turn, sells the weapons at discounted rates to JROTC programs in schools and to individual members of CMP-affiliated clubs. As Elder explained in his February 27, 2018 report for World Beyond War, although the CMP has so far only recirculated surplus rifles, it is poised to expand its program to include surplus handguns, such as the semi-automatic M1911 pistol. Reporting that the Army's cache of 100,000 of these handguns "could net the CMP more than $50 million," Elder noted that 20 years of silence by Congress on CMP weapons sales was "a testament to the lobbying fire-power of the NRA."

A number of corporate news outlets—including, for example, the *New York Times*, the *Washington Post*, and Fox News—reported on Cruz's JROTC affiliation.[101] Although the *Times* reported that the Pentagon "spends $370 million a year on Junior R.O.T.C. programs at about 3,400 high schools across the country," and the *Washington Post* noted that the NRA's "fundraising and charitable arm gave $10,827 in noncash assistance to the Douglas JROTC in 2016," both the NRA's strong influence over the Civilian Marksmanship Program and the role of the JROTC in the militarization of the country's schools were entirely left out of establishment media narratives.

22

Big Pharma's Biostitutes: Corporate Media Ignore Root Cause of Opioid Crisis

Abby Martin, "Death & Biostitutes—The US Opioid Crisis," *Empire Files*, teleSUR English, November 29, 2017, https://www.youtube.com/watch?v=iJjIewjgD1A.

Abby Martin, interview with Mike Papantonio, "Empire Files: Abby Martin Talks US Opioid Crisis with Mike Papantonio," teleSUR English, November 30, 2017, https://www.telesurtv.net/english/news/Empire-Files-Abby-Martin-Talks-US-Opioid-Crisis-With-Mike-Papantonio-20171130-0017.html.

Student Researcher: Zaynah Almaaita (College of Western Idaho)

Faculty Evaluator: Michelle Mahoney (College of Western Idaho)

At least 64,000 people died of drug overdoses in 2016, with more than 80 percent of those deaths attributed to opioid drugs, according to an August 2017 report from the Centers for Disease Control and Prevention.[102] Government officials say that the crisis is finally getting Washington's attention, as the *Wall Street Journal* reported in March 2018,[103] but debates over bigger budgets for law enforcement or drug addiction programs continue to feature most prominently in the corporate press. As Abby Martin of *The Empire Files* reported in November 2017, this focus potentially distracts from the root of the problem, which is gross misconduct by drug manufacturing giants and their distributors.

Martin's report featured an interview with Mike Papantonio, a partner in the law firm representing four Ohio counties that are suing pharmaceutical companies for their role in manufacturing the opioid crisis. As Papantonio told Martin, "Big Pharma has operated without any oversight or regulations."

The beginning of the opioid crisis, Martin reported, goes back to drug manufacturing companies hiring "biostitutes," a deroga-

tory term for biological scientists hired to misrepresent research or commit fraud in order to protect their employers' corporate interests. As Martin reported, research by biostitutes was used to make the (misleading) case that opioids could treat pain without the risk of addiction. Purdue Pharma, which manufactures OxyContin, and McKesson, Cardinal Health, and AmerisourceBergen, which distribute that drug and other opioids, suppressed research that showed how addictive opioids are, and they began to push doctors to write more prescriptions on behalf of the "needs" of consumers.

In particular, Papantonio said, distributors targeted the nation's poorer communities, including industrial cities with high unemployment rates, such as Detroit, and economically-stressed mining communities, as in West Virginia. Such mercenary practices not only impacted the individuals who became addicted, they also ravaged the finances of the targeted cities and counties. As Papantonio told *The Empire Files*, the opioid crisis has required local government expenditures for everything from new training for emergency medical responders, to the purchase of Naloxone (sold under the brand name Narcan) for treating opioid overdoses, to the expansion of dependency courts to handle the cases of neglected or abused children, and the retooling of jails as de facto rehabilitation centers—all of which have come out of city and county budgets. In his *Empire Files* interview, Papantonio estimated that the cost for a "typical community" fell between "ninety and two hundred million dollars—that's just the beginning number."

Although federal policies—including, most notably, the Comprehensive Drug Abuse Prevention and Control Act of 1970—should have prevented misconduct by Big Pharma manufacturers and distributors, the penalties for violations were too small. Companies literally treated the fines as business expenses, "leaving the federal government and taxpayers to 'flip the bill,'" teleSUR reported.

As *Censored 2019* went to press, Barry Meier reported in the *New York Times* that a confidential 120-page Justice Department report showed that federal prosecutors who investigated Purdue Pharma found that the company "knew about 'significant' abuse of OxyContin in the first years after the drug's introduction in 1996 and concealed that information."[104] According to the Justice Department report, Purdue officials had received information that the pills were being crushed and snorted, and stolen from pharmacies, and that some doctors were being charged with selling prescriptions, but the drug maker continued "in the face of this knowledge" to market OxyContin as less prone to abuse and addiction than other prescription opioids.

Prior to the revelations in Meier's *New York Times* report, the most significant coverage on the role of Big Pharma in the opioid crisis was from the *Guardian*, which ran an October 2017 story on how drug manufacturers have "poured close to $2.5bn into lobbying and funding members of Congress over the past decade"— but most of this report focused on members of Congress and prominent figures in the Trump administration who have received contributions from Big Pharma lobbyists.[105] The *Guardian*'s report did not address how drug manufacturers and distributors, such as Purdue Pharma and McKesson, have played a central role in creating the opioid epidemic.

23

New Restrictions on Prisoners' First Amendment Rights

Rand Gould, "New Mail Policy in Michigan Prisons: Billionaires Profit at the Expense of Prisoners, Their Families and Friends, and U.S. Postal Service," *San Francisco Bay View*, January 2, 2018, http://sfbayview.com/2018/01/new-mail-policy-in-michigan-prisons-billionaires-profit-at-the-expense-of-prisoners-their-families-and-friends-and-u-s-postal-service/.

Efren Paredes Jr., "MDOC Implements Strict New Prisoner Mail Policy Changes," Voice of Detroit, August 23, 2017, http://voiceofdetroit.net/2017/08/23/mdoc-implements-strict-new-prisoner-mail-policy-changes/.

Jon Swaine, "Acclaimed Book The New Jim Crow Banned in Some New Jersey Prisons," *The Guardian*, January 8, 2018, https://www.theguardian.com/us-news/2018/jan/08/new-jim-crow-banned-new-jersey-prisons.

Thu-Huong Ha, "Exactly What Gets a Book Banned from Prisons, in One US State's Spreadsheet," Quartz, January 17, 2018, https://qz.com/1176515/exactly-what-gets-a-book-banned-from-prisons-in-one-us-states-spreadsheet/.

Edward Helmore, "Texas Prisons Ban The Color Purple and Monty Python—But Mein Kampf is Fine," *The Guardian*, December 2, 2017, https://www.theguardian.com/us-news/2017/dec/02/texas-prisons-ban-books-mein-kampf-color-purple.

Shaun King, "ACLU Says New Jersey Prisons' Banning of 'The New Jim Crow' is Unconstitutional," The Intercept, January 8, 2018, https://theintercept.com/2018/01/08/new-jim-crow-ban-prisons-nj-new-jersey-aclu/.

Student Researchers: Courtney Hale (College of Western Idaho) and Anabel Sosa (University of Vermont)

Faculty Evaluators: Michelle Mahoney (College of Western Idaho) and Rob Williams (University of Vermont)

On November 1, 2017, the Michigan Department of Corrections (MDOC) implemented strict changes to its prison mail policy that discouraged inmates, their families, and friends from using the US Postal Service. Officially the policy aimed to stop the flow of contraband, including controlled substances, into state prisons. However, as Rand Gould reported for the *San Francisco Bay View*, the policy will actually "stop prisoners, their families and friends from sending mail via the U.S. Postal Service (USPS) and force them into buying email 'stamps' from JPay," allowing JPay and the MDOC to "rake in profits" and closely monitor all mail.

JPay is a private company, based in Florida, that provides money transfer, email, and video visitation services for prisoners and their families. According to a 2012 Bloomberg report, it services more than one million prisoners in at least 35 states.[106] As the *Bay View* reported, JPay is a subsidiary of Securus, the second-largest prison phone company in the United States.

Some of the new MDOC restrictions on incoming mail include mail being rejected if it is not in a white envelope, has any stain, sticker, or label on it, or is not addressed in blue or black ink or graphite pencil. Sending and receiving mail via the USPS is a US citizen's right, as the freedom of speech and press is protected by the First Amendment, Gould wrote, but for Michigan inmates use of that service will now be tightly controlled and possibly phased out by the MDOC. Further, critics speculate that the new policy is the first step on a slippery slope that will lead to the shutdown of prison mail rooms, forcing inmates to use the JPay system exclusively. As it stands, the new policies effectively restrict inmates' access to newspapers, magazines, and possibly court mailings, as Efren Paredes Jr. reported in an August 2017 article for the Voice of Detroit.

The new changes come disguised as an effort to curb contraband being smuggled into prisons, although there is little evidence or research to support the recent restrictions as effective measures. Meanwhile, little is done to stop what studies have shown to be significant contraband avenues: Data suggests prison employees are responsible for more than 80 percent of prison contraband traffic. Furthermore, discrepancies identified in the new policy hint at a blatant disregard for consistent lawmaking—for example, inmates' own funds (provided by friends and family) will be used to repackage all incoming envelopes, even ones which meet MDOC's criteria.

Meanwhile, in correctional facilities across the country, prison officials have banned thousands of books—including Michelle Alexander's bestselling book, *The New Jim Crow*, on the endemic racial bias of US prison systems. As Jon Swaine reported for the *Guardian*, through a public records request, the American Civil Liberties Union (ACLU) obtained a list of books banned in several New Jersey prisons. Those records led the ACLU to call for lifting the book ban because it violates inmates' rights under the First Amendment. In response to the ACLU's campaign, officials in New Jersey and North Carolina lifted bans; however, Texas, Pennsylvania, and Florida prisons have persisted in restricting inmates' access to numerous books.

The press secretary for the Pennsylvania Department of Corrections told Thu-Huong Ha at Quartz that the bans are intended to "ensure the safety, security and rehabilitation requirements inherent in the operation of a prison." That rationale might seem questionable if the books that *are* allowed to remain in prisons under the recent restrictions are considered; they include Adolf Hitler's autobiography, *Mein Kampf,* and two titles by former Ku Klux Klan leader David

Duke, as another *Guardian* article on the ban, by Edward Helmore, reported.

Banning *The New Jim Crow* is illustrative of precisely what Michelle Alexander's book on mass incarceration and "colorblindness" addressed: The contemporary criminal justice system is a modern-day version of past Jim Crow laws, which mandated racial segregation in all public facilities until 1965. As Alexander wrote, "As a criminal, you have scarcely more rights, and arguably less respect, than a black man living in Alabama at the height of Jim Crow. We have not ended racial caste in America; we have merely redesigned it."[107] In the case of prison officials banning particular books, the information in the books appears to be perceived as threatening to official power, as information obtained by inmates may lead to challenges to the very systems that oppress and incarcerate them.

During 2017–2018, the *New York Times*, Slate, and NBC News all reported that the book bans in prisons are unconstitutional, yet their coverage was minimal.[108] Without the ACLU's efforts, first to obtain records of prisons' banned books lists and then to publicize those bans as unconstitutional, it seems unlikely that any establishment news outlets would have covered this topic.

24
More Than 80,000 Stolen Guns Worsen Crime in Florida

Laura Morel, "82,000 Stolen Guns are Missing in Florida," Reveal (Center for Investigative Reporting), November 1, 2017, https://www.revealnews.org/article/82000-stolen-guns-are-missing-in-florida.

Laura Morel, "Thieves are Breaking into Florida Gun Stores, Often in Brazen Ways," Reveal (Center for Investigative Reporting), November 1, 2017, https://www.revealnews.org/article/thieves-are-breaking-into-florida-gun-stores-often-in-brazen-ways.

Laura C. Morel, "Unlocked and Loaded," *Tampa Bay Times*, November 1, 2017, http://project.tampabay.com/2017/special-report/unlocked-loaded/stolen-guns/.

Laura C. Morel, "Prime Targets," *Tampa Bay Times*, November 1, 2017, http://project.tampabay.com/2017/special-report/unlocked-loaded/gun-dealers/.

Laura C. Morel, "$36 Million Worth of Guns Stolen in Florida in Four Years," *Tampa Bay Times*, July 26, 2017, http://www.tampabay.com/news/publicsafety/report-36-million-worth-of-guns-stolen-in-florida-in-four-years/2331615.

Student Researcher: Samantha Ring (North Central College)

Faculty Evaluator: Steve Macek (North Central College)

Over the past ten years, more than 82,000 guns stolen in Florida remain missing, Laura Morel reported in November 2017 in joint reports for the *Tampa Bay Times* and the Center for Investigative Reporting's website, Reveal. The study, based on a ten-month investigation of "thousands of law enforcement records," found that in Tampa Bay alone at least 9,000 stolen guns have not been recovered. In 2016, on average, at least one gun was reported stolen every hour.

Those guns turn up in the hands of drug dealers and felons, Morel wrote, and some wind up killing people.

Experts say the figures likely underestimate the actual number of missing guns, in part because Florida law does not require gun owners to report gun thefts, and the Florida Department of Law Enforcement does not keep track of recovered guns. The *Tampa Bay Times*/Reveal study found that five law enforcement agencies in the state documented the theft of nearly 11,000 guns between 2014 and 2016. Based on this data, only about one in five guns has been recovered.

Burglaries of cars—many of which were unlocked—and of gun stores account for the great majority of stolen guns. A Jacksonville Sheriff's Office detective, Tom Martin, said criminals are not buying guns: "They're stealing them." As David Hemenway, a professor of health policy at Harvard whose focus is gun research, noted, "Basically, the gun owners are arming people we really don't want to have guns."

As Morel reported, "There are also more guns to steal." The number of people owning guns in the state of Florida has spiked over the last decade. In 2007, 438,864 Florida residents had permits to carry concealed weapons; in 2017 that figure reached 1.7 million.

There has been little corporate media coverage of this topic, despite widespread concern about Florida's crime rate. In November, WUSF, the Tampa Bay NPR station, ran a brief segment on the story, based on Morel's reports.[109]

25

Sheriffs Using Iris Recognition Technology along US–Mexico Border

George Joseph, "The Biometric Frontier," The Intercept, July 8, 2017, https://theintercept.com/2017/07/08/border-sheriffs-iris-surveillance-biometrics/.

Student Researcher: Jessica Paneral (North Central College)

Faculty Evaluator: Steve Macek (North Central College)

In April 2017, the Southwestern Border Sheriffs' Coalition (SBSC) unanimously approved use of new biometric identification technology as a defense against "violent unauthorized immigrants," George Joseph of the Intercept reported. All 31 US counties along the 1,989 miles of the US border with Mexico will receive a free three-year trial of the Inmate Recognition Identification System (IRIS), created by the company Biometric Intelligence and Identification Technologies, or BI2, according to Joseph's Intercept article.

IRIS software photographs and captures the details of an individual's eyes, collecting around 240 characteristic elements within seconds, then examines a database of nearly one million profiles for an identity match. When compared with the roughly 40 to 60 characteristic elements found in fingerprints, BI2's system is far more precise. SBSC hopes that both the stationary and mobile versions of the scanners will create a "digital wall" against criminals. BI2 plans on expanding the use of their system to law enforcement throughout the country. Analysis by the marketing research firm Tractica predicts an annual growth rate of 22.9 percent in biometric technology revenues, accounting for an estimated $69.8 billion in revenues over a ten-year period.[110]

As hopeful as SBSC is about the crime fighting potential of IRIS, critics of this system suggest that it will encourage racial profiling against immigrants and may be used to determine legal status. According to Nathan Wessler, staff attorney with the Speech, Privacy, and Technology Project of the American Civil Liberties Union, "Racial profiling is a serious concern . . . especially Latinos or people of color are at greater risk for iris checks simply for the color of their skin." Wessler told the Intercept, "In this country, we've long resisted being a 'show me your papers' society, but this moves us to that because you increasingly can't avoid your identity being scooped up in public."

Adam Schwartz, a senior staff attorney with the Electronic Frontier Foundation's civil liberties team, raised concerns about local law enforcement sharing information with federal immigration agencies such as US Immigration and Customs Enforcement (ICE). Schwartz told the Intercept, "Whatever legitimate interest police have in capturing biometrics to do ordinary law enforcement jobs, it is not proper to share that information with ICE." As Joseph's Intercept report noted, ICE currently has "direct access" to many law enforcement databases.

There has not been any establishment news coverage of the new border technology, with corporate media instead concentrating their reporting about border security on President Trump's proposed wall. A few local, specialized, and independent news sources have reported on this story, including the *San Antonio Express-News*, Business Wire, and MuckRock.[111]

Notes

1. Christopher Paul and Miriam Matthews, "The Russian 'Firehose of Falsehood' Propaganda Model," RAND, 2016, 1, https://www.rand.org/pubs/perspectives/PE198.html.
2. Ibid., 10.
3. See http://projectcensored.org/category/validated-independent-news/.
4. The idea of a networked news commons combines Yochai Benkler's concept of a "networked fourth estate" with the venerable history of research about the "commons," i.e., resources so fundamentally valuable to wellbeing that they should be actively protected and managed for the good of all, rather than treated as private property. See, respectively, Yochai Benkler, "WikiLeaks and the Networked Fourth Estate," in *Beyond WikiLeaks: Implications for the Future of Communications, Journalism and Society*, eds. Benedetta Brevini, Arne Hintz, and Patrick McCurdy (New York: Palgrave Macmillan, 2013), 11–34; and, e.g., "Introduction to the Commons," On the Commons website, undated, http://www.onthecommons.org/work/introduction-commons. In 2009, Elinor Ostrom, a political scientist, won the Nobel Prize for research that demonstrated the importance of the commons around the world.
5. See Andy Lee Roth and Project Censored, "Breaking the Corporate News Frame through Validated Independent News Online," in *Media Education for a Digital Generation*, eds. Julie Frechette and Rob Williams (New York: Routledge, 2016), 173–86.
6. On "information disorders," see, e.g., David M.J. Lazer, Matthew A. Baum, Yochai Benkler et al., "The Science of Fake News," *Science* 359, No. 6380 (March 9, 2018), 1094–96, http://science.sciencemag.org/content/359/6380/1094.full; and Liliana Bounegru, Jonathan Gray, Tommaso Venturini, and Michele Mauri, *A Field Guide to "Fake News" and Other Information Disorders* (Amsterdam: Public Data Lab, 2017), https://fakenews.publicdatalab.org/.
7. Paul and Matthews, "Russian 'Firehose of Falsehood,'" 2.
8. For evidence to back this claim, see the Junk Food News and News Abuse chapters in this and previous *Censored* volumes as well as the work of the late Edward S. Herman, including his "Still Manufacturing Consent: The Propaganda Model at Thirty," in *Censored 2018: Press Freedoms in a "Post-Truth" World*, eds. Andy Lee Roth and Mickey Huff with Project Censored (New York: Seven Stories Press, 2017), 209–23. The canonical reference on this perspective is Edward S. Herman and Noam Chomsky, *Manufacturing Consent: The Political Economy of the Mass Media* (New York: Random House, 2008 [1988]); for a recent reinterpretation, see Rob Williams, "*The Post* (Truth) World: Reviving the 'Propaganda Model of News' for Our Digital

Age," Project Censored, February 2018, http://projectcensored.org/post-truth-world-reviving-propaganda-model-news-digital-age/.

9. "Blind spots and lacunae": Andy Lee Roth, comp. and ed., Introduction to "The Top Censored Stories and Media Analysis of 2016–17," in Censored 2018: Press Freedoms in a "Post-Truth" World, eds. Andy Lee Roth and Mickey Huff with Project Censored (New York: Seven Stories Press, 2017), 31–37, 33.

10. See Peter Phillips, "How Mainstream Media Evolved into Corporate Media," Chapter 8 in this volume, for further discussion of why it is important to distinguish "corporate" media from "mainstream" media.

11. Herman and Chomsky, Manufacturing Consent.

12. For information on how to nominate a story, see "How to Support Project Censored" at the back of this volume.

13. Validated Independent News stories are archived on the Project Censored website at projectcensored.org/category/validated-independent-news.

14. For a complete list of the national and international judges and their brief biographies, see the Acknowledgments section at the back of this volume.

15. "WJP Rule of Law Index 2017–2018," World Justice Project, 2018, https://worldjusticeproject.org/our-work/wjp-rule-law-index/wjp-rule-law-index-2017%E2%80%932018.

16. Beatrice Dupuy, "Worsening Discrimination Leads U.S. to Drop in Global Ranking of Fundamental Human Rights, Report Finds," Newsweek, January 31, 2018, http://www.newsweek.com/fundamental-human-rights-are-diminishing-according-new-report-796325.

17. According to WikiLeaks, the first series of released CIA documents, titled "Year Zero," introduced "the scope and direction of the CIA's global covert hacking program, its malware arsenal and dozens of 'zero day' weaponized exploits against a wide range of U.S. and European company products, include Apple's iPhone, Google's Android and Microsoft's Windows and even Samsung TVs . . ." "Vault 7: CIA Hacking Tools Revealed," WikiLeaks, March 7, 2017, https://wikileaks.org/ciav7p1/.

18. Ibid. Examples of news coverage included Scott Shane, Matthew Rosenberg, and Andrew W. Lehren, "WikiLeaks Releases Trove of Alleged C.I.A. Hacking Documents," New York Times, March 7, 2017, https://www.nytimes.com/2017/03/07/world/europe/wikileaks-cia-hacking.html; and Greg Miller and Ellen Nakashima, "WikiLeaks Says It Has Obtained Trove of CIA Hacking Tools," Washington Post, March 7, 2017, https://www.washingtonpost.com/world/national-security/wikileaks-says-it-has-obtained-trove-of-cia-hacking-tools/2017/03/07/c8c50c5c-0345-11e7-b1e9-a05d3c21f7cf_story.html.

19. Tim Shorrock, "How Private Contractors Have Created a Shadow NSA," The Nation, May 27, 2015, https://www.thenation.com/article/how-private-contractors-have-created-shadow-nsa/.

20. Tim Shorrock, "5 Corporations Now Dominate Our Privatized Intelligence Industry," The Nation, September 8, 2016, https://www.thenation.com/article/five-corporations-now-dominate-our-privatized-intelligence-industry/. According to Shorrock's calculations, Booz Allen Hamilton employs an intelligence workforce of 12,000 cleared personnel; CACI International employs 10,000; Leidos Holdings and CRSA Inc. employ 8,000 each; and SAIC employs 6,600.

21. Ibid. See also Tim Shorrock, "The Spy Who Billed Me," Mother Jones, January/February 2005, https://www.motherjones.com/politics/2005/01/spy-who-billed-me/; and R.J. Hillhouse, "Outsourcing Intelligence," The Nation, July 24, 2007, https://www.thenation.com/article/outsourcing-intelligence/.

22. For one account of how early open-source intelligence contractors worked, see Benjamin Wallace-Wells, "Private Jihad," New Yorker, May 29, 2006, https://www.newyorker.com/magazine/2006/05/29/private-jihad.

23. Tim Shorrock, "Why Does WikiLeaks Keep Publishing U.S. State Secrets? Private Contractors," Washington Post, March 16, 2017, https://www.washingtonpost.com/posteverything/wp/2017/03/16/the-reason-wikileaks-receives-so-many-u-s-state-secrets-private-contractors/.

24. Noah Smith, "How the Top 1% Keeps Getting Richer," Bloomberg, August 28, 2017, https://www.bloomberg.com/view/articles/2017-08-28/how-the-top-1-keeps-getting-richer; and Aimee

Picchi, "The Rich Get Richer, and the Poor Get...," *MoneyWatch*, CBS, July 4, 2016, https://www.cbsnews.com/news/inequality-1-percent-99-percent-income-growth/.

25. See Feather Flores and Susanne Boden, with Andy Lee Roth, "Millions in Poverty Get Less Media Coverage Than Billionaires Do," in *Censored 2016: Media Freedom on the Line*, eds. Mickey Huff and Andy Lee Roth with Project Censored (New York: Seven Stories Press, 2015), 61–62, http://projectcensored.org/9-millions-in-poverty-get-less-media-coverage-than-billionaires-do/.

26. De-Kun Li, Hong Chen, Jeannette R. Ferber, Roxana Odouli, and Charles Quesenberry, "Exposure to Magnetic Field Non-Ionizing Radiation and the Risk of Miscarriage: A Prospective Cohort Study," *Scientific Reports* 7 (December 13, 2017), https://www.nature.com/articles/s41598-017-16623-8.

27. Sophie Haigney, "Radiation Typical of Cell Phones and Wi-Fi Linked to High Rate of Miscarriages," *San Francisco Chronicle*, December 16, 2017, https://www.sfchronicle.com/bayarea/article/Radiation-typical-of-cell-phones-and-Wi-Fi-linked-12436529.php. For previous Project Censored coverage of this topic, see Julian Klein and Casey Lewis, with Kenn Burrows and Peter Phillips, "Accumulating Evidence of Ongoing Wireless Technology Health Hazards," in *Censored 2015: Inspiring We the People*, eds. Andy Lee Roth and Mickey Huff with Project Censored (New York: Seven Stories Press, 2014), 62–64, http://projectcensored.org/14-accumulating-evidence-ongoing-wireless-technology-health-hazards/.

28. On "war-gaming," see, e.g., a 1994 Motorola memo, now published online: "Motorola, Microwaves and DNA Breaks: 'War-Gaming' the Lai-Singh Experiments," Microwave News, January/February 1997, https://www.rfsafe.com/wp-content/uploads/2014/06/cell-phone-radiation-war-gaming-memo.pdf.

29. F. Momoli, J. Siemiatycki, M.L. McBride et al., "Probabilistic Multiple-Bias Modeling Applied to the Canadian Data from the Interphone Study of Mobile Phone Use and Risk of Glioma, Meningioma, Acoustic Neuroma, and Parotid Gland Tumors," *American Journal of Epidemiology* 186, No. 7 (October 1, 2017): 885–93, https://www.ncbi.nlm.nih.gov/pubmed/28535174.

30. See "Cell Phone Safety Guidance from the California Department of Public Health Released by Court Order after Public Information Request," Environmental Health Trust, May 2017, updated January 2018, https://ehtrust.org/cell-phone-safety-guidance-california-health-department-released-court-order/.

31. "American Academy of Pediatrics Issues New Recommendations to 'Reduce Exposure to Cell Phones,'" Environmental Health Trust (via ReleaseWire), September 26, 2016, http://www.releasewire.com/press-releases/american-academy-of-pediatrics-issues-new-recommendations-to-reduce-exposure-to-cell-phones-726805.htm.

32. See, e.g., Gwyn Topham, Sean Clarke, Cath Levett, Paul Scruton, and Matt Fidler, "The Volkswagen Emissions Scandal Explained," *The Guardian*, September 23, 2015, https://www.theguardian.com/business/ng-interactive/2015/sep/23/volkswagen-emissions-scandal-explained-diesel-cars.

33. "France—Policy Recommendations on Cell Phones, Wireless Radiation & Health," Environmental Health Trust, 2017, https://ehtrust.org/france-policy-recommendations-cell-phones-wireless-radiation-health/.

34. Ibid. Emphasis in original.

35. "'Plus de téléphones portables dans les écoles et collèges à la rentrée 2018,' annonce Jean-Michel Blanquer," *Le Monde*, December 10, 2017, http://www.lemonde.fr/education/article/2017/12/10/plus-de-telephones-portables-dans-les-ecoles-et-colleges-a-la-rentree-2018-annonce-le-ministre-de-l-education-nationale_5227485_1473685.html.

36. Haigney, "Radiation Typical of Cell Phones."

37. Ryan Knutson, "Why the Largest Study Ever on Cellphones and Cancer Won't Settle the Debate," *Wall Street Journal*, February 2, 2018, https://www.wsj.com/articles/u-s-study-on-cellphone-radiation-wont-settle-debate-1517604284.

38. Rachel Feltman, "Do Cellphones Cause Cancer? Don't Believe the Hype," *Washington Post*, May 27, 2016, https://www.washingtonpost.com/news/speaking-of-science/wp/2016/05/27/do-cellphones-cause-cancer-dont-believe-the-hype/.

39. Whitney Webb, "Speculation Swirls over Sources of Trump Leaks, Yet No Mention of WaPo–CIA Ties," MintPress News, February 28, 2017, https://www.mintpressnews.com/speculation-swirls-over-sources-of-trump-leaks-yet-no-mention-of-wapo-cia-ties/225337/.

40. Norman Solomon, "Jeff Bezos is Doing Huge Business with the CIA, While Keeping His Washington Post Readers in the Dark," AlterNet, December 18, 2013, https://www.alternet.org/media/owner-washington-post-doing-business-cia-while-keeping-his-readers-dark.

41. Tracee Carrasco, "Washington Post Stirs Controversy with New Social Media Policy," Fox Business, July 14, 2017, http://video.foxbusiness.com/v/5507507651001/?#sp=show-clips.

42. James Freeman, "Bezos, Amazon and the Washington Post," Wall Street Journal, July 11, 2017, https://www.wsj.com/articles/bezos-amazon-and-the-washington-post-1499806742.

43. "Assessing Russian Activities and Intentions in Recent US Elections," Office of the Director of National Intelligence, January 6, 2017, https://www.dni.gov/files/documents/ICA_2017_01.pdf.

44. "2018 Nuclear Posture Review," U.S. Department of Defense, February 2018, 36, https://www.defense.gov/News/Special-Reports/0218_npr/.

45. Donie O'Sullivan, Drew Griffin, and Scott Bronstein, "The Unwitting: The Trump Supporters Used by Russia," CNNMoney, February 20, 2018, http://money.cnn.com/2018/02/20/media/internet-research-agency-unwitting-trump-supporters/index.html.

46. Sheera Frenkel and Katie Benner, "To Stir Discord in 2016, Russians Turned Most Often to Facebook," New York Times, February 17, 2018, https://www.nytimes.com/2018/02/17/technology/indictment-russian-tech-facebook.html.

47. See, e.g., Charles Eisenstein, "We Need Regenerative Farming, Not Geoengineering," The Guardian, March 9, 2015, https://www.theguardian.com/sustainable-business/2015/mar/09/we-need-regenerative-farming-not-geoengineering.

48. $486 billion in 2012: Carey L. Biron, "Global Agricultural Subsidies Near $500b, Favoring Large-Scale Producers," MintPress News, March 22, 2014, https://www.mintpressnews.com/global-agricultural-subsidies-near-500b-favoring-large-scale-producers/187275/.

49. $5.3 trillion a year: David Coady, Ian Parry, Louis Sears, and Baoping Shang, "How Large are Global Fossil Fuel Subsidies?" World Development 91 (March 2017), 11–27, https://www.sciencedirect.com/science/article/pii/S0305750X16304867.

50. Moises Velasquez-Manoff, "Can Dirt Save the Earth?" New York Times Magazine, April 18, 2018, www.nytimes.com/2018/04/18/magazine/dirt-save-earth-carbon-farming-climate-change.html; and Tom Roston, "Forget Sustainable Farming—Regenerative Agriculture is the New Frontier," Salon, May 4, 2018, www.salon.com/2018/05/04/forget-sustainable-farming-regenerative-agriculture-is-the-new-frontier/.

51. Lisa O. Monaco and John P. Carlin, "A 'Global Game of Whack-a-Mole': Overseas Data Rules are Stuck in the 19th Century," Washington Post, March 5, 2018, https://www.washingtonpost.com/opinions/a-global-game-of-whack-a-mole-overseas-data-rules-are-stuck-in-the-19th-century/2018/03/05/f24851e6-2096-11e8-86f6-54bfff693d2b_story.html.

52. Laura Hautala, "CLOUD Act Becomes Law, Increases Government Access to Online Info," CNET, March 23, 2018, https://www.cnet.com/news/cloud-act-becomes-law-increases-government-access-to-email-internet-microsoft/.

53. See, e.g., "Road Widening at Vilcabamba River and Recognition of Rights of Nature, Ecuador," Environmental Justice Atlas, undated (c. 2013), updated January 30, 2018, https://ejatlas.org/conflict/first-successful-case-of-rights-of-nature-ruling-vilcabamba-river-ecuador. For previous Project Censored coverage, see Chelsea Davis with Elaine Wellin, "Ecuador's Constitutional Rights of Nature," in Censored 2010: The Top 25 Censored Stories of 2008–09, eds. Peter Phillips and Mickey Huff with Project Censored (New York: Seven Stories Press, 2009), 83–86, http://projectcensored.org/18-ecuadors-constitutional-rights-of-nature/.

54. Bryant Rousseau, "In New Zealand, Lands and Rivers can be People (Legally Speaking)," New York Times, July 13, 2016, https://www.nytimes.com/2016/07/14/world/what-in-the-world/in-new-zealand-lands-and-rivers-can-be-people-legally-speaking.html.

55. Adam Taylor, "There are Now 3 Rivers that Legally Have the Same Rights as Humans," Washington Post, March 21, 2017, https://www.washingtonpost.com/news/worldviews/wp/2017/03/21/there-are-now-3-rivers-that-legally-have-the-same-rights-as-humans/.

56. Nirmala George, "India Gives Ganges, Yamuna Rivers Same Rights as a Human," *USA Today* (via Associated Press), March 21, 2017, https://www.usatoday.com/story/news/world/2017/03/21/court-gives-2-indian-rivers-same-rights-human/99439956/.

57. "Black Identity Extremists Likely Motivated to Target Law Enforcement Officers," Federal Bureau of Investigation Counterterrorism Division, August 3, 2017, https://www.documentcloud.org/documents/4067711-BIE-Redacted.html.

58. Andrew Rosenthal, "The F.B.I.'s Black Phantom Menace," *New York Times*, October 19, 2017, https://www.nytimes.com/2017/10/19/opinion/columnists/fbi-blacks-civil-rights.html.

59. "FBI Report: 'Black Identity Extremists' a Domestic Threat," Fox News, October 10, 2017, http://video.foxnews.com/v/5604525687001/?#sp=show-clips.

60. Chandelis R. Duster and Donna Owens, "'I Know They're Watching Us': Black Lawmakers, Activists Alarmed over FBI Report," NBC News, November 9, 2017, https://www.nbcnews.com/news/nbcblk/i-know-they-re-watching-us-black-lawmakers-activists-alarmed-n813221.

61. Henry Brean, "Air Force Seeks Comment on Plan to Expand Range into Wildlife Refuge," *Las Vegas Review-Journal*, December 7, 2017, https://www.reviewjournal.com/news/military/air-force-seeks-comment-on-plan-to-expand-range-into-wildlife-refuge/; and Henry Brean, "Air Force Plan to Expand Nevada Training Range Raises Concerns," *Las Vegas Review-Journal*, January 23, 2018, https://www.reviewjournal.com/news/military/air-force-plan-to-expand-nevada-training-range-raises-concerns/.

62. Nathan O'Neal, "Air Force Considers Expansion of Bombing Range into Nevada Wildlife Refuge," KSNV (NBC, Las Vegas, Nevada), January 17, 2018, http://news3lv.com/news/local/gallery/air-force-considers-expansion-of-bombing-range-into-nevada-wildlife-refuge.

63. Dahr Jamail, "Navy Secretly Conducting Electromagnetic Warfare Training on Washington Roads," Truthout, March 7, 2016, http://www.truth-out.org/news/item/35111-exclusive-navy-secretly-conducting-electromagnetic-warfare-training-on-washington-roads. See also Nora Kasapligil with Elaine Wellin, "The Toll of US Navy Training on Wildlife in the North Pacific," in *Censored 2018: Press Freedoms in a "Post-Truth" World* (New York: Seven Stories Press, 2017), 57–58, http://projectcensored.org/7-toll-us-navy-training-wildlife-north-pacific/.

64. Paighten Harkins, "Air Force Working with Bureau of Land Management to Temporarily Close Public Lands as Military Tests Weapons, including New 'Hypersonics,'" *Salt Lake Tribune*, April 13, 2018, https://www.sltrib.com/news/2018/04/13/air-force-working-with-bureau-of-land-management-to-temporarily-close-public-lands-as-military-tests-weapons-including-new-hypersonics/.

65. Nick Sobczyk, "Prospects for Sage Grouse Rider's Survival Improve," E&E News, May 21, 2018, https://www.eenews.net/stories/1060082171.

66. Otis R. Taylor Jr., "Mistreatment at the Richmond Jail? There is None, Sheriff Says," *San Francisco Chronicle*, January 5, 2018, https://www.sfchronicle.com/news/article/Mistreatment-at-the-Richmond-jail-There-is-none-12474841.php.

67. Caitlin Dickerson, "Trump Plan Would Curtail Protections for Detained Immigrants," *New York Times*, April 13, 2017, https://www.nytimes.com/2017/04/13/us/detained-immigrants-may-face-harsher-conditions-under-trump.html.

68. See John Upton, "Media Contributing to 'Hope Gap' on Climate Change," Climate Central, March 28, 2015, http://www.climatecentral.org/news/media-hope-gap-on-climate-change-18822.

69. For previous Project Censored coverage of "solutions journalism," see, e.g., Sarah van Gelder, "Solutions in a Time of Climate Meltdown: The Most Censored (and Indispensible) Story," in *Censored 2014: Fearless Speech in Fateful Times*, eds. Mickey Huff and Andy Lee Roth with Project Censored (New York: Seven Stories Press, 2013), 13–23. On the dangers of cynicism toward news, see Andy Lee Roth and Mickey Huff, "Introduction," *Censored 2014*, 25–34, 27–28.

70. "The Burden of Stress in America," NPR/Robert Wood Johnson Foundation/Harvard School of Public Health, 2014, 5, https://www.rwjf.org/content/dam/farm/reports/surveys_and_polls/2014/rwjf414295.

71. The first Intergovernmental Panel on Climate Change (IPCC) report, focused on problems related to climate change, was covered in 65 news stories; the third IPCC report, focused on

adaptations to climate change, was covered just 27 times. Saffron O'Neill, Hywel T.P. Williams, Tim Kurz, Bouke Wiersma, and Maxwell Boykoff, "Dominant Frames in Legacy and Social Media Coverage of the IPCC Fifth Assessment Report," *Nature Climate Change* 5 (March 25, 2015): 380–85, https://www.nature.com/articles/nclimate2535.

72. Upton, "Media Contributing to 'Hope Gap.'"

73. "About," Constructive Journalism Project, undated, https://www.constructivejournalism.org/about/.

74. Cathrine Gyldensted, *From Mirrors to Movers: Five Elements of Positive Psychology in Constructive Journalism* (Lexington, KY: GGroup Publishing, 2015). See also Cathrine Gyldensted, "News Media Kills Political Visions. Help: Prospective Psychology," Creativity Post, September 28, 2015, http://www.creativitypost.com/activism/news_media_kills_political_visions_help_prospective_psychology/.

75. John Authers, "Why Market Reporters Lean Towards Negative News," *Financial Times*, March 10, 2017, https://www.ft.com/content/c884defa-054a-11e7-aceo-1ce02efodef9.

76. Michael Smerconish, "The Real Media Bias: Negativity," CNN, May 27, 2017, https://www.cnn.com/videos/tv/2017/05/27/the-real-media-bias-negativity.cnn/.

77. Sean Emery, "Child Pornography Charges Dismissed in Case against Newport Beach Doctor that Involved FBI, Best Buy Techs," *Orange County Register*, November 28, 2017, https://www.ocregister.com/2017/11/28/child-pornography-charges-dismissed-in-case-best-buy-techs-tipped-fbi-agents-to-photo-on-newport-beach-doctors-computer/.

78. Natasha Bach, "The FBI has been Paying Geek Squad Repairmen to Turn Over Illegal Content on Your Computer," *Fortune*, March 7, 2018, http://fortune.com/2018/03/07/best-buy-geek-squad-fbi-informants/; and Tom Jackman, "Records Show Deep Ties between FBI and Best Buy Computer Technicians Looking for Child Porn," *Washington Post*, April 3, 2017, https://www.washingtonpost.com/news/true-crime/wp/2017/04/03/records-show-deep-ties-between-fbi-and-best-buy-computer-technicians-looking-for-child-porn/.

79. Cecilia Kang, "How to Give Rural America Broadband? Look to the Early 1900s," *New York Times*, August 7, 2016, https://www.nytimes.com/2016/08/08/technology/how-to-give-rural-america-broadband-look-to-the-early-1900s.html.

80. For Project Censored's previous coverage of the missing $6.5 trillion in US Army spending, see Elsa Denis with Mickey Huff, "Over Six Trillion Dollars in Unaccountable Army Spending," in *Censored 2018: Press Freedoms in a "Post-Truth" World*, eds. Andy Lee Roth and Mickey Huff with Project Censored (New York: Seven Stories Press, 2017), 44–47, http://projectcensored.org/2-six-trillion-dollars-unaccountable-army-spending/.

81. Laurence Kotlikoff and Mark Skidmore, "Has Our Government Spent $21 Trillion of Our Money without Telling Us?" *Forbes*, December 8, 2017, https://www.forbes.com/sites/kotlikoff/2017/12/08/has-our-government-spent-21-trillion-of-our-money-without-telling-us/.

82. See Solari's "The Missing Money" website for an archive of the documents: "DOD and HUD Missing Money: Supporting Documentation," The Missing Money (Solari), December 12, 2017, updated June 6, 2018, https://missingmoney.solari.com/dod-and-hud-missing-money-supporting-documentation/. Solari is a private company founded by Catherine Austin Fitts, who also serves as the company's president.

83. $2.4 trillion in assets: "Pentagon Announces First-Ever Audit," RT, December 8, 2017, updated December 9, 2017, https://www.rt.com/usa/412529-pentagon-first-ever-audit/. For previous coverage by Project Censored of this important but underreported news story, see Jeannette Acevedo with Peter Phillips, "Pentagon Awash in Money Despite Serious Audit Problems," in *Censored 2015: Inspiring We the People*, eds. Andy Lee Roth and Mickey Huff with Project Censored (New York: Seven Stories Press, 2014), 59–60, http://projectcensored.org/12-pentagon-awash-money-despite-serious-audit-problems/.

84. Kotlikoff and Skidmore, "Has Our Government Spent $21 Trillion"; and Bill Chappell, "Pentagon Announces First-Ever Audit of the Department of Defense," *The Two-Way* blog, NPR, December 8, 2017, https://www.npr.org/sections/thetwo-way/2017/12/08/569394885/pentagon-announces-first-ever-audit-of-the-department-of-defense.

85. "Teaching the Movement: The State Standards We Deserve," Southern Poverty Law Center's Teaching Tolerance Project, Montgomery, Alabama, March 2012, 9, https://www.splcenter.org/sites/default/files/d6_legacy_files/downloads/publication/Teaching_the_Movement_2_3.pdf.

86. Henry Louis Gates Jr., "What was the Civil Rights Movement?" The Root, August 12, 2013, https://www.theroot.com/what-was-the-civil-rights-movement-1790897669.

87. Evelyn Lirri, "Uganda Tightens Foreign Adoption Rules to Thwart Child Trafficking," Reuters, March 4, 2016, https://www.reuters.com/article/us-uganda-children-adoption/uganda-tightens-foreign-adoption-rules-to-thwart-child-trafficking-idUSKCN0W61OI.

88. Gita Aravamudan, "Child Trafficking, 'Manufactured Orphans': The Dark Underbelly of Inter-Country Adoption in India," Firstpost, September 3, 2017, https://www.firstpost.com/india/child-trafficking-manufactured-orphans-the-dark-underbelly-of-inter-country-adoption-in-india-4000837.html.

89. "The Universal Accreditation Act of 2012," US Citizenship and Immigration Services, July 14, 2014, updated February 21, 2018, https://www.uscis.gov/adoption/universal-accreditation-act-2012.

90. "Trafficking is not just an issue that happens to people in other countries. The United States is a source and transit country and is also considered one of the top destination points for victims of child trafficking and exploitation." See "Child Trafficking," UNICEF USA, undated, https://www.unicefusa.org/mission/protect/trafficking.

91. Joshua Philipp, "Child Trafficking through International Adoption Continues Despite Regulations," Epoch Times, March 15, 2018, updated March 28, 2018, https://www.theepochtimes.com/child-trafficking-through-international-adoption-continues-despite-regulations_2464370.html. See also the website of the US Institute Against Human Trafficking, https://usiaht.org/.

92. Abigail Niehaus, "The Underground Market of Internationally Adopted Children: Re-Homing and Questioning the Practice of International Adoption," Arkansas Journal of Social Change and Public Service, April 29, 2015, http://ualr.edu/socialchange/2015/04/29/underground-market-internationally-adopted-children-re-homing-questioning-practice-international-adoption/.

93. Amy Goodman and Nermeen Shaikh, interview with Alastair Gee, "'Bussed Out': How Cities are Giving Thousands of Homeless People One-Way Bus Tickets to Leave Town," Democracy Now!, December 28, 2017, https://www.democracynow.org/2017/12/28/bussed_out_how_cities_are_giving; and Hari Sreenivasan, interview with Alastair Gee, "Is Relocating Homeless People a Life Line or Broken System?" PBS NewsHour, PBS, December 23, 2017, https://www.pbs.org/newshour/show/is-relocating-homeless-people-a-life-line-or-broken-system.

94. Ali Velshi, interview with Alastair Gee, "The Guardian Investigation Reveals Flawed Homeless Relocation Program," NBC News, December 22, 2017, https://www.nbcnews.com/nightly-news/video/the-guardian-investigation-reveals-flawed-homeless-relocation-program-1122670659640; and Benjamin Oreskes and Shelby Grad, "Essential California: How Homelessness Became an Intractable Crisis," Los Angeles Times, March 4, 2018, http://www.latimes.com/newsletters/la-me-ln-essential-california-20180304-story.html.

95. Travis Fedschun, "Homeless Encampment Relocation Plan Has California Residents Outraged," Fox News, March 26, 2018, http://www.foxnews.com/us/2018/03/26/homeless-encampment-relocation-plan-has-california-residents-outraged.html.

96. Corinna C. Zygourakis, Seungwon Yoon, Victoria Valencia, Christy Boscardin, Christopher Moriates, Ralph Gonzales, and Michael T. Lawton, "Operating Room Waste: Disposable Supply Utilization in Neurosurgical Procedures," Journal of Neurosurgery 126, No. 2 (February 2017): 620–25, https://www.ncbi.nlm.nih.gov/pubmed/27153160.

97. Beth Jones Sanborn, "Hospitals Save Millions with Sustainability Programs, Cut Back on Waste," Healthcare Finance, March 14, 2017, http://www.healthcarefinancenews.com/news/hospitals-save-millions-sustainability-programs-cut-back-waste; and Paige Minemyer, "Hospitals' Wasted Supplies may Contribute to Growing Costs," FierceHealthcare, March 10, 2017, https://www.fiercehealthcare.com/finance/hospitals-wasted-supplies-may-contribute-to-growing-costs.

98. Marshall Allen, "Want to Cut Health-Care Costs? Start with the Obscene Amount of Waste," PostEverything (Washington Post), December 28, 2017, https://www.washingtonpost.com/news/posteverything/wp/2017/12/28/want-to-cut-health-care-costs-start-with-the-obscene-amount-of-waste/.

99. Anzish Mirza, "Hospitals Waste Billions of Dollars in Medical Supplies," U.S. News & World Report, March 9, 2017, https://www.usnews.com/news/healthcare-of-tomorrow/articles/2017-03-09/hospitals-are-wasting-billions-of-dollars-worth-of-medical-equipment.

100. John Woodrow Cox, Steven Rich, Allyson Chiu, John Muyskens, and Monica Ulmanu, "More than 215,000 Students have Experienced Gun Violence at School Since Columbine," *Washington Post*, May 25, 2018, https://www.washingtonpost.com/graphics/2018/local/school-shootings-database.

101. Neil Reisner and Dave Philipps, "Florida School's R.O.T.C. Lost 3 Cadets; Suspect was a Member," *New York Times*, February 20, 2018, https://www.nytimes.com/2018/02/20/us/jrotc-cadets-florida-shooting.html; Lori Rozsa, "'Selfless Service': JROTC Remembers Three Slain in Florida High School Shooting," *Washington Post*, February 19, 2018, https://www.washingtonpost.com/national/selfless-service-jrotc-remembers-three-slain-in-florida-high-school-shooting/2018/02/19/1e3138f2-158b-11e8-8b08-027a6ccb38eb_story.html; and Frank Miles, "Junior ROTC Leader Shocked that Florida School Shooting Suspect Nikolas Cruz was His Cadet," Fox News, February 18, 2018, http://www.foxnews.com/us/2018/02/18/junior-leader-shocked-that-florida-school-shooting-suspect-nikolas-cruz-was-his-cadet.html.

102. "Provisional Counts of Drug Overdose Deaths, as of 8/6/2017," National Center for Health Statistics, Centers for Disease Control and Prevention, August 6, 2017, https://www.cdc.gov/nchs/data/health_policy/monthly-drug-overdose-death-estimates.pdf.

103. Stephanie Armour, "Opioid Crisis Gets Washington's Attention," *Wall Street Journal*, March 8, 2018, https://www.wsj.com/articles/opioid-crisis-gets-washingtons-attention-1520514001.

104. Barry Meier, "Origins of an Epidemic: Purdue Pharma Knew Its Opioids were Widely Abused," *New York Times*, May 29, 2018, https://www.nytimes.com/2018/05/29/health/purdue-opioids-oxycontin.html.

105. Chris McGreal, "How Big Pharma's Money—and Its Politicians—Feed the US Opioid Crisis," *The Guardian*, October 19, 2017, https://www.theguardian.com/us-news/2017/oct/19/big-pharma-money-lobbying-us-opioid-crisis.

106. Nick Leiber, "JPay, the Apple of the U.S. Prison System," Bloomberg, September 13, 2012, https://www.bloomberg.com/news/articles/2012-09-13/jpay-the-apple-of-the-u-dot-s-dot-prison-system.

107. Michelle Alexander, *The New Jim Crow: Mass Incarceration in the Age of Colorblindness* (New York: The New Press, 2010/2012), 2.

108. Jonah Engel Bromwich, "Why are American Prisons So Afraid of This Book?" *New York Times*, January 18, 2018, https://www.nytimes.com/2018/01/18/us/new-jim-crow-book-ban-prison.html; Molly Olmstead, "Some New Jersey Prisons have Banned a Seminal Book about the Mass Incarceration of Black Men," Slate, January 8, 2018, https://slate.com/news-and-politics/2018/01/new-jim-crow-banned-new-jersey-prisons.html; and Jon Schuppe, "New Jersey Lifts Prison Ban of 'The New Jim Crow' after ACLU Criticism," NBC News, January 8, 2018, https://www.nbcnews.com/news/us-news/aclu-asks-new-jersey-lift-prison-ban-new-jim-crow-n835776.

109. Mary Shedden, "Unlocked Cars Provide Thieves Easy Access to Guns," WUSF News, November 15, 2017, http://wusfnews.wusf.usf.edu/post/unlocked-cars-provide-thieves-easy-access-guns.

110. "Global Biometrics Market Revenue to Reach $15.1 Billion by 2025," Tractica, February 6, 2017, https://www.tractica.com/newsroom/press-releases/global-biometrics-market-revenue-to-reach-15-1-billion-by-2025/.

111. Aaron Nelsen, "Sheriff Touts Biometric Technology in Fight against Cross-Border Crime," *San Antonio Express-News*, September 6, 2017, https://www.expressnews.com/news/local/article/Border-sheriff-touts-biometric-technology-in-12177779.php; "Southwestern Border Sheriffs' Coalition (SBSC) to Immediately Begin Improving the Biometric Identification Capabilities of the 31 Sheriffs' Offices along the U.S. and Mexico Border to Increase Border Security and Combat Criminal Activity," Business Wire, April 6, 2017, https://www.businesswire.com/news/home/20170406006132/en/Southwestern-Border-Sheriffs%E2%80%99-Coalition-SBSC-immediately-improving; and Grace Raih, "Biometric Firm Enters into Trial Agreement with Southwestern Border Sheriffs Coalition," MuckRock, December 21, 2017, https://www.muckrock.com/news/archives/2017/dec/21/border-iris/.

CHAPTER 2

Blurred Lines and Clickbait
The Sh*thole that is Junk Food News

Susan Rahman and Isabelle Snow, with Tonatiuh Beltran, Tate Dobbins, Jacqueline Gibbons, Maria Granados, Christina Hamilton, Whitney Howard, Katie Wong, and Kyle Zucker from the College of Marin

You guys love breaking news, and you did it, you broke it! Good work! The most useful information on CNN is when Anthony Bourdain tells me where to eat noodles.

—Michelle Wolff, 2018 White House Correspondents' Dinner[1]

The reality TV president has found his reality TV press. The sensationalist Fake News epidemic, with name-calling and partisan rancor from both major political parties, has helped to blur the lines between relevant news reports and Junk Food News. Project Censored founder Carl Jensen coined the term "Junk Food News" back in 1982 when referring to the trite, sensationalist stories that consumed the major news media. They were empty-calorie stories that often crowded out the kind of real investigative journalism required to maintain a healthy democracy. Project Censored has covered the phenomenon ever since and charted its unfortunate and meteoric rise. Not long after Jensen's coining of the phrase, media scholar Neil Postman addressed the broader concerns of this analysis in 1985 in one of the seminal works of media ecology, *Amusing Ourselves to Death: Public Discourse in the Age of Show Business.* Are we there yet? Our current media and political discourse suggest that perhaps we have arrived.

In 2017 and 2018, navigating news cycles became an Olympic sport, riddled with Junk Food News hurdles at every lap. At the drop of a "shithole," the corporate press dissected and dramatized stories with little substantive information or broader cultural relevance, known as "Junk Food News" stories, to the point that they overshadowed reporting on actually significant topics. Consumers of news were left to decipher the significance of each bombardment of alerts, dings, and hashtags, only to find that little lingered behind the flashy surface. The latest Kardashian stunt was debated by animated panelists, a puppy's fate was publicly mourned, porn-star-turned-whistleblower Stormy Daniels ruled the cable circuit, and Trump's infamous "shithole" comment was immortalized as a viral GIF.

The Junk Food headlines in this chapter, selected from the 2017–2018 news cycle, were all given priority by the corporate media over crucial investigative reporting. President Trump, the white whale of Junk Food News, manipulates the press much like a kindergartener during playtime. Policies are picked up just to be cast aside like building blocks. The press chases him down slides and across the monkey bars, subjected to his teasing and bullying all the way. The corporate media are, in effect, his playground.

With the weekly stockpile of White House gaffes, Junk Food News now shares the chair of the Oval Office with the sitting president. His tweet storms, his Stormy affair, and his voracious political accusations dominate the corporate media. With each staff turnover and conflict of interest, would-be news stories are sensationalized to the point that their legitimacy is worn down. By late 2017, corporate news organizations began to question the nature of the president's obtuse ramblings. *The Washington Post* published a story in October 2017 with a title that appeared to refer to Postman's—"Trump is Distracting Us to Death." Soon the *New York Times*, Vox, and The Hill followed suit with similarly titled op-eds. This series of pieces publicly wondered, "Is President Trump trying to distract us from more important issues?" *The Washington Post* recounted the viral moment when Trump threw paper towel rolls to hurricane victims in Puerto Rico. This served to distract from the increasing Republican support for gun background checks after the Las Vegas shooting.[2] In the fall of 2017, Trump publicly feuded with National Football League protestors on Twitter. This coincided with Secretary of the Interior Ryan Zinke's announcement that 76.9 million acres of federal waters were sold in the largest lease sale to the oil and gas industry in United States history.[3] We are pulled away from important issues to chase the idiocy and inanity of our president, often via Twitter and then onto the front pages and prime-time slots of the so-called news.

The corporate media has found its true love as it continues to be enamored by the latest follies of President Trump. Political commentators aggressively evaluate his every weekend in Mar-a-Lago to catch him in Gotcha! moments of contradiction that nonetheless seem to bear few, if any, consequences. Members of the press wait eagerly to find the next biggest scandal, churning out melodramatic op-eds right and left, generally to no avail. Even newsworthy stories are gutted by the 24-hour cycle and reduced to mere soundbites and GIFs. On March 26, 2018, Associated Press White House correspondent Zeke Miller asked White House deputy press secretary Raj Shah, "Why should we in this room—and more importantly, the American people—trust anything this administration is telling them?"[4] The existence of fake news itself is what dominates the headlines. Ambiguity shrouds whatever comes out of the White House, and the corporate press is left to spin gold out of straw. We are living in an age where clickbait is the norm. Misconduct is a benchmark for our leaders and double entendres are a CNN staple. When the apocalypse comes and we are too uninformed by the corporate press to notice, thanks to the late, great Anthony Bourdain at least we'll know where to get the best noodles.

STICKS AND STONES, BUT SH*THOLE HAS HURT SAFA

On January 11, 2018, President Trump met with lawmakers privately to discuss a bipartisan deal that would protect Deferred Action for Childhood Arrivals (DACA) participants. As he argued against restoring protections in the United States for people from El Salvador, Haiti, and a few African countries, President Trump reportedly asked, "Why are we having all these people from shithole countries come here?"[5] Corporate media revved up into overdrive to cover the *alleged* comment. News reports ran continuously for weeks. *Politico* reported that the Federal Communications Commission logged at least 162 indecency complaints regarding the verbatim use of the word "shithole" by major news networks. CNN received the predominant share of complaints, but other outlets, including NBC News, NPR, and MSNBC, were also named.[6]

The American public was furious over news coverage impropriety. Conservative and liberal pundits took to the airwaves with arguments and analyses of whether and how this latest Oval Office comment was racist, elitist, and/or just unkind profanity.[7] Both Republicans and Democrats were quick to condemn the comment, the Internet exploded with international responses, and #shithole topped Twitter's trending news for the week.[8] The remark came just after Trump's termination of Temporary Protected Status for migrants from El Salvador and Haiti, which spurred even more outrage. All the while, little attention was paid to the purpose of the meeting—immigration reform. On occasion, articles briefly mentioned that President Trump rejected the meeting's bipartisan proposal.[9] A week following the comment, Haiti was removed from the list of countries eligible for H-2A and H-2B temporary work visas. While there was debate as to whether Trump actually used the word "shithole," undoubtedly the word *not* used was SAFA.

Republican Bob Goodlatte's Securing America's Future Act (SAFA) received practically no coverage in the corporate media. Amidst heightened immigration contention, the bill was introduced to provide a legislative solution for the nearly 700,000 beneficiaries of DACA. SAFA was introduced in Congress on January 10, 2018, without so much as a mention in the corporate media.[10] The so-called solution provides only contingent nonimmigrant status and no consideration for those who will age into DACA eligibility, and it offers no pathway to legal permanent status or citizenship. The bill would limit family-based immigration to spouses and minor children, and would grant the government the right to use DNA verification. Excluding parents, siblings, and adult children further exacerbates the issue of separating families and leaves the fate of the parents of DACA participants undetermined.[11]

But DACA is only a small provision of the sweeping 400-page anti-immigration bill. Interior provisions propose to infringe upon state and local law enforcement sovereignty. The Department of Justice would be allowed to withhold grants from sanctuary cities. SAFA would require states to pay local law enforcement to perform the functions of immigration officers. This would be a violation of both the separation of powers and the Tenth Amendment of the US Constitution. Illegal entry and visa overstays would be criminalized under SAFA. Even if individuals have not violated any criminal or civil laws, they would face punishment consisting of fines and/or incarceration for anywhere from six months to 20 years.[12]

The diversity visa program would be eliminated under SAFA. This is the only means for nationals from some African countries, who don't qualify for refugee status, to even apply for immigration to the US in hope of a better life. SAFA would also restrict eligibility for those seeking asylum for humanitarian reasons. It is estimated that these provisions would reduce legal immigration levels by issuing 400,000 fewer visas than current policies mandate, which would have significant economic and social impacts.[13]

This only scratches the surface of SAFA, which also seeks to limit protection for unaccompanied alien children, appropriate $20 billion for a wall along the Mexican border, increase Customs and Border Protection by 5,000 new hires, and implement a biometric identification program for the employment of immigrant workers, amongst other Big Brother policies. DACA deadlines have come and gone without a glimpse of political compromise. Meanwhile, SAFA quietly gained 96 Republican co-sponsors, which further distanced any hope for a bipartisan bill.[14]

While the impending passage of a Big Brother–type bill looms over the legislature, all the press can do, it seems, is literally talk shit. On April 30, 2018, a reporter asked Nigerian president Muhammadu Buhari, the first leader from sub-Saharan Africa to visit the White House since the inauguration, the question still weighing on American minds: whether the two presidents have discussed Trump's "shithole" comment.[15]

KEEP UP WITH KYLIE AND NEGLECT BLACK INFANT MORTALITY

Makeup guru and social media icon Kylie Jenner gave birth to a daughter, Stormi Webster, on February 1, 2018.[16] In early September

2017, rumors began to spread about Jenner's pregnancy, but nothing was ever confirmed. For months fans had been chomping at the bit for any sign that the youngest sister of the Kardashian/Jenner family was actually pregnant—and, if she was, they demanded to know: Who was the father? The corporate press attempted to out Jenner's pregnancy for six months. It was featured among the trending headlines on almost every social networking site.[17] The Jenner story enticed us to forget the political disarray of our time, sweeping us up in the fantasy of her glamorous life. Our obsession with the Kardashian baby also helped divert attention from a startling new report on the black infant mortality rate.

With today's technological innovations, one would only assume high infant mortality in the United States was a thing of the past. The research suggests otherwise. According to recent data from the US Centers for Disease Control and Prevention, "For every 1,000 live births, 4.5 white infants die in the first year of life. For black babies that number is 11.7."[18] This begs the question: What could be causing this racially disproportionate infant mortality rate? Could it be the diet of black women? Or perhaps smoking/drinking habits? Poverty? Overall health and exercise? Education? Strikingly, even black women with advanced degrees and high-paying prestigious professions are more likely to lose infants than white women who haven't graduated from high school. Were it not for tennis star Serena Williams's childbirth complications making headlines, this story might have all but faded into oblivion.[19]

Although minimally covered in the corporate press, this infant mortality disparity has been under investigation since the 1990s. To much surprise, the collective findings conclude that the main culprit of the black infant mortality rate is, quite simply put, the stress of being a black woman in the US.[20] The lives of black women (and men) are filled with greater harassment, microaggressions, fear, and danger than the lives of their white counterparts. This increases the likelihood of health risks during pregnancies and childbirth.[21] Stress throughout the span of a woman's life can prompt biological effects that endanger the health of her future children. Stress can disrupt immune, vascular, metabolic, and endocrine systems, and cause cells to age more quickly.[22] Chronic stress raises levels of cortisol, a hormone that at elevated levels can induce early labor. Higher levels of cortisol can cause an inflammatory response that restricts blood flow to the placenta, which stunts infant growth and lowers the birth weight. Black mothers have a greater chance of early onset labor and are more likely to be unable to carry their child to full term.[23]

So, while little Stormi's entry into this world was anticipated with bated breath, we as a society missed identifying and addressing an entirely treatable, yet ongoing, health crisis, one that highlights why movements like Black Lives Matter and Showing Up for Racial Justice are so desperately needed. These groups call attention to the racial disparity of infant mortality while the corporate press continue to neglect the issue in favor of celebrity baby talk.

PUPPY EYES BEFORE HUMAN RIGHTS

On March 12, 2018, a ten-month-old French bulldog died during a United Airlines flight. The flight crew required that the dog stay in the overhead bin for the duration of the flight.[24] From the date the dog died, this story spread like wildfire across the corporate media. In April 2018, Fox News reported that the family was considering filing a lawsuit.[25] Human interest stories reign as Junk Food News; they are the zeitgeist for 21st-century establishment media, especially if they are aesthetically and emotionally appealing and pose no threat to corporate interests.

While the public cried foul on United Airlines and demanded animal rights, a fundamental human rights issue was all but ignored by the corporate media. Victims of human trafficking are frequently funneled into the agriculture industry with the help of the US government. This disgraceful oversight is neither cute nor cuddly. An April 2018 *Frontline* documentary on PBS highlighted an example of modern-day trafficked slavery in the United States. The documentary focused on a group of eight minors who were granted immigration status from Guatemala. Their trafficker set up a system of fake sponsors for the minors to pose for immigration officials at the border. The minors were then enslaved on a Trillium egg farm in Ohio to pay off the $15,000 fee their traffickers charged. When the workers refused to pay, the traffickers would threaten physical violence against them and their families.[26]

According to a 2016 Senate subcommittee investigation into the Department of Health and Human Services (HHS), immigration officials overlooked their responsibility to follow up on the cases of unaccompanied sponsored minors. HHS is unable to locate 19 percent of unaccompanied minors in cases from 2016 to 2017. More than half of these minors did not appear for their immigration hearings. The case highlighted by the *Frontline* documentary is not an isolated incident; the Permanent Subcommittee on Investigations has now heard 12 similar cases.[27] This investigation revealed ubiquitous exploitation throughout the agricultural industry and neglect by the US government, but the corporate media refuses to hold anyone accountable, ultimately failing in its role as a free press.

According to the National Human Trafficking Hotline, a majority of labor trafficking victims are forced to work in the agricultural industry.[28] One Green Planet reports that 72 percent of factory farm workers are born outside of the United States.[29] Captors exploit the isolation of farms and processing centers and the marginal status of seasonal workers to prevent captives from escape.[30] The harmful conditions of factory farms cause an employee turnover rate of more than 95 percent annually. There is a 50 percent chance of injury in factory farming jobs, with 70 percent of agricultural workers experiencing respiratory issues due to contact with ammonia, hydrogen sulfide, and bacteria. The income of factory farm workers falls below the federal poverty line, with shifts that last ten or more hours. Workers refrain from reporting workplace hazards because they risk impulsive firing or deportation.[31] This practice traps workers in a catch-22 position, forcing them to survive in debilitating working conditions.

Crucial investigations into the agricultural industry were eclipsed by the corporate media's sensationalized United Airlines story. Focus on a story about a puppy with cute, sad eyes, and it will dominate the news cycle. Once United resolved the issue, their corporate interest was protected by the press. United representatives were given a platform for sound bites and interviews by a variety of publications. It appears that this was by design. The *Frontline* investigation was largely unmentioned in lieu of the updated airline story, with United officials rewritten as heroes.[32] While busy protecting the interests of United Airlines, the corporate media simultaneously protected the interests of the agriculture industry by not calling out documented human rights violations. A well-worn idiom reminds us that every dog has its day. Today that might be taken quite literally: while the next air-traveling dog may be granted safe passage, where is the justice for victims of human trafficking?

SEX, LIES, AND SHARK WEEK

Live every week like it's Shark Week.

—Tracy Jordan, *30 Rock*[33]

Prior to 2018, few people without a vested interest in the porn industry knew the name of adult film actress Stormy Daniels. That all changed after January 12, when the *Wall Street Journal* reported that Daniels was allegedly paid $130,000 by Donald Trump's personal lawyer to deter her from publicly revealing an extramarital affair she had with Trump years earlier.[34] The lawyer in question, Michael Cohen, initially denied the story only to issue a statement to the *New York Times* a month later that he did in fact pay Daniels—but from his own pocket, stating that the exchange was lawful and not connected to the Trump campaign in any way.[35] Stormy Daniels was ubiquitously covered by major establishment and entertainment news sources for the first quarter of 2018.

Daniels's interview on *60 Minutes* in late March was a ratings blockbuster for CBS—the largest audience the news program had in a decade, with a higher viewership than that year's Grammy Awards and Golden Globes ceremonies.[36] There was no major new revelation or proof of the affair. We did learn that Trump liked being spanked and that he made Daniels watch hours of the Discovery Channel's famed Shark Week programming with him.[37] The most famous porn star on Earth is currently on her "Make America Horny Again" tour, making appearances at strip clubs across the country (a job it seems like the president wishes he had right about now).[38] It may be counterintuitive that someone who bragged that she could "describe [Trump's] junk perfectly"[39] would be a genuine threat to the presidency and not simply an extension of Trump's reality TV administration, but the Daniels story may be more than the *Cosmo* articles make it seem.

As scandals go, the Stormy Daniels saga has it all: sex, money, politics, abuse of power, threatening goons, lies and cover-ups, suits and countersuits . . . and possible federal crimes. *The Los Angeles Times* succinctly summed up the news story as "a tawdry tabloid tale that also happens to have potentially enormous political ramifications."[40] Corporate media did its due diligence in following the ever-changing narrative. More questions were raised after the Federal Bureau of Investigation raided Michael Cohen's New York office in connection with Daniels's payoff as well as other ongoing criminal investigations into charges that include bank fraud.[41] With Cohen under investigation, Trump's legal team needed new blood to defend the commander-in-chief. They acquired former New York City mayor Rudy Giuliani for the job. Giuliani confirmed to Fox News in May that President Trump reimbursed Cohen for the $130,000 paid to Daniels—a direct contradiction of Trump's earlier denials—in order to quell rumors that campaign funds were used for the payoff, which would amount to a federal offense.[42]

Amidst the personal and legal dramas surrounding the Daniels payoff, there was a dearth of coverage on two bills that raced through Congress. With near-unanimous approval, these bills threaten both sex workers and the future of freedom on the Internet. One week before Daniels's much-anticipated *60 Minutes* interview, the Stop Enabling Sex Traffickers Act (SESTA) passed by 97–2 in the Senate. While the bill was purportedly intended to protect victims of online trafficking, advocacy groups argued that it would endanger trafficking victims and sex workers.[43] Two months earlier, the House passed the bill's counterpart, the Allow States and Victims to Fight Online Sex Trafficking Act (FOSTA), which permitted authorities to hold websites used as platforms for solicitation liable to civil as well as federal prosecution "even if they were unaware of users promoting sex trafficking."[44]

Combined into one single bill with an unwieldy acronym, FOSTA-SESTA targeted sites known for solicitation ads. In spite of its aim of stopping sex trafficking, the bill faced an onslaught of criticism. Sex workers and human rights groups such as the American Civil

Liberties Union, The National Center for Transgender Equality, and Freedom Network USA, an alliance of advocates who say they support a human rights-based approach to human trafficking, spoke out against the bill. These critics claimed that the FOSTA-SESTA bill forces traffickers to go further underground, which makes it more difficult for the government to find them. This hinders law enforcement investigations of nonconsensual sex work and endangers consensual sex workers.[45]

What went underreported by the corporate media was how the bill will undermine a decades-old law that laid the foundation for "the basis of free internet as we know it": Section 230 of the Communications Decency Act of 1996.[46] Section 230 protects Internet sites "against laws that may hold them accountable for their users' content,"[47] but FOSTA-SESTA amended that provision so that victims of online trafficking could "legally pursue websites that facilitate trafficking . . . and [make] it easier for federal and state prosecutors and private citizens to go after platforms whose sites have been used by traffickers."[48] Website operators are now responsible for anything that users generate on their sites and are open to litigation. This impacts vital communication platforms that sex workers use to warn one another about dangerous clients, find emergency housing, and assist in screening potential clients.[49] Following the passage of FOSTA SESTA, Craigslist personal ads and Reddit subforums used by sex workers were expunged from the Internet in order to avoid future fallout. This pulls a vital safety net right out from under those who need it most, and raises serious concerns about free speech protections on the Internet.[50]

FOSTA-SESTA is an "enormous chilling of free speech," declared Senator Ron Wyden (D-OR), co-author of Section 230, and one of the two opposing votes for the Senate version of the combined bill.[51] Not only will FOSTA-SESTA endanger the very people it was supposed to protect, but it could potentially affect everyone who uses sites like Facebook and Yelp. This is a destabilization of free speech online and calls into question the future of the net neutrality debate. President Trump signed the bill into law on April 11, two days after the FBI raid of Cohen's office and hotel room.[52]

Stormy Daniels and FOSTA-SESTA as presented to the public

were simple and straightforward stories on their respective surfaces. The former appeared to involve a torrid sexual exploit with a very powerful man befitting tabloid covers, and the latter appeared to be a law to stop sex trafficking online. But much like Trump's binge-watch programming of choice, Shark Week, the frothy coverage of Stormy Daniels and FOSTA-SESTA had deeper, more perilous dangers lurking in the depths. The fangs of potential campaign fraud charges looming over the heads of Cohen and Trump were captured for all the world to see. Unfortunately, the coverage was not the same for FOSTA-SESTA. The press was unable or unwilling to exhume the facts about the bigger threat against sex workers, trafficking victims, and Internet freedom protections. As is often the case with corporate media's love of Junk Food News, Trump's past sexual exploits and TV-watching habits were the bigger stories. The corporate news media may have focused on the surface waters of the Stormy Daniels case, but the ripple effect from FOSTA-SESTA will be felt for a long time to come.

CONCLUSION

This chapter constitutes just a small selection of the innumerable accounts of the corporate media's willful censorship. The preponderance of published Junk Food News stories represents an ongoing disservice that news agencies perpetrate on the American public. The safeguarding of corporate interests, financial gains, and the total tally of eyes on a page or screen shapes the content of the corporate news cycle, not the utility of valuable information that is in the public interest. The Instagram karma of a Kardashian baby was given priority over a health crisis that reveals the extensive effects of racial inequality. The illicit Stormy Daniels affair garnered more attention than a bill that unjustly ignores the nuances of sex work in the 21st century. A cute puppy photo served as distracting clickbait to divert from the realities of human trafficking. One "shithole" meme attracted like flies more pundit analysis than two immigration bills with evident racial bias.

Entertainment has become the almighty answer for news media seeking ratings, a stark contrast to the purpose for which they were designed: to provoke questions and hold those in power accountable. In this time, we must turn to smaller, more independent agencies to dissect the nuances of our reality. We must approach the corporate media with the careful consideration of an Anthony Bourdain on the hunt for the next best noodle dish. A media-literate consumer will work to see past the brothy surface of our media landscape to find substance and be on the lookout for truth, whether it's digestible or not.

SUSAN RAHMAN is a mother and professor of behavioral sciences at the College of Marin. Her work toward social justice in her classes allows for student inquiry into the pressing issues of our times. In addition to her teaching, she humbly serves as the vice president of the Media Freedom Foundation. She resides in Northern California with her family.

IZZY SNOW is an incoming sophomore at the College of Marin. She graduated from the Communications Academy at Sir Francis Drake High School in 2016 and then took a gap year, working full-time at Revolution 9 in Fairfax, CA. Izzy hopes to transfer to a four-year university where she will study film and sociology. She adored working with Project Censored and hopes to collaborate with local media stations in the future.

Notes

1. Bethy Squires, "Michelle Wolf's Best Jokes at the 2018 White House Correspondents' Dinner," Vulture, April 29, 2018, www.vulture.com/2018/04/michelle-wolf-white-house-'correspondents-dinner-jokes.html.

2. Kathleen Parker, "Trump is Distracting Us to Death," Washington Post, October 6, 2017, www.washingtonpost.com/opinions/trump-is-distracting-us-to-death/2017/10/06/4dad7888-aaca-11e7-850e-2bdd1236be5d_story.html.

3. John Filostrat, "Secretary Zinke Announces Largest Oil & Gas Lease Sale in U.S. History," U.S. Department of the Interior, October 24, 2017, www.doi.gov/pressreleases/secretary-zinke-announces-largest-oil-gas-lease-sale-us-history.

4. Tim Hains, "Reporter to White House: Why Should We Trust Anything This Administration Tells Us?" RealClearPolitics, March 26, 2018, https://www.realclearpolitics.com/video/2018/03/26/reporter_to_white_house_why_should_we_trust_anything_this_administration_tells_us.html.

5. Josh Dawsey, "Trump Derides Protections for Immigrants from 'Shithole' Countries," Washington Post, January 11, 2018, https://www.washingtonpost.com/politics/trump-attacks-protections-for-immigrants-from-shithole-countries-in-oval-office-meeting/2018/01/11/bfc0725c-f711-11e7-91af-31ac729add94_story.html.

6. John Hendel, "Trump 'Shithole' Coverage Prompted More Than 160 Indecency Complaints," Politico, April 3, 2018, https://www.politico.com/story/2018/04/03/trump-shithole-media-coverage-indecency-complaints-454928.

7. Patrick Wintour, Jason Burke, and Anne Livsey, "'There's No Other Word but Racist': Trump's Global Rebuke for 'Shithole' Remark," The Guardian, January 13, 2018, https://www.theguardian.com/us-news/2018/jan/12/unkind-divisive-elitist-international-outcry-over-trumps-shithole-countries-remark.

8. Graeme McMillan, "While You were Offline: Twitter Has Thoughts on Trump's 'Shithole Countries' Talk," Wired, January 14, 2018, https://www.wired.com/story/internet-week-153.

9. Tal Kopan and Lauren Fox, "Trump Says Some Immigrants from 'Shithole Countries' as He Rejects Bipartisan Deal," CNN, January 11, 2018, https://www.cnn.com/2018/01/11/politics/daca-deal-obstacles-flake-white-house/index.html.
10. *H.R. 4760: Securing America's Future Act of 2018*, Congress.gov, January 10, 2018, https://www.congress.gov/bill/115th-congress/house-bill/4760/text.
11. Kristie De Peña and Jeremy L. Neufeld, "Review of the *Securing America's Future Act of 2018* and State-by-State Economic Effects," Niskanen Center, February 2, 2018, https://niskanencenter.org/blog/news/review-securing-americas-future-act-2018-state-state-economic-effects/.
12. Ibid.
13. Ibid.
14. Ibid.
15. Jaclyn Reiss, "A Reporter Asked the Nigerian President about Trump's 'S—hole Countries' Comment. Here's What He Said," *Boston Globe*, April 30, 2018, https://www.bostonglobe.com/news/politics/2018/04/30/reporter-asked-nigerian-president-about-trump-hole-countries-comment-here-what-said/M8Yg12PWOtWzOkObzcNREI/story.html.
16. Elahe Izadi, "Kylie Jenner Announces the Birth of a Baby Girl After Months of Pregnancy Rumors," *Washington Post*, February 4, 2018, https://www.washingtonpost.com/news/arts-and-entertainment/wp/2018/02/04/kylie-jenner-announces-the-birth-of-a-baby-girl-after-months-of-pregnancy-rumors/.
17. Isis Briones, "Everything That's Happened Since News of Kylie Jenner's Pregnancy Broke," *Billboard*, October 11, 2017, https://www.billboard.com/articles/news/lifestyle/7997543/kylie-jenner-pregnancy-timeline.
18. Rhitu Chatterjee and Rebecca Davis, "How Racism May Cause Black Mothers to Suffer the Death of Their Infants," *Morning Edition*, NPR, December 20, 2017, https://www.npr.org/sections/health-shots/2017/12/20/570777510/how-racism-may-cause-black-mothers-to-suffer-the-death-of-their-infants.
19. Carly Ledbetter, "Serena Williams Talks About the Terrifying Complications She Faced after Giving Birth," Huffington Post, January 10, 2018, updated February 21, 2018, https://www.huffingtonpost.com/entry/serena-williams-opens-up-about-her-terrifying-pregnancy-complications_us_5a5621fce4b0b117f8812c9f. For previous Project Censored coverage of this issue, see also story #8, Jane C. Hau and Hope Matheson, with Andy Lee Roth and Steve Macek, "Maternal Mortality a Growing Threat in the US," in chapter 1 of *Censored 2018: Press Freedoms in a "Post-Truth" World*, eds. Andy Lee Roth and Mickey Huff with Project Censored (New York: Seven Stories Press, 2017), 59–61, online at http://projectcensored.org/8-maternal-mortality-growing-threat-us/.
20. Linda Villarosa, "Why America's Black Mothers and Babies are in a Life-or-Death Crisis," *New York Times Magazine*, April 11, 2018, https://www.nytimes.com/2018/04/11/magazine/black-mothers-babies-death-maternal-mortality.html.
21. Zoë Carpenter, "What's Killing America's Black Infants?" *The Nation*, February 15, 2017, https://www.thenation.com/article/whats-killing-americas-black-infants/.
22. Villarosa, "Why America's Black Mothers and Babies are in a Life-or-Death Crisis."
23. Ibid.
24. Bill Chappell, "Dog Dies in Overhead Bin on United Flight; Airline Apologizes," NPR, March 14, 2018, https://www.npr.org/sections/thetwo-way/2018/03/14/593479827/dog-dies-in-over-head-bin-on-united-flight-airline-apologizes.
25. Michelle Gant, "Family of Dog Killed on United Flight Considering Lawsuit," Fox News, May 3, 2018, http://www.foxnews.com/travel/2018/05/03/family-dog-killed-on-united-flight-considering-lawsuit.html.
26. Daffodil Altan, correspondent, "Trafficked in America," *Frontline*, PBS, April 24, 2018, www.pbs.org/wgbh/frontline/film/trafficked-in-america/.
27. Ibid.
28. "Agriculture," National Human Trafficking Hotline, Polaris, undated, www.humantraffickinghotline.org/labor-trafficking-venuesindustries/agriculture.
29. Lindsay Patton, "The Human Victims of Factory Farming," One Green Planet, February 13, 2015, www.onegreenplanet.org/environment/the-human-victims-of-factory-farming/.

30. "Agriculture," National Human Trafficking Hotline.
31. Ibid.
32. Chappell, "Dog Dies."
33. "Jack the Writer," S01E04 of *30 Rock*, directed by Gail Mancuso, written by Robert Carlock, NBC, originally broadcast November 1, 2006.
34. Michael Rothfeld and Joe Palazzolo, "Trump Lawyer Arranged $130,000 Payment for Adult-Film Star's Silence," *Wall Street Journal*, January 12, 2018, https://www.wsj.com/articles/trump-lawyer-arranged-130-000-payment-for-adult-film-stars-silence-1515787678.
35. Maggie Haberman, "Michael D. Cohen, Trump's Longtime Lawyer, Says He Paid Stormy Daniels out of His Own Pocket," *New York Times*, February 13, 2018, https://www.nytimes.com/2018/02/13/us/politics/stormy-daniels-michael-cohen-trump.html.
36. John Koblin, "Stormy Daniels Attracts 22 Million Viewers to '60 Minutes,'" *New York Times*, March 26, 2018, https://www.nytimes.com/2018/03/26/business/media/stormy-daniels-60-minutes-ratings.html.
37. Anderson Cooper, "Stormy Daniels Describes Her Alleged Affair with Donald Trump," CBS News, March 28, 2018, https://www.cbsnews.com/news/stormy-daniels-describes-her-alleged-affair-with-donald-trump-60-minutes-interview/.
38. Emily Tillett, "Stormy Daniels to Make Appearance at D.C. Strip Club," CBS News, March 28, 2018, https://www.cbsnews.com/news/stormy-daniels-appearance-washington-dc-strip-club-cloakroom/.
39. "Stormy Daniels' Explosive Full Interview on Donald Trump Affair: 'I Can Describe His Junk Perfectly,'" *In Touch Weekly*, March 25, 2018, https://www.intouchweekly.com/posts/stormy-daniels-full-interview-151788.
40. Meredith Blake, "How Stormy Daniels' Candor and Humor in Her '60 Minutes' Interview Showed 'A Woman to be Reckoned With,'" *Los Angeles Times*, March 26, 2018, http://www.latimes.com/entertainment/tv/la-et-st-stormy-daniels-60-minutes-trump-20180325-story.html.
41. Matt Apuzzo, "F.B.I. Raids Office of Trump's Longtime Lawyer Michael Cohen; Trump Calls It 'Disgraceful,'" *New York Times*, April 9, 2018, https://www.nytimes.com/2018/04/09/us/politics/fbi-raids-office-of-trumps-longtime-lawyer-michael-cohen.html.
42. Eli Watkins, "What Rudy Giuliani Has Said on Donald Trump and Stormy Daniels," CNN, May 7, 2018, https://www.cnn.com/2018/05/06/politics/rudy-giuliani-stormy-daniels-interviews/index.html.
43. Casey Quinlan, "Sex Workers would be Endangered by Senate Bill, Advocates Say," Think-Progress, March 21, 2018, https://thinkprogress.org/senate-sesta-sex-workers-danger-f22f0383f6be/.
44. Ricky Riley, "New Legislation Forces Sex Workers Back to Streets and Strips Away Internet Freedoms in One Swoop," AlterNet, April 15, 2018, https://www.alternet.org/sex-amp-relationships/sesta-forces-sex-workers-back-streets-threatens-internet-freedoms.
45. Quinlan, "Sex Workers would be Endangered."
46. Emily Stewart, "The Next Big Battle over Internet Freedom is Here," Vox, April 23, 2018, https://www.vox.com/policy-and-politics/2018/4/23/17237640/fosta-sesta-section-230-internet-freedom.
47. Riley, "New Legislation Forces Sex Workers Back to Streets."
48. Ibid.
49. Quinlan, "Sex Workers would be Endangered."
50. Riley, "New Legislation Forces Sex Workers Back to Streets."
51. Stewart, "The Next Big Battle."
52. Apuzzo, "F.B.I. Raids Office of Trump's Longtime Lawyer Michael Cohen."

CHAPTER 3

The Magic Trick of Establishment Media
News Abuse in 2017–2018

John Collins, Nicole Eigbrett, Jana Morgan, and Steve Peraza

We know of course there's really no such thing as the "voiceless." There are only the deliberately silenced, or the preferably unheard.

—Arundhati Roy[1]

INTRODUCTION

As the work of Project Censored has demonstrated for decades, establishment media play a fundamental propaganda role in the United States by systematically ignoring important stories that deserve greater public attention.[2] Often the space that should be occupied by these stories is filled with the kind of sensationalist or titillating material that Project Censored founder Dr. Carl Jensen termed "Junk Food News." Even when important issues receive extensive coverage, however, they can be presented in a way that minimizes their deeper importance, distorts what is happening, or otherwise encourages the public to interpret the story in a way that falls into line with the interests of the power elite. Dr. Peter Phillips, former director of Project Censored, coined the term "News Abuse" to describe this "abuse" of the public trust by news outlets that offer "spin," and sometimes outright propaganda, instead of prioritizing proper investigation.

News Abuse perpetually operates like a magician's trick, using distraction to direct our attention away from what we really need to know. While the magician keeps us focused on one minor or misleading part of the story, the important things—the operation of power, the purchasing of influence, the daily injustices affecting ordinary people, the courageous movements for social change—continue moving forward, largely free from journalistic scrutiny and open public debate.

Throughout 2017, the troubling rhetoric and policies of the Trump administration, including vicious attacks on journalists, led to occasional signs that the establishment media were waking up and seeking to uphold their proper role as investigative watchdogs. More commonly, however, the American public was subjected to an ongoing torrent of News Abuse that served more to mislead and confuse than to educate.

In our investigation of News Abuse in 2017, we drew on our experience with the citizen journalism project Weave News (www.weavenews.org) to investigate a number of stories that clearly fit the News Abuse label. We examined the coverage of these stories by focusing on major establishment media outlets, including the *New York Times*, *Washington Post*, *Boston Globe*, *Wall Street Journal*, National Public Radio (NPR), CNN, MSNBC, and Fox News. We found repeated examples of the establishment media framing crucial public issues in ways that marginalize critical and grassroots perspectives, shield the powerful from scrutiny, and discourage the public from understanding the deeper forces that are shaping their lives. Whether in endless articles about Trump's "heartland" voters, "culture war"–style coverage of National Football League (NFL) quarterback Colin Kaepernick's principled stance against racist police violence, paper-thin discussions of corporate influence in the political system, or misleading coverage of colonial violence in Palestine, the magic trick of News Abuse was unfortunately on full display in 2017.

TRUMP VOTERS: CLASSIST MYTHOLOGY

Since the 2016 US presidential election, establishment media outlets have intensely focused on those who voted for Donald Trump: who they are, where they are living, why they made that decision, and how they have or haven't changed their minds. The media's classist mythology of Trump voters, constructed around the voters' psyche, circumstances, and motivations for supporting Trump, has further suppressed the stories of marginalized communities, whose livelihoods are unequivocally at a heightened risk of harm under this administration. Meanwhile, the voices of anti-racist or anti-deportation activists and advocates who always knew the election of Trump would bring little to the white working class, but would endanger the lives of people of color, remain underheard.

Leading up to the election and throughout 2017, Trump's voter base was often described by establishment media as consisting of people "from the heartland of America." The dominant narrative was that Trump voters are working class, blue collar, and not highly educated; their way of life is eroding; and they saw a leader in Trump, who is anti-establishment and will take a populist stand for the country. A survey of eight establishment media outlets in 2017 demonstrates this pattern, as the phrase "Trump voters" appeared in the headlines of 2,040 news stories. Of these stories on Trump voters, 49 percent included descriptors such as "poor" (340 stories), "working class" (241), "white working class" (90), "populist" (214), "Rust Belt" (75), and "heartland" (33). When considering the motivations of Trump supporters, 15 percent of stories included the terms "racism" (262), "nationalism" (74), or "nativism" (13).

Fox News provides an insightful glimpse into how Trump supporters describe themselves in the US political landscape. According to the Pew Research Center, at least 40 percent of Trump voters named Fox News as their "main source" of news during the 2016 presidential campaign.[3] Following the August 2017 incident in Charlottesville, Virginia, in which white supremacists and counter-protesters violently clashed over the removal of a Confederate monument, conservative commentator and author Wayne Allyn Root explained on Fox News how the incident was connected to Trump. Or rather, Root explicitly *distanced* the "typical Trump voter" and the president himself from the Charlottesville neo-Nazis and KKK members:

> The typical Trump voter is <u>NOT</u> a racist. I was opening speaker at all six Donald Trump campaign events in Las Vegas. I never saw or heard one instance of racism at any

Trump event . . . nor at any of the hundreds of Tea Party
events that I spoke at across America from 2009 to 2015.
The anger of almost every white middle class Trump voter
has nothing to do with racism . . . and everything to do with
economics. It's about financial survival, not race. The middle
class is being targeted for extinction. It is being persecuted
and wiped off the face of the earth by liberal/progressive/
socialist economic policies.[4]

Root further asserted that these middle-class voters are predominantly small business owners concerned with "big taxes, big regulations, big government, illegal immigration and using Obamacare,
climate change, and government agencies like the EPA and the IRS
to kill our jobs and redistribute our hard-earned income. Those are
the reasons middle class voters are angry."[5] Thus, by removing the
racialized component of Trump voters' behaviors and statistically evi-
denced biases, Fox News perpetuated a simplified class conflict.[6] Supporting Trump, therefore, was not racist; it was necessary resistance
against the unchecked liberal elite.

It quickly became apparent that, despite his populist message,
Trump's policies would not meet the material needs of working-class
voters; yet working-class voters were presented as uniquely responsible for his election. By creating this simplified conflict and narrative, establishment media outlets not only accentuated an earlier
narrative of "Blue vs. Red" partisan division, but also stereotyped and
scapegoated the white working class. What about the affluent Republican voters and activists who may actually have fueled the fire and
reaped the benefits?

To counter the prevailing narratives, the *Washington Post* examined
polling data and surveys of Trump voters' income and education in
June 2017. They found that only one-third of Trump voters made less
than $50,000, while two-thirds of white voters with and without col-
lege degrees voted for Trump:

According to the election study, white non-Hispanic voters
without college degrees making below the median house-
hold income made up only 25 percent of Trump voters.

That's a far cry from the working-class-fueled victory many journalists have imagined.[7]

This nuanced, outside-the-establishment narrative of Trump voters wasn't widely circulated until six months into his term as president. For the remainder of 2017, the *Post* was practically the only media outlet in this analysis that published regular counter-establishment narratives in coverage of Trump voters.

Consequently, this classist story of poor, uneducated white voters has remained in the mainstream, reinforcing longstanding class-based animosity and prejudice. Ultimately, it has reproduced the institutional hegemony of wealthy elites, many of whom are at the helm of establishment media outlets and other institutions of power. Moreover, the descriptions of Trump voters as white and working-class also overlooked the reality of many Midwestern communities that experienced economic revitalization and growth in the last two decades. This can be attributed to recent immigration from Asia, Africa, and Latin America, an increased workforce that has resulted in overall greater racial and ethnic diversity.[8] Stories and narratives of Trump's base almost always discounted these immigrant voices that are also very much "from the heartland."

Establishment media's coverage of Trump voters also largely excluded stories of marginalized communities, people of color, and activists and advocates at odds with Trump's policies and actions. Undoubtedly, these communities were among the most active in organizing major anti-Trump movements and events, such as the Women's March and the March for Science. Yet, overall, the individual, intimate attention given to Trump voters sharing their opinions was not granted to left-leaning individuals and movements. Several of the major outlets reviewed in this analysis—the *New York Times*,[9] NPR,[10] CNN,[11] and the *Boston Globe*[12]—published at least one "one year later" piece on Trump voters, mainly asking whether those same people had changed their minds about supporting the president. Such follow-up stories are important, but why wasn't similar, personalized attention paid to individual immigrants, Muslims, LGBTQ+ people, or their advocates, who were all directly targeted by Trump at several points in 2017? By not amplifying their voices to the same extent as Trump voters and supporters, the establishment media failed many of the most vulnerable communities.

In 2017, the *New York Times* widely circulated op-eds by columnist Nicholas Kristof, who also contributes to CNN. One particular piece, titled "Trump Voters are Not the Enemy," insisted on humanizing Trump supporters rather than those facing immediate harm.[13] In August 2017, the *Times* continued soliciting input from Trump voters regarding their views, but a reader solicitation form was never created for people opposed to Trump.[14] NPR, which is often considered a more liberal outlet and praised for its compassionate audio storytelling, published soundbites of Trump voters several times in 2017. In one particular story following the events in Charlottesville, a rural tradesman made sweeping, almost nonsensical statements about racial and ethnic identity, with a stream-of-consciousness frankness that almost seemed obtuse:

> Who cares what your ethnic background is? Great. You know, maybe we can learn something. Maybe I can teach a dish. You know, I'm fourth generation here, so I don't have a—I didn't have a grandmother teach me how to cook ethnic. But if you did, great. You know, come on over for a meal. I'll go over your house for a meal. And the left likes to teach us diversity, which is just a thinly veiled balkanization is what it is, you know. E pluribus unum—many one, and they teach the opposite.[15]

In contrast to the presentation of such unfiltered, accusatory remarks, it was very challenging to find a parallel piece on a left-leaning voter or activist, or simply an ordinary person opposed to Trump's policies, who made generalized negative statements about an entire community simply because of that community's support for Trump (reader comments were not included in this analysis).

Most interesting amid the "news abuse" coverage of Trump voters was how traditionally liberal media outlets fared in comparison with conservative outlets. In November 2017, the *New York Times*, a centrist, neoliberal, and highly regarded outlet for the upper and wealthy classes, published its now infamous profile of a white supremacist.[16]

The reporter followed his subject's daily schedule and conversations, picked at his ideology, and reviewed online postings of alt-right extremism, thus normalizing his visions of hate. *The Times* was harshly criticized by readers and other journalists for painting a picture of the "Nazi next door," but the editors staunchly defended the piece.[17] The problem, again, was that the story was never balanced with a similarly in-depth profile of a far-left activist. With the clashes in Charlottesville still in recent memory, establishment media could have captured readers' attention with a profile of an antifa (a term used to designate a range of anti-fascist movements) activist, but instead did a disservice to liberal, progressive, and left-wing groups by not providing them with a similar platform.

From a conservative perspective, Fox News published an opinion piece from Jean Card, a writer and communications consultant. In it she drew parallels between Trump voters and the #MeToo movement, arguing that each received a "megaphone this year" that "was good for America."[18] Card's comparison of women who are survivors of sexual harassment and assault with disenfranchised white Trump voters is an intensely false equivalence. How can the #MeToo "crowd" make any inroads against hegemonic institutions when Trump was elected president of the United States with 21 accusations of sexual misconduct against him, and essentially zero accountability?[19] Trump may have "candidly acknowledged that there is agony in America" for the working class, but he has simultaneously created agony for many *more* people.[20] Card also relied on the watered-down class narrative, stating that "[w]orking-class Americans have long known how the wealthy and powerful actually view them, and they have long known that elitism contributes to injustice."[21] Fox News and the *New York Times* have diverging brand reputations and audiences, yet similar, overtly compassionate takes on Trump supporters.

Near the end of 2017, Fox News published a poll from *Politico/ Morning Consult* conducted exactly one year after Trump's election, in which 82 percent of those who say they supported Trump said they would vote for him again.[22] Kyle Dropp, Morning Consult cofounder and chief research officer, concluded that "[v]oters who support President Trump have a markedly sunnier outlook on their own financial situation than those who don't," as 41 percent of those who strongly approve of Trump report that they're better off financially than they were the year before.[23] It begs the question of what the survey results would have been if the views of people of color, immigrants and refugees, LGBTQ+ people, and people with disabilities were examined with the same, captivated interest throughout the year.

While Trump's purported base may not have benefited in a materially significant way in 2017, classism is embedded so deeply into US society and establishment media that Trump's election symbolized a psychological, emotional, and moral victory—in other words, a reclamation of greatness—for the white working class. By not giving those who faced the greatest threats from Trump an equally nuanced, contextualized, and data-driven platform for their stories, establishment media collectively failed those communities. This abusive coverage from establishment outlets reinforced a system of racist, classist hegemony that ultimately harmed, and continues to harm, everyone.

COLIN KAEPERNICK: MISSING THE MESSAGE

While NFL players kneeled in protest against racial injustice in the United States, the establishment media presented a distorted narrative that marginalized their message and amplified critics' misperceptions of the protest. Nationwide, police killings continued to ravage predominantly black neighborhoods, and in response to the carnage NFL quarterback Colin Kaepernick began to engage in peaceful protest in 2016 by sitting or kneeling during the playing of the national anthem at football games. National correspondents, despite Kaepernick's articulate explanations, disconnected his protest from the social conditions that produced it. Instead of raising awareness of racial injustices in policing, journalists trained the nation's eyes on the ideological differences between NFL players and the fans and owners who objected to Kaepernick's protest and the protests of fellow players he inspired. The NFL kneeling controversy thus devolved into a 21st-century culture war over patriotism while the racially disproportionate police killings persisted.

San Francisco 49ers quarterback Colin Kaepernick chose to sit during the US national anthem during a preseason NFL football game in August 2016, a peaceful protest against what he perceived as racial injustice in US policing. Kaepernick explained, "I am not going to stand up to show pride in a flag for a country that oppresses black people and people of color . . . There are bodies in the street and people getting paid leave and getting away with murder."[24] He said he would stand for the anthem "[w]hen there's significant change and I feel that [the US] flag represents what it's supposed to represent."[25] The establishment media exploded with commentary on, and opposition to, Kaepernick's protest. Critics charged that Kaepernick offended the men and women who serve in the US armed forces when he sat for the anthem. For some veterans, Kaepernick's peaceful protest was a "form of rejection" because the US flag symbolizes the nation that soldiers swore to protect with their lives.[26]

Media pressure prompted a shift in tactics. Kaepernick decided to continue his protest but to kneel rather than sit. "I have family, I have friends that have gone and fought for this country," Kaepernick explained. "And they fight for freedom, they fight for the people, they fight for liberty and justice, for everyone." Out of respect for US soldiers, Kaepernick decided to kneel on one knee, but he refused to stand until the US began to honor its values: "People are dying in vain because this country isn't holding their end of the bargain up, as far as giving freedom and justice, liberty to everybody."[27]

Kaepernick's protest became a national soap opera in 2017 as the establishment media amplified the cultural tensions between protesters and their critics. No one stoked the fire of controversy like President Donald Trump, who argued that NFL players who knelt for the national anthem were "ruining the game" by disrespecting the US flag. "That's a total disrespect of our heritage," he proclaimed at a rally in Alabama. "That's a total disrespect of everything that we stand for." Trump called on NFL owners to fire players like Kaepernick for their lack of patriotism and directed fans to boycott NFL games in which players knelt during the anthem.[28]

Following Trump's invective, the national media focused much of their attention on the NFL's response to player protests. NFL franchise owners like Jerry Jones of the Dallas Cowboys prohibited their players from protesting during the national anthem. Players who decided to kneel would be in direct violation of team policy and risk fines, suspensions, or even termination of employment. The league as a whole sent a clear message that it would demonstrate its intolerance of player protest by closing its doors to Kaepernick. The former standout quarterback has not been able to find work in the NFL since opting out of his contract with the 49ers. "Colin Kaepernick is Unemployed. Is It Because of His Arm, or His Knee?" read one *New York Times* headline in March.[29] Later in the year, after the 2017–2018 NFL season had begun, the *Washington Post* reminded readers that Kaepernick, "the NFL's most talked-about player," was still unemployed.[30] Kaepernick is not the only player who risked his career by kneeling for the national anthem. In fact, the term "Kaepernicked" has entered the national lexicon to indicate when an employee loses opportunities due to expressing controversial views. *The Washington Post* reported that Eric Reid, strong safety for the 49ers, had been "Kaepernicked" for supporting the protest in its early days.[31] For his part, Kaepernick filed a collusion grievance against the NFL owners in October 2017, claiming that the owners have been working together to prevent NFL franchises from hiring him. To date, no NFL team has hired Kaepernick, and the owners' opposition to national anthem protests remains resolute.[32]

The establishment media deserve some commendation for attempting to contextualize Kaepernick's national anthem protest as part of a broader black American protest tradition. Without focusing on the social conditions that gave rise to this protest, however, even this progressive news coverage marginalized the athletes' message and rather ironically reified stereotypes of aggressive, disruptive black athletes. *The New York Times*, for example, reported on the long history of national anthem protests by black American athletes since sprinters Tommie Smith and John Carlos raised black-gloved fists in a Black Power salute during the medal ceremony at the 1968 Summer Olympics in Mexico City.[33] Other correspondents began to discuss Kaepernick in the context of civil rights activists like Muhammad Ali. In fact, for taking a courageous stance against racial injustice, Kaepernick won *Sports Illustrated*'s Muhammad Ali Legacy Award and a host of other awards, such as ESPN's Best Breakthrough Athlete ESPY and *GQ*'s Man of the Year.[34] Though Kaepernick deserved praise for his peaceful protest, comparing him to civil rights leaders of the past did not result in a nuanced discussion of the social conditions Kaepernick and his fellow athletes sought to change. The establishment media focused more attention on ranking Kaepernick among a growing list of black activist athletes than addressing the pervasiveness of racial inequality and injustice in 21st-century America. It bears noting that, according to the *Washington Post*'s Fatal Force database, there were more deadly police shootings in 2017 (987) than in 2016 (963).[35] Kaepernick's peaceful protest began in 2016 to highlight these tragedies and demand justice for the victims and their families. The establishment media picked his protest apart but rarely gave voice to the very message that Kaepernick hoped to send. Instead the media distracted from this message and encouraged cultural bickering. Although Kaepernick inspired a national conversation on race, the media failed him by making the story about the legitimacy of protest and not the need for social change.

CORPORATE CAPTURE: MISSING THE CONNECTIONS

Corporations and wealthy individuals have long had an outsized influence on government policy. Since the infamous 2010 *Citizens United* ruling and the release of unchecked dark money into the political system, wealth has encountered few barriers to purchasing political perks, and nowhere have there been fewer barriers than in the Trump administration. While establishment outlets reported on isolated conflicts of interest and corporate maneuvers to influence policy, they failed to report some key connections between various incidents that would give a sense of the enormity and pervasiveness of the problem.

Most Americans agree that corporations and the wealthy hold sway over too much US policy.[36] In fact, a much-discussed 2013 study found that the political system in the United States more closely resembles an oligarchy than a democracy due to the overwhelming influence of special interests.[37] A critical role of the fourth estate is to guard against this type of influence by keeping the public informed about it. However, reporting in establishment media often fails to connect the dots when the subject is deep corporate pockets and the regulatory, or corporate, capture of government officials and policies. When government officials and agencies regulate in the interest of corporations or wealthy influencers rather than, and often at the expense of, the interests of the public, they effectively disenfranchise citizens.[38]

While there are some establishment media journalists who choose to dig deeper with their reporting, too often articles regurgitate press release talking points rather than assess the veracity of the stakeholder's claims. This is, in part, a function of round-the-clock journalism, intended to sell the public's eyeballs to advertisers through easily digestible snippets instead of offering thorough, hard-hitting reporting. Furthermore, in this case, there is a consistent failure to name the problem shaping American politics today: *corporate capture.*

In early 2017, congressional Republicans instigated a flurry of regulatory rollbacks using an obscure law known as the Congressional Review Act (CRA). Although the law itself has since received a lot of coverage in establishment media, little attention has been paid to the question of which stakeholders won big as a result of these rollbacks—and why. Analysis conducted by the International Corporate Accountability Roundtable found that "the victims now lying in the CRA's regulatory graveyard leave no doubt about whose wishes were prioritized—Big Oil's."[39] Environmental protections, clean water requirements, and anti-corruption regulations opposed by natural resources companies—but broadly supported by US citizens—were just a few of the safeguards that were repealed at the behest of the extractive industries. The wins continued to roll in for the oil, gas, and mining sector throughout 2017 with the rollback of safety regulations meant to prevent another oil spill like BP's Deepwater Horizon disaster of 2010, the opening up of public lands for extraction by the Department of the Interior, and the passing of the GOP tax bill into law, which allowed oil and gas companies to reap $190.4 billion in benefits.[40]

Why do these companies have the influence they do? The answer, of course, is the money that they funnel into politics. But the establishment media consistently fails to acknowledge this as a systemic problem for democracy. Every article detailing a new "win" for the energy sector should include an evaluation of who made the decision to grant the "win," how much the interested companies spent on lobbying, whom their money enriched, and whether the decision was influenced by "revolving door" agreements—that is, political favors exchanged for securing future corporate positions.

The prevalence of the use of the terms "regulatory capture" and "corporate capture" was surveyed, using a Google News search, in news coverage published by eight establishment media outlets: the *New York Times, Washington Post, Boston Globe, Wall Street Journal,* CNN, MSNBC, Fox News, and NPR. The results were disappointing. In 2017 the term "regulatory capture" appeared only 11 times and "corporate capture" appeared only five times in articles available online. When "oil" was added to the search terms, there were only three relevant results—one each from the *Wall Street Journal,* CNN, and the *New York Times.*

The *Wall Street Journal*'s use of the term "regulatory capture" did not appear in a news article, but in an opinion piece about the influence of corporate capture on Environmental Protection Agency policy under Scott Pruitt's leadership.[41] The CNN article discussed "regulatory capture" in the Trump administration and how its deregulatory philosophy, which only considers the costs and not the benefits of regulations, will have a negative impact on the public.[42] Finally, the *New York Times* article detailed the 2017 climate talks in Germany, and noted representatives' concerns that corporate interests were being prioritized over the needs of developing nations. The terms "corporate interests" and "corporate power" were featured prominently in the article, but "corporate capture" was only used to refer to the words on a protester's sign.[43]

A search for the term "policy capture" in establishment media yielded no results at all; the term "state capture" appeared 17 times, but the term was only used in reference to issues in countries outside the United States. An even broader search for "corporate influence" yielded only 27 results, and, while "corporate power" yielded 97 results, those instances were often irrelevant to the topic at hand. When the term "oil" was added to these searches, moreover, very few relevant or viable results remained.

These results highlight a major failure of establishment media reporting in 2017. These influential news outlets failed to name, with consistency, the systematically disproportionate influence corporations—particularly among the energy sector—wield over regulators and policies when compared with that of citizens. Journalists must call this beast by its name—corporate capture, power, and influence—in a consistent way to highlight the ubiquity of the issue for those most affected by it. While the lack of results could partly be attributed to the fact that the terms "corporate capture" and "regulatory capture" have, to date, been used mostly by academics or Beltway insiders rather than the general public, that precedent is no excuse for journalists to shirk their duty to inform the public of such a pressing issue; connecting the dots of corporate capture—whether that be through "revolving door" agreements, cushy political appointments, lobbying, or campaign contributions—to favorable regulatory results for corporations is a critical public service and a central task of journalists. Unfortunately, in 2017, the establishment media fell short.

PALESTINE: INVISIBLE COLONIZATION, DECONTEXTUALIZED VIOLENCE

Palestine/Israel has long been the ultimate blind spot for the establishment news media in the United States, with the nearly unassailable US–Israeli alliance mirrored by a myopic and destructive pattern of news coverage. At best, coverage often takes refuge in the language of false equivalence, using the infamous "both sides" frame despite the extreme lack of equivalence between the two "sides'" abilities to inflict violence. At worst, the coverage openly adopts and naturalizes Zionist linguistic and ideological categories without any attempt at portraying alternative perspectives. While there have been some marginal improvements in recent years, 2017's coverage nonetheless displayed many of the patterns familiar from previous years that serve to hide the realities of what is happening on the ground.

At the root of establishment media coverage of Palestine/Israel is a dominant frame that uncritically accepts a number of interrelated assumptions:

▸ the situation is best understood as a "conflict" between two "sides"
▸ Israeli violence is only to be understood as a "response" to Palestinian violence
▸ the so-called "peace process" leading to a "two-state solution" is the only way to resolve the problem
▸ the US role in the situation is inherently benevolent and impartial

The coverage surveyed from 2017 starkly reflects these patterns. Of the nearly 3,000 stories from seven establishment media outlets (the *New York Times, Washington Post, Boston Globe,* CNN, NPR, MSNBC, and Fox News) that mentioned Palestine or Israel, a sizable number contained references to "the Israeli–Palestinian conflict" (439 stories), the "peace process" (530), and the "two-state solution" (540), with the exact phrase "both sides" appearing in more than 10 percent of all stories (366 out of 2,948).

By contrast, the coverage systematically ignored alternative frames that might call into question dominant categories or Zionism more generally. For example, the idea of a "one-state solution"—the extension of full democratic rights to all people who live in Palestine/Israel—is outnumbered by the "two-state solution" in the coverage by a factor of more than ten (45 vs. 540 references).

More generally, thanks to the binary "conflict" frame, the grievances of Palestinians were typically presented as opinions to be weighed against official Israeli talking points rather than as political expressions grounded in international law and empirical realities. A prime case is coverage of the fundamental right of Palestinian refugees to return to their homeland. While this right is well established under international law, the phrase "right of return" (which is ubiquitous in Palestinian political discourse) appeared in only 26 of the 2,938 stories surveyed—a paltry number when compared with the number of stories quoting Israeli officials and pro-Israel experts who are openly opposed to Palestinians' right of return.

Arguably the most glaring pattern in the coverage, however, is the failure to acknowledge the Zionist project as a case of settler colonialism. Critics and scholars have produced dozens of books, hundreds of articles, and numerous major international conferences devoted to the study of Palestine/Israel through the settler colonialism lens. Yet the 2017 establishment media coverage reviewed here contained exactly two references to settler colonialism in Palestine: one in a quote from Palestine Liberation Organization (PLO) Executive Committee member Hanan Ashrawi,[44] and the other in a discussion of a University of California, Berkeley, course that drew attention for employing "the lens of settler colonialism."[45]

When the search of establishment media coverage was broadened to include the terms "colonial," "colonization," and "colonize," the results were equally stark. Only 15 of the nearly three thousand articles on Palestine/Israel contained any of these terms in specific reference to Israel. Of those 15 instances, seven were news stories and eight were op-eds or interviews. In the seven news stories, all references were found in quotes from political officials or protesters/activists; not a single academic expert on settler colonialism was ever quoted.

The eight op-ed pieces referencing Israeli colonization included a prominent *New York Times* piece by jailed Palestinian activist Marwan Barghouti;[46] a follow-up in the *Times* two days later by public editor Liz Spayd giving voice to reader critiques of the Barghouti piece;[47] four pieces by pro-Israel authors who only acknowledged the colonial framework in the process of seeking to discredit it; an NPR interview with Palestinian lawyer and author Raja Shehadeh (who made one indirect reference to Israeli colonialism);[48] and a *Washington Post* piece by Israeli sociologist Gershon Shafir (which gave Shafir the distinction of being the only scholarly expert on settler colonialism to appear in the nearly 3,000 stories surveyed).[49]

In the 2004 documentary *Peace, Propaganda & the Promised Land*, filmmakers Sut Jhally and Bathsheba Ratzkoff identify "invisible colonization" as one of several key elements of Israel's "public relations" strategy that has a direct impact on US media coverage.[50] While Israel's colonization project has only accelerated since that time, and while the vast majority of the world views such actions as plainly illegal under international law, this survey of 2017's coverage suggests that little progress has been achieved in making colonization an explicitly visible part of the public narrative.

Finally, it is worth noting in particular that MSNBC's coverage on Palestine/Israel in 2017 was almost laughable in its myopia. In this case, however, the problem has less to do with the replication of dominant categories and more to do with the network's status as a de facto mouthpiece for the Democratic Party. Of the 15 MSNBC stories that referenced Palestine/Israel in any significant way, all 15 were primarily about President Donald Trump, either addressing his questionable approach to foreign policy or his late-2017 decision to recognize Jerusalem as Israel's capital. For MSNBC, it seems, the situation in Palestine/Israel is only relevant insofar as it connects with the cable audience's appetite for all things Trump. Any other issue, including the actual conditions facing Palestinians living under Israeli coloniza-tion backed by bipartisan US support, merits nary a mention.

CONCLUSION

This review of coverage from 2017 demonstrates that establishment media continue to serve as ideological magicians, consistently diverting the public's gaze away from some of the most important elements of key stories. The urgent perspectives of vulnerable communities fol-lowing the election of Donald Trump, the critiques of structural racism offered by Colin Kaepernick and other high-profile athletes, the corrosive influence of the fossil fuel industry and other corporations on the US political system, and the ongoing colonization of Palestine are realities hiding in plain sight, demanding our attention and concern. Yet they are starkly downplayed, sometimes to the point of being virtually absent, in the reporting of the most influential US news outlets. Far from simple censorship, these patterns reveal a deeper process of mass distraction, ex-nomination (the systematic failure to name certain processes and structures), and political manipulation whose detrimental impact on public discourse, and on democracy itself, cannot be overestimated.

JOHN COLLINS is Professor of Global Studies at St. Lawrence University. He is also a founder of Weave News (www.weavenews.org), which emerged out of his seminar on global news analysis, and he currently serves as the organization's director of develop-ment. He has written extensively on the Palestinian liberation struggle and its global ramifications, most recently in *Global Palestine* (Hurst/Oxford University Press, 2011).

NICOLE EIGBRETT serves as the director of communications for Weave News. Hailing from the Finger Lakes region of New York, she works at the intersection of public service, progressive policy, media, and community organizing. Nicole is dedicated to social equity and focuses on amplifying the voices and stories of underheard commu-nities. She graduated from St. Lawrence University in 2014 with a BA in global studies and languages.

JANA MORGAN is a founder of Weave News. She also serves as the director of advocacy and campaigns for the International Corporate Accountability Roundtable (ICAR), a coalition that fights to ensure that corporations respect human rights. Jana holds an MA in international relations from the Maxwell School of Syracuse University and resides in Washington, DC.

STEVE PERAZA is an assistant professor in the Department of History and Social Studies Education at SUNY College at Buffalo. He earned his PhD in US history, specializing in law and the transatlantic slave trade. For Weave News, Steve contributes to "The Poverty Report," which examines the multidimensional problem of poverty in the United States.

Notes

1. Arundhati Roy, "The 2004 Sydney Peace Prize Lecture," University of Sydney, November 4, 2004, http://sydney.edu.au/news/84.html?newsstoryid=279.

2. In this chapter we use the term "establishment media" to highlight the role of influential news media outlets—typically those that are corporate-owned or otherwise closely connected with private interests and with the power elite ("the establishment") more broadly—in setting the agenda for public debate. The "establishment media" privileges certain voices, perspectives, categories, and narratives at the expense of others, thereby creating and reinforcing "establishment" views. For more analysis of this terminology, and the use of "corporate" media vs. so-called "mainstream" media labels, see chapter 8 of this volume by Peter Phillips.

3. "Fox News Dominated as Main Campaign News Source for Trump Voters; No Single Source as Pronounced among Clinton Voters," Pew Research Center, January 17, 2017, accessed June 7, 2018, http://www.journalism.org/2017/01/18/trump-clinton-voters-divided-in-their-main-source-for-election-news/pj_2017-01-18_election-news-sources_0-01/.

4. Wayne Allyn Root, "Charlottesville, Trump and Angry White Males," Fox News, August 17, 2017, accessed June 7, 2018, http://www.foxnews.com/opinion/2017/08/17/charlottesville-trump-and-angry-white-males.html.

5. Root, "Charlottesville, Trump and Angry White Males."

6. See German Lopez, "The Past Year of Research Has Made It Very Clear: Trump Won Because of Racial Resentment," Vox, December 15, 2017, accessed June 7, 2018, https://www.vox.com/identities/2017/12/15/16781222/trump-racism-economic-anxiety-study; and Tom Jacobs, "More Evidence that Racism and Sexism were Key to Trump's Victory," Pacific Standard, April 4, 2018, accessed June 7, 2018, https://psmag.com/social-justice/more-evidence-that-racism-and-sexism-were-key-to-trump-victory.

7. Nicholas Carnes and Noam Lupu, "It's Time to Bust the Myth: Most Trump Voters were Not Working Class," Washington Post, June 5, 2017, https://www.washingtonpost.com/news/monkey-cage/wp/2017/06/05/its-time-to-bust-the-myth-most-trump-voters-were-not-working-class/.

8. MaryJo Webster, "Three Things the Latest Census Data Tells Us about the Upper Midwest," Star Tribune, December 15, 2017, accessed April 2, 2018, http://www.startribune.com/three-things-the-latest-census-data-tells-us-about-the-upper-midwest/462316983/; and Dan Keating and Laris Karklis, "The Increasingly Diverse United States of America," Washington Post, November 25, 2016, https://www.washingtonpost.com/graphics/national/how-diverse-is-america/.

9. Barbara Marcolini, "Trump Voters, One Year Later," New York Times, November 8, 2017, accessed April 2, 2018, https://www.nytimes.com/video/us/politics/100000005538314/trump-voters-one-year-later.html.

10. Ari Shapiro, "Trump Voter Reflects on First Year of Presidency," All Things Considered, NPR, December 29, 2017, accessed April 2, 2018, https://www.npr.org/2017/12/29/574693623/trump-voter-reflects-on-first-year-of-presidency.

11. Richa Naik and Logan Whiteside, "Michigan's Trump Voters, a Year Later," CNN, December 15, 2017, accessed April 2, 2018, http://money.cnn.com/2017/12/15/news/economy/michigan-trump-voters/index.html.

12. Julia Jacobs, "Trump Voters in N.H. Have Little Regret, Poll Indicates," Boston Globe, October 19, 2017, accessed April 2, 2018, https://www.bostonglobe.com/news/politics/2017/10/19/trump-voters-have-little-regret-poll-indicates/C7JpEk6I4WdZxkS206UnjP/story.html.

13. Nicholas Kristof, "Trump Voters are Not the Enemy," *New York Times*, February 23, 2017, accessed April 2, 2018, https://www.nytimes.com/2017/02/23/opinion/even-if-trump-is-the-enemy-his-voters-arent.html.

14. "Did You Stop Supporting Trump? We Would Like to Hear from You," *New York Times*, August 31, 2017, https://www.nytimes.com/interactive/2017/08/31/opinion/31trump-supporters-callout.html.

15. "After Charlottesville, Trump Supporters Stand by the President," *All Things Considered*, NPR, August 19, 2017, https://www.npr.org/2017/08/19/544727399/after-charlottesville-its-clear-america-is-still-dealing-with-complex-history.

16. Richard Fausset, "A Voice of Hate in America's Heartland," *New York Times*, November 25, 2017, accessed April 2, 2018, https://www.nytimes.com/2017/11/25/us/ohio-hovater-white-nationalist.html.

17. Marc Lacey, "Readers Accuse Us of Normalizing a Nazi Sympathizer; We Respond," *New York Times*, November 26, 2017, accessed April 2, 2018, https://www.nytimes.com/2017/11/26/reader-center/readers-accuse-us-of-normalizing-a-nazi-sympathizer-we-respond.html.

18. Jean Card, "The Incredible Thing that Trump Voters, Working Women Shared in 2017," Fox News, December 27, 2017, accessed June 7, 2018, http://www.foxnews.com/opinion/2017/12/27/incredible-thing-that-trump-voters-working-women-shared-in-2017.html.

19. Catherine Pearson, Emma Gray, and Alanna Vagianos, "A Running List of the Women Who've Accused Donald Trump of Sexual Misconduct," Huffington Post, December 12, 2017, accessed June 7, 2018, https://www.huffingtonpost.com/entry/a-running-list-of-the-women-whove-accused-donald-trump-of-sexual-misconduct_us_57ffae1fe4b0162c043a7212.

20. Card, "The Incredible Thing that Trump Voters, Working Women Shared."

21. Ibid.

22. "No Regrets: Trump Backers Say They'd Vote for Him Again, One Year after Election," Fox News, November 9, 2017, accessed June 7, 2018, http://www.foxnews.com/politics/2017/11/09/no-regrets-trump-backers-say-theyd-vote-for-him-again-one-year-after-election.html.

23. Steven Shepard, "Trump Voters: We'd Do It Again," *Politico*, November 9, 2017, accessed June 7, 2018, https://www.politico.com/story/2017/11/09/trump-voters-polling-election-244644.

24. Steve Wyche, "Colin Kaepernick Explains Why He Sat during the National Anthem," National Football League (NFL), August 27, 2016, updated August 28, 2016, accessed June 7, 2018, http://www.nfl.com/news/story/0ap3000000691077/article/colin-kaepernick-explains-why-he-sat-during-national-anthem.

25. Adam Stites, "Everything You Need to Know about NFL Protests during the National Anthem," SB Nation, October 19, 2017, accessed June 7, 2018, https://www.sbnation.com/2017/9/29/16380080/donald-trump-nfl-colin-kaepernick-protests-national-anthem.

26. Brian MacQuarrie, "Military Veterans are Divided Over NFL Protests," *Boston Globe*, September 25, 2017, accessed June 12, 2018, https://www.bostonglobe.com/metro/2017/09/25/military/MLjykBWSTbMlWqbaVUAGzI/story.html.

27. Mark Sandritter, "A Timeline of Colin Kaepernick's National Anthem Protest and the Athletes Who Joined Him," SB Nation, September 25, 2017, accessed June 7, 2018, https://www.sbnation.com/2016/9/11/12869726/colin-kaepernick-national-anthem-protest-seahawks-brandon-marshall-nfl.

28. Associated Press, "Trump Says N.F.L. Players Should be Fired for Anthem Protests," *New York Times*, September 23, 2017, accessed June 12, 2018, https://www.nytimes.com/2017/09/23/sports/trump-nfl-colin-kaepernick-.html.

29. Victor Mather, "Colin Kaepernick is Unemployed. Is It Because of His Arm, or His Knee?" *New York Times*, March 27, 2018, accessed June 12, 2018, https://www.nytimes.com/2017/03/27/sports/football/free-agent-colin-kaepernick-national-anthem-protest.html.

30. Kent Babb, "NFL's Most Talked-About Player is Also a Player without a Job," *Washington Post*, September 8, 2017, 1.

31. Tracy Jan, "Despite Risk of Being 'Kaepernicked,' 49ers Safety Eric Reid will Keep Kneeling," *Washington Post*, October 29, 2017, accessed June 12, 2018, https://www.washingtonpost.com/

news/wonk/wp/2017/10/29/despite-risk-of-being-kaepernicked-49er-safety-eric-reid-will-keep-kneeling/.

32. In May 2018, the NFL issued a new league policy that requires all players to stand for the national anthem. Those who choose not to stand must wait in the locker room until the national anthem has concluded. See Eli Rosenberg, "What the NFL's New Rules for Anthem Protests Really Mean for the First Amendment, According to Experts," *Washington Post*, May 24, 2018, accessed June 12, 2018, https://www.washingtonpost.com/news/early-lead/wp/2018/05/24/what-the-nfls-new-rules-for-anthem-protests-really-mean-for-the-first-amendment-according-to-experts/.

33. Zach Johnk, "National Anthem Protests by Black Athletes Have a Long History," *New York Times*, September 25, 2017, accessed June 12, 2018, https://www.nytimes.com/2017/09/25/sports/national-anthem-protests-black-athletes.html.

34. Michael Rosenberg, "Colin Kaepernick is Recipient of 2017 Sports Illustrated Muhammad Ali Legacy Award," *Sports Illustrated*, November 30, 2017, accessed June 12, 2018, https://www.si.com/sportsperson/2017/11/30/colin-kaepernick-muhammad-ali-legacy-award.

35. "Fatal Force Database," *Washington Post*, 2016–present, accessed June 7, 2018, https://www.washingtonpost.com/graphics/national/police-shootings-2017/.

36. Rebecca Riffkin, "Majority of Americans Dissatisfied with Corporate Influence," Gallup, January 20, 2016, accessed June 7, 2018, http://news.gallup.com/poll/188747/majority-americans-dissatisfied-corporate-influence.aspx.

37. "Study: US is an Oligarchy, Not a Democracy," *Echo Chambers* blog, BBC, April 17, 2014, accessed June 7, 2018, http://www.bbc.com/news/blogs-echochambers-27074746.

38. Will Baude, "Regulatory and Academic Capture," *Washington Post*, May 18, 2014, accessed June 7, 2018, https://www.washingtonpost.com/news/volokh-conspiracy/wp/2014/05/18/regulatory-and-academic-capture/.

39. Jana Morgan, "End the Corporate Hijacking: It's Time to Separate Oil & State," International Corporate Accountability Roundtable (ICAR), April 25, 2018, accessed June 7, 2018, https://www.icar.ngo/news/2018/4/25/end-the-corporate-hijacking-its-time-to-separate-oil-state.

40. Antonia Juhasz, "Inside the Tax Bill's $25 Billion Oil Company Bonanza," *Pacific Standard*, March 27, 2018, accessed June 7, 2018, https://psmag.com/economics/tax-bill-oil-company-bonanza.

41. Joe Árvai, "Letter: EPA Fund Recipients Side with the Agency," *Wall Street Journal*, July 28, 2017, accessed June 7, 2018, https://www.wsj.com/articles/epa-fund-recipients-side-with-the-agency-1501263968.

42. Andrew Koppelman, "Trump's 'Libertarianism' Endangers the Public," CNN, March 7, 2017, accessed June 7, 2018, https://www.cnn.com/2017/03/07/opinions/trumps-phony-libertarianism-endangers-the-public-opinion-koppelman/index.html.

43. Hiroko Tabuchi, "'Vulnerable Voices' Lash Out as Companies Sway Climate Talks," *New York Times*, May 16, 2017, accessed June 7, 2018, https://www.nytimes.com/2017/05/16/climate/corporations-global-climate-talks-bonn-germany.html.

44. Oren Liebermann, "Israel Approves Construction of First New Settlement in More Than 20 Years," CNN, March 31, 2017, accessed March 20, 2018, https://www.cnn.com/2017/03/30/middleeast/israel-approves-new-settlement/index.html.

45. Samantha Schmidt, "Berkeley Student Newspaper Apologizes for Cartoon Depicting Alan Dershowitz Stomping a Palestinian," *Washington Post*, October 27, 2017, accessed March 20, 2018, https://www.washingtonpost.com/news/morning-mix/wp/2017/10/27/berkeley-student-newspaper-apologizes-for-cartoon-depicting-alan-dershowitz-stomping-a-palestinian.

46. Marwan Barghouti, "Why We are on Hunger Strike in Israel's Prisons," *New York Times*, April 16, 2017, accessed March 20, 2018, https://www.nytimes.com/2017/04/16/opinion/palestinian-hunger-strike-prisoners-call-for-justice.html.

47. Liz Spayd, "An Op-Ed Author Omits His Crimes, and The Times Does Too," *New York Times*, April 18, 2017, accessed March 20, 2018, https://www.nytimes.com/2017/04/18/public-editor/an-op-ed-author-omits-his-crimes-and-the-times-does-too.html.

48. Robert Siegel, interview with Raja Shehadeh, "'We Felt Totally Defeated': Palestinian Writer Recalls Memories of 6-Day War," *All Things Considered*, NPR, June 7, 2017, accessed March 20, 2018, https://www.npr.org/2017/06/07/531945547/we-felt-totally-defeated-palestinian-writer-recalls-memories-of-6-day-war.

49. Gershon Shafir, "Israel's 'Temporary' Occupation Has Lasted 50 Years. A New Book Explains Why," *Washington Post*, June 9, 2017, accessed March 20, 2018, https://www.washingtonpost.com/news/monkey-cage/wp/2017/06/09/israels-temporary-occupation-has-lasted-50-years-a-new-book-explains-why.

50. Sut Jhally and Bathsheba Ratzkoff, directors, *Peace, Propaganda & the Promised Land* (Media Education Foundation, 2004). Online at https://shop.mediaed.org/peace-propaganda--the-promised-land-p117.aspx.

CHAPTER 4

Media Democracy in Action

Contributions by Samantha Parsons (UnKoch My Campus), Hans-
Joerg Tiede (American Association of University Professors),
Chenjerai Kumanyika (*Uncivil*), J. Spagnolo and Elle Aviv Newton
(*Poets Reading the News*), and Eleanor Goldfield (*Act Out!*);
compiled and with an introduction by Steve Macek

Since 2004, the Project Censored yearbook has featured a chapter
entitled "Media Democracy in Action" that showcases the voices of
organizations and individuals fighting against censorship, disinformation, and the corporate media's enormous influence over our culture and our politics. Over the years, contributors to the chapter have
included free speech activists, media reformers, radical TV journalists, investigative reporters, media literacy educators, documentary
filmmakers, and government watchdog groups. What all these people
and groups have in common is a shared determination to search out
and publicize often-suppressed truths and a shared faith that public
truth-telling can spark and sustain movements for social justice and
genuine democracy.

Such efforts have always been important. But they are arguably even
more important in the present moment. Today, the White House is
occupied by a pathological liar with authoritarian tendencies who has
nothing but contempt for facts, science, education, journalists, and the
First Amendment. Meanwhile, the corporate news media seem hell-
bent on lending credibility to Trump's accusations of "fake news" with
their endless rumor-mongering, groundless speculation, and thought-
less parroting of Republican and Democratic Party talking points.

The contributors to this year's chapter have each in their own way
worked to provide the rest of us with the knowledge, information,
insight, and critical analysis that are so vital to the struggle for a better
world.

In their contributions, Samantha Parsons of UnKoch My Campus and Hans-Joerg Tiede of the American Association of University Professors (AAUP) expose the current threats posed to academic freedom and the autonomous functioning of the university by conservative pressure groups, and they discuss some of the ways faculty and students have successfully resisted outside meddling in the internal affairs of the academy. Parsons examines some of the well-funded and often underhanded efforts by the billionaire Koch brothers to promote their "free market" ideology on campuses across the country and discusses how her group is successfully fighting back. Tiede's essay explains what academic freedom is and presents an overview of the various ways that the AAUP defends it.

The last three contributions to the chapter highlight creative media projects with a definite critical edge. In his piece, scholar and journalist Chenjerai Kumanyika explicates the philosophy behind his Peabody Award–winning history podcast *Uncivil*, which tells stories left out of standard narratives about the American Civil War and in the process debunks cherished Southern myths about the conflict and its origins. In their essay, J. Spagnolo and Elle Aviv Newton spell out how their online publication and event series, *Poets Reading the News*, harnesses the power of "journalism in verse" to respond to the buzzing confusion of daily events and the difficult, complex issues they raise. Finally, in her entry, Eleanor Goldfield lays out the aims of her innovative video newscast *Act Out!*, a show that combines politically charged spoken-word monologues with interviews featuring radical thinkers, activists, and artists who don't normally make it onto the *Meet the Press* guest list.

Together, the contributors to this year's chapter demonstrate what media democracy in action looks like. They show that fearless truth-telling in the service of social change is still alive and well, even though you would not know it from watching network TV news.

DARK MONEY AND THE PRODUCTION OF KNOWLEDGE

Samantha Parsons

Since the 2016 publication of Jane Mayer's book *Dark Money*, more and more people have been paying attention to how Charles and

David Koch, better known as "the Koch brothers," use their wealth to promote free-market causes and influence state and federal elections throughout the country.[1] Unfortunately, many remain unaware of how the Charles Koch Foundation (CKF) manipulates our nation's universities to serve this political agenda.

UnKoch My Campus seeks to expose and prevent donors like the Koch brothers from being able to buy undue academic influence to advance their libertarian ideology and corporate bottom-line. Established by a group of concerned students and activists, we conduct investigative research on the Kochs' higher education investments, track how CKF donations violate standard academic principles, and support students, faculty, and community members in a national effort to resist Koch-funded corrupt programs on their campuses.

By Charles Koch's own admission, universities are the most important thread in this web of influence. The CKF's financial investments are driven by a strategy known as the "Structure of Social Change," which seeks to establish an expansive infrastructure of universities, think tanks, and front groups that are meant to shape the media, all branches of government, and our education system. First, the Kochs fund universities to produce research and teach curricula that support the ideas they want to dominate local, state, and national policy narratives. This includes funding research and classes that explore the "virtues of free enterprise" through the creation of free-market centers and courses on the principles of economics, ethics and entrepreneurship, political economy, philosophy, and Western civilization.[2]

These ideas are then transformed into policy proposals at Koch-funded think tanks, championed by a network of front groups (such as Americans for Prosperity), and ultimately used to lobby elected officials who often receive direct campaign contributions from Koch Industries.

Since 2005, the CKF has spent $195 million on programs at nearly 500 colleges and universities, while coordinating $100 million from other donors. In 2014, recordings of Koch officials confirmed suspicions that Koch-supported academic programs were in fact being used as recruiting grounds to bring students into their "talent pipeline" of right-wing think tanks and front groups across the country. One official was recorded bragging that this "fully integrated" academic/

political project would "not just change the policies of those states, but also have a significant impact on the federal government."[3]

To make sure his university investments yield the results he wants, Charles Koch attaches expectations to his "philanthropy" that often require strict secrecy and violate long-standing principles of academic freedom and shared governance. This has included interfering with the hiring of faculty; influence over the creation of new programs, majors, and curricula; screening of graduate fellows; approval power over dissertation topics; and oversight of research.

But faculty and students have had enough. Since 2014, UnKoch My Campus has supported dozens of campuses in exposing the CKF's threats to both the integrity of universities and the long-standing principles that are meant to protect the production of knowledge.

Faculty Resistance

Faculty at Wake Forest University have issued two reports about their investigations into the creation of a Koch-funded center on their campus. Based on these reports, the WFU faculty senate passed a motion to cut ties with Koch and his network of political donors. This move was inspired by the efforts of faculty at Western Carolina University, where faculty voted to reject the creation of a Koch-backed center, and the University of Kentucky, where two faculty committees voted to reject a proposed Koch center's governance structure.

More recently, the faculty senate at George Mason University created a committee dedicated to improving the university's gift acceptance and institutional conflict of interest policies to prevent undue donor influence. After the release of a lengthy report on Florida State University's Koch-funded programs, the FSU faculty senate passed a motion to review the university's gift acceptance policies.

Faculty are also leading efforts to investigate donor influence at Syracuse University, University of Arizona, University of Utah, Montana State University, Brown University, Arizona State University, and Middle Tennessee State University.

Student Resistance

Students have been behind much of the resistance to Koch influence across the country, often helping to spark faculty opposition. The CKF has responded by funding initiatives to pass model legislation that would suppress student dissent on campus (as featured in *Censored 2018*).[4]

Students at George Mason University filed a lawsuit against their university and its fundraising foundation to obtain access to Koch donor agreements. George Mason University has received more than two-thirds of all CKF giving, totaling over $100 million.

The student newspaper at Chapman University released an in-depth investigative piece in response to their university's newly-proposed Koch-funded center, revealing that the Koch funding behind new hires in several departments went undisclosed. The newspaper's editorial board later concluded that "accepting this money is unethical and wrong."[5]

After our recent report on neo-Confederate professors featured a Koch-funded white supremacist political scientist at Florida Atlantic University with ties to private prisons, FAU students mobilized to educate peers and faculty while calling for a deeper investigation into donor influence and white supremacy on campus.

With resistance on the rise, the Charles Koch Foundation's legitimacy is fragile. Local fights can have much larger implications. To do your part to help destabilize the Koch network, visit www.unkochmycampus.org or contact Samantha Parsons at samantha@unkochmycampus.org.

SAMANTHA PARSONS is a grassroots campaign organizer and co-founder of UnKoch My Campus. She provides university stakeholders with the support needed to investigate, expose, and launch strategic grassroots campaigns to address undue donor influence on their campuses. She is an alumna of George Mason University with a degree in Conflict Analysis and Resolution and a research background in structural violence, social movements, and Western influence in international peace-building programs.

HOW THE AMERICAN ASSOCIATION OF UNIVERSITY PROFESSORS PROTECTS AND DEFENDS ACADEMIC FREEDOM

Hans-Joerg Tiede

In a recent survey of university provosts, 29 percent responded that faculty at their institution had been "unfairly attacked by conservative websites and politicians."[6] Such attacks, occurring on websites such as Campus Reform—which claims in solicitations for donations that it "exposes the liberal bias and abuse against conservatives on America's colleges and universities"[7]—are regularly followed by large numbers of threats against the targeted faculty member and the institution. In some cases, administrations have suspended or dismissed faculty members who were subject to online harassment. Although harassment campaigns are intended to silence and intimidate those who are targeted, because they have occurred so publicly, including on social media, they can also cause institutions or even other faculty members to censor themselves. Thus, over the course of the last year, targeted harassment of faculty members has emerged as a significant threat to academic freedom.[8]

Although academic freedom in the United States receives some protection—at public universities—from the First Amendment, the conception of academic freedom in this country predates its judicial recognition and has developed largely outside of it. The American Association of University Professors regards academic freedom as a right extended to members of the academic profession who fulfill their obligations in upholding professional ethics. The AAUP also recognizes that, if faculty members are actually to experience academic freedom, colleges and universities must adopt policies that define academic freedom and protect faculty members from adverse administrative actions that violate it. The AAUP has long argued that institutions of higher education in which academic freedom is insecure cannot adequately serve the common good.

The Association's Committee A on Academic Freedom and Tenure approved the following brief definition of academic freedom for incorporation into faculty handbooks and collective-bargaining agreements:

Academic freedom is the freedom to teach, both in and out-side the classroom, to conduct research and to publish the results of those investigations, and to address any matter of institutional policy or action whether or not as a member of an agency of institutional governance. Professors should also have the freedom to address the larger community with regard to any matter of social, political, economic, or other interest, without institutional discipline or restraint, save in response to fundamental violations of professional ethics or statements that suggest disciplinary incompetence.[9]

Of the four activities covered by academic freedom—teaching, research, intramural speech, and extramural speech—the last is the most controversial, because addressing the larger community does not necessarily relate directly to the expertise or professional function of faculty members. Although there are sound theoretical reasons for its inclusion, one reason is perhaps more pragmatic than all others: from cases of professors dismissed in the 1910s because they advocated against child labor, to dismissals in the 1950s because professors defended desegregation, to dismissals in the 1960s because professors advocated for less conservative codes of sexual morality at public institutions, to dismissals in the 1980s because professors advocated for less conservative codes of sexual morality at Catholic institutions, to cases of faculty members dismissed today because their posts on social media sparked outrage campaigns against them, extramural utterances are frequently cited as reasons for dismissing faculty members.

Since its founding in 1915, the AAUP has maintained that the best protection for academic freedom is tenure, which is defined as an indefinite appointment terminable only for adequate cause or under extraordinary circumstances, such as financial exigency. Tenure, in turn, is protected by academic due process. Thus, over the course of the last century, not only has the AAUP helped define and estab-lish the modern tenure system in the United States, but it has also spurred the widespread adoption of procedural safeguards for con-ducting dismissal and appeals hearings, for the imposition of sanc-tions, and for the adjudication of grievances. Documents containing these procedural standards are found in the AAUP Redbook, formally known as *Policy Documents and Reports.*[10]

The AAUP conducts investigations when it receives credible evidence that a serious departure from its key standards may have occurred. An investigation is conducted by an ad hoc committee of AAUP members who visit the institution, interview involved faculty members and administrative officers, and prepare a report of their findings. The goal of an investigation is to ascertain facts and interpret them in light of AAUP policy. For instance, in 2015 the Association conducted an investigation of the dismissal of Professor Steven Salaita from the University of Illinois for his Twitter posts criticizing in strong terms the war in Gaza. The AAUP's decision to conduct an investigation does not assume that a violation has occurred, and some published reports have actually exonerated the subject administrations. In the last century, the Association published more than 300 investigative reports. Not only are these reports a rich source of academic case law interpreting the AAUP's policies in specific circumstances, they also record the history of the development of academic freedom in the United States as it encountered a variety of challenges.

If Committee A finds that the investigative report has identified a serious violation of AAUP-supported standards of academic freedom and tenure, the Association's annual meeting can vote to censure the offending administration. For example, the above-cited investigation of the dismissal of Professor Salaita led to the censure of the University of Illinois administration. Since one condition for the removal of censure is the adoption of AAUP-supported procedural standards, which occurred at the University of Illinois just two years later, the institution of censure serves to facilitate the wider adoption of those standards.

Even though the Association works entirely in the realm of persuasion, its activities have helped shape higher education in the United States. Its recommended policies are included in thousands of faculty handbooks and collective-bargaining agreements. But perhaps more importantly, its central tenet—that academic freedom is essential for higher education—is widely accepted, even though challenges to academic freedom, both old and new, point to the continued need for an organization that serves to protect and defend it.

HANS-JOERG TIEDE is senior program officer in the Department of Academic Freedom, Tenure, and Governance of the American Association of University Professors (www. aaup.org). He is the author of *University Reform: The Founding of the American Association of University Professors* (Johns Hopkins University Press, 2015) and editor of the 11th edition of *AAUP's Policy Documents and Reports* (Johns Hopkins University Press, 2014). The opinions expressed in this essay are the author's.

PUNCHING CENSORED HISTORIES IN THE FACE: THE PHILOSOPHY BEHIND THE *UNCIVIL* PODCAST

Chenjerai Kumanyika

In 1634 a man of African descent listed in official records as "a molato" arrived in bondage in Maryland on a Jesuit ship named *The Ark*. Like the other men who had arrived on that ship, Mathias de Sousa toiled for the person that owned his labor for endless days, doing work such as harvesting crops and building houses. Then, in 1641, he did something that challenged the historical narrative that I have been taught: he campaigned and was elected to the Maryland General Assembly.

On October 21, 1909 legendary journalist Ida Tarbell of the *American Magazine* wrote to General F.C. Ainsworth of the United States Army, saying that she was "anxious to know whether your department has any record of the number of women who enlisted and served in the Civil War, or has it any record of any women who were in the service?" The reply came swiftly: ". . . no record of such cases is known to exist in the official files."[11] The truth is that there were more than 400 such cases.

There is a reason that I and most students in the United States have never learned these stories. The true answer to Ida Tarbell's question reveals a history of resistance in which women challenged essentialist gender categories and outwitted, outperformed, and killed men. As such, this history confirms what most women already know: women's subordinate place in society is not in any way natural, and women have never accepted it.

Mathias de Sousa's career trajectory shows that slavery and racism were not the product of "hate" or even inhumane ignorance, but hundreds of years of economic and political design. It demonstrates that racial delineations were not firm in early America. They were unstable legal and social categories, constructed and reworked for projects of capital accumulation, colonialism, and white domination that continue today.

In 2017 I joined Jack Hitt and Gimlet Media as co-host and executive producer of a new podcast devoted to telling stories like de Sousa's and Tarbell's. It is called *Uncivil* and it aims to explode the misconceptions and myths so many Americans have about the Civil War, slavery, and what those things have to do with contemporary America. The reverence for Confederate monuments and other "Lost Cause" propaganda currently shared by violent ethno-nationalists and high-level politicians reveals a deep commitment to an impoverished history.

In every society, powerful classes, groups, and individuals have reasons to suppress and censor certain kinds of history. The term "censored media" brings to mind discrete instances of pulled news reports, banned books and films, and redacted sentences on government white papers. But whole traditions of oppression, and entire legacies of resistance, like the black radical tradition, the American labor struggle, and the disability rights movement, are conspicuously absent from our popular collective memory.

When histories of resistance are suppressed, they are more challenging to recover than specific incidents. Even when historians and media producers are able to bring pivotal moments of revolutionary struggle to a broader public, those moments are too often cast as exceptional or random. Henry Highland Garnet's speech at the National Negro Convention of 1843 in which he exhorted his enslaved brethren to "arise, arise! Strike for your lives and liberties" can be understood as an inspiring anomaly. In truth, there were countless slave rebellions before 1861 and many similar speeches at some 200 conventions or meetings over the course of seven decades. Isolated from their roots and continuing legacy, traditions of struggle can wither.

The term "censorship" points to absences in our dominant historical narratives, curricula, and media. But those absences are hidden by the presence of other kinds of histories. The history of black American revolutionary solidarity with anti-colonial struggles in the Global South has been replaced with compelling individual stories of "achievement," which allow the powerful to celebrate diversity while bolstering false narratives of American progress.

When censored history is institutionalized in this way, it no longer requires the conscious or explicit ideological intention of any actor. Written into monuments, textbooks, films, flags, and the common language of "broken systems" or "founding principles," censored history becomes commonplace and even revered. It hides its face as propaganda and reproduces sexism, white domination, ableism, and other forms of oppression through people who may not be consciously bigoted or who may even side with the oppressed. It conceals economic interests that have had a crucial effect on history and its recounting, and it obscures major divisions within groups popularly portrayed as homogeneous; consider, for instance, how few popular histories even mention the massive transfer of land from poor white farmers to wealthy white planters that preceded the Civil War. With censored history's oppressive architecture silently erected, those who would pass down that history need only follow institutional norms and the paths of least resistance.

The stories we tell on *Uncivil* attempt to challenge this, but building explicit politics into an ad-funded narrative-nonfiction podcast is unwieldy business. *Uncivil*'s form is public radio–style nonfiction while its ethos is one of critical historiography.

There is no magic formula for creating *Uncivil*, but in contributing to a larger movement of critical pedagogy there are some practices that we have found useful and effective.

We tell listeners explicitly that they have been lied to, and that the truth is radical, knowable, and much more exciting. Our first episode, "The Raid," tackled the most successful covert operation of the Civil War, an attack led by a black woman and a regiment of mostly African American soldiers.[12] Told with the help of young living descendants of the soldiers and with research conducted by local historians, the piece functions as an essential oral archive, rendering this history as vivid and intimate.

We place the politics of history and memory at the center of the storytelling. Our fourth episode, "The Spin"—a favorite among listeners—treats the Lost Cause version of Civil War history as a 150-year public relations victory.[13]

Our show is character-driven, but through lived experience our characters show us structural oppression and collective resistance to it. Episode 2, "The Deed," begins at the conclusion of the Civil War. It tells the story of an African American woman named Nettye Handy and her as-yet-unsuccessful struggle to reclaim land on Sapelo Island.[14] In "The Deed," historians, residents, and Gullah historians like Cornelia Bailey demonstrate how racial capitalism resurfaces in each era using extralegal violence to accomplish what it cannot accomplish through law. More importantly, it shows how black land-owners have continually resisted this. Episode 7, "The Sentence," revisits the slow, intentional establishment of repressive laws that broke from English common law to create distinctly American racial categories that perpetuate various forms of injustice.[15]

Our current economic, political, and cultural reality, with its war-friendly, gendered, raced, capitalist character, is the product of censored histories. *Uncivil* was our attempt to see if we could use the techniques of investigative journalism, critical scholarship, oral history, and audio documentary to revive the histories occluded by censorship, and to create a wide community of citizens who can push history forward based on that knowledge.[16]

CHENJERAI KUMANYIKA is a researcher, journalist, and artist who works as an assistant professor in Rutgers University's Department of Journalism and Media Studies. His research and teaching focus on the intersections of social justice and emerging media in the cultural and creative industries. He is the co-executive producer and co-host of *Uncivil*, Gimlet Media's new podcast on the Civil War. He has also been a contributor to Transom, NPR's *Code Switch* podcast, *All Things Considered*, *Invisibilia*, and Vice, and he is a news analyst for *Rising Up with Sonali*, hosted by Sonali Kolhatkar.

HOW TO READ THE NEWS LIKE A POET

J. Spagnolo and Elle Aviv Newton

If you're apathetic about reading the news, you're in the majority. According to a study by the Media Insight Project, roughly six out of ten Americans don't read beyond the headlines.[17] In some ways, this makes sense: the news forces us to acknowledge daily the harsh realities of environmental destruction, war, systemic injustice, and corruption. This is important truth-telling, because the more aware and engaged a people are, the more powerful their actions might be. Still, who *wants* to be that witness to depravity? Who wants to keep confronting trauma? A common reaction to the news is a real and fervent desire to push it away—to shake off the complicities and complexities of the current moment.

Even if you're reading the news, you may have trouble finding content you trust. When news stories fail to connect to wider narratives, they preclude the public's ability to understand the complexities of the world's issues. For example, in a typical newspaper, economic and environmental sections exist independently of each other, even though environmental degradation is intricately linked with industry. Further, communities that face systematic injustice, such as communities of color, LGBTQ people, women, undocumented immigrants, and the poor and working class, regularly see their oppressions reinforced or neglected by the media platforms employed to tell *everyone*'s stories. When journalism fails to fundamentally seek out and articulate these connections, the work is incomplete.

Still, apathy is no solution. P.T. Barnum wrote, "He who is without a newspaper is cut off from his species."[18] Even if we stop reading the news, the world continues unfolding around us. The structures of power continue to cause incredible amounts of pain. The world continues to want for a legion of informed advocates.

So, the question remains: How can we witness a painful news cycle and still maintain the hope and resilience needed to pursue a better world?

In founding *Poets Reading the News*, we came upon an age-old response: Poetry is an incredible way for cultures to process violence, complexity, political change, and loss. *Poets Reading the News* is a newspaper written entirely by poets, distributed online and soon also in books.[19] Hundreds of talented poets have covered critical events in local, national, and international news. With the power of the genre we call "journalism in verse," poets claim their own subjective truths, link previously isolated stories, and create more integrated understandings of the world.

As an example of what this approach can achieve, take a look at our extensive gun violence coverage.[20] After the deadly shooting at a high school in Parkland, Florida, high school students and teachers wrote about the difficulty of abiding by lesson plans amidst active-shooter drills. Parents wrote about the futility and fear they felt while discussing gun violence with their children. After the historic March for Our Lives, many wrote in with their ideas, frustrations, and hopes for gun control. This is an emotional archive that carries historical import: these poets have captured how it feels to live through recurrent gun violence and political ineptitude in America.

As another example, the poem below, published on May 2, 2017, demonstrates how poetry can serve as a vehicle for truth-telling.

What is Family Detention?
by Abigail Carl-Klassen

A federal judge says it's suspended. The 21 day maximum
    stay is for processing, not detention.
The news says there are three remaining family holding
    facilities in the nation.
Google Maps says it's Leesport, Pennsylvania.
The for-profit prison administrator says it's a job creator.
Immigration and Custom Enforcement says it's a family
    residential center effective for maintaining family unity.
The Texas Department of Family and Protective Services
    wants to say it's a licensed childcare facility.
Google Maps says it's Karnes City, Texas.
The ACLU and Grassroots Leadership says it's baby jail.
The public affairs representative says it's meeting our gov-
    ernment partner's stated needs with dignity and safety.
The Texas House and Senate want to say it's exempt from
    childcare facility licensing requirements.
Google Maps says it's Dilley, Texas.
The American Academy of Pediatrics says it's inappropriate
    for children.
Border Patrol says it's getting the job done.
412 people call it home, for now.

Through this work, Carl-Klassen presented a variety of narratives about family detention. Not only are some statements contradictory, there's also an obvious abstraction: few of the statements concern the families at the heart of the issue, families whose words are noticeably absent. Carl-Klassen critiques not only the institution of family detention but also the discussion around it.

Poetry takes many forms, but above all it relies on creativity, which is a vehicle for hope. As poets rearrange language, erase words from news articles and press releases, and bring together history and the present, they are reconfiguring the news. Poetry compels critical thinking by rewarding those who re-read. Unlike many news articles, which are designed to be understood quickly, poetry asks its readers to look deeper and to question their assumptions.

It's through this confluence of active creativity, community connection, and fierce reckoning that we as writers and readers are changing the top-down approach of journalism. *Poets Reading the News* hands the megaphone to those who have something to say and to those who need to find safe and thoughtful spaces for expression. As a tool for both emotional processing and for reflective conversation, we believe poetry is uniquely situated to help heal the trauma of the world's many divides. At the same time, we believe this work contains essential teachings about the value of independent investigation, critical thought, media literacy, and creative expression. Contact us at editors@poetsreadingthenews.com or visit us online at www. PoetsReadingTheNews.com. This is a place for people who seek to more profoundly engage with the world's pressing issues.

ELLE AVIV NEWTON, a fourth-generation Oaklander, is the co-founder and editor of *Poets Reading the News*. She's also an art curator and regular contributor to KPFA Radio. She holds degrees in history and art criticism from Mills College.

J. SPAGNOLO is an activist, cultural producer, and poet living in California. Spagnolo has shared poetry through radio shows, film festivals, podcasts, and events around the country, and currently co-directs *Poets Reading the News*.

ACT OUT!

Eleanor Goldfield

"What can I do?" has to be the most common question I've gotten in my 15+ years of activism, with a close second being, "Why bother?"

Think of our body politic as an actual body made sick and beaten down by the actions of our oligarchical capitalist system. There are treatments and cures, but they are mostly ignored, censored, repressed, or otherwise shut down and shut up so as to maintain a sickly status quo. This status quo has a vested interest in also ensuring the disconnect between mind and body—or rather, the people and the structure of their sociopolitical lives. From behind a flimsy façade—a mirage democracy of smoke, mirrors, and flags—we observe politics as distant, disconnected spectators. We address sociopolitical ailments with vacant laissez-faire or a mild concern synonymous with treating cancer by tweeting about it. Not enough of us feel directly affected by the vicious diseases ravaging our rights, our lives. In spite of this, we are no less affected. That body politic is as much mine as it is yours as it is the white nationalist's in Kentucky, the immigrant's in Arizona, the oil rig worker's in Louisiana, the water protector's in Pennsylvania, and the political prisoner's in solitary confinement.

As a journalist and an activist, my aim is to combat this systemic disconnect that pulls the people from their own self-determination— a bit like a citizen personal trainer. Having been a personal trainer as well, I know that you can't change your body until you get to know and accept your body. With politics it's no different. We have to see how we fit into the suffering in Puerto Rico, how the bombs dropped in Yemen implicate us, how the bullshit infotainment peddled as news misinforms and divides us, and how the prisons built on Superfund sites compromise us. From there, we have to own it. We have to recognize that it is not up to others, particularly elected officials, to better the body politic. It is up to us.

Czech philosopher Jan Patočka called this idea "the solidarity of the shaken."[21] It's the notion that once we let go of the buoys of blind optimism, blind faith in officials, the system, or any other sociopolitical "higher power," we can actually and legitimately stand with each other. It will not be a steady or comfortable foundation, but it will be a real one—and one from which we can pointedly and powerfully act.

The history of people's victories is written on this unsteady ground. And today, people continue this work: of building and fighting together, of squaring with the ills of this system and conceiving of something better.

The goal of *Act Out!* is to highlight this work while simultaneously placing it in the context of the raw, uncensored, unredacted realities of our sick body politic. The show attempts to answer both of those permanently pressing questions: "What can I do?" and "Why bother?" It is there to build a bridge between caring and doing and to engage people who feel it's useless to fight. We cover stories that corporate media will never touch. Since you're holding this book, you have a rough idea of what kind of stories those are: the kind that don't fit into the capitalist confines of a consumerist infotainment paradigm built to manufacture consent on behalf of the powers that be. By bringing to light those censored, redacted, and ignored stories, we aim to expose as a means to engage.

It's not about converting people—after all, progress isn't a church. Rather, it's about exposure. It's about ripping that flimsy façade apart, but it is also about exposing the work of fighting and building. Indeed, highlighting the creative ways that people are building while resisting is the powerful and necessary follow-up to exposing the empire. It introduces us to alternatives, asks us to question, dares us to dream. For instance, why can't an abandoned parking lot be a community garden that promotes food sovereignty in marginalized communities? Another question outside the conventional confines of polite conversation: Why do we need cops? Are guns bad or is it the culture around them? By questioning the status quo, the smoke and mirrors begin to fade. By creatively considering alternatives, we bypass the abyss of nihilistic apathy and instead find the urge to build.

What that looks like is different in every community we've covered on the show. The objective isn't uniformity or indeed any kind of manufactured unity. The goal is solidarity. The goal is giving a fuck and doing something while accepting that it won't be perfect, easy, or anything like *V for Vendetta*. It will be fun and depressing, and it'll be hard work—from actively informing ourselves and bringing to light censored stories and their storytellers, to digging past programmed ideas for progress into deeper creative dreams of what could be, beyond the horizon of a capitalist empire in decline. It will require supporting each other in our work, dodging infighting and infiltration, and bucking the calls for purity, both in our movements and in society. It will entail striving with no guarantee of success. But as

Chris Hedges has stated, "I do not fight fascists because I will win. I fight fascists because they are fascists."[22] When we fight, when we build, we sustain hope. And we trigger the best in humanity—the qualities that overthrew kings, that looked at undefeated power and found a way to defeat it.

The most pressing questions therefore aren't "What can I do?" or "Why bother?" but rather "What should we build?" and "Who's with me?"

Act Out! airs weekly online via occupy.com and every weekend on Free Speech TV.

ELEANOR GOLDFIELD is a creative activist and journalist. In addition to hosting *Act Out!*, she writes for several alternative media outlets, assists in local organizing, facilitates trainings, and performs spoken word, music, and visual projections. Find her at ArtKillingApathy.com.

STEVE MACEK, who edited and compiled this chapter, is Professor of Communication and Chair of the Department of Communication and Media Studies at North Central College in Naperville, Illinois. He is the author of *Urban Nightmares: The Media, the Right, and the Moral Panic over the City* (University of Minnesota Press, 2006), and his op-eds and essays about the media, politics, and free speech issues have been published in a wide range of magazines and newspapers, including *Z Magazine, St. Louis Journalism Review, Atlanta Journal-Constitution, Columbus Dispatch*, and *News & Observer* (Raleigh, North Carolina).

Notes

1. Jane Mayer, *Dark Money: The Hidden History of the Billionaires Behind the Rise of the Radical Right* (New York: Penguin Random House, 2016).
2. "Virtues of free enterprise": See, e.g., the text of the grant agreement between Ball State University, the Ball State University Foundation, and the CKF, establishing the John H. Schnatter Institute for Entrepreneurship and Free Enterprise in March 2016, https://ia601208. us.archive.org/26/items/BallStateCKFAgreementMarch2016/Ball%20State%20CKF%20 Agreement%20March%202016.pdf.
3. "Koch's Political Strategy and the Role of Academia," UnKoch My Campus, undated, http:// www.unkochmycampus.org/the-donors/.
4. See Dawn M. Lucier and Emily von Weise, with Susan Rahman and Rob Williams, "Right-Wing Money Promotes Model Legislation to Restrict Free Speech on University Campuses," in *Censored 2018: Press Freedoms in a "Post-Truth" World*, eds. Andy Lee Roth and Mickey Huff with Project Censored (New York: Seven Stories Press, 2017), 73–75.
5. Panther Editorial Board, "UnKoch Our Campus," *The Panther* (Chapman University), November 12, 2017, http://www.thepantheronline.com/opinions/unkoch-our-campus.
6. Scott Jaschik, "The Pressure on Provosts," *Inside Higher Ed*, January 24, 2018, https://www. insidehighered.com/news/survey/2018-inside-higher-ed-survey-chief-academic-officers.

7. See, e.g., Bradley Devlin, "Protesters Nearly Derail Dave Rubin Speech at UNH," Campus Reform, May 3, 2018, https://www.campusreform.org/?ID=10858.

8. See, e.g., Jaschik, "Pressure on Provosts."

9. Robert M. O'Neil et al., "Protecting an Independent Faculty Voice: Academic Freedom after *Garcetti v. Ceballos*," AAUP, November–December 2009, 88, https://www.aaup.org/file/Protecting-Independent-Voice.pdf.

10. American Association of University Professors, *Policy Documents and Reports*, 11th ed. (Baltimore: Johns Hopkins University Press, 2014).

11. See, e.g., DeAnne Blanton, "Women Soldiers of the Civil War," *Prologue* (National Archives), Vol. 25, No. 1 (Spring 1993), https://www.archives.gov/publications/prologue/1993/spring/women-in-the-civil-war-1.html.

12. "The Raid," *Uncivil*, October 4, 2017, https://www.gimletmedia.com/uncivil/the-raid#episode-player.

13. "The Spin," *Uncivil*, November 8, 2017, https://www.gimletmedia.com/uncivil/the-spin#episode-player.

14. "The Deed," *Uncivil*, October 11, 2017, https://www.gimletmedia.com/uncivil/the-deed#episode-player.

15. "The Sentence," *Uncivil*, December 13, 2017, https://www.gimletmedia.com/uncivil/the-sentence#episode-player.

16. To download episodes of *Uncivil* for free, visit https://itunes.apple.com/gb/podcast/uncivil/id1275078406.

17. "How Americans Get Their News," from "The Personal News Cycle: How Americans Choose to Get Their News," Media Insight Project (American Press Institute and the Associated Press–NORC Center for Public Affairs Research), March 17, 2014, https://www.americanpressinstitute.org/publications/reports/survey-research/how-americans-get-news.

18. Phineas Taylor Barnum, "The Art of Money-Getting," in *The Life of P.T. Barnum: Written by Himself, Including His Golden Rules for Money-Making* (Buffalo: The Courier Company, 1888), 168–91, 183.

19. Visit us at www.PoetsReadingTheNews.com.

20. Category Archive: Gun Violence, *Poets Reading the News*, October 16, 2016–present, http://www.poetsreadingthenews.com/category/gun-violence.

21. Jan Patočka, *Heretical Essays in the Philosophy of History*, tr. Erazim Kohák, ed. James Dodd (Chicago: Open Court, 1996 [Czech orig. 1975]), 134.

22. Chris Hedges, "Revolt is the Only Barrier to a Fascist America," Truthdig, January 23, 2017, https://www.truthdig.com/articles/revolt-is-the-only-barrier-to-a-fascist-america/.

CHAPTER 5

Vetting Free Speech
How the United Kingdom Approaches
Freedom of Expression on Campus

Sally Gimson, Layli Foroudi, and Sean Gallagher

For all its intensity, the debate on free speech is a relatively recent phenomenon in the United Kingdom—bursting into common cultural consciousness during the tumultuous 1960s. In recent years, the debate has been fueled by identity politics and accusations that today's students are nothing more than "snowflakes" in need of safe spaces and trigger warnings to protect them from microaggressions. In the United Kingdom, this polarization has been fanned by traditional, social, and Internet-based outlets—on both the Right and the Left—further muddying the waters and leading to confusion.

What is clear is that many British universities are attempting to limit the speech of students, and are able to write these restrictions into university policy. Much of this has been done in more or less successful attempts to navigate difficult questions of bullying and inclusion, and to protect the universities' interests, but some of these new policies limiting free speech have been created in response to government anti-terror legislation. At the same time, student unions are attempting, not always successfully, to restrict some forms of speech on campus that they find offensive.

Almost all British universities are publicly funded, although student fees are changing the culture of institutions, so there is more of a commercial relationship developing between students and university authorities.[1] There is no First Amendment protection on speech in the United Kingdom as there is in the United States, which means the government is more likely to interfere in what can be said on campus, particularly on the grounds that some speech "promotes terrorism." Racial tensions in the United Kingdom and Europe are different from those in the United States, with greater focus on colonialism, apartheid, and Britain's relationships with former colonies, particularly South Africa.[2] Equality debates in the United Kingdom are also influenced by the recent debates about transgenderism and misogyny in the United States.

The 2017 Spiked online survey of 115 UK universities found that 63.5 percent of universities limited free speech in some ways.[3] Some had rules stipulating that speakers could not appear on university platforms unless their speeches were cleared by university authorities,[4] others banned such speakers as the former leader of the English Defence League, Tommy Robinson,[5] and others have codes of conduct that prescribe (with threats of disciplinary action) acceptable ways of talking about certain issues in order to "promote an atmosphere in which all students and staff feel valued."[6] Universities have argued that the latter are equality policies which state that homophobic, sexist, and racist language will not be tolerated and that their violations of freedom of speech are exaggerated by the "red ratings" given in the Spiked report.

In this chapter we examine the history and the impact of government policies and legislation on free speech on UK university campuses. While the fraught debate over free speech has been influenced by contemporaneous arguments taking place in the United States, the approaches of government, university administrations, and student unions place curbs on language in the United Kingdom in pursuit of anti-terror strategy, safety, and no-platforming, respectively. Looking at historical and contemporary debates, this chapter explores the impact that government legislation and directives, as well as student unions, have had on free speech.

Students in the United Kingdom, like those in the United States, have also been guilty of limiting speech: boycotting pro- and anti-Israel speakers; banning tabloid newspapers in student unions; and no-platforming feminists who have been critical of transgender people. Britain's colonial heritage is also being challenged. Oxford University students ran an as-yet-unsuccessful campaign demanding the removal of a statue of Cecil Rhodes because of his brutal legacy of imperialism and racism in southern Africa.[7] Sometimes the universities and students work in tandem to limit speech, as when a London School of Economics student union objected to T-shirts referencing the "Jesus and Mo" webcomic. Passersby complained to the student union, and the university's legal department ordered the T-shirts not to be worn.[8]

The UK government, while condemning bans on free speech, has put some free speech limitations into effect as part of Prevent, its anti-terrorism strategy. Prevent is a policy implemented across schools, colleges for further education, and universities to deny a platform to those who might encourage terrorism. The strategy also encourages teachers and lecturers to report those who may have been radicalized or who might radicalize others.[9] Further, King's College London in January 2017 told students that their emails could be retained and monitored as part of the college's Prevent obligations.[10] It is believed that other universities also monitor student and staff emails. Critics, including human rights lawyers, have said the policy is a catch-all for many types of political dissent and free speech—and encourages the demonization of Muslims.[11]

HISTORICAL CONTEXT

Demonstrations against speakers, boycotts on goods, and no-platforming have existed since the 1960s and '70s in the United Kingdom, though laws passed in the last 30 years have made political actions of this type more difficult to organize in universities today.

The British anti-apartheid movement, for instance, lobbied student unions in the 1960s. This campaign prompted the National Union of Students (NUS) in 1970 not only to pass a motion supporting the armed struggle in South Africa, but also to call for a total cultural, sporting, and academic boycott of South African goods and services.[12]

The policy of no-platforming was developed in the 1970s by Trotskyist groups, and their takeover of the NUS in 1974 led to the following resolution, aimed at the Far Right and the fascist National Front:[13] "[C]onference believes that in order to counter these [racist and fascist] groups, it is . . . necessary to prevent any member of these organisations or individuals known to espouse similar views from speaking in colleges by whatever means necessary (including disrupting of the meeting)."[14]

Many of the discussions from the 1970s and '80s up to the present day revolve around whether only fascist and racist groups should be no-platformed, or whether other people should likewise be targeted.

The 1970s and '80s was a time when overt racist rhetoric was being challenged, the Far Right was gaining support in elections, and immigration, particularly from Britain's former colonies, was changing the racial makeup of UK cities.

Some Trotskyist factions believed no-platforming should be extended to such Tory MPs as Enoch Powell, a government minister in the 1970s who said there would be "rivers of blood" in Britain because of mass immigration. Some factions also wanted to target members of a right-wing Conservative Party organization, the Conservative Monday Club, as well as psychologist Hans Eysenck, who had courted controversy with his assertions linking race with intelligence.

Later in the 1970s, there were also discussions about whether no-platforming should be applied to Zionists or defenders of Israel, and this debate still continues today. As a History & Policy blog post by Evan Smith highlights, in May 1977 Alan Elsner of the Union of Jewish Students protested in the *New Statesman* that the no-platforming policy "could be used as a means of silencing people whose views might be controversial or unpopular."[15]

Student leaders like Charles Clarke, who would later become the Labour Party home secretary, and Sue Slipman, a founding member of the Social Democratic Party (SDP), fought left-wing student leaders over free speech limitations and no-platforming. Both argued against such strategies, though Clarke believed that they could be selectively applied to racists and fascists and not to democratically elected politicians.[16]

No-platforming policy was criticized in the press at the time as a denial of free speech, with the *Guardian* warning in an editorial, "Students should perhaps remember that frustration which leads to a denial of the right of one section of society is not something new. It is a classic pattern of fascism."[17]

The attacks and demonstrations against Conservative Party politicians were naturally condemned by student Conservatives on campus, as well as the right-wing media.

It was in response to these clashes at university unions, particularly affecting Conservative MPs and supporters of Israel, that the House of Commons debated more legislation to protect free speech. In concert with a general campaign of union-busting,[18] the government of prime minister Margaret Thatcher passed Section 43 of the Education (No. 2) Act 1986, which places a statutory duty on the higher education sector to uphold freedom of speech in their institutions as far as is practical within the law. Section 43 has also meant, though, that any controversial speech becomes a designated event with extra costs associated with organizing it.[19] This law still governs free speech on campus in the United Kingdom today.[20]

Legislation

Free speech on British campuses is governed not only by Section 43 of the Education (No. 2) Act 1986, but also by Public Order Act 1986, which contains provisions on the prevention of racial and religious hatred.

Institutions must ensure events do not cause public disorder offenses, threaten violence, or cause fear, alarm, or distress. Universities and colleges must also comply with the Equality Act 2010, which prevents discrimination, and the Human Rights Act 1998, which further enshrines freedom of speech.

Furthermore, student unions are governed by the Education Act 1994, which restricts student unions' ability to campaign. As Alex Bols, deputy chief executive of GuildHE, one of the two formal representative bodies for higher education in the United Kingdom, wrote in a 2014 blog post, the Education Act 1994 "also enshrined the idea that students' unions should be supporting their 'students as students' i.e. limiting their ability to campaign on national and international issues such as the miners' strike or apartheid."[21] Student unions are also now regarded as educational charities, which imposes further legal obligations on balanced speaker panels and the kinds of political activities, including lobbying, they can undertake.[22]

All this legislation taken together guarantees, on the one hand, rights to free speech on UK campuses, but on the other hand it gives university authorities and student unions the power to limit such rights.

Prevent Strategy

The evolution of the United Kingdom's anti-terror strategies—including its CONTEST strategy, publicly established in 2006, and later amended by such legislation as the Counter-Terrorism and Security Act 2015—has resulted in a statutory duty imposed on universities and other public bodies to tackle radicalization. The government anti-terror guidance includes a catch-all phrase, requiring that universities make sure their students or staff are not "drawn into terrorism. This includes not just violent extremism but also non-violent extremism, which can create an atmosphere conducive to terrorism and can popularise views which terrorists exploit." It is a condition of funding that all further education and independent training providers must comply with relevant legislation and any statutory responsibilities associated with the delivery of education and safeguarding of learners.[23]

Where events on campus are concerned, the guidance contains an unequivocal statement: "Where [institutions] are in any doubt that the risk cannot be fully mitigated they should exercise caution and not allow the event to proceed."[24] Noting that "young people continue to make up a disproportionately high number of those arrested . . . for terrorist-related offences," the Prevent guidelines identify universities as places where young people risk "radicalisation,"[25] which can be facilitated through events held for extremist speakers or through other radicalized students on social media.[26]

Although the language of the government's anti-terror guidelines may seem overly alarmist, there have been several examples of UK university students committing acts of terror. Umar Farouk Abdulmutallab, who graduated from University College London (UCL) in 2008, attempted to detonate explosives on a transatlantic flight on Christmas Day in 2009. In 2016, a student at King's College London, Suhaib Majeed, was arrested for plotting a series of drive-by shootings.[27]

It is worth noting, however, that it remains unclear whether either of these individuals were radicalized at universities or through outside networks, and the magnitude of terrorist "radicalization" on campus continues to be a disputed subject.

The British Government and Its Commitment to Free Speech

On March 21, 2017, the *Times* published a report in which MP Jo Johnson, then minister for higher education, told universities that they will be "compelled to include a clear commitment to freedom of speech in their governance documents to counter the culture of censorship and so-called safe spaces."[28]

As indicated by this report, free speech on campus has become a high-profile issue. Reflecting the range of actors who have been affected by restrictions on speech on campus, Johnson said it was the "legal duty" of universities to ensure that freedom of speech is secured for "members, students, employees and visiting speakers."[29]

Yet, while Johnson's words recognize that the freedom of individuals to express themselves on campus is being called into question, the UK government has also played a major part in limiting speech on university campuses.[30]

Johnson said he wanted to remind students and university officials that freedom of speech "should be at the heart of a higher-education community," yet he also publicly backed the counter-terrorist Prevent strategy which bans certain speakers and events and encourages universities to monitor students' behavior.

Indeed, the NUS has been the main organization taking a stand against Prevent, arguing that it disproportionately targets Muslim students[31] and poses a challenge to free speech.[32] An NUS campaign, Students Not Suspects, has also been set up to challenge the legislation's effect on students.[33]

CONTEMPORARY DEBATES

As in the past, the debates over free speech in UK universities are fraught with personal and political difficulties. Students and universities tend to be on one side, while the popular press and conservative politicians tend to be on the other. All this is fueled by libertarian organizations, like Spiked, which believe in "freedom of speech with no ifs and buts, against the myriad miserabilists who would seek to wrap humans in red tape, dampen down our daring, restrain our thoughts, and police our speech."[34]

The Spiked Free Speech University Rankings (FSUR) have, since the project launched in 2015, tracked 129 bans in universities. Their April 2018 report showed that 10 universities have banned publications, 12 have banned speakers, 17 have punished students, and 11 have banned fancy dress.[35]

The row about free speech has concerned leading academics as well. In early 2016, on the day of her formal installation as the new vice-chancellor of Oxford University, the political scientist Louise Richardson professed her commitment to free speech. She said,

> Education is not meant to be comfortable. Education should be about confronting ideas you find really objectionable, figuring out why it is you should find them objectionable, fashioning a reasoned argument against them, confronting the person you disagree with and trying to change their mind, being open to them changing your mind. That isn't a comfortable experience, but it is a very educational one.[36]

The general popular narrative, in part picked up from the United States, is that universities are filled with "snowflake" millennials who do not want to hear other viewpoints and need safe spaces and trigger warnings.

In reality, the situation is complicated and the arguments are rather more nuanced. Students say they do want to hear other viewpoints, but are worried about hurting minorities in the student body, pointing out that student unions are now, by law, places where students should be supporting students. They are concerned that in today's divisive political environment everyone is operating in an echo chamber, only wanting to hear ideas that correspond to their own view of the world.[37]

On the Israel–Palestine debate, we find that neither side is particularly keen to encourage the free speech of the other; and that students see banning newspapers as one of the few tools with which they can protest what they see as the outlets' racist and sexist content.

Universities have also become risk-averse, worried, for instance, about how fancy dress parties involving blackface or Nazi uniforms might go against their equality policies, upset the wider student body, and discourage minority students from applying. It might also lead to their university being characterized in the press as a haven of racism.

In 2011, for instance, the Oxford University Conservative Association's fancy dress party featured Nazi uniforms, anti-Semitic songs, and students dressed as miners to mock the working classes.[38] Details of the party and the concerns of the authorities were leaked to the *Daily Telegraph*, and the university found itself at the center of a national scandal. An Oxford debating society also hit the headlines in 2015 when it offered "Colonial Comeback" cocktails for sale on a poster showing a slave's chained wrists.[39]

It was hardly surprising, then, that students at Pembroke College in Cambridge decided in 2016 they did not want to have an "Around the World in 80 Days" party, to prevent instances of "cultural appropriation."[40] Pictures from the previous themed party showed some students in Native American headdresses. Other students, according to reports, had to be turned away for mockingly wearing hijabs.

Many students on Facebook objected to the cancellation of the party, and the *Daily Telegraph*, ever adaptable, ran a sarcastic comment piece about political correctness and respect for ethnic diversity gone mad.[41]

This is typical of much of the problem. There are genuine debates going on in British universities about balancing the role of free speech and the protection of minorities, but there is also a press keen to jump on and oversimplify those debates and criticize students.

Not a day passes without some news article or commentator picking up the issue of free speech on campus, and some reporters or pundits are overly zealous in their commitment to the narrative of "censorious students," leading them to misreport the facts.

For instance, the protests at the School of Oriental and African Studies (SOAS) University of London calling for the "decolonisation of the curriculum," for greater representation of diverse voices in the philosophy curriculum, and for white philosophers and history to be taught in their colonial context, were gravely mischaracterized by the corporate press.[42]

Meera Sabaratnam, a lecturer in international relations at SOAS, explained in a blog post that the protests called for three things: challenging assumptions about culture and the way history is taught, putting philosophers and writers in their historical context, and thinking about "implications of a more diverse student body in terms of pedagogy and achievement."[43]

The newspaper reports of the protests, however, erroneously said that students wanted to "ban white philosophers." The headline in the *Daily Mail* ran "They Kant be Serious! PC Students Demand White Philosophers Including Plato and Descartes be Dropped from University Syllabus."[44]

In another case, a *Telegraph* article claimed that UCL students had started a campaign called "Galton Must Fall," to have the name of Victorian scientist Sir Francis Galton removed from university rooms.[45] It turned out, however, that the campaign never existed—the reporter, Camilla Turner, had made it up. It fit the narrative of students seeking to limit free speech, but it was entirely unfounded.

What had happened, according to the *Tab*, UCL's student newspaper, was that the provost had been challenged by students during an event called "Why isn't My Professor Black?"[46] Nathaniel Adam Tobias Coleman, UCL's first research associate on the philosophy of race, had also written a provocative article in 2014 in the *Times Higher Education* magazine about Galton's relationship to UCL.[47] However, to suggest that there was a "Galton Must Fall" campaign was taking the story too far, as the *Telegraph* subsequently acknowledged.

Both incidents, like the real "Rhodes Must Fall" campaign, reflect debates within British universities, not only among students but also among academics, about how to deal with a more diverse student population and changing attitudes to colonialism, race, and the history of the United Kingdom. It is also not surprising that these debates are being challenged by Conservative Party–dominated newspapers.

Mirroring Debates in the United States

These free-speech debates are similar to ones that have taken place in the United States in an environment where speech is protected through the First Amendment. Increasingly in universities the argument is put forward that structural inequality and ingrained patterns of harassment silence minority voices on a daily basis.

In a recent article, Keeanga-Yamahtta Taylor, an assistant professor of African American studies at Princeton University, argued that the conservative press in the United States is selective about which kinds of freedom of speech it chooses to defend, often harassing and silencing voices they do not approve of.[48] She cites how Fox News took a clip of her condemnation of President Trump and ran it for four days under the headline "Princeton Professor Goes on Anti-POTUS Tirade,"[49] so that she and her department were inundated with abuse, including threats of lynching, shooting, and raping.

Genuine freedom of speech entails the right to question, disagree with, and even condemn what others say. Philosophy professors Kate Manne and Jason Stanley, from Cornell and Yale Universities, respectively, differentiate between censure and censorship: "the right not to be censored by the government extends to the right to censure—that is, morally condemn—the speech acts of other people."[50]

The narrative of "censorious students" has resulted in some legitimate protests by students and faculty members against being categorized as attackers of freedom of speech and the right to freedom of expression. As Manne and Stanley wrote in the US *Chronicle of Higher Education*,

> The notion of freedom of speech is being co-opted by dominant social groups, distorted to serve their interests, and used to silence those who are oppressed and marginalised. All too often, when people depict others as threats to freedom of speech, what they really mean is, "Quiet!"[51]

No-Platforming

Speech must be countered with speech so that ideas are explored, viewpoints challenged, and arguments refined. Enlightenment principles prescribe that the natural limits of one's liberty lie at the point at which one's liberty begins to impose upon the liberty of another. Such are the principles of free debate. No-platforming, which seeks to stop certain people from speaking on the grounds that they hold views that are offensive, goes against this principle.

As discussed above, the NUS adopted a "no-platform" policy in

1974 in order to combat the influence of "openly racist and fascist organisations" like the National Front. The NUS position today is that student unions "have a right to refuse individuals and groups who threaten the safe environment students' unions provide for their members."[52] The policy also prevents representatives of the NUS from sharing a public platform with particular named individuals or groups, which officially include six "fascist and racist organisations": Al-Muhajiroun; British National Party; English Defence League; Hizb ut-Tahrir; Muslim Public Affairs Committee; and National Action.[53] One of these organizations, Al-Muhajiroun, is a proscribed terror organization under UK law, and speakers from the other groups might well be unable to speak at universities under the government's recent anti-terror and anti-extremism legislation.[54]

Individual university unions and student groups are not bound by this list and are permitted to formulate their own. According to a 2016 survey of 1,001 students conducted by ComRes, 63 percent of university students support the NUS "no-platform policy," and 54 percent think that the policy should be enforced against people who could be found intimidating.[55]

In practice, no-platforming has been extended to other speakers whom student unions find offensive, such as, for instance, feminist Julie Bindel, who was not allowed to speak at a campus event by Manchester University's student union due to her views on transgender people.[56] Bindel wrote that her experience was part of a wider trend of feminists being shut down for talking about violence against women. Bindel's exclusion could also be understood as part of a wider debate within the feminist movement about the identity of trans women, which has drawn in second-wave feminist Germaine Greer, gay rights campaigner Peter Tatchell, and, most recently, the Nigerian novelist Chimamanda Ngozi Adichie.[57]

Both Tatchell and Greer have found themselves crossing student unions or their representatives due to their views. For instance, in early 2016 NUS lesbian, gay, bisexual, and transgender (LGBT) representative Fran Cowling refused to share a platform with gay rights activist Peter Tatchell at an event at Canterbury Christ Church University, because of his racist and "transphobic" views, and because he signed a letter in the *Observer* in support of free speech in 2015.[58] As a result, Tatchell spoke at the event and Cowling did not attend. Both sides laid out their cases on blogs and in the press, with Tatchell benefiting from much more favorable coverage than Cowling.[59]

There were also calls to no-platform Greer, who has been very vocal about her position that trans women are not women. Cardiff University women's officer Rachael Melhuish initiated a petition against Greer for demonstrating "misogynistic views towards trans women, including continually misgendering trans women and denying the existence of transphobia altogether." The petition received more than three thousand signatures, but after a statement from the university, which said, "We in no way condone discriminatory comments of any kind," Greer went ahead and gave her planned lecture at the university.[60]

Speakers deemed to be Islamophobic have also found themselves the victims of no-platforming. Nick Lowles, chief executive of the anti-fascist organization HOPE Not Hate, claimed that "ultra left" NUS students did not want him to speak on an anti-racist platform because he is "Islamophobic." He believes that is why he was not invited to an anti-racism conference at Canterbury Christ Church University.[61]

Somewhat ironically, HOPE Not Hate originally supported no-platforming as a strategy to combat fascism, but in 2013 Nick Lowles wrote a blog post, since taken down, stating that their traditional position was no longer adequate and that "we need to do more to debate the ideas we oppose."[62]

Student opposition to controversial speakers has led universities to err on the side of caution. In many institutions, because of legal requirements on universities and unions, student societies are charged a security fee for organizing potentially disruptive events; they are required to give notice for inviting "controversial" speakers; and they must pass a number of checks before an event can be approved.

In 2016, on the BBC Victoria Derbyshire program, Richard Brooks, one of the NUS's vice presidents at the time, differentiated between disinviting a speaker under a "safe space" policy and no-platforming. The no-platform policy refers to six specific organizations, but the safe space policy, he explained, is "based on the idea that every single person has freedom of speech [and] we are making sure that marginalised groups get their views heard."[63]

Zoe Williams, in a column for the *Guardian*, wrote that she was puzzled by the "rigidity and conventionality of [Germaine] Greer's stance" on transgenderism, but felt that, in the final analysis, no-platforming speakers with potentially offensive or hurtful views was not a necessary path of action:

> The application of this to the no-platforming debate is as follows: it is precisely because there is still so much prejudice against trans people that nobody should be silenced. In terms of social ideas, you progress from A to B—from saying homosexuality is aberrant, for instance, towards homosexuality is normal—not by shutting down homophobes but by argument, persuasion, rage and ridicule, openness and candour.[64]

History shows us that the casualties of anti–hate speech legislation and no-platforming are often the minorities that advocates seek to protect.

For instance, the first casualty of a Canadian anti-obscenity law was a gay and lesbian bookshop in Toronto; and in 1993, *Black Looks: Race and Representation* by bell hooks was confiscated by the Canada Border Services Agency as potential "hate literature."[65]

As writer and lecturer Kenan Malik has pointed out, the extremist politician Geert Wilders tried to outlaw the Koran in Holland because it "promotes hatred," as, he argued, "Each Holy Book blasphemes against the other."[66] According to Malik, "Hate speech restriction is a means not of tackling bigotry but of rebranding certain, often obnoxious, ideas or arguments as *immoral*. It is a way of making certain ideas illegitimate without bothering politically to challenge them. And that is dangerous."[67]

Safe Spaces

The term "safe space" is contested, and it has come to mean anything from a specific space on campus where students of a certain background feel comfortable, to the banning of speakers, ideas, and publications from the university campus as a whole.

Broadly speaking, "safe space policies" include guidelines that promote a safe environment for students to engage in discussions free from interrogation and judgment.

This may result in individuals in breach of such guidelines being asked to leave the discussion or the particular space. One of the predominant arguments for safe spaces is that these spaces enhance freedom of speech for minority groups, whose voices are usually undermined by traditional and dominant narratives. Safe spaces are thus understood as an equality mechanism to address power imbalances.

Although safe spaces naturally exist on a micro and informal level, among interest groups and societies where likeminded individuals may come together and support each other,[68] having a formal university safe space policy may result in chilling free speech on campus or disrupting events.

When Iranian secularist Maryam Namazie spoke at Goldsmiths University in 2015 on the subject of "blasphemy and apostasy," her talk was interrupted by students from the Islamic Society, who shouted "Safe space! Safe space! Intimidation!" ten minutes into the event. The event continued despite the interruption, but it is indicative of the potential abuse of the safe space concept.

At a St. George's House event for academics on the subject of freedom of expression on campus, speakers proclaimed that "safe space" policies create a "tyranny of the majority" in the classroom, where those with dissenting views may be dissuaded from speaking out. In addition to this, one participant commented that, "in debates about a particular minority group or experience, safe space policies may hinder students not of that group from commenting"—for example, white students may be discouraged from contributing to discussions about colonialism.[69]

At the same event, participants noted that safe space policies may block opportunities for the development of critical thinking among students, as they may result in restricting students' exposure to different points of view. As we have noted earlier, the idea that a university student union is a "safe space" has been used to no-platform and disinvite speakers.

There is a long history of "safe spaces" being instrumental to the growth and development of ideas and thinking that challenge societal norms; however, these ideas must also be brought into the public arena to be challenged, refined, and debated. Furthermore, some views that would not be expressed in public may gain legitimacy in a "safe space" away from public scrutiny.

It is through dialogue between different ideas that preconceptions are challenged and ideas are refined. This practical fact is repeated again and again in the literature on and coverage of censorious students or the disinviting of allegedly extremist speakers in universities.

The challenge to those advocating for free speech is to respond to arguments for safe spaces and to understand their root causes, as that will, in turn, help refine their own arguments for free speech. For example, it is important to attribute legitimate motivations to the actors involved and to avoid reducing individuals to their presumed deficiencies or dismissing grievances rooted in social inequality and the historical marginalization of groups. Furthermore, protest is a legitimate means of expression and is naturally to be encouraged.

It is also important to respond to arguments put forward for limiting speech that may be deemed hateful in the campus context. A third-year law student at the London School of Economics (LSE), Maurice Banerjee Palmer, wrote a blog post in 2016 criticizing the LSE free speech group Speakeasy for its naïve approach to freedom of expression, saying that "they pretty much endorse hate speech (which is illegal)." He continued, "they don't seem to have put any effort into understanding the rationale behind safe spaces, or their effect. And for a supposedly pro-debate organisation they don't seem awfully keen on putting across the other side of the argument." In a tongue-in-cheek move, Banerjee Palmer put forward a motion to the student union to ban Speakeasy altogether for being "self-important and ill-informed."[70]

Trigger Warnings

Trigger warnings, safe spaces, and other similar terms have been imported from campus free speech debates that have taken place in the United States. Altogether, these hot-button terms have been attributed to the so-called "snowflake generation," who are allegedly unable to hear or discuss difficult or disturbing subjects and are accused of being oversensitive to criticism. Many universities and individual lecturers in the United Kingdom have prefaced their coursework with trigger warnings, which are applied mostly to subject matter dealing with violence against women, general violence, and subject matter to do with racism and colonialism.

Defenders of the warnings say they are not about shutting down debate or letting students evade requirements, but about signaling difficult subjects so that students do not relive trauma. Those against trigger warnings believe this "mollycoddles" students.

The University of Oxford, London School of Economics, University of Edinburgh, University of London's Goldsmiths, and many other universities have included trigger warnings in their lectures, with Oxford coming under particular criticism for its trigger warnings at the beginning of criminal law lectures.

Omni Gust, an assistant professor at the University of Nottingham who teaches the history of monstrosity in the 18th-century British Empire, wrote an article in the *Guardian* defending their use, and saying it was not about mollycoddling students:[71] "A trigger warning does not give permission for students to skip class, avoid a topic or choose alternative readings. What it does do is signal to survivors of abuse or trauma that they need to keep breathing. It reminds them to be particularly aware of the skills and coping strategies that they have developed and to switch them on."

Similarly, as Izzy Gurbuz, wellbeing officer at the University of Manchester Students' Union, told the student newspaper, the *Mancunion*, "Trigger warnings simply allow those whose mental health could be significantly affected by certain topics to make informed decisions about their health. For example, adequately preparing themselves so they're able to take part in [a] particular discussion, or avoiding a situation which would cause them flashbacks or a panic attack."[72]

Meanwhile, Cambridge classics professor Mary Beard told the *Sunday Times* that she completely disapproved of the trend: "It would be dishonest, fundamentally dishonest, to teach only Roman history and to miss out not just the rape of the Sabines but all their rapes. We have to encourage students to be able to face that, even when they find they're awkward and difficult for all kinds of good reasons."[73]

Assaultive speech is increasingly being defined not by its content, but by its effect: "experienced as a blow, not a proffered idea."[74] In effect, words can result in violence or can move people to commit violence, but increasingly words are being viewed as violent in and of themselves.

David Aaronovitch, journalist and chair of the Index on Censorship board of trustees, wrote, "There is a substantial argument that trigger warnings, sensitivity training, safe spaces, no platforms are all based on an assumption of fragility—an assumption that can do harm to those supposedly being protected."[75]

Dismissive psychological readings of student behavior have become common in this debate, explored in depth in a widely-read *Atlantic* article by First Amendment lawyer Greg Lukianoff and psychologist Jonathan Haidt titled "The Coddling of the American Mind." They chronicled campus movements that, in an attempt to create "safe spaces" and to avoid triggering memories of trauma that some students might be harboring, call for restrictions to speech and bans on content in classroom discussions. Lukianoff and Haidt, in reviewing such situations, suggest that restricting speech, imposing trigger warnings, or banning difficult content is not an effective solution. "A discussion of violence is unlikely to be followed by actual violence, so it is a good way to help students change the associations that are causing them discomfort," Lukianoff and Haidt wrote.[76] In the same article, the authors pointed to a rise in political polarization on campus, with each side demonizing the other.

CONCLUSION

Free speech on campus is under pressure from a variety of actors in the United Kingdom. On the one hand, the government stresses its commitment to free speech by reminding university administrations that they have a statutory responsibility to protect it; yet, on the other hand, universities are also required to adhere to a raft of legislation and policies that can be interpreted as restricting speech. Students claim to want to hear differing viewpoints, but they seek to protect minorities in the student body from being hurt or excluded from discussion. The popular press and political interests use examples of no-platforming to claim that free speech is under threat. Commentary and social media-driven outrage—whether genuine or manufactured—further cloud the issue.

Historically, the struggle over free speech is nothing new, but over the last 30 years the introduction of legislation in the United Kingdom has made navigating contemporary discussions around controversial ideas and language a very difficult prospect. In recent days, Sam Gyimah, universities minister, suggested that the Department for Education should oversee the creation of a new set of guidelines on free speech that would apply to both students and institutions. At the time of writing, it is unclear how such guidelines would be implemented or what they would entail.

These debates, which call for nuanced and considered arguments, often reflect the polarized political dialogues taking place on both sides of the Atlantic—most notably around gender identity and race relations—and they are easily hijacked by uninvolved parties interested in their own agendas.

Taken together, all of this has generated a risk-averse culture that is increasingly reliant on the vetting of speakers and controversial ideas on university campuses through legislation, reflecting divisions found in the larger society, both within the United Kingdom and throughout the world today.

AUTHORS' NOTE: In Summer 2018, Index on Censorship released "Free Speech on Campus," a report exploring the United Kingdom's legislative framework and its impact at the university level.

SALLY GIMSON is a London-based writer who contributes to *Index on Censorship* magazine, the *Guardian*, and the *New Statesman*.

LAYLI FOROUDI is a journalist.

SEAN GALLAGHER is the head of content at Index on Censorship.

Notes

1. Paula Cocozza, "The Party's Over—How Tuition Fees Ruined University Life," *The Guardian*, July 11, 2017, https://www.theguardian.com/education/2017/jul/11/the-partys-over-how-tuition-fees-ruined-university-life.
2. Amit Chaudhuri, "The Real Meaning of Rhodes Must Fall," *The Guardian*, March 16, 2016, https://www.theguardian.com/uk-news/2016/mar/16/the-real-meaning-of-rhodes-must-fall.
3. Tom Slater, "Free Speech University Rankings: Traffic-Light Ranking System," Spiked, 2018, http://www.spiked-online.com/free-speech-university-rankings#.WZgutSiGOyI.
4. Ibid.

5. Steven Hopkins, "Tommy Robinson Speaking Events Cancelled at Edinburgh and Durham Universities after Pegida Speech," Huffington Post UK, October 22, 2015, http://www.huffingtonpost. co.uk/2015/10/22/universities-cancel-tommy-robinson-speaking-events_n_8357950.html.
6. Courtney Manning, Justin Ellick, and Madeline Domenichella, "Is Free Speech in Jeopardy on UK Campuses?" Index on Censorship, March 17, 2017, https://www.indexoncensorship. org/2017/03/is-free-speech-in-jeopardy-on-uk-campuses/.
7. Peter Scott, "Oxford Students' Fight to Topple Cecil Rhodes Statue was the Easy Option," *The Guardian*, February 2, 2016, https://www.theguardian.com/education/2016/feb/02/ students-cecil-rhodes-statue-campaign-oxford-oriel-college.
8. Alice Kirkland, "Five Things Banned from University Campuses," Index on Censorship, February 12, 2014, https://www.indexoncensorship.org/2014/02/five-things-banned-universities/.
9. "Prevent Duty Guidance: Prevent Duty Guidance for Scotland and England and Wales," Government of the United Kingdom website, March 12, 2015, updated March 23, 2016, https:// www.gov.uk/government/publications/prevent-duty-guidance.
10. Sally Weale, "London University Tells Students Their Emails may be Monitored," *The Guardian*, January 20, 2017, https://www.theguardian.com/uk-news/2017/jan/20/university-warns-students-emails-may-be-monitored-kings-college-london-prevent.
11. Jenny Jones et al., "Prevent isn't Making Anyone Safer. It is Demonising Muslims and Damaging the Fabric of Trust in Society," *The Guardian*, February 10, 2016, https://www. theguardian.com/politics/2016/feb/10/prevent-isnt-making-anyone-safer-it-is-demonising-muslims-and-damaging-the-fabric-of-trust-in-society.
12. "The British Anti-Apartheid Movement," South African History Online, November 13, 2012, updated July 27, 2017, http://www.sahistory.org.za/topic/british-anti-apartheid-movement.
13. Evan Smith, "A Policy Widely Abused: The Origins of the 'No Platform' Policy of the National Union of Students," History & Policy, March 23, 2016, http://www.historyandpolicy.org/ opinion-articles/articles/a-policy-widely-abused.
14. Ibid.
15. Ibid.
16. Jim Dickinson, "Freedom to Speak or Freedom from Harm? The History of the No Platform Debate," Wonkhe, February 17, 2016, http://wonkhe.com/blogs/freedom-to-speak-or-freedom-from-harm-the-history-of-no-platform/.
17. Quoted by Smith, "A Policy Widely Abused."
18. Alan Travis, "National Archives: Margaret Thatcher Wanted to Crush Power of Trade Unions," *The Guardian*, July 31, 2013, https://www.theguardian.com/uk-news/2013/aug/01/margaret-thatcher-trade-union-reform-national-archives.
19. Dickinson, "Freedom to Speak."
20. "Education (No. 2) Act 1986," Government of the United Kingdom Legislation website, November 7, 1986, http://www.legislation.gov.uk/ukpga/1986/61/section/43.
21. Alex Bols, "The 1994 Education Act and Students' Unions," Wonkhe, June 26, 2014, http:// wonkhe.com/blogs/the-1994-education-act-and-students-unions/.
22. "OG 48 Students' Unions," Charity Commission Operational Guidance, May 2, 2018, http:// ogs.charitycommission.gov.uk/g048a001.aspx.
23. "*Prevent* Duty Guidance: For Higher Education Institutions in England and Wales," Government of the United Kingdom website, March 2015, 5, https://www.legislation.gov.uk/ ukdsi/2015/9780111133309/pdfs/ukdsiod_9780111133309_en.pdf.
24. Ibid., 4.
25. Ibid.
26. St George's House, "Freedom of Speech in Universities," St George's House and School of Oriental and African Studies (SOAS) University of London, October 31–November 1, 2016, https:// www.stgeorgeshouse.org/wp-content/uploads/2017/03/Freedom-of-Speech-in-Universities-Report.pdf.
27. Press Association, "Two British Students Jailed for Plotting Isis-Style Drive-By Shootings," *The Guardian*, April 22, 2016, https://www.theguardian.com/uk-news/2016/apr/22/british-students-jailed-plotting-isis-style-drive-by-shootings-tarik-hassane-suhaib-majeed.

28. Rosemary Bennett, "Universities Told They Must Protect Freedom of Speech," *The Times*, March 21, 2017, https://www.thetimes.co.uk/article/universities-told-they-must-protect-freedom-of-speech-fzqhx7vqt.

29. Ibid.

30. Emily Dinsmore, "Codes won't Defeat Campus Censorship," Spiked, March 27, 2017, http://www.spiked-online.com/newsite/article/codes-wont-defeat-campus-censorship/19603.

31. Jasmin Gray, "NUS Launches Helpline for Students Affected by 'Racist' and 'Ineffective' Prevent Strategy," Huffington Post, November 30, 2016, http://huff.to/2ngeA6b.

32. Patrick Wintour, "Government Warns NUS to Stop Opposition to Prevent Strategy," *The Guardian*, September 16, 2015, https://www.theguardian.com/education/2015/sep/17/government-nus-stop-opposition-prevent-strategy.

33. "Preventing Prevent—We are Students Not Suspects," National Union of Students, undated (c. 2017), https://www.nusconnect.org.uk/campaigns/preventing-prevent-we-are-students-not-suspects.

34. "About *Spiked*," Spiked, undated, http://www.spiked-online.com/newsite/about/336/.

35. "Free Speech University Rankings," Spiked, February 2018, http://bit.ly/2nLo9hr.

36. Andrew Anthony, "Is Free Speech in British Universities Under Threat?" *The Guardian*, January 24, 2016, https://www.theguardian.com/world/2016/jan/24/safe-spaces-universities-no-platform-free-speech-rhodes.

37. Tom Cheshire, "Social Media 'Echo Chamber' Causing Political Tunnel Vision, Study Finds," Sky News, February 6, 2017, http://news.sky.com/story/social-media-echo-chamber-causing-political-tunnel-vision-study-finds-10755219.

38. Gordon Rayner and Richard Alleyne, "Oxford Tories' Nights of Port and Nazi Songs," *The Telegraph*, November 4, 2011, https://www.telegraph.co.uk/education/universityeducation/8870909/Oxford-Tories-nights-of-port-and-Nazi-songs.html.

39. Abby Young-Powell, "Oxford Union Accused of Racism for Sale of 'Colonial Comeback' Cocktail," *The Guardian*, May 29, 2015, https://www.theguardian.com/education/2015/may/29/oxford-union-accused-of-racism-for-sale-of-colonial-comeback-cocktail.

40. Telegraph Reporter, "Cambridge University College Cancels 'Racist' Around the World in 80 Days Party," *The Telegraph*, March 10, 2016, http://www.telegraph.co.uk/news/newstopics/howaboutthat/12190238/Cambridge-University-college-cancels-racist-Around-the-World-in-80-Days-party.html.

41. Michael Deacon, "Students are Right—You Never Know When a Party Might Turn Accidentally Racist," *The Telegraph*, March 11, 2016, http://www.telegraph.co.uk/comment/12190743/Students-are-right-you-never-know-when-a-party-might-turn-accidentally-racist.html.

42. Meera Sabaratnam, "Decolonising the Curriculum: What's All the Fuss About?" School of Oriental and African Studies (SOAS) University of London, January 18, 2017, https://www.soas.ac.uk/blogs/study/decolonising-curriculum-whats-the-fuss/.

43. Ibid.

44. Jonathan Petre, "They Kant be Serious! PC Students Demand White Philosophers Including Plato and Descartes be Dropped from University Syllabus," *Daily Mail*, January 7, 2017, updated January 11, 2017, http://www.dailymail.co.uk/news/article-4098332/They-Kant-PC-students-demand-white-philosophers-including-Plato-Descartes-dropped-university-syllabus.html.

45. Pippa Vanderplank and Paddy Baker, "Fake News? Lecturer Calls Telegraph Article about Galton Must Fall 'Entirely Misinformed,'" *The Tab*, February 28, 2017, https://thetab.com/uk/london/2017/02/28/fake-news-telegraph-article-ucl-students-campaign-slammed-untruea-28290.

46. Jess Murray and Ollie Phelan, "How Does a University Deal with Its Legacy of Eugenics?" Runnymede, April 10, 2015, http://www.runnymedetrust.org/blog/how-does-a-university-deal-with-its-historic-legacy-of-eugenics.

47. Nathaniel Adam Tobias Coleman, "Eugenics: The Academy's Complicity," *Times Higher Education*, October 9, 2014, https://www.timeshighereducation.com/comment/opinion/eugenics-the-academys-complicity/2016190.article.

48. Keeanga-Yamahtta Taylor, "The 'Free Speech' Hypocrisy of Right-Wing Media," *New York Times*, August 14, 2017, https://www.nytimes.com/2017/08/14/opinion/the-free-speech-hypocrisy-of-right-wing-media.html.

49. "Princeton Professor Goes on Anti-POTUS Tirade," Fox News, May 28, 2017, http://video.foxnews.com/v/5451382191001/.

50. Kate Manne and Jason Stanley, "When Free Speech Becomes a Political Weapon," *Chronicle of Higher Education*, November 13, 2015, https://www.chronicle.com/article/When-Free-Speech-Becomes-a/234207.

51. Ibid.

52. "NUS' No Platform Policy," National Union of Students (NUS), February 13, 2017, https://nusdigital.s3-eu-west-1.amazonaws.com/document/documents/31475/NUS_No_Platform_Policy_information_.pdf.

53. Ibid.

54. UK Home Office, "Proscribed Terrorist Organisations," Government of the United Kingdom website, December 22, 2017, https://www.gov.uk/government/uploads/system/uploads/attachment_data/file/612076/20170503_Proscription.pdf.

55. Sarah Bell, "NUS 'Right to Have No Platform Policy,'" BBC, April 25, 2016, http://www.bbc.co.uk/news/education-36101423.

56. Julie Bindel, "No Platform: My Exclusion Proves This is an Anti-Feminist Crusade," *The Guardian*, October 9, 2015, https://www.theguardian.com/commentisfree/2015/oct/09/no-platform-universities-julie-bindel-exclusion-anti-feminist-crusade.

57. David Smith, "Chimamanda Ngozi Adichie on Transgender Row: 'I Have Nothing to Apologise For,'" *The Guardian*, March 21, 2017, https://www.theguardian.com/books/2017/mar/21/chimamanda-ngozi-adichie-nothing-to-apologise-for-transgender-women.

58. Tracy McVeigh, "Peter Tatchell: Snubbed by Students for Free Speech Stance," *The Guardian*, February 13, 2016, https://www.theguardian.com/uk-news/2016/feb/13/peter-tatchell-snubbed-students-free-speech-veteran-gay-rights-activist.

59. Zoe Williams, "Peter Tatchell: 'Attacks from the Left are Incredibly Painful,'" *The Guardian*, February 19, 2016, https://www.theguardian.com/2016/feb/19/peter-tatchell-attacks-from-the-left-are-incredibly-painful-nus.

60. Steven Morris, "Germaine Greer Gives University Lecture Despite Campaign to Silence Her," *The Guardian*, November 18, 2015, https://www.theguardian.com/books/2015/nov/18/transgender-activists-protest-germaine-greer-lecture-cardiff-university.

61. Aftab Ali and Jamie Merrill, "HOPE Not Hate Chief Executive, Nick Lowles, 'No-Platformed' by NUS for being 'Islamophobic,'" *The Independent*, February 18, 2016, http://www.independent.co.uk/student/news/hope-not-hate-chief-executive-nick-lowles-no-platformed-by-nus-for-being-islamophobic-a6881831.html.

62. Nick Lowles, "Why 'No Platform' Means Something Different Today," HOPE Not Hate, January 6, 2013, https://web.archive.org/web/20130108234003/http://www.hopenothate.org.uk/blog/article/2410/why-no-platform-means-something-different-today.

63. George Bowden, "NUS No Platform Policy Prompts Lively Debate on BBC Victoria Derbyshire Programme," Huffington Post UK, April 25, 2016, https://www.huffingtonpost.co.uk/entry/nus-no-platform-policy-prompts-controversial-debate-on-bbc-victoria-derbyshire-programme_uk_571dc5dee4b018a884dcfe2c.

64. Zoe Williams, "Silencing Germaine Greer will Let Prejudice against Trans People Flourish," *The Guardian*, October 25, 2015, https://www.theguardian.com/commentisfree/2015/oct/25/germaine-greer-prejudice-trans-people.

65. Henry Louis Gates Jr., "War of Words: Critical Race Theory and the First Amendment," in *Speaking of Race, Speaking of Sex: Hate Speech, Civil Rights, and Civil Liberties*, ed. Henry Louis Gates Jr. et al. (New York: New York University Press, 1994), 17–58, 43.

66. Peter Molnar, "Interview with Kenan Malik," in *The Content and Context of Hate Speech: Rethinking Regulation and Responses*, eds. Michael Herz and Peter Molnar (Cambridge, UK: Cambridge University Press, 2012), 81–91, 83.

67. Ibid, 81.

68. Kieran Yates, "Freshers: Carry Forward the Fight for Safe Spaces at University," *The Guardian*, September 22, 2015, https://www.theguardian.com/education/2015/sep/22/freshers-carry-forward-the-fight-for-safe-spaces-at-university.

69. St George's House, "Freedom of Speech in Universities."

70. Katie King, "LSE Law Student Files Motion to Ban Student Society Set Up to Stop University Banning Things," Legal Cheek, February 5, 2016, https://www.legalcheek.com/2016/02/lse-law-student-files-motion-to-ban-student-led-society-set-up-to-stop-university-banning-things/.

71. Onni Gust, "I Use Trigger Warnings—But I'm Not Mollycoddling My Students," *The Guardian*, June 14, 2016, https://www.theguardian.com/higher-education-network/2016/jun/14/i-use-trigger-warnings-but-im-not-mollycoddling-my-students.

72. Elrica Degirmen, "British Universities Use Trigger Warnings to Help Students' Mental Health," *The Mancunion*, October 17, 2016, http://mancunion.com/2016/10/17/british-universities-increasingly-using-trigger-warnings-help-students-mental-health/.

73. Rosie Kinchen, "Mary Beard: When in Rome, She Does All the Gruesome Bits," *The Times*, April 17, 2016, https://www.thetimes.co.uk/article/mary-bearch-when-in-rome-she-does-all-the-gruesome-bits-65s7xdnjc.

74. Henry Louis Gates Jr., "War of Words," 24, quoting Charles R. Lawrence III.

75. David Aaronovitch, "Being Offended is Often the Best Medicine," *The Times*, February 15, 2017, https://www.thetimes.co.uk/article/being-offended-is-often-the-best-medicine-nnbmxmjh5.

76. Greg Lukianoff and Jonathan Haidt, "The Coddling of the American Mind," *The Atlantic*, September 2015, https://www.theatlantic.com/magazine/archive/2015/09/the-coddling-of-the-american-mind/399356/.

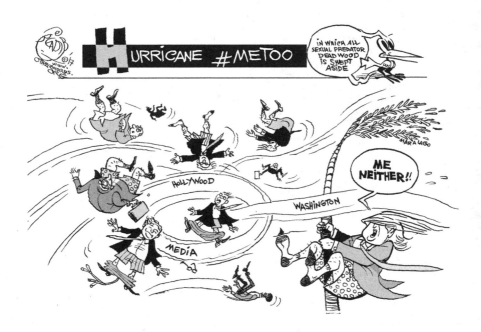

CHAPTER 6

#TimesUp
Breaking the Barriers of Sexual Harassment in Corporate Media for You and #MeToo

Julie Frechette

TRUMP'S WAR ON WOMEN USHERS IN THE FOURTH WAVE OF FEMINISM

In 2017, the first Women's March was held, with millions of people coming together to defy the sexist, misogynistic, racist, xenophobic, and elitist ideologies of then newly elected president Donald Trump. The shout heard round the world was a resounding "Not My President" from women donning knit pink "pussy hats" in Washington, DC, and at 600 marches held all across the globe. While grassroots and corporate media alike provided coverage of the Women's March, hegemonic elites were blindsided and unprepared for the solidarity and strength of women mobilizing en masse and ushering in a new movement to defy Trump's political agenda. Defined by some as "fourth-wave feminism," women coalesced in numbers hitherto unprecedented to speak truth to power.[1] In their unified resistance to Trump, women joined in solidarity with others to address the long-standing inequalities, abuses, violations, and social injustices facing them and other oppressed groups, particularly those targeted by Trump's administration and his Republican Party.

Holding the Women's March so early in Trump's presidency proved prescient, for Trump's administration wasted no time declaring its war on women. Among his first acts as president, Trump reinstated—and massively expanded—the global gag rule, "an executive order . . . barring US foreign aid from going to any nongovernmental organization (NGO) that either provides abortion services, or even *discusses* abortion with its patients as an option for family planning."[2] The impact of Trump's policy is projected to lead to the death of thousands of women throughout the world, and millions will lose access to both safe abortion and birth control.[3]

As part of his attempt to dismantle the Affordable Care Act, Trump and Republican neo-conservatives signed legislation to cut off federal funding to Planned Parenthood and other women's health groups in a move to overturn the Obama administration's law prohibiting state and local governments from withholding "federal funding for family planning services related to contraception, sexually transmitted infections, fertility, pregnancy care, and breast and cervical cancer screening from qualified health providers—regardless of whether they also performed abortions."[4]

Over the summer and into the fall of 2017, Trump and his Republican supporters took direct aim at birth control coverage "for more than 62 million American women, eliminating the guarantee they had for coverage for birth control regardless of who they work for."[5] The sweeping new rule eliminated "the Affordable Care Act's requirement that all insurance plans must cover birth control without a co-pay or otherwise ensure access to birth control coverage for women whose employers or schools can legally opt out of providing coverage."[6]

Trump's cabinet, more than four-fifth of whom were men, went further in its anti-women, anti-families agenda by "eroding family economic security; putting children at risk; attacking reproductive rights; undermining women's legal rights; weakening protections against gender-based violence; undermining women's leadership; tearing families apart; and slashing health benefits."[7] A comprehensive study conducted by the Center for American Progress (CAP) found that, in just a mere 100 days, Trump's administration harmed women and families in 100 different ways.[8] Listed among the report's findings were the specific ways that Trump's administration fails to advance women's equal pay; denies women's reproductive, educational, and counseling services by limiting Title X availability; limits coverage of abortion by calling for the Hyde Amendment to become permanent in restricting Medicare and Medicaid coverage; stacks the courts with anti-choice judges; expands religious exemptions for health care providers, allowing them to deny preventative health services for women, including contraception; restricts adoption for LGBTQ families; interferes with doctor–patient relationships; promotes misinformation about reproductive health care; and undermines pregnancy discrimination protections.

According to the CAP report, Trump's war on women includes weakening protections against gender-based violence by threatening to defund civil rights enforcement, cutting the National Domestic Violence Hotline budget by 18 percent, refusing to fight sexual assault in schools, defending accused sexual harassers (including the president himself and Bill O'Reilly in public tweets), cutting programs that are intended to reduce violence against women, endangering Muslim women, silencing victims of domestic abuse, cutting requirements that insurers cover domestic violence screenings, and undoing the Fair Pay and Safe Workplaces Executive Order.[9]

Trump's budget also cut the Family and Medical Leave Act by 21 percent or $2.5 billion, threatened child care assistance programs, slashed nutrition assistance for Women, Infants, and Children (WIC) by $200 million, cut after-school programs by $1.2 billion, slashed Head Start funding and jobs by 18 percent, stripped public school funding, and harmed transgender students.[10]

While Trump's cronies waged their war against women and families from the comfort of their executive offices, women fought back on the streets, at voting booths, in legislative offices, in news stories and op-eds, in entertainment, and online. One of the swiftest and most notable countercultural movements came in the form of the #MeToo movement on Twitter, along with online petitions and protests organized by women decrying sexual harassment and sexual assault in a range of industries and organizations. The movement began to coalesce in the summer of 2016, when allegations of sexual harassment at Fox News were being litigated and leaked to the press. A *New York Times* investigative exposé validated longstanding accusations against Fox News's former CEO, Roger Ailes, and mounting public pressure to fire him resulted in his departure. Investigations into other claims of sexual harassment left even the most insulated goliaths at Fox News, like the caustic Bill O'Reilly, exposed to public scrutiny.[11] When the *New York Times* investigated the $13 million that the right-wing corporate news channel had paid to defend O'Reilly in five sexual harassment lawsuits, feminist groups like UltraViolet launched an effective public campaign to fire the predator. Not only did these efforts work, they set off a chain reaction.

The toppling of Fox News's Papa Bear was the amalgamation of a renewed feminist movement stemming from 1) the courage of female journalists at Fox News to speak out against top male offenders by seeking recourse and litigation in spite of reprisal; 2) investigative news coverage by the *New York Times* and other sources to uncover the extent and longevity of sexual harassment claims at Fox News; 3) organized efforts by women's groups, like UltraViolet, to pressure advertisers and the board of directors of Fox News's parent company to fire O'Reilly; and 4) pressure from citizens signing petitions and persuading advertisers to drop their funding for O'Reilly's program.

With stories about sexual harassment toppling the kingpins of Fox News, attention shifted to prominent players at the top echelons of the film production industries.

At the same time that the Trump administration cut access to reproductive care and contraception for 62 million women, two female reporters at the *New York Times* broke the story that, for more than three decades, undisclosed allegations of sexual harassment and unwanted physical contact with film industry workers had implicated Harvey Weinstein during his reign at Miramax and the Weinstein Company.[12] With at least eight settlements by women on record dating back to the 1990s, Ashley Judd's October 2017 revelation that she, too, was harassed by Weinstein launched what would become a swift and powerful crusade against him.

Five days after Judd went public with her story, the *New York Times* published a follow-up under the headline "Gwyneth Paltrow, Angelina Jolie and Others Say Weinstein Harassed Them."[13] This investigative piece exposed a greater extent of Weinstein's history of sexual harassment through the corroborating testimony of several other women. A deluge of similar stories in the following days forced the board of the film studio The Weinstein Company, a production house that Harvey Weinstein had himself co-founded, to terminate his position.[14]

Increased reporting of sexual harassment cases by prominent

figures and celebrities in news and entertainment helped publicize the #MeToo movement, which had originated more than a decade earlier when Tarana Burke "coined the phrase 'Me Too' as a way to help women who had survived sexual violence."[15] The movement was popularized when actress Alyssa Milano tweeted a call-out to victims to provide the public with a sense of the seriousness and magnitude of the problems of sexual harassment and assault.[16] As more women spoke out, and their experiences were legitimized within news coverage and on the #MeToo site, victims gained strength in numbers to tell their own personal stories about sexual harassment and assault within and beyond the film, television, and music industries. Social media campaigns emerged from a plethora of women's groups that invited the wider public to join them in validating women who have experienced degradation, inequity, and oppression. What began as a campaign against sexual harassment and assault grew to include other forms of sexual abuse and discrimination affecting women, young adults, children, minorities, members of the LGBTQ community, and others.

Given its subsequent scope and duration, how can we measure the impact of the #MeToo movement? Structurally, the sexual wrongdoings of the hegemonic elites in corporate media have exposed the degree to which powerful media industries have worked for decades as closed-door systems that protect and reward those running and owning them. #MeToo has demanded that industry leaders and their boards conduct investigations and dismiss the old regime of harassers, assaulters, and misogynists.

In both its original and expanded form, #MeToo's organizational goals and outcomes are multifold: to share the personal stories of victims as a means to acknowledge the social injustice of these experiences; to expose the pervasive and systemic reality and impact of sexual harassment and sexual assault shared by women as a class; and to show that women who work in solidarity together and with others can usher in a more equitable generation of organizational practices and ethics across all sectors.

As it continues to rapidly gain momentum, the #MeToo countercultural movement has gone on to impact athletics, politics, business, education, medicine, farming, and many other professions. In the news industries, Matt Lauer was fired from NBC News and the *Today* show for sexual harassment;[17] Charlie Rose was fired by CBS and PBS for sexual misconduct;[18] and NPR Chief News Editor David Sweeney was ousted following allegations of sexual harassment filed against him by at least three female journalists.[19] Garrison Keillor was fired from Minnesota Public Radio after accusations of sexual misconduct.[20] At the Boston NPR affiliate station WBUR, a steady stream of women and men came forward "with allegations against *On Point* radio host Tom Ashbrook and WBUR managers who they say failed to stop Ashbrook's alleged bullying" and sexual harassment.[21] Ashbrook was put on leave as a result of the station's ongoing investigation, and, two months later, was fired. By the end of November 2017, Russell Simmons was forced to step down from his companies after writer Jenny Lumet accused him of sexual assault in the *Hollywood Reporter*.[22] Two weeks later, Dylan Farrow penned an op-ed about Woody Allen, asking again "why the slew of sexual misconduct allegations against her adoptive father haven't made more of an impact on his career."[23]

In the film and entertainment industries, allegations of sexual misconduct and improprieties dethroned Kevin Spacey, Louis C.K., and Bill Cosby, among others. In politics, the *Washington Post* published an investigative piece about Republican Senate nominee Roy Moore and his alleged history of preying upon and sexually assaulting underage girls.[24] Media scrutiny, online campaigns, and protests by those within and outside politics were credited with his electoral loss. Amidst pressure from his party, US Senator Al Franken (D-MN) resigned from Congress over allegations of sexual misconduct.[25] Even President Donald Trump, whose "grab 'em by the pussy" comments did not manage to keep him from winning the top presiding seat in the nation, received long overdue excoriation for his lewd sexual behavior, harassment, and assault when many of his accusers held a press conference on December 11, 2017 to demand a congressional investigation. At the event, the women questioned why Trump had seemed to escape scrutiny over multiple sexual harassment and/or assault claims at a time when other politicians and Hollywood producers were forced to resign amidst the momentum of the #MeToo movement. Senators Kirsten Gillibrand, Bernie Sanders, and Cory Booker joined the call for an investigation and for Trump's resignation.[26]

In athletics, after "Olympic gymnast McKayla Maroney tweeted that she was sexually assaulted by former team doctor Lawrence G. Nassar" (who had previously been sentenced to 60 years in federal prison on child pornography charges), more than 150 young girls and women testified that he sexually molested or assaulted them.[27] Within the Women's National Basketball Association, 23-year-old star Breanna Stewart joined the #MeToo movement, revealing personal accounts of the sexual assault she endured as a child. Like so many survivors, she joined #MeToo for personal and political reasons.[28] Other key cultural figures who were put on leave or investigated for sexual harassment included Mario Batali, who was removed from his show and restaurants after four women came forth and he apologized for his wrongdoing, though seven additional women have since shared their own stories of his sexual misconduct.[29] In late December, the *Los Angeles Times* broke the story of seven men accusing the "successful theater prodigy Gary Goddard of molesting or attempting to molest them as boys."[30]

While the number of cases against the Hollywood and political elite continues to grow, the #TimesUp anti-harassment action plan was announced in early January 2018 as a means to enlarge the scope and depth of sexual harassment discussions by highlighting the frequency and pervasiveness of these issues in women's daily lives. Announced at the Golden Globe Awards by Oprah Winfrey as she accepted the Cecil B. DeMille Award for lifetime achievement, #TimesUp was inspired by #MeToo, with the goal of going beyond sharing stories of sexual harassment and abuse to changing the power structure and preventing future sexual misconduct. The anti-harassment action plan was formed by "300 prominent actresses and female agents, writers, directors, producers, and entertainment executives" to "fight systemic sexual harassment in Hollywood and in blue-collar workplaces nationwide.[31] The initiative includes:

▸ A legal defense fund, backed by $13 million in donations, to help less privileged women—like janitors, nurses and workers at farms, factories, restaurants and hotels—protect themselves from sexual misconduct and the fallout from reporting it.

- Legislation to penalize companies that tolerate persistent harassment, and to discourage the use of nondisclosure agreements to silence victims.
- A drive to reach gender parity at studios and talent agencies that has already begun making headway.
- And a request that women walking the red carpet at the Golden Globes speak out and raise awareness by wearing black.[32]

In seeking change, the #MeToo movement and #TimesUp anti-harassment action plans have worked to "speak truth to power" symbolically, ethically, emotionally, educationally, and materially. Across all occupations and walks of life, women and girls have used these grassroots efforts to mobilize women and men to challenge all forms of sexism, sexual harassment, sexual abuse, and violence against women, children, immigrants, LGBTQ people, and the mentally ill, among others.

UNIFYING "THE SECOND SEX" THROUGH GRASSROOTS ORGANIZING

Without question, the Hollywood and media sex scandals have ushered in a watershed moment for women to share their varied narratives and experiences of sexual harassment and assault. In less than a year, the sexual harassment scandals in corporate news, entertainment, athletics, politics, and beyond have emerged as front-burner issues on the national and global landscape. Since last year, there has been a great outpouring of additional cases from women coming forth with allegations and evidence against other male harassers and assaulters, including President Trump, thereby creating a domino effect among the formerly dominant male patriarchal elite. Despite centuries of normalization of the everyday abuse of common people, the issue of sexual harassment is getting more attention because of the corporate media's infatuation with celebrity and scandal. As a result, the issues of sexual harassment and sexual assault have trickled down into the public consciousness, affecting organizational and workplace culture, social media conversations, and online consciousness-raising campaigns.

#MeToo and #TimesUp have forced systemic change at the structural level, as journalists and whistleblowers have used grassroots organizing to take down offenders and perpetrators at the highest echelons of cultural and economic power. Not only have prominent male harassers and abusers been summarily fired from positions of power, but some of them have publicly acknowledged their culpability and apologized for their wrongdoing to those they victimized. Additionally, male supporters of the movement have verified what the women and girls in their lives have gone through, with some accepting responsibility for their roles as bystanders who didn't speak out or do enough to rectify the problem in their work, familial, and social spheres. Recent public admonishment against harassers at large has also uprooted the premise that "boys will be boys," that sexual harassment is just "locker room talk" (as claimed by President Trump), and that sexual harassment is normal and acceptable within the culture. In fact, as prominent feminist scholar Catherine MacKinnon retorts after a lifetime of research devoted to the subject,

> the #MeToo movement is accomplishing what sexual harassment law to date has not. This mass mobilization against sexual abuse, through an unprecedented wave of speaking out in conventional and social media, is eroding the two biggest barriers to ending sexual harassment in law and in life: the disbelief and trivializing dehumanization of its victims . . . Sexual harassment law prepared the ground, but it is today's movement that is shifting gender hierarchy's tectonic plates.[33]

UNDERSTANDING THE ECONOMICS OF CONSENT

Hollywood producers and directors have been getting away with power abuses for far too long, as justifications for sexual abusers and harassers have included blind reverence for their "genius" and "avantgarde" creativity.[34] Within the industry, abusers were given a pass for their sexist attitudes by critics who praised them for their "juvenile love for provocation."[35] #MeToo and #TimesUp have exposed the impact of such harassment and brutality by exposing perpetrators and justi-fiers. Prior to these forms of hashtivism, the culture in Hollywood and in corporate media made it hard for victims of abuse to speak up too loudly without risking their own employment. #TimesUp indicates that those in the film and entertainment industry are joining forces to say "enough is enough." For instance, when musician and actress Björk accused *Dancer in the Dark* director Lars von Trier of sexual harassment and provocation, journalists were prompted to scrutinize the power that male directors, producers, and owners of cultural production have been allowed to abuse.[36]

So why are sexual harassment and sexual assault so prevalent in corporate media? Structural power, such as patriarchy, serves as the political and economic source of inequality and oppression. In the media and entertainment sectors, among others, there are a lot of young talents who want to break through whatever industry they are trying to get into. This has led to a systematic pattern in which those in power (mostly men) take advantage of young girls and women in vulnerable moments, with sexual harassment and sexual assault serving as manifestations of patriarchal power. Young women in particular face an invisible kind of oppression as they are pressured to "go along to get along," and the repression of their experiences represents a mass psychological burden. A necessary antidote to this structural inequity is to provide equal opportunities and employment to women as owners, gatekeepers, producers, and executives across all cultural industries. Until there are more female producers holding power positions throughout the media, the system is not going to change in the long term.

In an article featured in the *Atlantic*, actress and writer Brit Mar-ling documents the economics of consent in the film industry.[37] As she rightfully contends, the complexity of sexual harassment and sexual assault cannot be reduced to consent alone, with women and girls instructed to "just say no" to sexual advances as if it's a level playing field. Even though Marling holds more power as a writer than others seeking stardom in the film industry, she explains how that wasn't enough to shield her from Weinstein's predations. As with all present-day systems designed to create and maintain a pecking order, men are the ones who wield the most political and economic power.

In order to stay afloat and advance in the industry, many of those working beneath the top tier of this system knowingly turn a blind eye to abuses of power (just as Weinstein's female assistant did when relocating Marling's meeting from a hotel bar to the producer's private suite). As Marling implores, it's the system of those in power, the gatekeepers, that we have to scrutinize, as well as the power imbalance that results when they overwhelmingly control the means of production and distribution. Weinstein held power over Marling and other women's careers, and he denied women who opposed his abuse the opportunity to get ahead in the system. While Marling and some other women were able to escape Weinstein's sexual advances, most victims noted that it took them a long time to recover from their abuse. For many other women, refusal to acquiesce to Weinstein's sexual advances was met by attempts to damage their careers, surveil their private lives, and suppress their stories of his abuse. And for every woman who got away, plenty of others did not, reflecting an unequal distribution of sociocultural, political, and economic power among women and girls, even as women as a class are oppressed by men in power.

THE IMBALANCED POLITICAL ECONOMY OF CORPORATE MEDIA

As media owners and producers, men serve as the dominant storytellers and gatekeepers who determine what cultural narratives are worth telling, while deciding who will be featured in a particular film, program, sound recording, or other popular medium. They control the technological means of production and distribution to get their stories and perspectives out in the culture at large to reap commercial profit. "The storytellers—the people with economic and artistic power—are, by and large, straight, white men. As of 2017, women make up only 23 percent of the Directors Guild of America and only 11 percent are people of color."[38] And even with a few more women behind the camera today than in the past, "the cinematic perspective of straight white men is still largely considered the *better* one in Hollywood and beyond—the more artistic and more meaningful lens through which to see the world."[39]

With men overwhelmingly controlling these important cultural power positions, women remain marginalized in the media at the level of ownership, production, storytelling, and distribution. For instance, even though women account for more than half of moviegoers, of the top 100 grossing films of 2017, women accounted for only 8 percent of directors, 10 percent of writers, 2 percent of cinematographers, 24 percent of producers, and 14 percent of editors.[40] According to the Center for the Study of Women in Television and Film, during the 2016–2017 broadcast network TV season,

▸ Women accounted for only 28 percent of all creators, directors, writers, producers, executive producers, editors, and directors of photography working on broadcast network, cable, and streaming programs
▸ 97 percent of programs had no women directors of photography, 85 percent had no women directors, 75 percent had no women editors, 74 percent had no women creators, 67 percent had no women writers, 23 percent had no women producers, [and] 20 percent had no women executive producers
▸ 66 percent of female characters were white; 19 percent were Black, 5 percent were Latina, 6 percent were Asian, and 1 percent were of another race or ethnicity
▸ On programs with at least one woman creator, females accounted for 51 percent of major characters
▸ On programs with exclusively male creators, females comprised only 38 percent of major characters.[41]

The inequities are staggering. Of the *New York Times*'s "25 Best Films of the 21st Century So Far," men directed 21 of them, while only "two (white) women have ever won Best Director at Cannes in its 71-year history, and only one (white) woman has ever won Best Director at the Oscars."[42] As a timely BuzzFeed article invokes, "it's not just who gets recognized as 'great' that bears out a gender bias, but how the mainstream language around directing film remains centered on expressions of masculinity as well."[43]

Men serve as the arbiters of cultural taste and public opinion by shaping narratives that impose patriarchal views and opinions upon other people's experiences. Across all cultural platforms, they tell stories about women through their own gendered lens and point of view, while asserting their power as cultural producers, distributors, and creators. Under such circumstances, they hold and wield the power to tell the stories that (re)constitute women and girls as "the second sex." As Brit Marling explains,

> Straight, white men tend to tell stories from their perspective, as one naturally does, which means the women are generally underwritten. They don't necessarily even need names; "Bikini Babe 2" and "Blonde 4" are parts I auditioned for. If the female characters are lucky enough to have names, they are usually designed only to ask the questions that prompt the lead male monologue, or they are quickly killed in service to advancing the plot.[44]

In the top 100 films of 2016, women represented less than a third of the protagonists. They are not even the main characters for most mass media content. Similarly, within

> the top 250 grossing films of 2017, women comprised 3 percent of composers. This represents no change since 2016. (Center for the Study of Women in Television and Film); Kathryn Bigelow is the only woman to ever win the Academy Award for Best Director. Only five women have ever been nominated (Lina Wertmüller, Jane Campion, Sofia Coppola, Bigelow, and Greta Gerwig). In 2018 "Mudbound's" Rachel Morrison became the first woman ever nominated for the Academy Award for Cinematography. 76 percent of all female characters were white in the top 100 films of 2016. 14 percent were Black, 6 percent were Asian, and 3 percent were Latina.[45]

Since most cultural production is conducted by elite, white, heterosexual males, it's no wonder that stories of male power achieved through sexual conquest get told over and over again. Often times, such stories are told through visual signifiers that reduce a woman's worth to her sex appeal for male subjects both on- and off-screen. In her groundbreaking essay "Visual Pleasure and Narrative Cinema," Laura Mulvey wrote about the cinematic "male gaze" within Hollywood, and how, as a result of the repeated use of semiotic conventions invoked by the camera, the visual codes used to define women and their bodies become a form of internalized conditioning that objectifies women through male subjectivity.[46] These visual signifiers have become so powerful throughout the media that women and girls have learned to judge themselves and their bodies according to the "male gaze," often leading to their subjugation. Similarly, corporate media promote narratives that depict sexual harassment as commonplace and even welcomed, along with a glut of exploitative stories that condone violence against women.

In the article "How Has Rape Become Such a Common Trope of Television Drama?," Ellen Vanstone offers a revelatory glimpse into how Hollywood, as a superstructure, is part of an ideological and economic system of conditioning. As a TV writer, she describes how content that she's written has been twisted to fetishize and sexualize the rape and victimization of young, attractive women. She describes her "rage over how much female rape there is on TV in general."[47] For example, in an analysis of the prevalence of rape in the critically acclaimed TV series *Game of Thrones*, researchers found 50 acts of rape and 29 rape victims on the show, while George R.R. Martin's books (from which the series is derived) contained 214 rape acts and 117 rape victims.[48] In what has become the clichéd narrative device of this popular trope, "rape is used as a back story (usually with graphic flashbacks) for characters," as well as "a device to motivate male heroes" for anguish and revenge.[49] Visually, sexual harassment and rape are "aestheticized for the camera," with "massive amounts of time and money . . . spent on hair, makeup and lighting to sexualize rape victims."[50]

In this closed system, what kinds of stories are told by men about women and girls for a male target audience? As mentioned, the stories are generally very misogynistic and sexist, with sexual harassment and sexual assault shown and justified, ad nauseam. Across all media, female victims of harassment and violence are subject to ridicule and re-victimization when their experiences are questioned or invalidated, or worse, when they are the ones punished (through "victim blaming") instead of the male perpetrators. According to a 2016 national study in Australia that examined the nature of reporting about violence against women,

nearly one in six news reports imply the victim is to blame: 14.8 percent of the news reports included information to exonerate or excuse men; 14.5 percent included information about the behavior of women; and 16 percent of the reports about sexual assault and rape implied women had placed themselves at risk.[51]

The research shows that the victim's perspective is often overlooked and victim impact statements get minimal attention in news media. In the United States, "research shows one barrier to social change is the way the media sustains the misconception that women are responsible for men's use of violence and that women can play a role in prevention by modifying their own behavior."[52]

An analysis of the rape trial of Luke Lazarus last year in [New South Wales] highlights the disproportionate attention given to the perpetrator. Prominence was given to his claims that his life was "completely destroyed." This is as opposed to the harrowing victim statement in the Brock Turner case, in which she described how she "sat in the bath for days after the attack" and, two years after the attack, she "cried so hard that she could not breathe."[53]

Invariably, people's attitudes and behaviors are shaped by the way narratives are told in the media, and from whose vantage point they are told. As feminist TV writer Ellen Vanstone explains, "When women behind the camera are treated as second-class citizens, and women on camera are seen primarily as sex objects," it's not surprising that male justifications for sexual harassment and sexual assault are overrepresented.[54] Consequently, a lot of the mass media narratives that teach young boys and men how they're supposed to act and become socially integrated promote the sexist and misogynist myths that are generated by predominantly male media producers. As Imran Siddiquee contends, "The dominance of white men is the centuries-long story of the world we live in and the movies have long played a role in celebrating and maintaining patriarchy. For nearly 100 years, Americans have gone to the cinema, sat in the darkness beneath a massive screen, and stared up at the dreams of men."[55] If and when stories of sexual harassment and sexual assault are told within this system, women have to face reprisal and risk their careers by coming out. Even then, the media's focus on the story is usually a "blame the victim" narrative that criticizes women for being hyper-sensitive, naïve, provocative through their dress or words, or unfamiliar with the norms of professional relationships. Women and girls are told that they shouldn't have been in that field, or on the streets, or out in the bar at night, or wherever they were provoked or attacked, instead of focusing on the perpetrators and the injustice of their acts of personal and political violence.

Until the system opens up to let women tell their own varied and enriching stories, Marling and others urge us to stop watching those films, programs, and genres in which women are exploited and victimized. "If you don't want to be a part of a culture in which sexual abuse and harassment are rampant, don't buy a ticket to a film that promotes it . . . maybe it's time to imagine more films that don't use exploitation of female bodies or violence against female bodies as their selling points."[56] Films with gender and racial balance, for instance, would be worth supporting. Likewise, cultural acclaim shouldn't be awarded for content in which women are shown being sexually abused, harassed, or humiliated. To change the corporate media system of sexual oppression, we have to look at the power that men have as gatekeepers, and the types of stories they tell and sell that support patriarchy.

GOING BEYOND THE "USE AND ABUSE STORIES"

While the #MeToo movement has empowered a growing number of women to share their experiences about harassment and assault, the corporate media have often reduced these issues to "news abuse" stories focused on whetting audience appetites for the latest Hollywood gossip on who will be implicated next. In luring people to watch clickbait, corporate media have driven up their ratings with stories that expose and excoriate the "bad apples" rather than examining the pervasive structural roots of sexual harassment and sexual assault. Within this kind of spectacle, media narratives rehash "gotcha" moments or the clichéd "she said, he said" duel profitable to both the tabloids and hard news industries. For instance, breaking news stories about actor Aziz Ansari's alleged sexual harassment of a fan led to a lot of tabloid coverage and commentary that focused on the "she said, he said" trope, which was mockingly featured in a *Saturday Night Live* skit. In essence, corporate media have taken very serious stories of sexual harassment and assault and sensationalized them in inappropriate ways for profit rather than focusing on the structural roots of economic and political inequalities.

Instead of encouraging us to ask, "Why is this happening? What are the systematic issues that we should be addressing? And how can we come up with better laws, policies, or education?," the media have goaded us into guessing "Who's the next person that's going to be implicated?" and "Are they guilty or innocent?" These are the wrong sets of questions to be asking, and such sensationalism exposes the limits of the for-profit, ads-and-ratings-driven corporate media, highlighting their inability to cover substantive issues with historical context and analysis. When ratings dictate content, the corporate media often steer the conversations about sexual harassment and sexual assault into a ditch, with an erroneous focus on individuals rather than the overall political criticisms raised by fourth-wave feminism.

In contrast, independent news and analysis puts people's needs before profits, providing the depth and scope needed to understand the important issues of the day. Far from the lives of the rich and famous, Jane Slaughter explores how "[s]exual harassment doesn't happen just to glamorous women in glamorous industries. Since sexual harassment is about power, not sex, it's not surprising that low-wage women in lousy jobs get a lot of it."[57] Based on reports from the Equal Employment Opportunity Commission, she notes that the restaurant industry is the largest source of sexual harassment claims:

In a national survey of 4,300 restaurant workers by the worker center Restaurant Opportunities Centers United, more than one in 10 workers reported that they or a co-worker had experienced sexual harassment. ROC says even this creepy figure is likely an undercount . . . The Restaurant Opportunities Centers United notes, in a 2014 report, that "a majority-female workforce must please and curry favor with customers to earn a living." Men take advantage with harassing questions, gestures, groping, even stalking.

"Unfortunately, it's just become the societal norm, and we have all accepted it and we all hate it," a woman bartender told ROC.[58]

Similarly, "a 2010 study of farmworker women found 80 percent had experienced sexual harassment at work," while female janitors are vulnerable because they are "often working late at night in isolated workplaces."[59] As documented in the 2015 PBS *Frontline* episode "Rape on the Night Shift," the frequency and magnitude of the problem among female janitors stems from the pressure not to report the issue for fear of being fired.[60] Likewise, hotel cleaners are "perhaps the women workers most vulnerable to actual assault . . . [because] apparently male guests reason that if there's a woman in a bedroom, she must be available."[61] According to Jenny Brown, "Workers report that male customers expose themselves, attempt to buy sexual services, grab and grope them and, in some cases, attempt to rape them."[62] Labor reports and independent media coverage like Slaughter's remind us that #MeToo and #TimesUp are about bringing the conversations about sexual harassment beyond Hollywood or Washington, DC, and considering the daily experiences of vulnerable women who endure a disproportionate amount of such injustices because they are seen as an accepted part of the culture.

When you examine the hegemonic paradigms of masculine power, and the ways that they have led to centuries of domination, you can expose how women in general, and particularly those from the working classes and middle classes, have been experiencing the brunt of sexual harassment. You can address how their experiences become normalized and are not usually subject to scrutiny or vindication. The reason sexual harassment functions as a normalized part of the culture is because it is constituted and reconstituted by the hegemonic elite. As Antonio Gramsci reminds us, the very ways that the ruling elite tell their stories are designed to gain footing in the culture as "common sense," or "just the way things are." When people consent to these political ideologies, power is maintained by the ruling class, which in this case largely consists of the men who own and control most means of capital production and power across all sectors in society. Whether you're looking at business, the military, education, politics, sports, or corporate media, sexual harassment and sexual assault are often enacted, justified, and condoned, alongside homophobia, xenophobia, and other sorts of discrimination. As #MeToo, #TimesUp, and feminist standpoint theory indicate, we need to carefully examine other sectors outside Hollywood and Washington, DC, as their power structures also affect women and other oppressed groups from all walks of life.

Institutionalized power masks itself in many ways, including language and the very ways we frame and discuss issues. For a long time, sexual harassment wasn't even a named phenomenon, making it difficult to articulate that this was an issue or a problem. In the 1960s and '70s, cases making their way through the court system in the United States gave people a chance to ask, "What is sexual harassment?" and "What does it entail?" At first, a lot of the discussions of sexual harassment revolved around quid pro quo arguments which claimed that harassed women "knew what they were getting into," as professional advancement was expected in return for sexual "favors." So in any work environment, particularly for people who don't have a lot of power or status, examining the kinds of conditions they were put through in order to maintain and keep their jobs, or even obtain them in the first place, was crucial. Thereafter, "[e]arly recognition of blatant quid pro quo harassment was supplemented by recognizing that more subtle behaviors and intimidating and hostile work environments are sexually harassing. Thus, court opinions gradually etched out an alternative discourse which defined sexual harassment as sex discrimination and a prosecutable and punishable offense."[63]

Decades later, in the fall of 1991, Professor Anita Hill came forward to speak about the sexual harassment she had endured while working for a judge later nominated for the Supreme Court, Clarence Thomas. Hill's testimony against Thomas was historic because it gave the country a chance to finally hear about sexual harassment from the perspective of a black female professiónal who made her case before the American public in televised congressional hearings.

Since that time, cases of sexual harassment have been correlated with attitudes and behaviors surrounding social encounters as well as structural power. This brings us back full circle to examine how stories about men and women are told within corporate media. We need to ask, where did these stories about men abusing their power over women in these ways come from? Why are these stories normalized and justified? Whether we're looking at gaming culture, online culture, the culture of pornography, or the culture of filmmaking, television, radio, or other industries, they all reinforce sexist messages that cultivate attitudes and beliefs which, in turn, are normalized and go unquestioned as consensus narratives. #MeToo and #TimesUp indicate that now is the time to unveil these narratives and injustices as they affect all victims, and not just the elite individuals featured in gossip columns.

CONCLUSION: #CRITICALMEDIALITERACYEDUCATION

While the system of cultural production in corporate media remains tilted in favor of white men, women from all walks of life have unified to balance the scales through #MeToo and #TimesUp, Women's Marches, protest rallies, and other grassroots organizing. In order to sustain the ideals of the "fourth wave" of the feminist movement, critical media literacy education is needed to help enable social justice activism aimed at dismantling structural power.

Critical media literacy education (CMLE) encourages people to analyze, deconstruct, and overthrow the hegemonic power structures that control corporate media production and dissemination. It investigates the owners, producers, directors, and distributors of corporate media; how they define and tell the stories of our culture and society; to whom they target their content; and with what effect they impact social attitudes and behaviors. CMLE also encourages people to use new media technologies to tell their own stories from their intersectional perspectives by "becoming the media," uniting and changing their communities through independent media production.

Comprehensively, these critical inquiries and practices help us explore how power manifests itself structurally in corporate media through gatekeeping, narrative production, advertising, and targeted distribution. CMLE encourages us to understand the framing devices and consensus narratives used across genres and channels to keep white men in social, political, and economic power. It invites us to challenge hegemonic power through creative and accessible technological means that represent the voices and perspectives of people marginalized in the culture. It encourages us to examine the patterns and practices that define social consciousness and behavior in the cultural industries, politics, business, education, and all organizational structures of society, so that we can become empowered to enact the change we wish to see in the world.

In light of the successes of the #MeToo movement, CMLE encourages us to critique the power imbalances and inequalities that are the direct result of corporate media structures and practices that have worked historically, contextually, and systematically to exclude women and non-dominant groups. If we are going to change the ways that power is institutionalized and operationalized in society, we need to focus on more than just the "bad apples" in the system, because that kind of media coverage is designed to profit off of celebrity exposés through tabloid-style gossip. Instead, we need stories that expose the broader matrices of power that lead to abuses and social injustices from the top down. Through personal and political testimony, #MeToo and #TimesUp represent non-dominant voices that expose such power imbalances by challenging the consensus narratives that normalize patriarchy in everyday life.

Since consent is a function of power, women must be afforded institutional power as executives, owners, and key leaders across all tiers and platforms. In order to implement change within the media industries and beyond, women need to be able to tell their stories and shape socio-cultural meaning as journalists, news anchors, field reporters, and correspondents; as sports editors and commentators; as film, TV, radio, music, and Internet producers, directors, cast and crew members, and talent scouts; as camera and technology operators; as advertisers, marketers, public relations leaders, and all other key positions in the cultural industries. Through CMLE, we must continue to analyze the ways that sexist and misogynist ideologies seep into the culture, get normalized, and are enacted in everyday life. We must challenge the ways that organizational power discriminates, harasses, and abuses women and girls. Given the unique patriarchal and misogynist challenges of the Trump era, the hope is that hashtivism, grassroots campaigns, and critical media literacy will represent a tipping point for structural power, and that people will continue to work together to stand up for the rights and equality of all.

JULIE FRECHETTE, PHD, is Professor and Chair of the Department of Communication at Worcester State University. Her book, *Media Education for a Digital Generation*, provides a framework for developing critical digital literacies by exploring the necessary skills and competencies for engaging students as citizens of the digital world. She is the co-editor and co-author of the book *Media in Society*, and has published numerous articles and book chapters on media literacy, critical cultural studies, and gender and media. Her first book, *Developing Media Literacy in Cyberspace*, explores the multiple literacies approach for the digital age. She serves as co-president of the Action Coalition for Media Education, and is a cofounder of the Global Critical Media Literacy Project.

Notes

1.   Ealasaid Munro, "Feminism: A Fourth Wave?" Political Studies Association (PSA), undated, www.psa.ac.uk/insight-plus/feminism-fourth-wave.
2.   Emily Crockett, "Trump Reinstated the Global Gag Rule. It Won't Stop Abortion, But It will Make It Less Safe," Vox, January 23, 2017, updated January 25, 2017, https://www.vox.com/identities/2017/1/23/14356582/trump-global-gag-rule-abortion.
3.   Ibid.
4.   Julie Hirschfeld Davis, "Trump Signs Law Taking Aim at Planned Parenthood Funding," April 13, 2017, *New York Times*, https://www.nytimes.com/2017/04/13/us/politics/planned-parenthood-trump.html.
5.   "Trump Administration Takes Direct Aim at Birth Control Coverage for 62 Million Women," Planned Parenthood, October 6, 2017, https://www.plannedparenthood.org/about-us/newsroom/press-releases/trump-administration-takes-direct-aim-at-birth-control-coverage-for-62-million-women-2.
6.   Ibid.
7.   Sunny Frothingham and Shilpa Phadke, "100 Days, 100 Ways the Trump Administration is Harming Women and Families," Center for American Progress, April 25, 2017, https://www.americanprogress.org/issues/women/reports/2017/04/25/430969/100-days-100-ways-trump-administration-harming-women-families/.
8.   Ibid.
9.   Ibid.
10.   Ibid.
11.   Julie Frechette, "Tip of the Day: The Unfair and Imbalanced Culture of Sexual Harassment at Fox News," Project Censored, May 9, 2017, http://projectcensored.org/tip-day-unfair-imbalanced-culture-sexual-harassment-fox-news/.
12.   Jodi Kantor and Megan Twohey, "Harvey Weinstein Paid Off Sexual Harassment Accusers for Decades," *New York Times*, October 5, 2017, https://www.nytimes.com/2017/10/05/us/harvey-weinstein-harassment-allegations.html.

13. Jodi Kantor and Rachel Abrams, "Gwyneth Paltrow, Angelina Jolie and Others Say Weinstein Harassed Them," *New York Times*, October 10, 2017, https://www.nytimes.com/2017/10/10/us/gwyneth-paltrow-angelina-jolie-harvey-weinstein.html.

14. Caitlin Moore, "Harvey Weinstein Fired from Film Studio He Co-Founded after Recent Harassment Allegations," *Washington Post*, October 8, 2017, https://www.washingtonpost.com/news/arts-and-entertainment/wp/2017/10/08/harvey-weinstein-fired-from-film-studio-he-co-founded-after-recent-harassment-allegations/.

15. Christen A. Johnson and K.T. Hawbaker, "#MeToo: A Timeline of Events," *Chicago Tribune*, January 25, 2018, updated May 25, 2018, http://www.chicagotribune.com/lifestyles/ct-me-too-timeline-20171208-htmlstory.html.

16. See Ed Mazza, "#MeToo: Alyssa Milano's Call for Sexual Abuse Victims to Come Forward Goes Viral," Huffington Post, October 16, 2017, updated October 17, 2017, https://www.huffingtonpost.com/entry/me-too-victims-come-forward_us_59e4271ae4b03a7be5817b3f.

17. David Bauder, "NBC Fires Matt Lauer over 'Inappropriate Sexual Behavior,'" *Chicago Tribune*, November 29, 2017, http://www.chicagotribune.com/news/nationworld/ct-matt-lauer-fired-sexual-behavior-20171129-story.html.

18. Richard Gonzales, "Charlie Rose Fired by CBS, After 8 Women Accused Him of Sexual Harassment," NPR, November 20, 2017, https://www.npr.org/sections/thetwo-way/2017/11/20/565542031/charlie-rose-is-accused-of-sexual-harassment-by-eight-women.

19. Merrit Kennedy and David Folkenflik, "NPR Chief News Editor Departs after Harassment Allegations," NPR, November 28, 2017, https://www.npr.org/sections/thetwo-way/2017/11/28/567026934/npr-chief-news-editor-departs-in-wake-of-harassment-allegations.

20. Camila Domonoske, "Garrison Keillor Accused of 'Inappropriate Behavior,' Minnesota Public Radio Says," NPR, November 29, 2017, https://www.npr.org/sections/thetwo-way/2017/11/29/567241644/garrison-keillor-accused-of-inappropriate-behavior-minnesota-public-radio-says.

21. Martha Bebinger, "More Allegations Made Against 'On Point' Host Ashbrook and WBUR," WBUR, December 19, 2017, http://www.wbur.org/news/2017/12/19/more-allegations-ashbrook.

22. Daniel Victor, "Russell Simmons Steps Down from Businesses after Sexual Misconduct Report," *New York Times*, November 30, 2017, https://www.nytimes.com/2017/11/30/arts/russell-simmons-sexual-harassment.html.

23. Cited in Johnson and Hawbaker, "#MeToo: A Timeline of Events."

24. Johnson and Hawbaker, "#MeToo: A Timeline of Events."

25. Sheryl Gay Stolberg, Yamiche Alcindor, and Nicholas Fandos, "Al Franken to Resign from Senate Amid Harassment Allegations," *New York Times*, December 7, 2017, https://www.nytimes.com/2017/12/07/us/politics/al-franken-senate-sexual-harassment.html.

26. Heidi M. Przybyla, "Trump Sex Harassment Accusers Demand Congress Investigate as Lawmakers Resign," *USA Today*, December 11, 2017, https://www.usatoday.com/story/news/politics/2017/12/11/trump-sex-harassment-accusers-demand-congress-investigate-lawmakers-resign/940051001/.

27. Will Graves, "Gymnast McKayla Maroney Alleges Sexual Abuse by Team Doctor," *Chicago Tribune*, October 18, 2017, http://www.chicagotribune.com/sports/breaking/ct-mckayla-maroney-larry-nassar-metoo-20171018-story.html.

28. Dave Zirin, "WNBA Star Breanna Stewart Joins the #MeToo Movement, Saying 'Courage is Contagious,'" *The Nation*, November 1, 2017, https://www.thenation.com/article/wnba-star-breanna-stewart-joins-the-metoo-movement-saying-courage-is-contagious/.

29. Christine Hauser, Kim Severson, and Julia Moskin, "Mario Batali Steps Away from Restaurants Amid Sexual Misconduct Allegations," *New York Times*, December 11, 2017, https://www.nytimes.com/2017/12/11/dining/mario-batali-sexual-misconduct.html; and Greg Evans, "Mario Batali Accused of Misconduct by Seven Additional Women," Deadline, May 30, 2018, https://deadline.com/2018/05/mario-batali-sexual-misconduct-seven-additional-women-report-1202400450/.

30. Johnson and Hawbaker, "#MeToo: A Timeline of Events."

31. Cara Buckley, "Powerful Hollywood Women Unveil Anti-Harassment Action Plan," *New York Times*, January 1, 2018, https://www.nytimes.com/2018/01/01/movies/times-up-hollywood-women-sexual-harassment.html.

32. Ibid.

33. Catharine A. MacKinnon, "#MeToo has Done What the Law Could Not," *New York Times*, February 4, 2018, https://www.nytimes.com/2018/02/04/opinion/metoo-law-legal-system.html.

34. Imran Siddiquee, "Why Do We Let 'Genius' Directors Get Away with Abusive Behavior?" BuzzFeed, October 25, 2017, https://www.buzzfeed.com/imransiddiquee/hollywood-abusive-auteur-problem.

35. Ibid.

36. See ibid.

37. See Brit Marling, "Harvey Weinstein and the Economics of Consent," *The Atlantic*, October 23, 2017, https://www.theatlantic.com/entertainment/archive/2017/10/harvey-weinstein-and-the-economics-of-consent/543618/.

38. Ibid.

39. Siddiquee, "Why Do We Let 'Genius' Directors Get Away with Abusive Behavior?"

40. "Facts to Know about Women in Hollywood," 2017, https://womenandhollywood.com/resources/statistics/.

41. Ibid.

42. Siddiquee, "Why Do We Let 'Genius' Directors Get Away with Abusive Behavior?"

43. Ibid.

44. Marling, "Harvey Weinstein and the Economics of Consent."

45. "Women in Hollywood."

46. Laura Mulvey, "Visual Pleasure and Narrative Cinema," in *Film Theory and Criticism: Introductory Readings*, eds. Leo Braudy and Marshall Cohen (New York: Oxford University Press, 1999 [this version of the essay was originally published in 1975]), 833–44.

47. Ellen Vanstone, "How Has Rape Become Such a Common Trope of Television Drama?" *The Globe and Mail*, September 16, 2016, updated June 5, 2017, https://www.theglobeandmail.com/arts/television/how-has-rape-become-such-a-common-trope-of-television-drama/article31931181/.

48. Ibid.

49. Ibid.

50. Ibid.

51. Natasha Stott Despoja, "The Media is Reporting Rape Stories All Wrong," Huffington Post, June 16, 2016, updated July 15, 2016, http://www.huffingtonpost.com.au/natasha-stott-despoja/one-in-six-news-reports-imply-the-victim-is-to-blame-for-rape_a_21396130/.

52. Ibid.

53. Ibid.

54. Vanstone, "How Has Rape Become Such a Common Trope of Television Drama?"

55. Siddiquee, "Why Do We Let 'Genius' Directors Get Away with Abusive Behavior?"

56. Marling, "Harvey Weinstein and the Economics of Consent."

57. Jane Slaughter, "No Casting Couch for Low-Wage Women, But Lots of Sexual Harassment," Truthout, October 21, 2017, http://www.truth-out.org/news/item/42327-no-casting-couch-for-low-wage-women-but-lots-of-sexual-harassment.

58. Ibid.

59. Ibid.

60. Lowell Bergman, correspondent, "Rape on the Night Shift," *Frontline*, PBS, June 23, 2015, updated January 16, 2018, https://www.pbs.org/wgbh/frontline/film/rape-on-the-night-shift/.

61. Slaughter, "No Casting Couch for Low-Wage Women."

62. Ibid.

63. Julia T. Wood, "Saying It Makes It So: The Discursive Construction of Sexual Harassment," in *Conceptualizing Sexual Harassment as Discursive Practice*, ed. Shereen G. Bingham (Westport, CT: Praeger, 1994), 17–30, 20.

CHAPTER 7

Data Activism through Community Mapping and Data Visualization

Dorothy Kidd

INTRODUCTION

One of the most robust trends in Project Censored's annual reports of important but underreported news stories is the massive use and abuse of people's personal data by national security organizations, government agencies, and the giant Silicon Valley corporations. In *Censored 2016*, the big story, at #18, was the leak by whistleblower Edward Snowden, which documented ICREACH, the National Security Agency (NSA)'s Google-like search engine that made some 850 million personal records accessible to US intelligence and law enforcement agencies.[1] Story #4 in *Censored 2017* highlighted the use of algorithms in the manipulation of search engine rankings to influence election outcomes.[2] And *Censored 2018* featured a trio of related stories: story #5, on the influences of Big Data and dark money in the 2016 election;[3] #14, about how judges in courtrooms across the United States are using algorithms to rate the risks of defendants committing further crimes, with black defendants far more likely to be identified as risks than their white counterparts;[4] and #23, which detailed Facebook's multibillion-dollar business model. Updating the old media's practice of delivering audiences to advertisers, Facebook sells the personal data of users (combining Facebook's own online data with information collected offline bought from data brokers) to advertisers who want to target specific types of users for their products and services.[5]

Julia Angwin and her colleagues at ProPublica produced the reports on Facebook and racially-biased software which Project Censored independently verified, and the ProPublica team's work on algorithmic injustice has been exemplary. ProPublica is an independent, nonprofit investigative unit that is funded by the Knight, MacArthur, Ford, and Open Society Foundations, the Pew Charitable Trusts, and other major grant-making institutions, and regularly works with legacy news media organizations such as PBS, the *Washington Post*, and the *New York Times*. ProPublica has reported on systemic injustices, from race discrimination in housing ads and car insurance rates, to the exclusion of older workers from job ads by Amazon, Verizon, UPS, and Facebook, to the ways that Facebook and other sites help to aggregate and monetize extremist hate groups.[6]

These reports on digital surveillance are extraordinarily important as the 24/7 *datafication* of our communications, financial transactions, physical movements, and interactions with government are increasingly tracked. In addition, Big Data has become the new "oil" for the Silicon Valley giants such as Facebook, Google, and Amazon—companies refining ways to monetize aspects of our daily lives, such as our interpersonal connections and emotions, that have never before been quantified and sold. US digital corporations are also racing to secure markets in regions such as India and China, where the great majority of people live and, importantly, operate most of the world's seven billion mobile phones.[7]

As a result, rapid changes in our domestic and public infrastructure, including the "Internet of Things" and "smart" homes and cities, mean that this systematic monitoring of citizens and the collection, analysis, and application of Big Data will only become even further normalized, monetized, and entrenched.

ProPublica's reports have been important in detailing the systemic biases of much of this data surveillance; Big Data, superimposed on structural biases, often results in extremely biased knowledge. A range of interacting characteristics—race, ethnicity, religion, gender, location, nationality, and socioeconomic status—determine how individuals become administrative and legal subjects through their data and, consequently, how the intersecting sets of data can be used by policymakers and commercial firms, separately and in combination, to act upon them. In the case of much Big Data, knowledge is created by and for corporate giants who are only concerned with how to monetize the most valuable consumer niches, and the skew is multiplied incrementally. As Virginia Eubanks and the grassroots research group Our Data Bodies has reported, the greatest burden of dataveillance (surveillance using digital data) is borne by the poor, which in the United States often intersects with oppression based upon race, ethnicity, gender, and age.[8]

DATA ACTIVISM

What's missing in much of the dominant media and alternative media coverage of Big Data has been any systematic reporting on data activism. This global, if highly decentralized, movement includes two interconnected sets of practices. The first type of data activism involves groups whose tactics focus on identifying and resisting mass surveillance. This includes individual whistleblowers such as Edward Snowden and whistleblower platforms such as GlobaLeaks and Publeaks, which transfer data to journalists and the citizenry at large, usually with the aim of monitoring powerful actors and uncovering malfeasance. In addition, organizations such as the Electronic Frontier Foundation (EFF) focus on policy development, legal initiatives, and educational efforts to defend free speech online and challenge surveillance practices; while the Media Action Grassroots Network (Mag-NET) focuses its efforts on educating members and circulating information about the increasing surveillance of African Americans, Muslims, migrants, and social and political justice activists enabled by predictive policing's use of Big Data and interconnected technologies such as facial recognition, Stingrays, and other devices.

Social movements in many countries are also resisting the efforts of governments to implement centralized mega-databases of citizens' biometrics (fingerprints, voice records, eye scans, etc.) which can be used for surveillance and/or hacked by third parties.[9] In 2013, as South African communications professor Jane Duncan has reported, a Mauritian coalition of opposition parties, trade unionists, artists, and other activists mounted a massive anti-surveillance campaign that politicized the issues beyond concerns of individual privacy.[10] The government in

Mauritius, a tiny island nation off the southeast coast of Africa, tried to implement a smart ID card system and to require citizens to carry the ID cards at all times, arguing that this would eliminate identity fraud and theft. Drawing parallels between the coercive plan for digital social control and their lived experience of being forced to carry identity cards during slavery and colonial times, the coalition linked anti-surveillance to workers' rights and called for the government to dismantle the database. Combining public demonstrations, legal actions, and a media campaign, the coalition forced the government to dismantle the centralized database. Although the Mauritian government created, in turn, a more limited one-to-one system, where an individual's data is compared to only previously submitted data, the movement was effective in educating citizens about digital data, government surveillance, and their rights to their own biometric data.

A second type of data activism involves civic and nongovernmental organizations, individual hackers, and social and political movements proactively using data to organize for social, economic, and political change. These activists are requesting, assessing, analyzing, modeling, and creating data sets in order to critique the injustices of dominant narratives and policies and to create, support, and circulate different social imaginaries and forms of truth-telling based on the public good. They are also innovatively adapting and utilizing information technologies to create spaces of participation and counter-evidence that speak to corporate and state power, especially for groups who have been systemically marginalized by states and corporate media alike.

While a wide range of important and inspiring data activism is taking place throughout the world today, in this chapter I will focus on one particular type of proactive data activism: the use of community mapping and data visualization. I begin with a brief rehearsal of the backstory of Big Data, and then discuss a variety of projects and campaigns that are working to shift the narrative.

COUNTER-PLANNING

Big Data is not new. The massive collection of personal data by governments has a long history, as Virginia Eubanks described in her interview with Tanvi Misra in the *Atlantic*.[11] During World War I, the

US government, together with IBM, collected reams of data about US troops. The Cold War was a watershed period for the development of computational geographical methods by government defense and intelligence agencies. Technologies such as geographic information systems (GIS), reconnaissance satellites, geodetic models of the Earth for intercontinental ballistic missile targeting, and the Global Positioning System (GPS) were first developed by the US military. However, during the last decade those technologies have been modified for the world consumer market, providing a significant new technological capacity for ordinary citizens, but at the same time leaving us vulnerable to intensive monitoring at all times and places.[12]

Even as it allows for indiscriminate surveillance, Big Data has never been about equal opportunity. As Yeshimabeit Milner, the executive director of Data for Black Lives, wrote in an open letter to Facebook, "In the United States, racism has always been numerical. The decision to make every Black life count as three-fifths of a person was embedded in the electoral college . . . Histories of redlining, segregation, voter disenfranchisement and state sanctioned violence have not disappeared, but have been codified and disguised through new data regimes."[13]

Nevertheless, if the use of data in government and corporate planning has a long history, so too does counter-planning, the bottom-up practices of social and political movements that challenge dominant systems of knowledge. Readers may know about the people's budget process of Porto Alegre, also adopted in New York, Chicago, San Francisco, and many other cities, in which citizens requested public information, which they then analyzed in order to counter unrepresentative municipal planning and budget processes.[14] Less well known is the work of the Detroit Geographic Expedition and Institute, which from 1968 to 1970 taught more than 500 African American community members to produce numerous maps that challenged school decentralization, healthcare discrimination, and other important prejudices affecting civic issues.[15] In locations throughout the world, there are venerable (but often underappreciated) histories of civic, labor, and health activists, citizen science initiatives, and nongovernmental organizations launching do-it-ourselves grassroots processes of critiquing the official data of policy decisions, offering alternative narratives and political demands based upon their own realities.

THE NEW EXTRACTIVISM

In 2014 I reported for Project Censored on the growing global movement against extractivism, in which indigenous groups, who are the stewards and protectors of 80 percent of the planet's biodiversity, mobilize with environmental and other social justice movements to protect their water and territories from mining, oil, and natural gas companies.[16] Not surprisingly, then, one of the fastest growing networks of data activism has been developing among indigenous movements. For example, the US Indigenous Data Sovereignty Network was recently set up to provide information and advocacy for safeguarding the rights and promoting the interests of indigenous nations and peoples in relation to data, to ensure that indigenous nations "govern the collection, ownership and application of [their] own data" as part of their "inherent right to govern their peoples, lands and resources."[17] This is one part of the legacy of indigenous groups developing and safeguarding their own data that goes back several decades.

If the exploitation of data is sometimes called the new extractivism, it is strongly linked to the centuries of old extractivism and its exploitation of natural resources, most of which took place on indigenous lands. In 1968, oil was discovered in Alaska's Prudhoe Bay. Arctic Gas (a consortium of Exxon, Gulf, Shell, and other energy companies) and the Foothills Pipeline consortium both proposed pipeline routes to the Canadian government, without any consideration or consultation with the indigenous Dene communities whose territories the pipelines would cross. The Dene, together with environmental organizations, launched protests and lawsuits; in response, the Canadian government established a Royal Commission of inquiry under the noted justice Thomas Berger.[18] In an important precedent, rather than allowing outsiders to control the research process, the Dene decided to take back control of their own knowledge and produce evidence for the Commission that would also have longstanding value for their own livelihoods.

Coordinated by Phoebe Nahanni, a team of 20 Dene researchers set out to establish a collective form of research and advance the Dene Nation's land claim negotiations. As they were fluent in the Dene language, they were able to gather information from a greater number of people than previous efforts.[19] They interviewed 546 people, carefully recording their trapping, hunting, gathering, and other economic practices and uses of the land, via audio recordings and hard-copy maps.[20] They then took the finished maps back to the communities to be re-checked, ensuring greater accuracy and much wider community collaboration in the larger project.[21] The maps not only provided the Commission with important visual evidence of the Denes' longstanding historical occupancy, but they also constituted a new medium for connecting the Denes' collective use of land to their stories of individual and community life, thus challenging notions of individual property.[22] The mapping project, according to Phoebe Nahanni, was also vital in promoting discussion among the Dene communities about their past and future paths of development.[23] The Dene were successful at stopping the construction of pipelines in their community in the 1970s. Their mobilization ultimately led to a modicum of indigenous sovereignty, with a land claims agreement with the government of Canada established in 1994.

In 1980, together with academics from the University of Alberta, the Dene researchers organized the maps into one of Canada's first geographic information systems (GIS).[24] Recently, the Dene researchers decided to once again use the maps as part of their wildlife management, land use planning, and regulation of development. In 2014, the Sahtú Renewable Resources Board (SRRB) began a research project to create a new GIS point data set with the old maps. They are particularly interested in understanding the geography and trends in caribou–harvester relationships. They are also planning to map indigenous harvester responses to oil and gas exploration and development from traditional knowledge and scientific perspectives.[25]

The Dene collective research actively contributed to the mobilization of national and transnational movements by indigenous nations. Their modeling of indigenous mapping has been taken up by First Nations across Canada as part of land claim negotiations; it was instrumental, for instance, in the establishment of Nunavut, the Inuit-governed territory in northern Canada. More recently, indigenous groups have utilized critical practices of mapping and, more importantly, control over their own research and knowledge, in protecting their territories from mining projects and oil and gas pipelines.

THE UNIST'OT'EN

The Unist'ot'en band is part of the Wet'suwet'en First Nation in northern British Columbia, Canada. Their territory is still relatively whole, with intact forests, abundant wildlife, and relatively pure water. In 2010 they used GPS to locate pit houses and solidarity camps right on the GPS center point of Chevron Canada's Pacific Trail Pipeline. Since then, the Unist'ot'en have continued their "indigenous reoccupation" with local people and volunteers from all over the world.[26] Together, they are actively cultivating and protecting their territory from three proposed oil and natural gas pipelines managed by Chevron, TransCanada, and Enbridge. The Unist'ot'en combine knowledge from their elders about effective practices for healthy living on the land with digital mapping and other data activism and solidarity-building practices. On one hand, they actively resist the surveillance and incursions of the police and extraction companies. On the other hand, educating themselves and their allies, they have created novel alternative maps that show the interconnection of neighboring First Nations together with the important waterways, and fish and animal habitats, necessary to sustain lives throughout the entire region. As of Spring 2018, all energy company contractors and representatives have been confronted and peacefully turned away, so no pipeline work has yet been completed on Unist'ot'en territory.[27]

THE ENVIRONMENTAL JUSTICE ATLAS

Indigenous and environmental groups in many regions of the world are sharing critical GIS and counter-mapping strategies to plot the impacts of mining and/or pipelines in local communities, further aiding transnational movements opposed to extractivism. From 2011 to 2015, a group of European and Latin American academic researchers created the Environmental Justice Atlas as a new medium to document and circulate community-sourced knowledge about, and resistance to, the social and environmental impacts of mining and extractivism, particularly in Latin America and Europe.[28] Describing themselves as social historians, akin to others who recorded details of peasant uprisings or labor union strikes, the researchers used data resources in teaching and training workshops, and for policy advice, among academic and activist organizations working in a variety of disciplines and movements.[29]

Working together with the Observatory of Mining Conflicts in Latin America (OCMAL), Oilwatch, World Rainforest Movement, Oswaldo Cruz Foundation (Fiocruz), Brazilian Network of Environmental Justice, Global Alliance for Incinerator Alternatives (GAIA), and Centro di Documentazione sui Conflitti Ambientali (CDCA), the Environmental Justice Atlas researchers plotted key campaigns and place-based struggles that were significant because of the organizing of environmental, indigenous, and other activists; the size of the media coverage; and/or the size of the project, the amount of investment, and the scale of the impact or intensity of the conflict. They culled their information from public institutions, company materials, local activist groups, academics, blogs, and media reports. All the details—including the description of the conflict; the commodities in question; the environmental, health, and socioeconomic impacts; the social actors and their repertoires of activism; and the outcomes of the conflicts—were entered on digital maps. They also included in the atlas a section that provided sources and references, with links to photographs and videos of protagonists and their banners, slogans, and songs.

Although the researchers who created the atlas are no longer active as a group, the knowledge gained from the project is still being analyzed and shared, demonstrating the scope of extractivism in regions throughout the world. More importantly, it shows the number of communities where people are mobilizing, either to stop a project or to mitigate its worst toxic effects. The atlas, still online, also clearly shows the inequality in the distribution of pollution and destructive environmental impacts within specific countries and among indigenous peoples and poor communities across all regions. For example, although indigenous populations constitute only 5 percent of the global population, they are affected in no less than 40 percent of the cases documented in the atlas, and subject to far more repression, violence against women, criminalization, and death for defending their territories.[30]

SAN FRANCISCO ANTI-EVICTION MAPPING PROJECT

More recent people's mapping projects have built on the knowledge of the older counter-planning initiatives. They continue the practices that previous social, economic, and political justice movements contributed to the wider movements of information activism and media justice. Describing themselves as a "data-visualization, data analysis, and storytelling collective," the San Francisco Anti-Eviction Mapping Project began by documenting the physical displacement of people via evictions.[31] Using an intersectional analysis that examines the cross-cutting factors of race, ethnicity, and gender, they combined digital maps with official government data from corporate filings and national, state, and municipal records, and with data visualization, oral history, film, murals, and community events.[32] Their data sets are extensive and include the entire chain of historical processes from the first contact of white settlers with the indigenous Ohlone peoples in the 18th century up to the present day, with updates on major social and political events involved in more contemporary urban redevelopment. Their maps not only show the foreclosures caused by the global financial crisis of 2008 and the subsequent wave of evictions, broken down by neighborhood and demographics; they also provide pictures of key local and national housing and industry developers, including Wall Street landlords, Airbnb, absentee landlords, and local politicians. The group also provides important resources for further research by tenants and others affected by gentrification, including tips on how to do property research and the names and contacts of supportive organizations.

More recently, their info-activism has become more proactive, using their visual data skills to work with communities to map and plan how they might develop their own neighborhoods. In an important community-building initiative in Oakland, the Anti-Eviction Mapping Project worked with youth and other community members to map the sites of community power.[33] The key question was "What places in Oakland sustain you spiritually, culturally, and creatively?" Groups created maps and produced videos that documented the richness of their neighborhoods.

MUNICIPAL STRUGGLES

Counter-mapping is an approach that is being used in many other locations throughout the world. In Jakarta, Indonesia, citizens in the *kampungs*, or high-density, poor neighborhoods near the waterfront, are working together with the Urban Poor Consortium (UPC), a national grassroots organization, and employing data to resist gentrification and redevelopment by multinational property developers. Although the citizens of the kampungs have paid taxes, and have occupied their homes in some cases for more than 30 years, lack of official recognition of their tenure leaves them highly vulnerable to displacement. As available land becomes scarce, and development pressures build, their waterfront neighborhoods have become increasingly attractive to developers. In response, as Alessandra Renzi has written, the UPC has utilized counter-maps to educate residents about the city and commercial plans for redevelopment.[34] The UPC has also combined census information with the personal and local histories of the neighborhood as part of a campaign to expose the problems to local media, and to aid negotiations with local government. The overall aim is to create a counter-model of community development.

FROM INFORMATION ACTIVISM TO DATA JUSTICE

The proactive movement of information activism is still small, highly decentralized, and working against the combined might of the new military–digital industry combine. There is little consistent corporate or alternative media coverage of it anywhere. Nevertheless, these case studies demonstrate the value of this growing grassroots transnational data activism movement.

Sharing practices such as critical mapping with open sources, online platforms and data portals, on- and off-line hackathons, workshops, and other public engagements, activists are combining approaches from multiple social and political justice movements and media justice practices. They are not only watching the watchers and providing important counter-surveillance information, techniques, and apps; they are also significantly shifting the focus to the social needs and everyday practices of ordinary people, as part of broader movements that create alternative knowledge and inspiration necessary for the sustainability of the planet. The vision, as Massachusetts Institute of Technology professor and media and data activist Sasha Costanza-Chock expressed in May 2018 at the Data Justice Conference in Cardiff, Wales, is to "optimize our liberation rather than the market's," using data as part of larger projects of redistributive, transformative, and restorative justice.[35]

DOROTHY KIDD documents the use of communications by social and political justice movements. Her current research projects concern how communities are responding to extractivism. She teaches media studies at the University of San Francisco.

Notes

1. Kori Williams with Nick Sedenquist, "ICREACH: The NSA's Secret Search Engine," in *Censored 2016: Media Freedom on the Line*, eds. Mickey Huff and Andy Lee Roth with Project Censored (New York: Seven Stories Press, 2015), 78–79.

2. Brandy Miceli and Amanda Woodward, with Kenn Burrows and Rob Williams, "Search Engine Algorithms and Electronic Voting Machines Could Swing 2016 Election," in *Censored 2017: Fortieth Anniversary Edition*, eds. Mickey Huff and Andy Lee Roth with Project Censored (New York: Seven Stories Press, 2016), 49–53.

3. Maura Rocio Tellez and Olivia Jones, with Kenn Burrows and Rob Williams, "Big Data and Dark Money behind the 2016 Election," in *Censored 2018: Press Freedoms in a "Post-Truth" World*, eds. Andy Lee Roth and Mickey Huff with Project Censored (New York: Seven Stories Press, 2017), 51–54.

4. Hector Hernandez with Andy Lee Roth, "Judges across US Using Racially Biased Software to Assess Defendants' Risk of Committing Future Crimes," in *Censored 2018: Press Freedoms in a "Post-Truth" World*, eds. Andy Lee Roth and Mickey Huff with Project Censored (New York: Seven Stories Press, 2017), 75–77.

5. Jonnie Zambrano with Andy Lee Roth, "Facebook Buys Sensitive User Data to Offer Marketers Targeted Advertising," in *Censored 2018: Press Freedoms in a "Post-Truth" World*, eds. Andy Lee Roth and Mickey Huff with Project Censored (New York: Seven Stories Press, 2017), 94–95.

6. For reports on these and other topics, see the investigative series "Machine Bias: Investigating Algorithmic Injustice," ProPublica, September 1, 2015–April 10, 2018 [to date], https://www.propublica.org/series/machine-bias.

7. Linnet Taylor, "What is Data Justice? The Case for Connecting Digital Rights and Freedoms Globally," *Big Data & Society* 4, No. 2 (July–December 2017), 1–14, 2, http://journals.sagepub.com/doi/abs/10.1177/2053951717736335.

8. See, e.g., Tanvi Misra's interview with Virginia Eubanks, "When Welfare Decisions are Left to Algorithms," *The Atlantic*, February 15, 2018, https://www.theatlantic.com/business/archive/2018/02/virginia-eubanks-automating-inequality/553460/.

9. Marc Davies, "Biometrics, Surveillance Technologies and the Rise of the 'Security State' in South Africa," *Africa at LSE* blog, March 22, 2017, http://blogs.lse.ac.uk/africaatlse/2017/03/22/biometrics-surveillance-technologies-and-the-rise-of-the-security-state-in-south-africa/.

10. Jane Duncan, "Doing Anti-Surveillance Activism Differently," openDemocracy, April 30, 2018, https://www.opendemocracy.net/digitaliberties/jane-duncan/doing-anti-surveillance-activism-differently.

11. Misra, "When Welfare Decisions Are Left to Algorithms."

12. Ibid.

13. Yeshimabeit Milner, "An Open Letter to Facebook from the Data for Black Lives Movement," Medium, April 4, 2018, https://medium.com/@YESHICAN/an-open-letter-to-facebook-from-the-data-for-black-lives-movement-81e693c6b46c.

14. On participatory budgeting, see Gianpaolo Baiocchi and Ernesto Ganuza, "Participatory Budgeting as if Emancipation Mattered," *Politics & Society* 42, No. 1 (March 2014), 29–50, http://journals.sagepub.com/doi/abs/10.1177/0032329213512978; and Hollie Russon Gilman, *Democracy Reinvented: Participatory Budgeting and Civic Innovation in America* (Washington, DC: Brookings Institution Press, 2016).

15. Kanarinka, "The Detroit Geographic Expedition and Institute: A Case Study in Civic Mapping," Center for Civic Media (MIT), August 7, 2013, http://civic.mit.edu/2013/08/07/the-detroit-geographic-expedition-and-institute-a-case-study-in-civic-mapping/.

16. Dorothy Kidd, "'We Can Live without Gold, But We Can't Live without Water': Contesting Big Mining in the Americas," in *Censored 2015: Inspiring We the People*, eds. Andy Lee Roth and Mickey Huff with Project Censored (New York: Seven Stories, 2014), 221–41. See also story #9, "Indigenous Communities around World Helping to Win Legal Rights of Nature," in Chapter 1 of this volume.

17. "About Us," US Indigenous Data Sovereignty Network (hosted by the Native Nations Institute at the University of Arizona), undated, http://usindigenousdata.arizona.edu/about-us-0.

18. Joe Bryan and Denis Wood, *Weaponizing Maps: Indigenous Peoples and Counterinsurgency in the Americas* (New York: Guilford Press, 2015).

19. Sophie McCall, *First Person Plural: Aboriginal Storytelling and the Ethics of Collaborative Authorship* (Vancouver, Canada: UBC Press, 2011), 54.

20. Bryan and Wood, *Weaponizing Maps*.

21. McCall, *First Person Plural*, 55.

22. Ibid.

23. Ibid., 56.

24. Camilia Zoe-Chocolate, "Dene Mapping Project," Borders in Globalization, June 21, 2016, http://biglobalization.org/sites/default/files/uploads/files/dene_mapping.pdf.

25. "Dene Mapping," Sahtú Renewable Resources Board, undated, http://www.srrb.nt.ca/index.php?option=com_content&view=article&id=137&Itemid=833.

26. For history and news updates, see the Unist'ot'en Camp website, https://unistoten.camp/.

27. "Background of the Campaign," Unist'ot'en Camp, undated, https://unistoten.camp/no-pipelines/background-of-the-campaign/.

28. Begüm Özkaynak, Beatriz Rodríguez-Labajos, and Cem İskender Aydın, with Ivonne Yanez and Claudio Garibay, "Towards Environmental Justice Success in Mining Resistances: An Empirical Investigation," EJOLT Report No. 14 (April 2015), http://www.ejolt.org/wordpress/wp-content/uploads/2015/04/EJOLT_14_Towards-EJ-success-mining-low.pdf.

29. Leah Temper, Federico Demaria, Arnim Scheidel, Daniela Del Bene, and Joan Martinez-Alier, "The Global Environmental Justice Atlas (EJAtlas): Ecological Distribution Conflicts as Forces for Sustainability," *Sustainability Science* 13 (May 2018): 573–84, https://doi.org/10.1007/s11625-018-0563-4, 573.

30. Ibid., 578.

31. "About," Anti-Eviction Mapping Project, undated, https://www.antievictionmap.com/about/.

32. See "Resources," Anti-Eviction Mapping Project, undated, https://www.antievictionmap.com/how-to-research/.

33. Terra Graziani, Erin McElroy, Mary Shi, Leah Simon-Weisberg, "Alameda County Eviction Report," Anti-Eviction Mapping Project and Tenants Together, September 2016, https://antievictionmapd.maps.arcgis.com/apps/Cascade/index.html?appid=53bb2678ff2d41ff8f287cb7e84a6f4d.

34. Alessandra Renzi, "Entangled Data: Modelling and Resistance in the Megacity," Open! Platform for Art, Culture & the Public Domain, Technology / Affect / Space (T/A/S) Issue, February 20, 2017, http://www.onlineopen.org/entangled-data-modelling-and-resistance-in-the-megacity.

35. Sasha Costanza-Chock, "Data and Discrimination," Keynote Plenary II, Data Justice Conference: Exploring Social Justice in an Age of Datafication, Cardiff University, Wales, May 22,

2018, https://cardiff.cloud.panopto.eu/Panopto/Pages/Viewer.aspx?id=d132281d-8bbc-4980-8013-a8e8007c788d.

CHAPTER 8

How Mainstream Media Evolved into Corporate Media

A Project Censored History

Peter Phillips

Historically the term "mainstream media" referred to the largest media outlets in the United States. Numbering in the hundreds, these newspapers and broadcast media outlets collectively reached a majority of the public. That was certainly the case in 1976 when Carl Jensen founded Project Censored. His concern was that the mainstream press increasingly left out important news stories; and, with Project Censored student researchers, he began to produce annual reports of the most important news stories ignored by the mainstream media. From the original photocopied reports to the first of the Project's yearbooks published in 1993, Project Censored referred to the US media collectively as the press, mass media, or mainstream media. In the Project's 20th anniversary yearbook, Carl wrote, "The Censored Yearbook is published annually in response to a growing national demand for news and information not published nor broadcast by the mainstream media in America."[1]

In the 1980s two important analyses of how mainstream media was changing in the US transformed the study of media and communications. In 1982, when Ben Bagdikian completed research for his book, *The Media Monopoly*, he found that 50 corporations controlled at least half of the media business.[2] By December 1986, when he finished revisions for the book's second edition, the concentration of power had shifted from 50 corporations down to just 29. Bagdikian noted that 98 percent of the nation's 1,700 daily newspapers were local monopolies, with fewer than 15 corporations controlling most of the country's print media.

The second major turning point in the evolution of media studies was the publication of Edward S. Herman and Noam Chomsky's book, *Manufacturing Consent*, in 1988.[3] Herman and Chomsky claimed that, because media is firmly imbedded in the market system, it reflected the class values and concerns of its owners and advertisers. They reported that the media maintains a corporate class bias through five systemic filters they referred to as the "Propaganda Model": concentrated private ownership; a strict bottom-line profit orientation; over-reliance on governmental and corporate sources for news; a primary tendency to avoid offending the powerful; and an almost religious worship of the market economy, strongly opposing alternative beliefs. These filters limit what becomes news in American society and set parameters on acceptable coverage of daily events.

In 1997, under my directorship and influenced by the research of Bagdikian, Herman, and Chomsky, Project Censored began to express the idea that mainstream media was in transition, becoming increasingly corporate and consolidated. In *Censored 1997*, Ivan Harsløf and I used the term "mainstream corporate media" to describe the continuing rapid consolidation of media in the US and the forms of censorship they imposed.[4] We cited Herbert Schiller's concerns in *Culture, Inc.* regarding the corporate takeover of public expression through the internationalization of media.[5]

The following year, in *Censored 1998*, we took a strong stance against self-censorship, especially when organizational cultures within corporate media bureaucracies influence journalists' choices and coverage of specific news stories.[6] In addition, we researched the interlocking directorships of the six major media organizations, finding that 81 corporate directors (89 percent of whom were male) also held 104 director positions on the boards of businesses identified as *Fortune* 1,000 corporations.[7] It was becoming very clear that what we had called *mainstream* media no longer existed, having transformed into simply *corporate* media.

In *Censored 1999* I wrote, "The US media has lost its diversity and ability to present different points of view . . . . Every corporate media outlet in the country spent hundreds of hours and yards of newsprint to cover Bill Clinton's sexual escapades and in the process ignored many important news stories."[8] By the millennium, "mainstream" media had entirely disappeared from the US as far as Project Censored was concerned. In its place arose an increasingly concentrated, controlled, and propagandized corporate structure that had abandoned the time-honored commitment to inform and serve the American people. To illustrate the extent of the media's corporate transformation, in *Censored 2006* a team of Project Censored student interns from Sonoma State University identified 118 board members of ten major US media organizations, from newspaper to television to radio, and traced their direct ties to other corporate boards. Based on this network analysis, the team concluded that "[i]n corporate-dominated capitalism wealth concentration is the goal and the corporate media are the cheerleaders."[9]

Today, after a dozen years of further consolidation, corporate media have become a monolithic power structure that serves the interests of empire, war, and capitalism. A chapter I co-authored with Ratonya Coffee, Robert Ramirez, Mary Schafer, and Nicole Tranchina for *Censored 2017*, titled "Selling Empire, War, and Capitalism: Public Relations Propaganda Firms in Service to the Transnational Capitalist Class," laid bare how public relations propaganda, and corporate media more generally, work to promote capital growth as their primary goal through the "hegemonic psychological control of human desires, emotions, beliefs, and values."[10]

For those of us interested in opposing the destructive agenda of empires of concentrated wealth, it's clearly time to stop using the term "mainstream media" when "corporate media" is both more accurate and revealing.

PETER PHILLIPS served as Project Censored director for 14 years, from 1996 to 2010. He officially retired from Project Censored's board of directors in 2018. He is a professor of political sociology at Sonoma State University. Seven Stories Press published his new book, *Giants: The Global Power Elite*, in August 2018.

Notes

1. Carl Jensen, "20 Years of Raking Muck, Raising Hell," in *Censored: The News That Didn't Make the News—and Why*, 20th ann. ed., eds. Carl Jensen and Project Censored (New York: Seven Stories Press, 1996), 9–20, 9.
2. Ben Bagdikian, *The Media Monopoly* (Boston: Beacon Press, 1983).
3. Edward S. Herman and Noam Chomsky, *Manufacturing Consent: The Political Economy of the Mass Media* (New York: Pantheon Books, 1988).

4. Peter Phillips and Ivan Harsløf, "Censorship within Modern, Democratic Societies," in *Censored 1997: The News That Didn't Make the News*, eds. Peter Phillips and Project Censored (New York: Seven Stories Press, 1997), 139–58.

5. Herbert I. Schiller, *Culture, Inc.: The Corporate Takeover of Public Expression* (New York: Oxford University Press, 1989).

6. Peter Phillips, Bob Klose, Nicola Mazumdar, and Alix Jestron, "Self-Censorship and the Homogeneity of the Media Elite," in *Censored 1998: The News That Didn't Make the News*, eds. Peter Phillips and Project Censored (New York: Seven Stories Press, 1998), 141–52.

7. Ibid., 145.

8. Peter Phillips, "Building Media Democracy," in *Censored 1999: The News That Didn't Make the News*, eds. Peter Phillips and Project Censored (New York: Seven Stories Press, 1999), 129–35, 129.

9. Bridget Thornton, Brit Walters, and Lori Rouse, "Corporate Media is Corporate America: Big Media Interlocks with Corporate America and Broadcast News Media Ownership Empires," in *Censored 2006: The Top 25 Censored Stories*, eds. Peter Phillips and Project Censored (New York: Seven Stories Press, 2005), 245–62, 246.

10. Peter Phillips, Ratonya Coffee, Robert Ramirez, Mary Schafer, and Nicole Tranchina, "Selling Empire, War, and Capitalism: Public Relations Propaganda Firms in Service to the Transnational Capitalist Class," in *Censored 2017: Fortieth Anniversary Edition*, eds. Mickey Huff and Andy Lee Roth with Project Censored (New York: Seven Stories Press, 2016), 285–315, 307.

CHAPTER 9

Campus–Newsroom Collaborations
Building Bridges for Investigative Journalism

Patricia W. Elliott

Quality investigative journalism is incredibly difficult to produce and, these days, it is almost always a team effort. In a time of declining newsroom resources, success often hinges on how many researchers and reporting contributors can be pooled together. As a journalism educator, my classroom increasingly mirrors this collaborative environment. I teach at the University of Regina School of Journalism in Saskatchewan, Canada. We are an undergraduate and graduate professional school specializing in long-form documentary and investigative journalism, as well as newsroom reporting. Since 2014, I've been a Project Censored collaborator and have had good results using the Validated Independent News (VIN) process in assignments for my undergraduate investigative journalism course. Going to alternative sources for underreported news improves my students' ability to recognize good reporting in practice. More elementally, the assignment familiarizes students with what James C. Scott calls "hidden social transcripts,"[1] exposing them to undercurrents of resistance and change brewing beneath the dominant order. Students enjoy the assignment, and offer positive feedback similar to the many testimonials received by Project Censored:

> Time and again . . . we hear from our colleagues about how excited students are to work on a project that may result in contributing to some greater social good. The prospect of sharing their work—on the Internet and potentially through the Project Censored yearbooks—motivates students to do their best on the assignment.[2]

I am proud to say students from our small (but mighty) prairie institution have found their way into the pages of the annual Project Censored yearbooks, and contributed Validated Independent News articles to the Project Censored website. Yet it's fair to say the work of Project Censored is at times an uncomfortable fit in my classroom. Every year, when it comes time to play "that video" to introduce the assignment, I wince inwardly. *Project Censored The Movie* contains a scathing critique of the corporate news media.[3] To be sure, our students are well steeped in propaganda theory, framing, and the media's place within capitalist, racist, colonial power structures. Fostering social and political understanding, along with empathy for society's underdogs, is as important to our curriculum as learning to edit a video file; indeed, to teach one without the other is a dangerous prospect. In addition, our students spend time exploring cooperative, nonprofit, Indigenous, and independent media models as worthy avenues for their future journalism work. In short, they are no strangers to either the critiques of corporate media or its alternatives. Nonetheless, one can't ignore that the majority of our undergraduates enter our doors in search of career inroads into the world of corporate newsrooms, and that our bachelor's program is designed to provide just that. The majority of our teaching faculty, myself included, retain a foothold in that world. Watching the video, though, it's clear our romantic vision of the hero reporter is dogged by external criticism and fraught with internal contradictions. Thus, beyond broadening students' lists of sources, the assignment works to "break the frame" of our journalism world, as the project's founders intended.[4] So, yes, engaging in Project Censored is unsettling. As it should be.

Unsettlement goes both ways, though. I believe the presence of journalism schools within the Project Censored network naturally unsettles the framework of professional journalists as lock-step participants in corporate censorship. Indeed, Project Censored itself recognizes that the boundaries of corporate media are blurred, as it's had a long history of successful collaborations with journalists working in corporate media environments. Throughout my working life, I have slipped back and forth between the worlds of the academy, alternative media, and corporate media. From these multiple vantage points, one sees that the unassailable iron system of media oppression envisioned by Max Horkheimer and Theodor Adorno is filled with fissures and cracks.[5] These cracks are widening each day that the free market fails to adequately support the guiding directive of every journalism grad: to go forth and hold power to account. In recent years we have also seen a variety of emergent collaborations between establishment journalists, alternative journalists, universities, nonprofit foundations, and progressive research centers. This chapter considers such instances of collaboration, where common ground has been found between various independent and institutional sources to promote quality investigative journalism capable of supporting democratic accountability.

CAMPUS–COMMUNITY MEDIA COLLABORATIONS

Campus–community media collaborations are nothing new. Historically, however, they have been mainly embedded in community-based "voice for the voiceless" projects rather than investigative journalism initiatives. This is an incredibly valuable foundation for democratic collaboration. Beyond serving mutual communications needs, such collaborations, according to Isobel Findlay and Len Findlay, engender solidarity among community-based media practitioners, which the Findlays view as one of many potential steps toward the decolonization of universities and toward the development of a co-creative class.[6] A good example of campus–community media collaboration is the University of the Western Cape (UWC)'s role in sparking the development of South Africa's Bush Radio in the early 1990s, described by community radio activist Zane Ibrahim as "a new media model for South Africa" that was "in line with UWC's transformation programme, intended to ensure community participation in university life."[7]

Similarly, the University of Hyderabad in India helped establish Bol Hyderabad 90.4 FM, a radio station administered by a board of campus and community representatives, under a mandate that includes "the development of a culture of critical and constructive debate . . . to ensure that all sectors of this community get a fair opportunity to state their views and concerns on air."[8]

There are numerous further examples of collaborative institutions throughout North America, such as the Center for Community

Media housed at Worcester State University in Massachusetts,[9] as well as participatory media initiatives such as the Mapping Memories project, a five-year multimedia collaboration with refugee youth supported by researchers at Concordia University in Montreal.[10] "Community media work has always been hard to fund, and it's only getting tougher with today's economy. Meanwhile, universities are looking for creative ways to reach out to the communities that surround them and have the resources to do it," explained jesikah maria ross, founder of the Art of Regional Change media project at the University of California, Davis, a project that brought members of the university and community together to make digital media art.[11]

In recent years, partnerships with newsrooms have begun to grow from this foundation, similarly motivated by the prospect of pooling resources and sharing peoples' stories and public concerns. Previously, interactions with commercial media outlets and state broadcasters were largely siloed within schools of journalism, and often limited to unpaid or marginally-paid internship programs. That model is now changing, with the emergence of co-productions that draw on universities' capacity for interdisciplinary research, with journalism schools helping to build inroads and linking to the research capacity of other faculties and departments. The movement is spurred to no small extent by the gutting of local newsrooms by rapacious, indebted media conglomerates. To Robert W. McChesney, this constitutes an important moment for media reform activists and scholars:

> What is striking about the current critical juncture is how strongly journalists and media workers feel alienated from the corporate system. I believe it is crucial that we establish and maintain close ties to the media professions and draw their perspectives into our work.[12]

Another significant "fit" is the indelible link between press freedom and academic freedom, particularly appropriate in that academic freedom and public university funding are also under considerable stress throughout the world today.[13]

For academics, though, the fit is not always obvious. As Christopher Anderson has noted, there is much critique of journalistic practice, offered equally by the political Left and the Right, but very few critics seek a more complete understanding of how journalists actually do their work or what drives them to remain in increasingly punishing working conditions.[14] Although often obscured by the heat and noise of North American–style infotainment, there are established methods of journalistic research that lend themselves to the furtherance of progressive social change, not to mention journalists around the world who risk their lives to expose state corruption and oppression. The Committee to Protect Journalists reported that no less than forty-six journalists were killed while doing their jobs in 2017.[15]

James L. Aucoin identified investigative journalism as a social practice,[16] one that Brant Houston further described as "analyzing and revealing the breakdown of social or justice systems and documenting the consequences."[17] Robert Cribb, Dean Jobb, David McKie, and Fred Vallance-Jones add that the desired outcome is "a real opportunity to foster change."[18] Thus, though entrapped in corporate structures, investigative journalists align their work as social/political projects aimed at righting power imbalances and achieving social justice.[19] This is reflected in the codes of conduct laid out by professional associations, such as the Canadian Association of Journalists (CAJ)'s Ethics Guidelines:

> We serve democracy and the public interest by reporting the truth. This sometimes conflicts with various public and private interests, including those of sources, governments, advertisers and, *on occasion, with our duty and obligation to an employer* [emphasis added]. Defending the public's interest includes promoting the free flow of information, exposing crime or wrongdoing, protecting public health and safety, and preventing the public from being misled.[20]

Around the world, journalists form and join labor unions that actively challenge the status quo of their workplaces, as members of the Washington-Baltimore News Guild did in June 2017, after management at the *Washington Post* implemented a new social-media policy that banned employees from using their own social media accounts to criticize the newspaper's advertisers, vendors, or partners.[21] Journalists also form grassroots professional networks, such as

Investigative Reporters and Editors, the National Association of His-panic Journalists, the Native American Journalists Association, the Canadian Association of Aboriginal Broadcasters, and myriad others dedicated to improving the quality and diversity of newsrooms. This organizing activity among journalists indicates a far more nuanced picture of life inside the machine. For journalists who feel con-strained by understaffing and the right-wing or, at best, timid edito-rial positions of their employers, the opportunity to collaborate with university researchers offers a promise of greater research resources and an important validation of their work's credibility. For university researchers, it is an opportunity to move their work from the ivory tower to a mass audience. For educators, it's a chance to give students real-life, socially impactful learning experiences, much as the Project Censored VIN assignment accomplishes.

Along these lines, in 2005 the Walter Cronkite School of Jour-nalism and Mass Communication at Arizona State University became the launch pad for News21, a Carnegie-Knight-funded initia-tive designed to spur collaborations. To date, 500 students and their professors have participated in News21 collaborations, diving into topics ranging from environmental issues to incarceration rates.[22] A 2011 *Washington Post*–led News21 collaboration, for example, saw 27 students help produce "dozens of stories, interactive graphics, photo galleries, videos and searchable databases showing how the nation's fragmented, underfunded and overwhelmed food safety system fails to prevent food-borne illnesses from striking tens of millions of Americans each year, killing thousands and hospitalizing hundreds of thousands more."[23] Supervising editor Leonard Downie Jr. wrote, "What was most exciting for me was the fire in their belly. They really wanted to do accountability journalism, and they understood its importance for our society."[24] In addition, two of the *Washington Post* investigative interns had the opportunity to travel to Guatemala to trace cantaloupes from their source to the consumers.

When it comes to international reporting, the Global Reporting Centre at the University of British Columbia (UBC) emphasizes building links with journalists in the countries reported on. The Centre emerged out of the UBC School of Journalism's Interna-tional Reporting Program in 2008 as a means to address declining international news coverage, and within one year produced its first Emmy-winning documentary. Under the leadership of former *60 Minutes* producer Peter W. Klein, the Centre combines the forces of academics, student researchers, and news reporters, and publishes with both establishment and alternative media outlets.[25]

On the heels of these early successes, other collaborations have followed. In 2010, for example, the US-based Center for Investigative Reporting, the University of Southern California (USC) Annenberg School for Communication and Journalism, newspapers, and radio and television stations throughout California collaborated on a multimedia investigation, "Hunger in the Golden State." The investigation revealed, among other things, that nearly one in 11 Californians were receiving food stamps while many other undernourished residents remained outside the system, with just 48 percent of eligible recipients registered for the program.[26] According to Russ Stanton, editor of the *Los Angeles Times*, "The combined effort sheds light on a significant public policy issue facing the state. At the same time, the team reporting approach has allowed us to help in training . . . the next generation of California journalists."[27] An Annenberg School media statement added, "With the weight of [Center for Investigative Reporting] professionals behind them, the walls between academic work and real-world journalism broke down."[28]

One of the first university–newsroom partnerships to draw significant national attention in Canada was "Code Red," a 2010 investigative collaboration between Steve Buist, an investigative reporter with the *Hamilton Spectator*; Neil Johnston, a researcher at McMaster University's faculty of medicine; and Patrick DeLuca, a spatial analyst at McMaster's school of geography and earth sciences.[29] Through the collaboration, Buist melded the university-based researchers' data-gathering work on the social determinants of health with a journalist's shoe-leather work of knocking on doors for human interest stories and confronting political leaders. Their combined efforts drew a clear link between poor health and poverty in Hamilton, and garnered a Hillman Prize, a major annual award founded by labor activist Sidney Hillman for "journalists who pursue investigative reporting and deep storytelling in service of the common good."[30]

THE NATIONAL STUDENT INVESTIGATIVE REPORTING NETWORK

The common good underpins a collaborative investigative project I am currently involved in, via a partnership between Canada's nascent National Student Investigative Reporting Network (NSIRN) and the Corporate Mapping Project (CMP), a Canada-wide network of researchers exploring the power structures behind carbon extractive industries. The project was sparked when the CMP was contacted by the recipient of an academic fellowship for working journalists, 2016 Michener-Deacon Fellow Patti Sonntag, who has since become head of the newly-created Institute for Investigative Journalism at Concordia University in Montreal. NSIRN's pilot project, launched in 2017, grew to include a wide constellation of participants: the National Observer, an environment-focused independent online publication; Global TV, a mainstream corporate broadcaster; the *Toronto Star*, a national newspaper; the Corporate Mapping Project and its partners, including the Canadian Centre for Policy Alternatives and the Parkland Institute, two progressive think tanks; and four Canadian journalism schools (University of British Columbia, University of Regina, Concordia University, and Ryerson University), with financial support from the Social Sciences and Humanities Research Council, a federal research funding agency, and the Michener Foundation.

Through the collaboration, University of Regina journalism students in our Investigative Journalism and Intermediate Broadcast Journalism courses were able to bring local voices—namely, rural and Indigenous people suffering from the health and environmental impacts of Saskatchewan's poorly regulated oil and gas industries—to national attention. Their coursework included producing a student documentary, *Crude Power: An Investigation into Oil, Money and Influence in Saskatchewan* (see www.crudepower.jschool.ca), and research toward an ongoing investigative series carried out by all the project partners, called *The Price of Oil*.[31]

The researchers found, among other things, that the Saskatchewan government had not fined any oil companies in the past ten years, despite multiple safety infractions, thousands of spills and pipeline breaches, and the ongoing flaring and venting of lethally dangerous gas byproducts.[32] Significantly, the project broke a long-held code of silence among rural and Indigenous communities that are economically dependent on the industry. "Just to see universities across Canada come together and put all of their efforts into this one project, this one issue in Saskatchewan has really been something," said student Janelle Blakley, adding that it was an opportunity to gain a range of skills, from data mining to interviewing.[33]

For students in their first year of journalism school, it was challenging work on many levels. Faculty advisor and broadcast lecturer Trevor Grant observed,

> Over and above the challenge for the university instructors in managing this complex project there was the reality that the students would be going into the field to film and conduct interviews. A primary challenge was to ensure our students were prepared, editorially and emotionally, to conduct face-to-face interviews with people who had suffered emotional devastation and also to conduct accountability interviews. There was concern about this step, but the accountability interviews were often insightful, informative and engaging.[34]

Meanwhile, students at Ryerson and Concordia Universities investigated emissions in what is known as Chemical Valley, a collection of industrial refineries bordering the Aamjiwnaang First Nation reserve and the city of Sarnia, Ontario. In addition, Ryerson, Concordia, and UBC students together tackled the intricate networks of government subsidies and banking cross-ownership that prop up Canada's oil industry at great expense to the public purse. "We aggregated and analyzed data, populating spreadsheets and ledgers—more specifically, we mapped oil wells in Saskatchewan, discovering which ones got tax breaks," said Concordia University student Matt Gilmour. "Everyone's work fed into the bigger picture. We learned so much alongside veteran reporters and professionals."[35] All told, 34 students helped gather thousands of background files, made nearly 400 interview requests, and assisted with 118 freedom of information requests.[36]

Partnerships aren't easy, especially the first time out. The collaborators operate in different arenas and platforms; there are various academic protocols to navigate, and each media partner has its own reporting style and guidelines. Then there is the matter of a mutually agreeable release date, with different media outlets having different peak-audience days. For our collaboration, all of this involved many late-night phone conversations and hundreds of emails. As journalists, we were working within what, to us, was an incredibly short turnaround time. Without a large collaboration, investigations of this scope normally take years to publish. Students on their first investigative outing, however, were doubtless frustrated that the final "reveal" they'd hoped for in April was not scheduled until October, with professional journalists and paid student assistants working over the summer to polish and add to the reporting.

When the long-awaited moment arrives, "Everyone hits the 'publish' button at the agreed upon time, then a social media frenzy ensues. We stay in communication to share feedback we've received on the work, craft follow-up pieces collaboratively and move on to the next chapter," explained Elizabeth McSheffrey, a journalist from the National Observer team.[37]

For the most part, any lost sleep was soon eclipsed by the success of the series. Within the first month of publication, the articles, television broadcasts, and student documentary had garnered a combined audience of three million viewers, or one in 12 Canadians.[38] Among numerous awards and accolades, the project as a whole received a Hillman honorable mention and was short-listed for a Canadian Journalism Foundation award. *Canada's Toxic Secret*, a *Price of Oil* documentary on Chemical Valley, earned a New York Festivals silver award for Best Investigative Report, while the University of Regina students' *Crude Power* documentary won 2017's Investigative Reporters and Editors award for a large student production. More importantly, Saskatchewan's provincial government was forced to answer publicly for years of complacency in the face of industry negligence. Rural dwellers and oil workers who had long held their silence felt empowered to come forward with further stories of the harmful impacts of a loosely regulated industry. In Ontario, residents living in the shadow of Chemical Valley finally saw some action.[39] Citing the qualities that earned the project an honorable mention, the Hillman Foundation noted,

As a result of this reporting, the Ontario government committed to funding a study examining the health impacts of industrial pollution in the region—a study the community had requested in vain for 10 years. The series drove two weeks of debate in Ontario's legislature, marked by calls for action and declarations of environmental racism as the Aamjiwnaang suffered. Long-demanded regulations for sulphur dioxide—which hadn't been updated in 43 years—were introduced and, after an eight-year delay, the government announced it would finally regulate the cumulative effects of air pollution in Sarnia's "Chemical Valley."[40]

There were also impacts for Canadian journalism, as described by Peter W. Klein, a faculty advisor who worked with the UBC student journalists:

Journalism schools have a responsibility and an opportunity here. We're seeing more and more excellent reporting coming out of universities, often integrating scholars who have substantive knowledge about issues in which reporters are interested. While training and offering mentorship to students, universities can also fill the growing void in high-level journalism throughout the country.[41]

Though still in development, the National Student Investigative Reporting Network has already provided numerous students with hands-on training alongside working professionals, and this collaboration has resulted in both awards and meaningful social change. The program offers a model that university faculty and journalists from other institutions could follow, broadening the potential for cross-border partnerships.

CONCLUSION: "TIME TO MAKE A DIFFERENCE"

In conclusion, campus–media collaborations offer an important counterpoint to the "obnoxious media frames" identified and opposed by Project Censored.[42] In an echo of Project Censored's mandate to expose missing news stories, *Price of Oil* series producer Patti Sonntag stated that campus–newsroom collaboration constitutes "excellent work experience for the students, and it serves the community by pursuing underreported stories."[43] Collaboration with working investigative journalists can serve to bring censored and underreported stories to a mass audience, at a time when journalism is struggling to redefine itself as a public good.

To be sure, this model would not be worth pursuing if it served only to prop up shaky corporate media models beyond their sell-by date. My participation is guided by a belief that the process offers long-term transformative potential toward a more democratic future. As media models of the past few centuries begin to collapse upon themselves, new networks linked to the public sphere are building capacity to pick up the shards. To some extent this process mirrors the trajectory of a networked mediascape described by Yochai Benkler as "several intersecting models of production, whose operations to some extent complement and to some extent compete with one another."[44] Leonard Downie Jr., whose career has migrated from the newsroom to the academy, sees a broadened potential for this type of collaborative work, one that involves alternative nonprofit media, small local projects, and larger-scale investigations housed in public institutions, using public platforms:

> Universities, despite their own financial challenges, can help provide nonprofit sustainability and produce professional-level journalism and digital news innovation. They can collaborate with both for-profit and nonprofit news media. Those that hold public broadcasting licenses, as many do, can steadily transform their public radio and television stations into platforms for local news. Journalism schools, too many of which have retreated into academic isolation, can play the same productive and developmental role in news coverage as other professional schools do in medicine, business, law, engineering, science and technology. This is their time to make a difference.[45]

Indeed, the opportunity to make a difference is what draws collaborators to venture out of their disparate spheres and come together to create something new. Campus–newsroom collaborations offer a step toward a reimagined media ecology that serves the needs of people rather the profits of corporations.

PATRICIA W. ELLIOTT is an investigative journalist and associate professor of journalism at the University of Regina in Saskatchewan, Canada. Her investigations have ranged from international drug-trade politics to fraudulent Canadian charities, while her academic research focuses on exploring nonprofit and independent journalism. Additionally, she authored a book on the roots of the Shan ethnic insurgency in Myanmar, *The White Umbrella* (Friends Books, 2005), and co-edited *Free Knowledge: Confronting the Commodification of Human Discovery* (University of Regina Press, 2015), a collection dedicated to reclaiming the knowledge commons from private interests.

Notes

1. James C. Scott, *Domination and the Arts of Resistance: Hidden Transcripts* (New Haven, CT: Yale University Press, 1990).
2. Andy Lee Roth and Project Censored, "Breaking the Corporate News Frame through Validated Independent News Online," in *Media Education for a Digital Generation*, eds. Julie Frechette and Rob Williams (New York: Routledge, 2016), 173–86, 183.
3. Doug Hecker and Christopher Oscar, directors, *Project Censored The Movie: Ending the Reign of Junk Food News* (Hole in the Media Productions, 2013). Online at http://www.projectcensoredthemovie.com.
4. Roth and Project Censored, "Breaking the Corporate News Frame," 183.
5. Max Horkheimer and Theodor Adorno, *The Dialectic of Enlightenment*, tr. John Cumming (New York: Continuum, 1972/1986). Originally published in German as *Dialektek der Aufklärung* (New York: Social Studies Association, 1944).
6. Isobel Findlay and Len Findlay, "Revisionary Civics, Reciprocal Relations: Development of a Co-Creative Class," Living Knowledge Conference. Copenhagen. April 10, 2014.
7. Zane Ibrahim, "The Road to Community Radio," *Rhodes Journalism Review* 24 (September 2004), 40–41, 40, http://www.rjr.ru.ac.za/n024.html.
8. "About Us," Bol Hyderabad 90.4 FM, University of Hyderabad, Gachibowli, India, undated, http://bolhyd.commuoh.in/about-us/.
9. "Center for Community Media," Worcester State University, undated, https://www.worcester.edu/Center-for-Community-Media/.
10. Michele Luchs and Elizabeth Miller, "Not So Far Away: A Collaborative Model of Engaging Refugee Youth in the Outreach of Their Digital Stories," *Area* 48, No. 4 (December 2016): 442–48, https://doi.org/10.1111/area.12165. See also the Mapping Memories project website at http://www.mappingmemories.ca.
11. jesikah maria ross, "Bringing Community Media into the University: A Strategy for Developing Media Arts Programs," National Alliance for Media Arts and Culture, November 20, 2009; available online at http://old.gfem.org/node/700. See also the Art of Regional Change project website at http://artofregionalchange.ucdavis.edu.
12. Robert W. McChesney, *Communication Revolution: Critical Junctures and the Future of Media* (New York: The New Press, 2007), 25.
13. Len M. Findlay and Paul M. Bidwell, eds. *Pursuing Academic Freedom: "Free and Fearless"?* (Saskatoon, Saskatchewan: Purich Publishing, 2001).
14. Christopher Anderson, "Journalism: Expertise, Authority, and Power in Democratic Life," in *The Media and Social Theory*, eds. David Hesmondhalgh and Jason Toynbee (New York: Routledge, 2008), 248–64.

15. "46 Journalists Killed," Committee to Protect Journalists (CPJ), 2017, accessed April 17, 2018, https://cpj.org/data/killed/2017/?status=Killed&motiveConfirmed%5B%5D=Confirmed&typ e%5B%5D=Journalist&end_year=2017&group_by=location. For past coverage by Project Censored of the threats faced by journalists in the course of doing their jobs, see Qui Phan with Andy Lee Roth, "Journalism Under Attack Around the Globe," story #16 in *Censored 2014: Fearless Speech in Fateful Times*, eds. Mickey Huff and Andy Lee Roth with Project Censored (New York: Seven Stories Press, 2013), 56–57; and Brian Covert's follow-up discussion in "Whistleblowers and Gag Laws," 75–77 in the same book. "Journalism Under Attack Around the Globe" is available online at http://projectcensored.org/journalism-under-attack-around-the-globe/.

16. James L. Aucoin, *The Evolution of American Investigative Journalism* (Columbia, MO: University of Missouri Press, 2005).

17. Brant Houston and Investigative Reporters and Editors, Inc., *The Investigative Reporter's Handbook: A Guide to Documents, Databases and Techniques*, 5th ed. (Boston/New York: Bedford/St. Martin's, 2009).

18. Robert Cribb, Dean Jobb, David McKie, and Fred Vallance-Jones, *Digging Deeper: A Canadian Reporter's Research Guide* (Don Mills, Ontario: Oxford University Press, 2006).

19. Ibid.

20. "Ethics Guidelines," Canadian Association of Journalists, June 2011, http://caj.ca/ethics-guidelines.

21. Andrew Beaujon, "The *Washington Post*'s New Social Media Policy Forbids Disparaging Advertisers," *Washingtonian*, June 27, 2017, https://www.washingtonian.com/2017/06/27/the-washington-post-social-media-policy/. See also "*Washington Post* Bans Employees from Using Social Media to Criticize Sponsors," story #5 in Chapter 1 of this volume.

22. "About News21," News21, undated, accessed May 29, 2018, https://news21.com/about/.

23. Leonard Downie Jr., "Big Journalism on Campus," *American Journalism Review*, December 2, 2011, para 6, http://ajrarchive.org/Article.asp?id=5200.

24. Ibid., para 13.

25. Global Reporting Centre, undated, accessed April 14, 2018, https://globalreportingcentre.org/.

26. Alexandra Zavis and Emilie Mutert, "California's Food Stamp Participation Rate is Nation's Second-Lowest," *Los Angeles Times*, March 21, 2010, http://www.latimes.com/local/la-me-food-stamps21-2010mar21-story.html.

27. Russ Stanton, cited in "USC Annenberg and Center for Investigative Reporting Produce Multimedia Series 'Hunger in the Golden State,'" USC Annenberg School for Communication and Journalism, March 15, 2010, updated June 12, 2015, https://annenberg.usc.edu/news/classes/usc-annenberg-and-center-for-investigative-reporting-produce-multimedia-series-"hunger.

28. Ibid.

29. See Paul Berton, "Code Red is Journalism at Its Best," *Hamilton Spectator*, October 26, 2013, https://www.thespec.com/opinion-story/4177158-berton-code-red-is-journalism-at-its-best/. View the Code Red project at http://thespec-codered.com/.

30. "The Sidney Hillman Foundation," undated, http://hillmanfoundation.org/sidney-hillman-foundation.

31. For a list of publications in the *Price of Oil* series, see the National Student Investigative Reporting Network (NSIRN) website at http://jpress.journalism.ryerson.ca/nsirn/publications/.

32. Since the series was published, Husky Energy may now face a fine of up to $1 million under the provincial Environmental Management and Protection Act, pending the outcome of a court case relating to a 225,000-liter spill that impacted the North Saskatchewan River. See David Baxter, "Husky Energy Facing up to $1M Fine for 2016 Oil Spill from Sask., Plus Nine Federal Charges," Global News, March 26, 2018, https://globalnews.ca/news/4105785/husky-energy-fine-2016-north-saskatchewan-oil-spill/.

33. Costa Maragos, "Crude Power Documentary a Bonanza for Journalism Students and Investigative Reporting," University of Regina External Relations, October 1, 2017, para 5, https://www.uregina.ca/external/communications/feature-stories/current/2017/10-01.html.

34. Trevor Grant, cited in Abdullah Shihipar, "Stronger Together: How Journalists Can Collaborate," J-Source, October 27, 2017, para 16, http://j-source.ca/article/stronger-together-journalists-can-collaborate/.

35. Matt Gilmour, cited in J. Latimer, "What Happens When 50 Reporters and 3 Media Outlets Team Up to Investigate the Price of Oil?" Concordia University News, October 2, 2017, para 18–19, http://www.concordia.ca/cunews/main/stories/2017/10/02/patti-sonntag-concordia-nationwide-student-powered-investigative-journalism.html.

36. "Hillman Prizes—Honourable Mention: The Price of Oil," Sidney Hillman Foundation, 2018, http://hillmanfoundation.org/canadian-hillman-prize/2018-winners#honourable1.

37. Quoted in Shihipar, "Stronger Together," para 20.

38. Corporate Mapping Project, Price of Oil Journalism Component, *Phase 1 Report* (unpublished report, 2017).

39. "Hillman Prizes—Honourable Mention," Sidney Hillman Foundation.

40. Ibid.

41. Peter Klein, cited in Thandi Fletcher, "The Future of Journalism Lies in Collaboration," University of British Columbia, October 11, 2017, https://news.ubc.ca/2017/10/11/the-future-of-journalism-lies-in-collaboration/.

42. Roth and Project Censored, "Breaking the Corporate News Frame," 174.

43. Patti Sonntag, cited in Latimer, "What Happens," para 24.

44. Yochai Benkler, "WikiLeaks and the Networked Fourth Estate," in *Beyond WikiLeaks: Implications for the Future of Communications, Journalism and Society*, eds. Benedetta Brevini, Arne Hintz, and Patrick McCurdy (New York: Palgrave Macmillan, 2013), 13.

45. Downie Jr., "Big Journalism on Campus," para 48.

CHAPTER 10

The Public and Its Problems
"Fake News" and the Battle for Hearts and Minds

Susan Maret

Following the major political events of 2016–2017 and the Facebook/ Cambridge Analytica revelations, phrases such as "alternative facts," "post-fact," "post-truth," and "fake news" have deluged global channels of communication. Of these terms, the use of "fake news" is now so commonplace—and vulgarized—that it has been included on the annual "List of Words Banished from the Queen's English for Misuse, Over-use and General Uselessness" as of January 1, 2018.[1] These fuzzy terms point to larger social problems that not only concern the authority, credibility, and believability of information, but its very manipulation.[2]

Under the guise of facts, shades of false, unvetted information, plagiarized stories, and clickbait from nation-states, contractors, advertisers, social media, news conglomerates, and hidden actors flood public communication spaces, usurping the traditional 24-hour news cycle. The technological ability to influence information choices, as well as to predict, persuade, and engineer behavior through algorithms (a "recipe" or set of instructions carried out by computer) and bots (applications that run automated, repetitive tasks) now blurs the line between potentially meaningful information and micro/targeted messaging.[3]

Several research studies illustrate the deleterious effects of false information on public communication.[4] For example, a survey by Pew Research Center and Elon University's Imagining the Internet Center found that the "fake news ecosystem preys on some of our deepest human instincts."[5] A Pew Research Center Journalism and Media survey of 1,002 US adults revealed two-in-three Americans (64 percent) find that "fabricated news stories" create confusion over current issues and events and believe that this confusion is "shared widely across incomes, education levels, partisan affiliations, and most other demographic characteristics."[6] This survey also revealed that "16% of US adults say they have shared fake political news inadvertently, only discovering later that it was entirely made up."[7] Still other research uncovered the influence of fake news, propagated by algorithms and bots, on the 2016 US election[8] and Cambridge Analytica's role in the Brexit and Leave.EU movements.[9]

But there is something more telling about the influence of fake news, which pertains to global perceptions of the media and trust in their sources. An investigation of approximately 18,000 individuals across the United States, United Kingdom, Ireland, Spain, Germany, Denmark, Australia, France, and Greece found reduced trust in the media due to "bias, spin, and agendas."[10] That is, a "significant proportion of the public feel that powerful people are using the media to push their own political or economic interests"; moreover, "attempts to be even-handed also get the BBC and other public broadcasters into trouble. By presenting both sides of an issue side by side, this can give the impression of false equivalence."[11]

In this chapter, I briefly outline the ways fake news is characterized in the research literature. I then discuss how fake news is manufactured and the global entities responsible for its propagation. I close the chapter by reporting on ongoing technological and educational initiatives and suggest several avenues in which to explore and confront this controversial, geopolitical social problem.

FAKE NEWS: AN UNSTABLE CONCEPT

The term "fake news" was reported as early as the 6th century CE, and persisted into the 18th century as a means of "diffusing nasty news . . . about public figures."[12] Merriam-Webster, however, situates fake news as "seeing general use at the end of the 19th century," and defines it as *news* ("material reported in a newspaper or news periodical or on a newscast") that is *fake* ("false, counterfeit").[13] The term "fake news" is "frequently used to describe a political story, which is seen as damaging to an agency, entity, or person . . . [I]t is by no means restricted to politics, and seems to have currency in terms of general news."[14] This expanded description by the esteemed dictionary allows for falsehood to be viewed within the sphere of harm, fallout, and consequence.

In addition to Merriam-Webster's definition, scholars have divided "fake news" into categories such as commercially-driven sensational content, nation state–sponsored misinformation, highly-partisan news sites, social media, news satire, news parody, fabrication, manipulation, advertising, and propaganda.[15] The use of the term "fake news" is now so prevalent that it is considered a "catch-all phrase to refer to everything from news articles that are factually incorrect to opinion pieces, parodies and sarcasm, hoaxes, rumors, memes, online abuse, and factual misstatements by public figures that are reported in otherwise accurate news pieces."[16]

Fake news is often framed as *misinformation, disinformation,* and *propaganda* in mainstream and scholarly literature, which complicates collective understanding of what constitutes "counterfeit" information and the actors behind its manufacture. Misinformation, for example, is defined as "information that is initially assumed to be valid but is later corrected or retracted . . . [though it] often has an ongoing effect on people's memory and reasoning."[17] Misinformation is either *intentional* (e.g., manufactured for some sort of gain) or *unintentional* (e.g., incomplete fact-checking, "hasty reporting," or sources who were misinformed or lying).[18] Misinformation has been identified with outbreaks of violence.[19] Misinformation is also described in relation to disinformation as "contentious information reflecting disagreement, whereas disinformation is more problematic, as it involves the deliberate alienation or disempowerment of other people."[20]

Disinformation, as characterized by the European Commission's High Level Expert Group (HLEG), "goes well beyond the term fake news."[21] Similar to Merriam-Webster's definition of "fake news" and its emphasis on damage and resulting harm, the HLEG likens fake news to disinformation to include "all forms of false, inaccurate, or misleading information designed, presented and promoted to intentionally cause public harm or for profit."[22]

To further muddy the waters, in an analysis of "mainstream and social media coverage" during the 2016 US election, disinformation was linked to "propaganda as the 'intentional use of communications to influence attitudes and behavior in the target population'"; disinformation is the "communication of propaganda consisting of materially misleading information."[23] But such characterizations are not as seamless as they at first appear. A specific category of propaganda called *black propaganda* is described as "virtually indistinguishable" from disinformation and "hinges on absolute secrecy . . . usually supported by false documents."[24] These particular definitions perhaps supplement longstanding descriptions of propaganda as a "consistent, enduring effort to create or shape events to influence the relations of the public to an enterprise, idea or group" and as a "set of methods employed by an organized group that wants to bring about the active or passive participation in its actions of a mass of individuals, psychologically unified through psychological manipulations and incorporated in an organization."[25]

Perhaps the most dramatic evolution in the study of fake news as it applies to Internet society is the proposal by Samuel C. Woolley and Philip N. Howard, who offer the term *computational propaganda* as the "assemblage of social media platforms, autonomous agents, and big data tasked with the manipulation of public opinion."[26] Computational propaganda—a mashup of technology, ideology, and political influence, coupled with deception and secrecy—results in calculated messaging designed to influence opinion and beliefs. Here it is critical to interject that some researchers find the term "fake news" "difficult to operationalize" and instead suggest in its place *junk news*, or content consisting of "various forms of propaganda and ideologically extreme, hyper-partisan, or conspiratorial political news and information."[27]

Under certain conditions, "fake news" may be infused with noise or classed as information distortion. Described as "undoubtedly the most damaging to the clarification of a catastrophe,"[28] information distortion occurred, for example, during the Las Vegas shootings when Google prominently displayed search results derived from 4chan, Twitter, and Facebook as "news."[29] Distortion also featured in the media coverage of Devin Patrick Kelley, who opened fire on 26 people in a Sutherland Springs, Texas, church on November 5, 2017. During the early hours of the disaster, Kelley was described as both a "liberal, Antifa communist working with ISIS" and a supporter of Bernie Sanders, creating "noise"—a conspiratorial, inaccurate, rumor-fed, politically-charged news stream run amok.[30] A similar scenario occurred during the aftermath of the Parkland shootings. Researchers found that individuals

> outraged by the conspiracy helped to promote it—in some cases far more than the supporters of the story. And algorithms—apparently absent the necessary "sentiment sensitivity" that is needed to tell the context of a piece of content and assess whether it is being shared positively or negatively—see all that noise the same.[31]

Sidestepping well-worn terms such as misinformation, disinformation, and propaganda, *truth decay* was recently suggested as a vital model for understanding the "increasing disagreement about facts and analytical interpretations of facts and data" and diminishing trust in sources of factual information.[32]

From this overview, it is apparent that "fake news" and related conditions of information suffer from epistemic fluidity. On one hand, recent attempts to flesh out fake news in relation to misinformation, disinformation, and propaganda potentially advance our previously-held notions. On the other hand, the lack of universally-established definitions and refinement of concepts creates Babel-like complexity in the journalism and research communities, resulting in a kitchen-sink approach to the study of falsehood and the disordered information-communication ecosystem where it thrives.

Falsehood—fake news—as misinformation, disinformation, and/or propaganda, is a crisis of collective knowledge. Whatever definitions or concepts with which we choose to categorize the phenomenon, the reality is that falsehood contributes to a cacophonous, polluted information-sharing environment. The infosphere now resembles a light-pollution map. In confronting fake news, we now face the challenge described by Karl Mannheim in his *Ideology and Utopia*: "not how to deal with a kind of knowledge which shall be 'truth in itself,' but rather how man deals with his problems of knowing."[33]

HOW FAKE NEWS HAPPENS

It is critical to acknowledge that fake news as counterfeit information is created by humans and/or humans tasking technologies to moderate information and/or disrupt communications. Often this moderation and disruption is conducted in secret by anonymous actors. For example, patented algorithms construct a search engine results page (SERP)'s appearance and content (e.g., ad words, knowledge panels, news boxes, rating stars, reviews, snippets), thus directing an individual's information-seeking and research gaze; hackers or "pranksters" manipulate search results through the practice of "Google bombing";[34] and algorithms and bots fabricated by troll factories and/or nation-states actively engage in the shaping of information in order to sow confusion and discord. In the following section, I briefly illustrate how fake news is promoted by these search features and global entities.

The Invisible Hand

One product of a SERP, the snippet, is "extracted programmatically" from web content to include a summary of an answer based on a search query. Google describes the snippet as reflecting "the views or opinion of the site" from which it is extracted.[35] The DuckDuckGo search engine also supplies snippets in the form of "Instant Answers" or "high-quality answers" situated above search results and ads. Instant Answers are pulled from news sources such as the BBC, but also include Wikipedia and "over 400 more community built answers."[36] The Russian web search engine Yandex also provides "interactive snippets," or an "island," to supply individuals with a "*solution* rather than an *answer.*"[37] Although the snippet is not entirely "counterfeit information," it is designed to confederate knowledge from across the web to make it appear "more like objective fact than algorithmically curated and unverified third-party content."[38]

More to the point, third-party advertising networks connect advertisers with website creators to attract paid clicks by producing often misleading, sensational, tabloid-like information or ads that mimic news stories.[39] To stem the rising tide of fake news monetization,

Google disabled a total of 112 million ads that "trick to click," with Facebook following suit with new guidelines that informed "creators and publishers" that they must have an "authentic, established presence."[40] However, Facebook's "Content Guidelines for Monetization" do not include a category for false or deceptive information that would disqualify this type of content from monetization.[41] In the end, "deciding what's fake news can be subjective, and ad tech tends to shrug and take a 'who am I to decide'" stance.[42]

At the Halifax International Security Forum in November 2017, Eric Schmidt, former executive chairman of Alphabet, Google's parent company, disclosed that "it was easier for Google's algorithm to handle false or unreliable information when there is greater consensus, but it's more challenging to separate truth from misinformation when views are diametrically opposed."[43] To address this technological quandary, Google altered its secret patented algorithm to de-rank "fake news," relegating it to a lower position on subsequent search result pages. The search giant also revised its "Search Quality Evaluator Guidelines" to assist its legion of search quality raters with "more detailed examples of low-quality webpages for raters to appropriately flag, which can include misleading information, unexpected offensive results, hoaxes and unsupported conspiracy theories."[44] Referring to Google's multi-pronged approach, Schmidt stated that he is "strongly not in favour of censorship. I am very strongly in favour of ranking. It's what we do."[45] In direct response to reports of Russia's alleged election interference, Google de-ranked content from Russia Today (RT) and Sputnik.[46] Contesting Google's actions, an op-ed published on RT argued "there is nothing good or noble about de-ranking RT. It's not a war against 'fake news' or misinformation. It's a war of ideas on a much, much wider scale."[47]

Google's techno-fix may have artificially repaired one problem while posing others. First, research on information-seeking behavior suggests that individuals tend to focus on the first page of search results, often not venturing to "bottom" layers or pages that may potentially contain meaningful links to sites representing a diversity of views.[48] Secondly, it is not only reactionary censorship we must guard against in the "war of ideas." It is gatekeeping as well.[49] In allowing behind-the-curtain algorithmic technology—the invisible hand—to distinguish "true" from "false" information without agreement, nuance, or context, the open pursuit of knowledge and ideas without boundaries is challenged on a fundamental level.[50] In this regard, "the human right to impart information and ideas is not limited to 'correct' statements." This information right also "protects information and ideas that may shock, offend and disturb."[51]

Information Warfare and Information Operations

In addition to behind-the-curtain assemblages of information by search engines and algorithmic determination of search results, "fake news" is produced by way of information warfare and information operations (also known as influence operations).[52] Information warfare (IW) is the "conflict or struggle between two or more groups in the information environment";[53] information operations (IO) are described in a Facebook security report as

> actions taken by governments or organized non-state actors to distort domestic or foreign political sentiment, most frequently to achieve a strategic and/or geopolitical outcome. These operations can use a combination of methods, such as false news, disinformation, or networks of fake accounts (false amplifiers) aimed at manipulating public opinion.[54]

With its emphasis on damage, it is possible to apply Merriam-Webster's definition of "fake news" (and possibly the High Level Expert Group's as well) to IW and IO, as they are conducted by cyber troops, or "government, military or political-party teams committed to manipulating public opinion."[55] These often anonymous actors from around the globe—invisible to oversight and regulation—are involved in delivering weaponized falsehoods to unwitting consumers of information via fake accounts.[56] In these cases, deception is a key element in the manipulation of information.[57]

The earliest reports of organized social media manipulation came to light in 2010, with revelations in 2017 that there are "offensive" organizations in 28 countries.[58] Less is known about corporations, such as Facebook's global government and politics team, and private actors that moderate information and troll critics in order to influence public perceptions.[59] With concealed geographic locations and secret allegiances, cyber troops engineer information machines to produce an embattled Internet. For instance, paid disinformation agents at the Internet Research Agency in St. Petersburg operated the "Jenna Abrams" Twitter account, which had 70,000 followers.[60] Coined "Russia's Clown Troll Princess," "Abrams" produced tweets that were covered by the BBC, Breitbart News, CNN, InfoWars, the *New York Times*, and the *Washington Post*.[61] The Internet Research Agency is also implicated in more than 400 fake Twitter accounts used to influence UK citizens regarding Brexit.[62] In addition, the *Guardian* and BuzzFeed reported that the Macedonian town of Veles was the registered home of approximately 100 pro-Trump websites, many reporting fake news; "ample traffic was rewarded handsomely by automated advertising engines, like Google's AdSense."[63] And to support the "infowar," Alex Jones, founder of the alternative media sites infowars.com, newswars.com, prisonplanet.com, and europe.infowars.com, likened purchases from his online store to purchasing "war bonds, an act of resisting the enemy to support us and buy the great products."[64]

Both IW and IO are useful in framing widespread allegations of "fake news" and micro/targeted messaging during major political events, including the 2016 US election,[65] the French election coverage in 2016–17,[66] the 2017 UK and German elections,[67] and the 2018 Italian election.[68] IW and IO potentially fueled "purported" fake news posted on the Qatar News Agency's website (which inflamed relations between Iran and Israel),[69] the spread of a false story about a $110 billion weapons deal between the US and Saudi Arabia (reported as true in such outlets as the *New York Times* and CNBC),[70] and "saber-rattling" between Israel and Pakistan after a false report circulated that Israel had threatened Pakistan with nuclear weapons.[71]

The conceptual framework of IW/IO has profound implications for the transgressions of Cambridge Analytica, whose techniques influenced the US and Nigerian elections.[72] Information warfare and/or information operations as high-octane opposition research certainly describes Donald Trump's former campaign manager Paul Manafort's alleged involvement in a covert media operation. This operation included revision of Wikipedia entries "to smear a key opponent" of former Ukrainian president Viktor Yanukovych and activating a "social media blitz" aimed at European and US audiences.[73] Ahead of the May 25, 2018 vote to repeal the 8th amendment to the Irish Constitution on a woman's right to terminate her pregnancy, journalist Rossalyn Warren wrote that "Facebook and the public have focused almost solely on politics and Russian interference in the United States election. What they haven't addressed is the vast amount of misinformation and unevidenced stories about reproductive rights, science, and health."[74]

THE PUBLIC AND ITS PROBLEMS: ADDRESSING FAKE NEWS

In 1927, philosopher John Dewey remarked that, "until secrecy, prejudice, bias, misrepresentation, and propaganda as well as sheer ignorance are replaced by inquiry and publicity, we have no way of telling how apt for judgment of social policies the existing intelligence of the masses might be."[75] In the age of "post-truth" and "fake news," Dewey's comments might be construed as patronizing or perhaps elitist. But embedded in his remarks is respect for democratic values, which recognize the power of openness and the essential role of education in transforming social action. Below I report on ongoing technological and educational initiatives and suggest several interconnected steps to address the fake news challenge.

Educational Initiatives

Echoing John Dewey's confidence in the formative power of education and literacy, several approaches originating from higher education can be employed across educational settings to address fake news. Since 1976, Project Censored's faculty–student partnerships have developed the Validated Independent News (VIN) model, subjecting independent news stories to intense evaluation in order to validate them as "important, timely, fact-based, well documented, and under-reported in the corporate media."[76] Supporting multiple literacies, the Association of College & Research Libraries (ACRL)'s "Framework for Information Literacy for Higher Education" offers tools for librarians and faculty to emphasize "conceptual understand-ings that organize many other concepts and ideas about information, research, and scholarship into a coherent whole."[77] Both Project Cen-sored's VIN model and the ACRL's "Framework" encourage the devel-opment of metaliteracies and metacognition, leading to increased awareness and skill regarding the creation of collective knowledge and the reporting of facts.[78]

Government Response to Fake News

Governmental response to the fake news problem varies interna-tionally. In the US, for instance, the State Department's Global Engagement Center (GEC), established during the Obama adminis-tration, aims to "counter the messaging and diminish the influence of international terrorist organizations and other violent extremists abroad."[79] The 2017 National Defense Authorization Act expanded the GEC to

> identify current and emerging trends in foreign propa-ganda and disinformation in order to coordinate and shape the development of tactics, techniques, and procedures to expose and refute foreign misinformation and disinforma-tion and proactively promote fact-based narratives and poli cies to audiences outside the United States.[80]

The US Congress also convened several high-profile hearings on combatting fake news and foreign disinformation.[81]

On a state level, the *Internet: Social Media: False Information Stra-tegic Plans* (SB-1424), introduced into the California State Legislature in February 2018, would require "any person who operates a social media, as defined, Internet Web site with a physical presence in California" to create a strategic plan to "mitigate" the spread of false news. The proposed legislation, which duplicates numerous ongoing educational-literacy programs and NGO activities that address "fake news," mandates the use of fact-checkers to verify news stories and outreach to social media users regarding stories that contain "false information" (which the proposed bill does not define), and requires social media platforms to place a warning on news that contains false information.[82]

European governmental agency responses to counterfeit news include legislation and regulatory stopgap measures. For example, Croatia, Ireland, Malaysia, and South Korea proposed legislation to counter fake news; legislation in France includes an emergency procedure that allows a judge to delete web content, close a user's account, or block access to a website altogether.[83] During its 2018 elections, the Italian government launched an online "red button" system for people to report "fake news" to the postal police, the federal agency responsible for monitoring online crime.[84] Sweden created a "psychological defence" authority to counter fake news and disinformation,[85] while the German Ministry of the Interior proposed a "Center of Defense Against Disinformation."[86] Linking fake news with national security concerns, and subtly with IO/IW, the United Kingdom is in the process of creating a national security communications unit to battle "disinformation by state actors and others."[87] In early February 2018, the UK Parliament's 11-member Committee on Digital, Culture, Media and Sport traveled to Washington, DC, to convene an "evidence session" with Facebook, Google, and Twitter executives on the subject of fake news, and to meet with members of the US Senate Intelligence Committee regarding Russian influence on social media during the 2016 election.[88]

Going several steps further, Chinese President Xi Jinping appeared to suggest increasing control and censorship of China's digital communications system when he remarked that "without Web security there's no national security, there's no economic and social stability, and it's difficult to ensure the interests of the broader masses."[89] The Russian Federation's Security Council recommended an alternate Domain Name System (DNS) for BRICS countries (Brazil, the Russian Federation, India, China, and South Africa), citing "increased capabilities of western nations to conduct offensive operations in the informational space."[90] If implemented, the new DNS would essentially create another layer of a walled-off, compartmentalized Internet in these countries.

NGOs and Social Media Companies

Nongovernmental organizations (NGOs) and social media companies have responded to the spread of counterfeit information by forming fact-checking programs and initiatives. Fact Tank, the International Fact-Checking Network at Poynter, Media Bias/Fact Check, Metabunk, Mozilla Information Trust Initiative, PolitiFact, and Snopes.com analyze specific, often memetic, news stories, while Google News and Google's search engine now include a "fact check" tag that alerts information consumers that a particular slice of information was scrutinized by organizations and publishers. Google is now partnering with the Trust Project, which—much like food ingredient labels for fat and sugar content—developed a "core set" of indicators for news and media organizations that range from best practices to the use of citations, references, and research methodologies, to having a "commitment to bringing in diverse perspectives."[91] Facebook now requires political ads to reveal their funding sources, and the creation of a nongovernmental, voluntary accreditation system to "distinguish reliable journalism from disinformation" is another proposal toward stemming the creation and dissemination of fake news.[92]

Technological Solutions

Technological approaches to curbing fake news include the formation of the World Wide Web Consortium (W3C)'s Credible Web Community Group, which investigates "credibility indicators" as these apply to structured data formats. MisinfoCon is a "global movement focused on building solutions to online trust, verification, fact checking, and reader experience in the interest of addressing misinformation in all of its forms."[93] Browser add-ons, such as Project FiB, a Chrome-based extension, detect fake news on Facebook, Reddit, and Twitter, while the controversial PropOrNot browser plugin misreports websites as delivering "Russian propaganda" targeted toward Americans. The Hamilton 68 Dashboard, a project of the German Marshall Fund's Alliance for Securing Democracy, monitors 600 Twitter accounts linked to Russian influence efforts online, "but not all of the accounts are directly controlled by Russia. The method is focused on understanding the behavior of the aggregate network rather than the behavior of individual users."[94]

In the following discussion, I suggest additional interconnected steps to bring clarity to public and academic investigations of false information and to combat fake news on a local, national, and global scale.

Defend Journalistic Integrity and Protect Journalists

The preponderance of fake news traversing public channels of communication challenges established editorial practices, information and media ethics, transparency, publicity, and the public right to know. In addition to the proliferation of fake news, newsbots created and employed by media organizations have shifted human authorship to algorithmic or "robo-journalism."[95] The rise of elected officials claiming that the media spreads "fake news" by "lying" to the public increases "the risk of threats and violence against journalists" and undermines the public's trust and confidence in members of the Fourth and Fifth Estates.[96]

Global Public/Information Policy

In the US, Congress must reconstitute the Office of Technology Assessment (OTA). For 23 years, OTA policy analysis included research on adult literacy, information security, emerging technologies, and US information infrastructure.[97] On an international level, a nonpartisan body of stakeholders (e.g., the Tallinn Manual Process) should be formed to address the policy implications of tech platforms, algorithms, bots, and their use in weaponizing information.[98] Above all, as Marietje Schaake suggests, "regulators need to be able to assess the workings of algorithms. This can be done in a confidential manner, by empowering telecommunications and competition regulators."[99] This proposed international body might also address the global implications of algorithmic accountability and algorithmic justice in order to confront "dissemination of knowingly or recklessly false statements by official or State actors" within the established framework of international human rights.[100] Both OTA v.2 and the proposed international body suggested above would address the influence of fake news and other information conditions that impact the right to communicate and freedom of expression.

Re-Imagine Education and the Curriculum

Institutional support and funding for inter/multi/transdisciplinary courses and initiatives that address intermeshed literacies across the curriculum, continuing education, and community is *imperative*. Studies of how editorial practices and ethics contribute to the construction of knowledge in crowdsourced and academic reference works would be an essential part of this proposed curriculum. Such initiatives can only be realized through global partnerships of "intermediaries, media outlets, civil society, and academia."[101]

Research as a Necessity and Global Social Good

Dewey observed that "tools of social inquiry will be clumsy as long as they are forged in places and under conditions remote from contemporary events."[102] Using Dewey as our North Star, theoretical forays into how "fake news" differs from various information conditions (e.g., misinformation, disinformation, or propaganda) serve to build a common language for deeper studies. Evidence-based research on those factors that influence the public's information-seeking and media habits is essential. This research would go a long way toward explaining how and why individuals adopt certain ideas and are influenced by specific information. For example, research suggests that "the greater one's knowledge about the news media . . . the less likely one will fall prey to conspiracy theories."[103] There is also a need for intensive qualitative and quantitative investigations into those actors who manipulate information for sociopolitical gain and to cause damage; one study indicates that "robots accelerated the spread of true and false news at the same rate, implying that false news spreads more than the truth because humans, not robots, are more likely to spread it."[104]

Support Local Media Through Citizen/Community Journalism

One solution to the problem of fake news, media conglomeration, and prepackaged news is community-based journalism. In forging educational partnerships with communities (see above), universities, libraries, and organizations have the opportunity to cultivate a climate focused on freedom of information and skill building. These partnerships allow citizens, including student journalists, to investigate local perspectives, stories, and events that national, corporate media ignore, marginalize, or abbreviate. According to one account, citizen journalism "ranks low on revenues and readers. It ranks high on perceived value and impact. While it aspires to report on community, it aspires even more to build community."[105]

In his book *The Public and Its Problems*, Dewey established that knowledge is *social*. As such, knowledge is a function of communication and association, which depend "upon tradition, upon tools and methods socially transmitted, developed, and sanctioned."[106] As discussed in this chapter, "fake news" as falsehood disrupts established ways of knowing and communication. In its wake, fake news destabilizes the very trust in information required to sustain relationships across the social world.

SUSAN MARET, PHD, is a lecturer in the School of Information at San José State University, where she teaches courses on information secrecy and information ethics. Maret is the editor/author of several works on government secrecy and a founding member of the peer-reviewed online journal *Secrecy and Society*.

Notes

1. "List of Words Banished from the Queen's English for Mis-use, Over-use and General Uselessness," Lake Superior State University, 2018, https://www.lssu.edu/banished-words-list/.
2. From its roots, informatio: *in* (within) *forma* (form, shape, pattern) *tio* (action, process). Information can be thought of as giving form to meaning, ideas, knowledge, and action; this powerful thing called information is crucial to decision-making, self-determination, and social trust. Based on this "special nature" of information, unique moral dilemmas arise in its use. For a discussion of information ethics, see Richard O. Mason, Florence M. Mason, and Mary J. Culnan, *Ethics of Information Management* (Thousand Oaks, CA: SAGE Publications, 1995); and Luciano Floridi, "Information Ethics, Its Nature and Scope," *ACM SIGCAS Computers and Society* 36, No. 3 (September 2006): 21–36, http://pages.uoregon.edu/koopman/courses_readings/phil123-net/intro/floridi_info-ethics_nature_scope.pdf.
3. None of my discussion in this chapter is meant to suggest a "golden age" of manipulation- and bias-free communications. Numerous theorists and journalists have documented media bias and tampering: C. Wright Mills, Marshall McLuhan, Carl Bernstein, Noam Chomsky and

Edward S. Herman, Michael and Christian Parenti, Robert McChesney, Chris Hedges, Carl Jensen, Project Censored, and the Senate Select Committee to Study Governmental Operations with Respect to Intelligence Activities (Church Committee).

4. Susan Maret, "Intellectual Freedom and Government Secrecy," in *The Library Juice Press Handbook of Intellectual Freedom: Concepts, Cases, and Theories*, eds. Mark Alfino and Laura Koltutsky (Sacramento, CA: Library Juice Press, 2014), 247–81.

5. Janna Anderson and Lee Rainie, "The Future of Truth and Misinformation Online," Pew Research Center, October 19, 2017, http://www.pewinternet.org/2017/10/19/the-future-of-truth-and-misinformation-online/.

6. Michael Barthel, Amy Mitchell, and Jesse Holcomb, "Many Americans Believe Fake News is Sowing Confusion," Pew Research Center, December 15, 2016, http://www.journalism.org/2016/12/15/many-americans-believe-fake-news-is-sowing-confusion/.

7. Ibid.

8. For example, Yochai Benkler, Robert Faris, Hal Roberts, and Ethan Zuckerman, "Breitbart-Led Right-Wing Media Ecosystem Altered Broader Media Agenda," *Columbia Journalism Review*, March 3, 2017, https://www.cjr.org/analysis/breitbart-media-trump-harvard-study.php; Rob Faris, Hal Roberts, Bruce Etling, Nikki Bourassa, Ethan Zuckerman, and Yochai Benkler, "Partisanship, Propaganda, and Disinformation: Online Media and the 2016 U.S. Presidential Election," Berkman Klein Center for Internet & Society at Harvard University, August 16, 2017, https://cyber.harvard.edu/publications/2017/08/mediacloud; and Chengcheng Shao, Giovanni Luca Ciampaglia, Onur Varol, Kaicheng Yang, Alessandro Flammini, and Filippo Menczer, "The Spread of Low-Credibility Content by Social Bots," arXiv.org, May 24, 2018, https://arxiv.org/pdf/1707.07592.pdf. See also Maura Rocio Tellez and Olivia Jones, with Kenn Burrows and Rob Williams, "Big Data and Dark Money behind the 2016 Election," in *Censored 2018: Press Freedoms in a "Post-Truth" World*, eds. Andy Lee Roth and Mickey Huff with Project Censored (New York: Seven Stories, 2017), 51–54.

9. See University of Essex lecturer Dr. Emma L. Briant's research, which unearthed how "Leave. EU sought to create an impression of 'democracy' and a campaign channeling public will, while creating deliberately 'provocative' communications to subvert it and win by channeling hateful propaganda." Emma L. Briant, "Three Explanatory Essays Giving Context and Analysis to Submitted Evidence," UK Parliament's Digital, Culture, Media and Sport Committee: Evidence, April 16, 2018, https://www.parliament.uk/documents/commons-committees/culture media and sport/Dr%20Emma%20Briant%20Explanatory%20Essays.pdf. See also Tellez and Jones, with Burrows and Williams, "Big Data and Dark Money," in *Censored 2018*, 53.

10. Nic Newman and Richard Fletcher, "Bias, Bullshit and Lies: Audience Perspectives on Low Trust in the Media," Digital News Project, 2017, 5, https://reutersinstitute.politics.ox.ac.uk/our-research/bias-bullshit-and-lies-audience-perspectives-low-trust-media.

11. Ibid.

12. Robert Darnton, "The True History of Fake News," *New York Review of Books*, February 13, 2017, https://www.nybooks.com/daily/2017/02/13/the-true-history-of-fake-news/. See also David Uberti, "The Real History of Fake News," *Columbia Journalism Review*, December 15, 2016, https://www.cjr.org/special_report/fake_news_history.php.

13. "The Real Story of 'Fake News,'" Merriam-Webster, March 23, 2017, https://www.merriam-webster.com/words-at-play/the-real-story-of-fake-news.

14. Ibid.

15. James Titcomb and James Carson, "Fake News: What Exactly is It—and Can It Really Swing an Election?" *The Telegraph*, November 14, 2017, http://www.telegraph.co.uk/technology/0/fake-news-exactly-has-really-had-influence/ [updated, and renamed "Fake News: What Exactly is It—and How Can You Spot It?" on May 30, 2018]; and Edson C. Tandoc Jr., Zheng Wei Lim, and Richard Ling, "Defining 'Fake News': A Typology of Scholarly Definitions," *Digital Journalism* 6, No. 2 (2018): 137–53.

16. Jen Weedon, William Nuland, and Alex Stamos, "Information Operations and Facebook," Facebook, April 27, 2017, v.1.0, 4, https://www.mm.dk/wp-content/uploads/2017/05/facebook-and-information-operations-v1.pdf.

17. Ullrich K.H. Ecker, Stephan Lewandowsky, Olivia Fenton, and Kelsey Martin, "Do People Keep Believing Because They Want To? Preexisting Attitudes and the Continued Influence of Misinformation," *Memory & Cognition* 42, No. 2 (February 2014): 292–304, 292.
18. See Melanie C. Green and John K. Donahue, "The Effects of False Information in News Stories," in *Misinformation and Mass Audiences*, eds. Brian G. Southwell, Emily A. Thorson, and Laura Sheble (Austin: University of Texas Press, 2018), 109–23. Information design and organization may also influence the integrity and veracity of information. This important detail goes unmentioned in most discussions.
19. See, for example, Amanda Taub and Max Fisher, "Where Countries are Tinderboxes and Facebook is a Match: False Rumors Set Buddhist against Muslim in Sri Lanka, the Most Recent in a Global Spate of Violence Fanned by Social Media," *New York Times*, April 21, 2018, https://www.nytimes.com/2018/04/21/world/asia/facebook-sri-lanka-riots.html.
20. Brian G. Southwell, Emily A. Thorson, and Laura Sheble, "Misinformation among Mass Audiences as a Focus for Inquiry," in *Misinformation and Mass Audiences*, eds. Brian G. Southwell, Emily A. Thorson, and Laura Sheble (Austin: University of Texas Press, 2018), 1–11, 2.
21. According to the HLEG, as a term, "fake news" "has been appropriated and used misleadingly by powerful actors to dismiss coverage that is simply found disagreeable." High Level Expert Group, "Final Report of the High Level Expert Group on Fake News and Online Disinformation," European Commission, March 12, 2018, 5, https://ec.europa.eu/digital-single-market/en/news/final-report-high-level-expert-group-fake-news-and-online-disinformation.
22. Ibid.
23. Faris et al., "Partisanship, Propaganda, and Disinformation," 19.
24. Victor Marchetti and John D. Marks, *The CIA and the Cult of Intelligence* (New York: Alfred A. Knopf, 1974), 165.
25. Edward L. Bernays, *Propaganda* (New York: H. Liveright, 1928), 25; and Jacques Ellul, *Propaganda: The Formation of Men's Attitudes*, trs. Konrad Kellen and Jean Lerner (New York: Vintage Books, 1965 [French orig. 1962]), 61.
26. Samuel C. Woolley and Philip N. Howard, "Political Communication, Computational Propaganda, and Autonomous Agents," *International Journal of Communication* 10 (2016): 4882–90, 4886.
27. Philip N. Howard, Samantha Bradshaw, Bence Kollanyi, Clementine Desigaud, and Gillian Bolsover, "Junk News and Bots during the French Presidential Election: What are French Voters Sharing over Twitter?" COMPROP Data Memo, April 22, 2017, 3, http://comprop.oii.ox.ac.uk/wp-content/uploads/sites/93/2017/04/What-Are-French-Voters-Sharing-Over-Twitter-v10-1.pdf.
28. José Vicente García-Santamaría, "The Crisis of Investigative Journalism in Spain: The Journalism Practice in the Spanair Accident," *Revista Latina de Comunicación Social* 65 (2010), http://www.revistalatinacs.org/10/art3/916_UC3M/38_Santamaria.html [author translation]; see also Claude E. Shannon, "Communication in the Presence of Noise," *Proceedings of the IEEE* 86, No. 2 (1949/1998), 447–57.
29. Alfred Ng, "How Social Media Trolls Capitalized on the Las Vegas Shooting," CNET, October 2, 2017, https://www.cnet.com/news/las-vegas-shooting-fake-news-hoax-social-media-facebook-twitter/.
30. Dana Liebelson and Paul Blumenthal, "The Texas Shooter was Called a Liberal, Antifa Communist Working with ISIS—Before Anyone Knew Anything," Huffington Post, November 7, 2017, updated November 8, 2017, https://www.huffingtonpost.com/entry/texas-shooter-conspiracy-theories_us_5a01ed2be4b092053058499e; and Christal Hayes, "Texas Church Shooter was a Bernie Sanders Supporter, Alt-Right Claims in Latest Lie," *Newsweek*, November 16, 2017, http://www.newsweek.com/texas-church-shooter-was-bernie-sanders-supporter-alt-right-claims-latest-lie-713677.
31. Molly McKew, "How Liberals Amped Up a Parkland Shooting Conspiracy Theory," *Wired*, February 27, 2018, https://www.wired.com/story/how-liberals-amped-up-a-parkland-shooting-conspiracy-theory/.

32. Jennifer Kavanagh and Michael D. Rich, "Truth Decay: An Initial Exploration of the Diminishing Role of Facts and Analysis in American Public Life," RAND Corporation, 2018, https://www.rand.org/pubs/research_reports/RR2314.html.

33. Karl Mannheim, *Ideology and Utopia: Introduction to the Sociology of Knowledge* (New York: Harcourt, Brace & Co, 1954), 168.

34. Techniques that artificially increase a site's page rank. See Karen Wickre, "Google Bombs are Our New Normal," *Wired*, October 11, 2017, https://www.wired.com/story/google-bombs-are-our-new-normal/.

35. "Featured Snippets in Search," Google, undated, https://support.google.com/webmasters/answer/6229325?hl=en.

36. Adam S. Cochran, answer to the question "What Search Algorithm Does DuckDuckGo Run in Order to Search? Is It Similar to PageRank?" Quora, May 20, 2015, https://www.quora.com/What-search-algorithm-does-DuckDuckGo-run-in-order-to-search-Is-it-similar-to-PageRank.

37. "Yandex Takes Leap with Its New Interactive Search Platform—First in Turkey," Yandex, June 5, 2013, https://yandex.com/company/blog/22/.

38. Jamie Condliffe, "Google's Algorithms May Feed You Fake News and Opinion as Fact," *MIT Technology Review*, March 6, 2017, https://www.technologyreview.com/s/603796/googles-algorithms-may-feed-you-fake-news-and-opinion-as-fact/.

39. Joshua Gillin, "The More Outrageous, the Better: How Clickbait Ads Make Money for Fake News Sites," PunditFact (PolitiFact), October 4, 2017, http://www.politifact.com/punditfact/article/2017/oct/04/more-outrageous-better-how-clickbait-ads-make-mone/.

40. Scott Spencer, "How We Fought Bad Ads, Sites and Scammers in 2016," Google, January 25, 2017, https://blog.google/topics/ads/how-we-fought-bad-ads-sites-and-scammers-2016/; and Nick Grudin, "Standards and Guidelines for Earning Money from Your Content on Facebook," Facebook, September 13, 2017, https://media.fb.com/2017/09/13/standards-and-guidelines-for-earning-money-from-your-content-on-facebook/. Monetization is a source of major controversy for established brands that find their ads on certain YouTube channels. A CNN investigation discovered that ads from approximately 300 companies (e.g., Adidas, Amazon, Cisco, Facebook, LinkedIn, Netflix, Nordstrom) and organizations (e.g., the US Department of Transportation, Centers for Disease Control and Prevention) "may have unknowingly helped finance" channels promoting white nationalism, Nazis ideology, "conspiracy theories," and pedophilia. See Paul P. Murphy, Kaya Yurieff, and Gianluca Mezzofiore, "YouTube Ran Ads from Hundreds of Brands on Extremist Channels," CNN Tech, April 20, 2018, http://money.cnn.com/2018/04/19/technology/youtube-ads-extreme-content-investigation/.

41. "Content Guidelines for Monetization," Facebook, undated, https://www.facebook.com/facebookmedia/get-started/monetization_contentguidelines.

42. Lucia Moses, "'The Underbelly of the Internet': How Content Ad Networks Fund Fake News," Digiday, November 28, 2016, https://digiday.com/media/underbelly-internet-fake-news-gets-funded/.

43. Liam Tung, "Google Alphabet's Schmidt: Here's Why We Can't Keep Fake News out of Search Results," ZDNet, November 23, 2017, http://www.zdnet.com/article/google-alphabets-schmidt-heres-why-we-cant-keep-fake-news-out-of-search-results/.

44. Ben Gomes, "Our Latest Quality Improvements for Search," The Keyword (Google), April 25, 2017, https://blog.google/products/search/our-latest-quality-improvements-search/; and Mark Bergen, "Google Rewrites Its Powerful Search Rankings to Bury Fake News," Bloomberg, April 25, 2017, https://www.bloomberg.com/news/articles/2017-04-25/google-rewrites-its-powerful-search-rankings-to-bury-fake-news.

45. Tung, "Google Alphabet's Schmidt."

46. In its report, the Office of the Director of National Intelligence labeled RT as the "Kremlin's principal international propaganda outlet" and cited its involvement with WikiLeaks in influencing the 2016 US election. See "Background to 'Assessing Russian Activities and Intentions in Recent US Elections': The Analytic Process and Cyber Incident Attribution," Office of the Director of National Intelligence, January 6, 2017, 3, https://www.dni.gov/files/documents/ICA_2017_01.pdf.

47. Danielle Ryan, "Google's De-Ranking of RT in Search Results is a Form of Censorship and Blatant Propaganda," RT, November 26, 2017, https://www.rt.com/op-edge/410981-google-rt-censorship-propaganda/.

48. Bing Pan, Helene Hembrooke, Thorsten Joachims, Lori Lorigo, Geri Gay, and Laura Granka, "In Google We Trust: Users' Decisions on Rank, Position, and Relevance," *Journal of Computer-Mediated Communication* 12, No. 3 (April 2007): 801–23. In addition, a report by Amy Gesenhues notes that a study by SurveyMonkey found that some individuals appear to trust search results labeled "Google" rather than "Bing," even when search results were swapped out. Taken together, research on individuals not scanning past the first page of search results, their preference for Google's brand, and Google's decision to de-rank results raises many questions regarding the depth of web users' information/knowledge-seeking habits. See Amy Gesenhues, "Study: Many Searchers Choose Google Over Bing Even When Google's Name is on Bing's Results," Search Engine Land, April 15, 2013, https://searchengineland.com/users-prefer-google-even-when-155682.

49. Engin Bozdag, "Bias in Algorithmic Filtering and Personalization," *Ethics and Information Technology* 15, No. 3 (September 2013): 209–27.

50. For example, Facebook came under attack for tagging as "child pornography" Nick Ut's award-winning 1972 Vietnam War photograph of then nine-year-old Phan Thi Kim Phuc fleeing from a napalm attack. This points to the inability of algorithms to clearly discriminate between types of information. See Mark Scott and Mike Isaac, "Facebook Restores Iconic Vietnam War Photo It Censored for Nudity," *New York Times*, September 9, 2016, https://www.nytimes.com/2016/09/10/technology/facebook-vietnam-war-photo-nudity.html. For another example, see Dutch Parliament member Marietje Schaake's video, which mentioned the word "torture" and was subsequently flagged by a Google algorithm as "spam" and removed from YouTube. Marietje Schaake, "Algorithms Have Become So Powerful We Need a Robust, Europe-Wide Response," *The Guardian*, April 4, 2018, https://www.theguardian.com/commentisfree/2018/apr/04/algorithms-powerful-europe-response-social-media.

51. Organization for Security and Co-operation in Europe, "Joint Declaration on Freedom of Expression and 'Fake News', Disinformation and Propaganda," March 3, 2017, 1, https://www.osce.org/fom/302796.

52. Martin C. Libicki writes that information warfare, "as a separate technique of waging war, does not exist." Libicki organizes seven distinct categories of information warfare, "each laying claim to the larger concept": command-and-control warfare, intelligence-based warfare, electronic warfare (radio-electronic or cryptographic techniques), psychological warfare (in which information is used to change the minds of friends, neutrals, and foes), "hacker" warfare (in which computer systems are attacked), economic information warfare (blocking information or channeling it to pursue economic dominance), and cyberwarfare ("a grab bag of futuristic scenarios"). See his *What is Information Warfare?* ([Washington, DC]: Center for Advanced Concepts and Technology, Institute for National Strategic Studies, National Defense University, 1995), http://www.dtic.mil/get-tr-doc/pdf?AD=ADA367662.

53. Isaac R. Porche III, Christopher Paul, Michael York, Chad C. Serena, Jerry M. Sollinger, Elliot Axelband, Endy M. Daehner, and Bruce Held, *Redefining Information Warfare Boundaries for an Army in a Wireless World* (Santa Monica, CA: RAND Corporation, 2013), xv, https://www.rand.org/pubs/monographs/MG1113.html.

54. Weedon, Nuland, and Stamos, "Information Operations and Facebook," 5.

55. Samantha Bradshaw and Philip N. Howard, "Troops, Trolls and Troublemakers: A Global Inventory of Organized Social Media Manipulation," Working Paper No. 2017.12, Computational Propaganda Research Project, University of Oxford, 2017, 4, http://comprop.oii.ox.ac.uk/wp-content/uploads/sites/89/2017/07/Troops-Trolls-and-Troublemakers.pdf.

56. Ibid.; Emerson T. Brooking and P.W. Singer, "War Goes Viral: How Social Media is being Weaponized Across the World," *The Atlantic*, November 2016, https://www.theatlantic.com/magazine/archive/2016/11/war-goes-viral/501125/; and Sara Fischer, "How Bots and Fake Accounts Work," Axios, October 31, 2017, https://www.axios.com/how-bots-and-fake-accounts-work-2503972339.html.

57. In her classic account of deception, Sissela Bok wrote that "deceptive messages, whether or not they are lies," are affected by self-deception, error, and "variations in the actual intent to deceive." Further, and this is central to the matter at hand, Bok identified three "filters"—thickness, distortion, and color—that alter how a message is experienced by *both the deceived and the deceivers*. Importantly, Bok stated that "someone who intends to deceive can work *with* these filters and manipulate them; he can play with the biases of some persons, the imagination of others, and on errors and confusion throughout the system." See her *Lying: Moral Choice in Public and Private Life* (New York: Vintage Books, 1978/1989), 15.

58. Bradshaw and Howard, "Troops, Trolls and Troublemakers," 3.

59. Lauren Etter, Vernon Silver, and Sarah Frier, "How Facebook's Political Unit Enables the Dark Art of Digital Propaganda," Bloomberg, December 21, 2017, https://www.bloomberg.com/news/features/2017-12-21/inside-the-facebook-team-helping-regimes-that-reach-out-and-crack-down. See also Facebook CEO Mark Zuckerberg's April 10, 2018 revelations before the Senate Committee on the Judiciary that Facebook not only collects data on nonusers for "security reasons," but doesn't provide any opt-out for non-Facebook subscribers. "Transcript of Zuckerberg's Appearance before House Committee," *Washington Post*, April 11, 2018, https://www.washingtonpost.com/news/the-switch/wp/2018/04/11/transcript-of-zuckerbergs-appearance-before-house-committee/.

60. See Ben Collins and Joseph Cox, "Jenna Abrams, Russia's Clown Troll Princess, Duped the Mainstream Media and the World," Daily Beast, November 2, 2017, https://www.thedailybeast.com/jenna-abrams-russias-clown-troll-princess-duped-the-mainstream-media-and-the-world; and Maya Kosoff, "The Russian Troll Farm that Weaponized Facebook Had American Boots on the Ground: The Shadowy Internet Research Agency Duped American Activists into Holding Protests and Self-Defense Classes," *Vanity Fair*, October 18, 2017, https://www.vanityfair.com/news/2017/10/the-russian-troll-farm-that-weaponized-facebook-had-american-boots-on-the-ground.

61. Collins and Cox, "Jenna Abrams."

62. Robert Booth, Matthew Weaver, Alex Hern, Stacee Smith, and Shaun Walker, "Russia Used Hundreds of Fake Accounts to Tweet about Brexit, Data Shows," *The Guardian*, November 14, 2017, https://www.theguardian.com/world/2017/nov/14/how-400-russia-run-fake-accounts-posted-bogus-brexit-tweets.

63. Samanth Subramanian, "Inside the Macedonian Fake-News Complex," *Wired*, February 15, 2017, https://www.wired.com/2017/02/veles-macedonia-fake-news/.

64. Alex Jones, *The Alex Jones Show (Infowars)*, episode of November 29, 2017 (podcast on iTunes), http://rss.infowars.com/20171129_Wed_Alex.mp3, at 1:40:34. See also *Cyberwar*, S02E01, titled "The Great Meme War," Viceland, October 3, 2017, https://www.viceland.com/en_us/video/cyberwar-the-great-meme-war/595f95afd978e31b73496a7e, where alt-right blogger and founder of GotNews Charles C. (Chuck) Johnson calls for the creation of a "citizen troll" army to make "journalism indistinguishable from trolling." Perhaps we can add "culture war" to the scope of IW and IO.

65. Office of the Director of National Intelligence, "Background to 'Assessing Russian Activities'"; Senate Intelligence Committee, "Facebook, Google, and Twitter Executives on Russia Election Interference," C-SPAN video of the hearing in Washington, DC, November 1, 2017, https://www.c-span.org/video/?436360-1/facebook-google-twitter-executives-testify-russias-influence-2016-election&live [the text of which is also available as Senate Report 105-1]; and Kent Walker and Richard Salgado, "Security and Disinformation in the U.S. 2016 Election," The Keyword (Google), October 20, 2017, https://www.blog.google/topics/public-policy/security-and-disinformation-us-2016-election/.

66. "Fake News: Five French Election Stories Debunked," BBC News, March 15, 2017, http://www.bbc.com/news/world-europe-39265777.

67. See, for example, Horand Knaup and Gerald Traufetter, "Innenministerium will Abwehrzentrum gegen Falschmeldungen einrichten" ("Ministry of the Interior Wants to Set Up a Defense Center against False Reports"), *Der Spiegel*, December 23, 2016, http://www.spiegel.de/netzwelt/netzpolitik/fake-news-bundesinnenministerium-will-abwehrzentrum-ein-

richten-a-1127174.html; and Peter Walker, "New National Security Unit Set Up to Tackle Fake News in UK," *The Guardian*, January 23, 2018, https://www.theguardian.com/politics/2018/jan/23/new-national-security-unit-will-tackle-spread-of-fake-news-in-uk.

68. Yasmeen Serhan, "Italy Scrambles to Fight Misinformation Ahead of Its Elections," *The Atlantic*, February 24, 2018, https://www.theatlantic.com/international/archive/2018/02/europe-fake-news/551972/.

69. Jon Gambrell, "Hack, Fake Story Expose Real Tensions Between Qatar, Gulf," Associated Press, May 24, 2017, https://apnews.com/f5da3293be1840a1954d48249f75394e.

70. Bruce Riedel, "The $110 Billion Arms Deal to Saudi Arabia is Fake News," Brookings Institution, June 5, 2017, https://www.brookings.edu/blog/markaz/2017/06/05/the-110-billion-arms-deal-to-saudi-arabia-is-fake-news/.

71. Russell Goldman, "Reading Fake News, Pakistani Minister Directs Nuclear Threat at Israel," *New York Times*, December 24, 2016, https://www.nytimes.com/2016/12/24/world/asia/pakistan-israel-khawaja-asif-fake-news-nuclear.html.

72. Carole Cadwalladr, "Revealed: Graphic Video Used by Cambridge Analytica to Influence Nigerian Election," *The Guardian*, April 4, 2018, https://www.theguardian.com/uk-news/2018/apr/04/cambridge-analytica-used-violent-video-to-try-to-influence-nigerian-election.

73. Luke Harding, "Former Trump Aide Approved 'Black Ops' to Help Ukraine President," *The Guardian*, April 5, 2018, https://www.theguardian.com/us-news/2018/apr/05/ex-trump-aide-paul-manafort-approved-black-ops-to-help-ukraine-president.

74. Rossalyn Warren, "Facebook is Ignoring Anti-Abortion Fake News," *New York Times*, November 10, 2017, https://www.nytimes.com/2017/11/10/opinion/facebook-fake-news-abortion.html. See also Laura Hazard Owen, "Can Facebook Beat Back the Fake News in Ireland's Upcoming Vote on Abortion?" NiemanLab, April 20, 2018, http://www.niemanlab.org/2018/04/can-facebook-beat-back-the-fake-news-in-irelands-upcoming-vote-on-abortion/.

75. John Dewey, *The Public and Its Problems: An Essay in Political Inquiry* (Chicago: Gateway Books, 1927/1946), 209.

76. "Validated Independent News," Project Censored, undated, https://projectcensored.org/category/validated-independent-news/. See also Andy Lee Roth and Project Censored, "Breaking the Corporate News Frame through Validated Independent News Online," in *Media Education for a Digital Generation*, eds. Julie Frechette and Rob Williams (New York: Routledge, 2016), 173–86.

77. The "Framework" is organized as "a cluster of interconnected core concepts" (or "frames") that include authority as constructed and contextual, information creation as a process, information as valuable, research as inquiry, scholarship as conversation, and searching as strategic exploration. See "Framework for Information Literacy for Higher Education," Association of College & Research Libraries (American Library Association), January 11, 2016, http://www.ala.org/acrl/standards/ilframework.

78. Ibid.

79. Barack Obama, "Executive Order 13721: Developing an Integrated Global Engagement Center to Support Government-Wide Counterterrorism Communications Activities Directed Abroad and Revoking Executive Order 13584," Federal Register, March 14, 2016, published March 17, 2016, https://www.federalregister.gov/documents/2016/03/17/2016-06250/developing-an-integrated-global-engagement-center-to-support-government-wide-counterterrorism.

80. It is not clear how the Global Engagement Center counters fake news on the Internet. See the Senate Committee on Armed Services, *National Defense Authorization Act for Fiscal Year 2017*, S. 2943, § 1287: Global Engagement Center, PL 114-328, December 23, 2016, Congress.gov, last updated December 23, 2016, https://www.congress.gov/bill/114th-congress/senate-bill/2943/text#toc-H533D0AE113D24D90A6BD9F8A0B9D679C. See also Samuel Mathias Ditlinger and Tom Field, with Andy Lee Roth and Mickey Huff, "US Quietly Established New 'Anti-Propaganda' Center," in *Censored 2018: Press Freedoms in a "Post-Truth" World*, eds. Andy Lee Roth and Mickey Huff with Project Censored (New York: Seven Stories Press, 2017), 71–73.

81. US House of Representatives Permanent Select Committee on Intelligence, "Russia Investigative Task Force Hearing with Former Secretary of Homeland Security Jeh Johnson," C-SPAN video of the hearing in Washington, DC, June 21, 2017, https://www.c-span.org/

video/?c4674447/trump-unwitting-agent-russia-2016-election; and the November 1, 2017 hearing by the Senate Intelligence Committee, "Facebook, Google, and Twitter Executives on Russia Election Interference." The latter hearing investigated "incendiary" Russian ads. See Nicholas Fandos, Cecilia Kang, and Mike Isaac, "House Intelligence Committee Releases Incendiary Russian Social Media Ads," *New York Times*, November 1, 2017, https://www.nytimes.com/2017/11/01/us/politics/russia-technology-facebook.html.

The 2015 House Committee on Foreign Affairs, *Confronting Russia's Weaponization of Information: Hearing Before the Committee on Foreign Affairs, House of Representatives*, 114-1, April 15, 2015 (Washington, DC: US Government Publishing Office, 2015), online at House.gov, https://docs.house.gov/meetings/FA/FA00/20150415/103320/HHRG-114-FA00-Transcript-20150415.pdf, undeservedly received less media scrutiny.

82. *SB-1424 Internet: Social Media: False Information Strategic Plans*, February 16, 2018, amended in the California State Senate, March 22, 2018, published on California Legislative Information on May 25, 2018, https://leginfo.legislature.ca.gov/faces/billTextClient.xhtml?bill_id=201720180SB1424.

83. Reuters Staff, "Macron Plans Law to Fight 'Fake News' in 2018," Reuters, January 3, 2018, https://www.reuters.com/article/us-france-macron/macron-plans-law-to-fight-fake-news-in-2018-idUSKBN1ES1LJ.

84. Angela Giuffrida, "Italians Asked to Report Fake News to Police in Run-Up to Election," *The Guardian*, January 19, 2018, https://www.theguardian.com/world/2018/jan/19/italians-asked-report-fake-news-police-run-up-election.

85. "Sweden to Create New Authority Tasked with Countering Disinformation," The Local, January 15, 2018, https://www.thelocal.se/20180115/sweden-to-create-new-authority-tasked-with-countering-disinformation.

86. Knaup and Traufetter, "Innenministerium will Abwehrzentrum gegen Falschmeldungen einrichten."

87. Walker, "New National Security Unit Set Up."

88. As this chapter goes to publication in May 2018, there is little public information available on this meeting.

89. Adam Jourdan, "China's Xi Says Internet Control Key to Stability," Reuters, April 21, 2018, https://www.reuters.com/article/us-china-internet/chinas-xi-says-internet-control-key-to-stability-idUSKBN1HS0BG.

90. Patrick Tucker, "Russia will Build Its Own Internet Directory, Citing US Information Warfare," Defense One, November 28, 2017, http://www.defenseone.com/technology/2017/11/russia-will-build-its-own-internet-directory-citing-us-information-warfare/142822/.

91. "Who We Are, What We Do," The Trust Project, 2017, https://thetrustproject.org.

92. Anna Gonzalez and David Schulz, "Helping Truth with Its Boots: Accreditation as an Antidote to Fake News," *Yale Law Journal Forum*, October 9, 2017: 315–36, https://www.yalelawjournal.org/pdf/GonzalezandSchulz_b6fvqdro.pdf.

93. "About," MisinfoCon, undated, https://misinfocon.com/about. One fly in the ointment here is that "misinformation" does not distinguish between disinformation, propaganda, and other conditions of information.

94. Hamilton 68 monitors "accounts likely controlled by Russian government influence operations," "'patriotic' pro-Russia users that are loosely connected or unconnected to the Russian government, but which amplify themes promoted by Russian government media," and "users who have been influenced by the first two groups and who are extremely active in amplifying Russian media themes. These users may or may not understand themselves to be part of a pro-Russian social network." For additional details on methods, see "The Methodology of the Hamilton 68 Dashboard," Alliance for Securing Democracy, August 7, 2017, http://securingdemocracy.gmfus.org/publications/methodology-hamilton-68-dashboard.

95. Shelley Podolny, "If an Algorithm Wrote This, How Would You Even Know?" *New York Times*, March 7, 2015, https://www.nytimes.com/2015/03/08/opinion/sunday/if-an-algorithm-wrote-this-how-would-you-even-know.html; and Joe Keohane, "What News-Writing Bots Mean

for the Future of Journalism," *Wired*, February 16, 2017, https://www.wired.com/2017/02/robots-wrote-this-story/.

96. Organization for Security and Co-operation in Europe, "Joint Declaration."
97. "The OTA Legacy," Office of Technology Assessment, Princeton University, undated, https://www.princeton.edu/~ota/.
98. Michael N. Schmitt, ed., *Tallinn Manual 2.0 on the International Law Applicable to Cyber Operations*, prepared by the International Groups of Experts at the invitation of the NATO Cooperative Cyber Defence Centre of Excellence (New York: Cambridge University Press, 2017).
99. Schaake, "Algorithms Have Become So Powerful."
100. "Algorithmic Accountability: Applying the Concept to Different Country Contexts," World Wide Web Foundation, July 2017, https://webfoundation.org/docs/2017/07/Algorithms_Report_WF.pdf; and Organization for Security and Co-operation in Europe, "Joint Declaration," 1.
101. Organization for Security and Co-operation in Europe, "Joint Declaration," 5.
102. Dewey, *The Public and Its Problems*, 181.
103. Stephanie Craft, Seth Ashley, and Adam Maksl, "News Media Literacy and Conspiracy Theory Endorsement," *Communication and the Public 2*, No. 4 (2017): 388–401, 388, 395.
104. Soroush Vosoughi, Deb Roy, and Sinan Aral, "The Spread of True and False News Online," *Science 359*, No. 6380 (2018): 1146–51, 1146.
105. Jan Schaffer, "Citizen Media: Fad or the Future of News?—The Rise and Prospects of Hyperlocal Journalism," J-Lab: The Institute for Interactive Journalism (Philip Merrill College of Journalism, University of Maryland, College Park), 2007, 7, http://www.j-lab.org/wp-content/pdfs/citizen-media-report.pdf.
106. Dewey, *The Public and Its Problems*, 158.

Acknowledgments

Mickey Huff and Andy Lee Roth

We are indebted to everyone who helped bring *Censored 2019*—the Project's 26th annual book—to completion.

This book represents the collective efforts of multiple groups of people, including the courageous journalists who report on vital issues beyond the pale of the corporate press, and the independent news outlets that make these reports available to the public; the faculty evaluators and student researchers at the Project's college and university affiliate campuses who help us to cover the increasingly extensive networked news commons; the authors who wrote chapters and sections of *Censored 2019* to inspire us with challenging questions and new perspectives; and our international panel of judges who ensured that this year's Top 25 list includes only the best, most significant validated independent news stories.

We are fortunate to work with Michael Tencer, who is an extraordinary editor. His encyclopedic knowledge, penetrating eye, and keen ear sharpened and improved this volume. We are also thankful for the continued expertise of Veronica Liu, who is always there when we need her.

At Seven Stories Press in New York, we thank our publisher, Dan Simon, along with Stewart Cauley, Sanina Clark, Jon Gilbert, Lauren Hooker, Noah Kumin, Allison Paller, Silvia Stramenga, Elena Watson, and Ruth Weiner, all of whom have our respect and gratitude for their commitment to publishing the Project's research.

Anson Stevens-Bollen provided the strikingly original cover art for *Censored 2019*. We also thank Khalil Bendib, whose cartoons again grace our book with his inimitable wit and wisdom.

The Media Freedom Foundation (MFF)'s board of directors, whose members are identified below, help to sustain Project Censored and its mission by providing invaluable counsel and crucial organizational structure.

The Project's mission benefits from the resolute guidance and deep insights of our webmaster, Adam Armstrong. In addition to making sure the Project's research and reports remain accessible to our global audience, Adam oversees the production of the Project's online video series, as well as our radio and podcast of *The Project Censored Show*; and he maintains the operation of our Patreon page.

We thank Christopher Oscar and Doug Hecker of Hole in the Media Productions for their ongoing support of the Project as they work with and inspire a new generation of documentary filmmakers. In this same vein, we thank MFF board member Nolan Higdon, who this past year has followed their lead by starting, with his student interns, a new Project documentary focused on the phenomenon of fake news.

We are grateful to the friends and supporters of *The Project Censored Show* as we embark on our eighth year of broadcasting. We thank senior producer Anthony Fest and our live broadcast engineers at KPFA Pacifica Radio. We also wish to thank everyone who supports the overlapping missions of Project Censored and Pacifica, including Bob Baldock and Ken Preston, for their tireless work on public events, and the 40-plus stations from Maui to New York that air the program each week. Peter Phillips, the program's cofounder and original cohost with Mickey Huff, continues to host several shows each year, while Nolan Higdon, Nicholas Baham III, Desiree McSwain, Aimee Casey, and Chase Palmieri comprise our expanding on-air team. Mitch Scorza, at California State University, East Bay, and Dennis Murphy, at KPCA in Petaluma, serve as steadfast associate producers.

We are grateful to the people who have hosted Project Censored events or helped to spread the word about the Project's mission in 2017–2018, including John Bertucci and videographer Dennis Murphy of Petaluma Community Access Television; John Crowley, the late Paul Coffman, and everyone at Aqus Café; Dave Adams and James Bray at QPS, Inc.; Larry Figueroa, Jennifer Jensen, and the crew at Lagunitas Brewing Company; Chase Palmieri and family at Risibisi; Raymond Lawrason, Grace Bogart, and all at Copperfield's Books; Kevin Herbert at Common Cents; James Preston Allen and the team at *Random Lengths News* in San Pedro, as well as Jason Zaragoza at the Association of Alternative Newsmedia (AAN); Michael

Nagler, Stephanie Van Hook, and the Metta Center for Nonviolence; Margli and Phil Auclair, Rick Sterling, and everyone at the Mount Diablo Peace and Justice Center in Lafayette; Attila Nagy, the Petaluma Progressives, and all those at the Peace and Justice Center of Sonoma County; the Sociology Social Justice and Activism Club at Sonoma State University; Amy Orr, president of the Pacific Sociological Association, who invited us to make a featured presentation at the 2018 PSA meetings in Long Beach, as well as Heidi Esbensen of Portland State University, who served as our session's presider; Steve Macek at North Central College, and our allies in the Union for Democratic Communications; D'vorah Grenn at Napa Valley College; Mark Crispin Miller; Pat Fahey; Marc Pilisuk; Davey D; Abby Martin of *The Empire Files* and Media Roots; Mnar Muhawesh and the team at MintPress News; Eleanor Goldfield of *Act Out!*; Free Speech TV; Lee Camp and *Redacted Tonight*; Krish Mohan; Sharyl Attkisson of *Full Measure*; Arlene Engelhardt and Mary Glenney, the hosts of *From a Woman's Point of View*; Eric Draitser and *CounterPunch Radio*; Bill Bigelow (Rethinking Schools), Deborah Menkart (Teaching for Change), and everyone involved in the Zinn Education Project; Michael Sukhov; John Barbour; J.P. Sottile (the Newsvandal); Jon Gold; John Collins of St. Lawrence University and the team at Weave News; Chase Palmieri, Jared Fesler, and the Tribe at Tribeworthy.com; Maggie Jacoby, Betsy Gomez, and everyone involved in the Banned Books Week Coalition, including those at the National Coalition Against Censorship and the American Library Association's Office for Intellectual Freedom; Ralph Nader and the Center for Study of Responsive Law; and Peter Ludes, Hektor Haarkötter, and Marlene Nunnendorf at the German Initiative on News Enlightenment—each of whom helps the Project to reach a broader audience.

We continue to be grateful for our relationships with the Action Coalition for Media Education (ACME) and the graduate program in Media Literacy and Digital Culture at Sacred Heart University (SHU), as well as our collaborative effort, the Global Critical Media Literacy Project (gcml.org), which officially launched at the Media Freedom Summit for Project Censored's 40th anniversary in October 2016.

In anticipation of a great event in October 2018, we thank everyone helping to organize Project Censored's Media Freedom Summit 2.0:

Critical Media Literacy for Social Justice at the College of Marin, especially Susan Rahman, Dawn Lucier, Elle Dimopoulos, Lakhvir Singh, and Jenifer Satariano. We also thank the College's senior vice president of student learning and student services, Jonathan Eldridge, for his support, as well as the United Professors of Marin Executive Council. We also thank Mary Fitzpatrick, adjunct college skills instructor at the College of Marin, for editorial assistance on our annual book.

At Diablo Valley College, Mickey thanks Lisa Martin, and History Department cochairs Matthew Powell and Melissa Jacobson, as well as John Corbally, Bridgitte Schaffer, Lyn Krause, Greg Tilles, Katie Graham, Mary Ann Irwin, Marcelle Levine, Adam Bessie, David Vela, Mark Akiyama, Jacob Van Vleet, Steve Johnson, Jeremy Cloward, Amer Araim, John Kropf, Ted Blair, Scott MacDougall, Dorrie Mazzone, Toni Fannin, Adam Perry, Mary Mazzocco, Albert Ponce, and Sangha Niyogi, along with everyone involved in the Social Justice program, English and Social Sciences dean Obed Vazquez, vice president of student services Newin Orante, and the Student Equity Committee. Mickey also thanks current and former teaching and research assistants and Project interns Stephanie Richter, Kelly Van Boekhout, Lewis Joseph Smith, Isela Chavez, Bethany Surface, Amber Yang, Gavin Rock, Claudia Bistrane, Jason Bud, and Aimee Casey. At California State University, East Bay, Mickey specifically thanks Danuta Sawka and the chair, Mary Cardaras, in the Department of Communications; and at Sonoma State University, Mickey thanks Emily Kyle, Monique Morovat, Damont Partida, and the chair, James Dean, all in the Department of Sociology.

Nolan Higdon, the Project's critical media literacy officer who represents the Project as faculty at several Bay Area colleges, thanks the following students and interns for their work in support of the Project this past year: Stephanie Razo, Ryan Wilson, Gabe Reyna, Caitlin Rokov, Brendan Wilson, Janice Domingo, Jamie Silva, Kristen van Zyll de Jong, Luke Zakedis, Scott Ault, Nia Williams, Daniel McGuire, Justin Mutch, Chelsea Corby, Kestutis Rushing, Michael Fisher, Katherine Epps, Janelle Christine Laberinto, Niklavs Zols, Caitlyn Harper, Tera Thompson-Garner, Monika Richards, Mariel McMindes, Claudia Cortez, Jamie DaSilva, Vincent Farley, Allison Weseman, Gabriel

Cox, Sage Healy, Laura Flores, Eliza Otto, Matthew Aldea, Samantha Buono, Stephanie Maniche, Jessica Chapman, Gabriella Custodio, Ananya Hindocha, Jenny Hill, Alexandra Archuleta, Mike Hotaling, Jorge Ayala, Mark Yolangco, and Josine Torres.

Mickey would also like to thank all of his students for the inspiration they provide, as they are a constant reminder of the possibilities of the future and how privileged we are as educators to have such an amazing role in contributing to the public sphere.

Andy thanks the students from the Honors section of his Fall 2017 Introduction to Sociology course at Citrus College. At Citrus, Dana Hester, Brian Waddington, Gayle Allen, and Olivia Canales provided the best support and collegial inspiration.

Continuing financial support from donors sustains the Project. This year, we are especially thankful to Marcia Annenberg, Sharyl Attkisson, Margli and Phil Auclair, Sandra Cioppa, Dwain A. Deets, Jan De Deka, Michael Hansen, Gillian G. Hearst, Neil Joseph, Sheldon Levy, Sergio and Gaye Lub, Robert Manning, James March, Sandra Maurer, Harry Mersmann, Nate Mudd, David Nelson, Christopher Oscar, Lynn and Leonard Riepenhoff, John and Lyn Roth, Basja Samuelson, Marc Sapir, David Schultz, T.M. Scruggs, Bill Simon, Elaine Wellin, Derrick West and Laurie Dawson, and Raymond Ziarno.

With sadness, we note the passing of two giants of media scholarship and independent journalism, Edward S. Herman and Robert Parry. Each has been a champion for a free press and an inspiration to all of us at Project Censored.

Mickey thanks his family for their ongoing support, especially his wife, Meg, for her amazing work, counsel, and patience; and Andy thanks Liz Boyd for encouragement and inspiration.

Finally, we thank you, our readers, who continue to cherish a truly free press. Together, we make a difference.

MEDIA FREEDOM FOUNDATION/PROJECT CENSORED BOARD OF DIRECTORS

Nicholas Baham III, Ben Boyington, Kenn Burrows, Allison Butler, Mary Cardaras, Doug Hecker, Nolan Higdon, Mickey Huff (president), Christopher Oscar, Susan Rahman (vice president), Andy Lee

Roth, T.M. Scruggs, Bri Silva, and Elaine Wellin; with bookkeeper Michael Smith.

PROJECT CENSORED 2017–18 JUDGES

ROBIN ANDERSEN. Professor of Communication and Media Studies, Fordham University. She has written dozens of scholarly articles and is author or co-author of four books, including *A Century of Media, A Century of War* (2006), winner of the Alpha Sigma Nu Book Award. She recently published *The Routledge Companion to Media and Humanitarian Action* (2017), and *HBO's* Treme *and the Stories of the Storm: From New Orleans as Disaster Myth to Groundbreaking Television* (2017). Writes media criticism and commentary for the media watch group Fairness & Accuracy In Reporting (FAIR), The Vision Machine, and the *Antenna* blog.

JULIE ANDRZEJEWSKI. Professor Emeritus of Human Relations and cofounder of the Social Responsibility program, St. Cloud State University. Publications include *Social Justice, Peace, and Environmental Education* (2009).

OLIVER BOYD-BARRETT. Professor Emeritus of Media and Communications, Bowling Green State University and California State Polytechnic University, Pomona. Publications include *The International News Agencies* (1980), *Contra-flow in Global News: International and Regional News Exchange Mechanisms* (1992), *The Globalization of News* (1998), *Media in Global Context* (2009), *News Agencies in the Turbulent Era of the Internet* (2010), *Hollywood and the CIA: Cinema, Defense, and Subversion* (2011), *Media Imperialism* (2015), and *Western Mainstream Media and the Ukraine Crisis* (2017).

KENN BURROWS. Faculty member at the Institute for Holistic Health Studies, Department of Health Education, San Francisco State University. Founder and director of the Holistic Health Learning Center and producer of the biennial conference, Future of Health Care.

ERNESTO CARMONA. Journalist and writer. Chief correspondent, teleSUR Chile. Director, Santiago Circle of Journalists. President of the Investigation Commission on Attacks Against Journalists, Latin American Federation of Journalists (CIAP-FELAP).

ELLIOT D. COHEN. Professor of Philosophy and chair of the Humanities Department, Indian River State College. Editor and founder of the *International Journal of Applied Philosophy*. Recent books include *Technology of Oppression: Preserving Freedom and Dignity in an Age of Mass, Warrantless Surveillance* (2014), *Theory and Practice of Logic-Based Therapy: Integrating Critical Thinking and Philosophy into Psychotherapy* (2013), and *Philosophy, Counseling, and Psychotherapy* (2013).

GEOFF DAVIDIAN. Investigative reporter, war correspondent, legal affairs analyst, editor, photojournalist, data analyst, educator, and media captain for Wisconsin gubernatorial candidate Mike McCabe. Founding publisher and editor of the *Putnam Pit* and *Milwaukee Press*. Contributor to Reuters, UPI, magazines, newspapers, and online publications.

JOSÉ MANUEL DE PABLOS COELLO. Professor of Journalism, Universidad de La Laguna (Tenerife, Canary Islands, Spain). Founder of *Revista Latina de Comunicación Social* (RLCS), a scientific journal based out of the Laboratory of Information Technologies and New Analysis of Communication at Universidad de La Laguna.

LENORE FOERSTEL. Women for Mutual Security, facilitator of the Progressive International Media Exchange (PRIME).

ROBERT HACKETT. Professor Emeritus of Communication, Simon Fraser University, Vancouver. Codirector of NewsWatch Canada since 1993. Cofounder of Media Democracy Days (2001) and OpenMedia.ca (2007). Publications include *Remaking Media: The Struggle to Democratize Public Communication* (with W.K. Carroll, 2006) and *Journalism and Climate Crisis: Public Engagement, Media Alternatives* (with S. Forde, S. Gunster, and K. Foxwell-Norton, 2017).

KEVIN HOWLEY. Professor of Media Studies, DePauw University. His work has appeared in the *Journal of Radio Studies, Journalism: Theory, Practice and Criticism, Social Movement Studies*, and *Television and New Media*. He is author of *Community Media: People, Places, and Communication Technologies* (2005), and editor of *Understanding Com-*

munity Media (2010) and *Media Interventions* (2013). His latest book is *Drones: Media Discourse and the Public Imagination* (2018).

NICHOLAS JOHNSON.* Author, *How to Talk Back to Your Television Set* (1970). Commissioner, Federal Communications Commission (1966–1973). Former media and cyber law professor, University of Iowa College of Law. More online at www.nicholasjohnson.org.

CHARLES L. KLOTZER. Founder, editor, and publisher emeritus of *St. Louis Journalism Review* and *FOCUS/Midwest*. The *St. Louis Journalism Review* has been transferred to Southern Illinois University, Carbondale, and is now the *Gateway Journalism Review*. Klotzer remains active at the *Review*.

NANCY KRANICH. Lecturer, School of Communication and Information, and special projects librarian, Rutgers University. Past president of the American Library Association (ALA), and convener of the ALA Center for Civic Life. Author of *Libraries and Democracy: The Cornerstones of Liberty* (2001) and "Libraries and Civic Engagement" (2012).

DEEPA KUMAR. Associate Professor of Journalism and Media Studies, Rutgers University. Author of *Outside the Box: Corporate Media, Globalization, and the UPS Strike* (2007) and *Islamophobia and the Politics of Empire* (2012). Currently working on a book on the cultural politics of the war on terror.

MARTIN LEE. Investigative journalist and author. Cofounder of Fairness & Accuracy In Reporting, and former editor of FAIR's magazine, *Extra!*. Director of Project CBD, a medical science information nonprofit. Author of *Smoke Signals: A Social History of Marijuana—Medical, Recreational, and Scientific* (2012), *The Beast Reawakens: Fascism's Resurgence from Hitler's Spymasters to Today's Neo-Nazi Groups and Right-Wing Extremists* (2000), and *Acid Dreams: The Complete Social History of LSD: The CIA, the Sixties, and Beyond* (with B. Shlain, 1985).

DENNIS LOO. Professor of Sociology, California State Polytechnic University, Pomona. Co-editor (with Peter Phillips) of *Impeach the President: The Case Against Bush and Cheney* (2006).

PETER LUDES. Professor of Mass Communication, Jacobs University, Bremen, 2002–2017. Visiting Professor at the University of Cologne, 2018–2021. Founder of the German Initiative on News Enlightenment (1997) at the University of Siegen (Project Censored, Germany). Recent publications include *Brutalisierung und Banalisierung Asoziale und soziale Netze* (Brutalization and Banalization in Asocial and Social Networks) (Springer Essentials, 2018) and "Distorted Knowledge and Repressive Power," in *Media, Ideology and Hegemony*, ed. Savaş Çoban (Brill, 2018).

WILLIAM LUTZ. Professor Emeritus of English, Rutgers University. Former editor of the *Quarterly Review of Doublespeak*. Author of *Doublespeak: From Revenue Enhancement to Terminal Living: How Government, Business, Advertisers, and Others Use Language to Deceive You* (1989), *The Cambridge Thesaurus of American English* (1994), *The New Doublespeak: Why No One Knows What Anyone's Saying Anymore* (1996), and *Doublespeak Defined* (1999).

SILVIA LAGO MARTÍNEZ. Professor of Social Research Methodology and codirector, Research Program on Information Society at the Gino Germani Research Institute, Faculty of Social Sciences, Universidad de Buenos Aires.

CONCHA MATEOS. Professor of Journalism, Department of Communication Sciences, Universidad Rey Juan Carlos, Spain. Journalist for radio, television, and political organizations in Spain and Latin America. Coordinator for Project Censored research in Europe and Latin America.

MARK CRISPIN MILLER. Professor of Media, Culture, and Communication, Steinhardt School of Culture, Education, and Human Development, New York University. Author, editor, and activist.

JACK L. NELSON.* Distinguished Professor Emeritus, Graduate School of Education, Rutgers University. Former member, Committee on Academic Freedom and Tenure, American Association of University Professors. Recipient, Academic Freedom Award, National Council for Social Studies. Author of 17 books, including *Critical Issues in Education: Dialogues and Dialectics*, 8th ed. (with S. Palonsky and M.R. McCarthy, 2013), *Human Impact of Natural Disasters* (with V.O. Pang and W.R. Fernekes, 2010), and about 200 articles.

PETER PHILLIPS. Professor of Political Sociology, Sonoma State University, since 1994. Director, Project Censored, 1996–2010. President, Media Freedom Foundation, 2010–2016. Editor or co-editor of 14 editions of *Censored*. Co-editor (with Dennis Loo) of *Impeach the President: The Case Against Bush and Cheney* (Seven Stories Press, 2006). Author of *Giants: The Global Power Elite* (Seven Stories Press, 2018), as well as four chapters in recent *Censored* yearbooks.

T.M. SCRUGGS. Professor Emeritus (and token ethnomusicologist), University of Iowa. Executive producer, the Real News Network.

NANCY SNOW. Pax Mundi Professor of Public Diplomacy, Kyoto University of Foreign Studies, Japan. Professor Emeritus of Communications, California State University, Fullerton. Public affairs and media relations advisor to Langley Esquire, a leading Tokyo public affairs firm. Author or editor of 11 books, including *Japan's Information War* (2016) and *The Routledge Handbook of Critical Public Relations* (with J. L'Etang, D. McKie, and J. Xifra, 2015).

SHEILA RABB WEIDENFELD.* President of DC Productions Ltd. Emmy Award–winning television producer. Former press secretary to Betty Ford.

ROB WILLIAMS. Founding president of the Action Coalition for Media Education (ACME). Teaches media, communications, global studies, and journalism at the University of Vermont and Champlain College. Author of numerous articles on critical media literacy education. Publisher of the *Vermont Independent* online news journal. Co-editor of *Media Education for a Digital Generation* (with J. Frechette, 2016) and *Most Likely to Secede* (with R. Miller, 2013), about the Vermont independence movement.

*Indicates having been a Project Censored judge since our founding in 1976.

ANNUAL REPORT FROM THE MEDIA FREEDOM FOUNDATION PRESIDENT

As we conclude another volume in the *Censored* series with Seven Stories Press in New York, there are myriad developments in politics and business that present growing threats to our press freedoms and civil liberties, in the United States and around the world. Yet there is also much to embrace and celebrate as many individuals and organizations rise to the occasion, fighting against the fake news invasion and the impending civic collapse it could bring. While it is true we have many challenges to face, we also have substantial tools to help us meet those challenges and even transcend them.

In the past two years, public interest in so-called "fake news" has spiked. In that time, so too have invitations for the Project to speak about our work fighting censorship and raising awareness around critical media literacy education as an antidote to propaganda. The number one question we are *still* asked when we speak around the country is, "Whom do you trust in the news media?" Although there is no single, simple *answer* to this question, there is a *process*—one we have taught for more than 40 years now—centered around critical media literacy and involving fact-checking, source transparency and veracity, and basic critical thinking skills. It is not up to anyone to tell the public *what* to think or whom to trust. It is, however, our job as educators to help people understand *how* to think about the news, including how to form critical questions about news content and how to establish whether or not a news outlet's coverage of any specific news story or issue is trustworthy. More specifically, we are working to help empower not only our students but also the general public to exercise good judgment about the veracity of news stories, based on the aforementioned critical pedagogical principles.

As Andy Lee Roth and I noted in the introduction to this volume, during the 1938 "War of the Worlds" broadcast, "'critical ability,' employed by wary audience members who successfully 'checked up' on the broadcast's veracity, saved the day, as it were, preventing the eruption of widespread panic." We need to apply similar critical skills today. The age of radio gave way to the rise of the screen, from movies to television, and now from the Internet to the personal screens of our mobile devices, which persistently buzz to alert us to happenings in the outside world. As with the "smart" phones that so many of us bring along everywhere we go, we need to keep in constant contact with our critical ability to "check up" on the news we consume. As Project Censored develops to meet both new technological challenges, such as digital manipulation, and other, enduring forms of propaganda and censorship, it seems obvious that the work we have been doing since 1976 is now more necessary than ever.

When Carl Jensen founded Project Censored at Sonoma State University (SSU) more than four decades ago, his mission was to report on the news that didn't make the news while analyzing the reasons for those omissions. Twenty years later, Peter Phillips, Jensen's successor as director, expanded the vision and scope of the Project. In 2000, Phillips created the Media Freedom Foundation (MFF), a 501(c)(3) nonprofit organization, to oversee and promote the mission of Project Censored and to ensure its independence. Phillips grew the Project and began expanding beyond the borders of SSU as early as 2003. In 2010, Phillips, along with Andy Lee Roth and I, expanded our educational outreach to colleges across the United States through Project Censored's Campus Affiliates Program. Since 2012, I have worked with associate director Andy Lee Roth on producing the annual *Censored* volumes, working in conjunction with our academic affiliates and civically-engaged community allies.

Since 2010, the Project has operated independently of any specific campus, being funded exclusively from donations raised through the MFF—which is why we depend on our readers for various types of support, including especially financial contributions. Thanks to this support, we can continue to promote critical media literacy through an ever-growing array of platforms and public outreach programs. One of the most significant of these is *The Project Censored Show*, a weekly public affairs program that Phillips and I began in 2010, the same year I became the Project's third director. The show now airs on nearly 50 stations around the United States, from Maui to New York, and has a staff of ten, including cohosts, producers, and interns, as well as a growing audience both in terrestrial radio and the podcast world. Although most of the broadcast staff work as volunteers, production of our weekly show also depends on resources that come out of the Project's limited financial budget.

Beyond the annual book, weekly radio show, and Campus Affiliates Program, we are increasingly making use of film and video to heighten the Project's impact. Christopher Oscar and Doug Hecker's *Project Censored The Movie: Ending the Reign of Junk Food News*, the second feature film about the Project, debuted at film festivals in 2013 and won numerous awards. Both *Project Censored The Movie* and its predecessor, Steven Keller's *Is the Press Really Free?* (1998), are excellent for community and classroom use and are available online. They helped inspire our new video series, produced by Project Censored's Nolan Higdon and his student interns, with the assistance of our webmaster, Adam Armstrong, and they serve as important models for our next film project, which focuses on the challenge of fake news and what is to be done about it.

As with the radio programs, the film projects are areas where the Project could use more financial support. Interested parties can donate to these multimedia endeavors through projectcensored.org, or directly at our Patreon page at patreon.com/projectcensored.

Over the years, MFF has supported media literacy education in many ways alongside the direct work of Project Censored. In 2015, MFF members oversaw and assisted in the creation of a joint educational effort, the Global Critical Media Literacy Project (GCMLP), with the Action Coalition for Media Education (ACME) and the graduate program in Media Literacy and Digital Culture at Sacred Heart University. The GCMLP website is an online platform for faculty and students to bring their research, essays, and video content to a wider public. Through the website, we also make available the GCMLP's *Educators' Resource Guide*, which members of the aforementioned parties, including Project Censored, co-edited and co-authored.

In addition, MFF continues to partner with numerous community organizations, cosponsoring many public events in efforts to raise awareness of the importance of a truly free press. The Project continues to support anti-censorship efforts, including Banned Books Week, the National Coalition Against Censorship, Open the Government, and Government Information Watch. In collaboration with these and additional, similarly aligned organizations, we promote awareness of censorship and petition government agencies and educational institutions in support of transparency, academic freedom, and free expression.

In 2016, the MFF board elected me as its second president. With that appointment came a growing set of responsibilities, not least of which is the task of propelling the Project into the future and ensuring its sustainability for the next generation. Of course, we welcome a time when Project Censored would no longer be necessary. Unfortunately, given the state of our so-called free press, and the themes explored in this volume, that may be a distant prospect. In the meantime, we have our work cut out for us.

Project Censored persists in its many endeavors through MFF, but we cannot do so without the dedication of a small but committed core group, including one part-time staff member, bookkeeper, and webmaster. Most of the people who work with us do so as a labor of love, with little to no financial compensation, but that alone is not enough to sustain the Project. Over the past few years, we have built up a modest number of dedicated monthly supporters (most of whom pledge five to ten dollars per month) and a smaller pool of generous donors. MFF does not receive or accept corporate funding or advertising money—not only to avoid conflicts of interest, but also to remain truly independent. As a result, over the years, many luminaries have heralded Project Censored's work and significance, including I.F. Stone, Walter Cronkite, Ralph Nader, Diane Ravitch, Noam Chomsky, Howard Zinn, Medea Benjamin, Daniel Ellsberg, Henry Giroux, Peter Kuznick, and Naomi Wolf, to name just a few.

Nevertheless, remaining truly independent comes with financial consequences that increasingly challenge the Project's sustainability. Despite the Project's long and vaunted history, financial pressures increasingly push us to focus on fundraising efforts in order to continue and expand the Project's vital work. We do all that we do on a five-figure budget, but in order to sustain all that we do we must double our current support levels.

In light of these practical realities, I humbly ask for support for our educational endeavors, as we work with hundreds of students and dozens of faculty at colleges and universities around the United States each year in an ongoing effort to increase critical media literacy and support a truly free and independent press. Our students learn about critical media literacy and the value of a free press through our Validated Independent News curriculum, which teaches them to think critically about media and to research and vet news stories while honing their journalistic skills. Furthermore, our Junk Food News and News Abuse curricula continue to show students how to distinguish sensationalist stories from substantive ones, and to detect, deconstruct, and counter increasingly sophisticated forms of propaganda while recognizing both Junk Food News and News Abuse as forms of censorship. Our model is one of inclusion and cooperation. We cannot do all that we do alone, nor do we want to. We need all the help we can get to create a more well-informed, and thus better, world for our posterity.

It is my assumption that you, dear reader—whether you are holding this book in your hands or reading it online—appreciate the craft of research and writing, as well as the importance of critical thinking and higher education. It is my hope that you will consider supporting Project Censored's work however you can. Whether that means purchasing a book for yourself, a family member, or friend, or donating a copy to your library or school; becoming a monthly supporter; or, for those who are more financially well-endowed, making a tax-deductible donation, your financial support ensures that Project Censored will be able to continue fighting the fake news invasion and media censorship in its many guises. Through your support, we will continue to advocate for the maintenance of a free press and to educate the next generation of intrepid muckraking journalists so that, together, we can create a more informed, inspired, and equitable society.

Sincerely,

Mickey Huff
President, Media Freedom Foundation
Director, Project Censored

HOW TO SUPPORT PROJECT CENSORED

NOMINATE A STORY

To nominate a *Censored* story, send us a copy of the article and include the name of the source publication, the date that the article appeared, and the page number. For news stories published on the Internet, forward the URL to mickey@projectcensored.org or andy@projectcensored.org. The deadline for nominating *Censored* stories is March 15 of each year.

Criteria for Project Censored news story nominations:

A censored news story reports information that the public has a right and a need to know, but to which the public has had limited access.

The news story is recent, having been first reported no earlier than one year ago. For *Censored 2019* the Top 25 list includes stories reported between April 2017 and March 2018. Thus, stories submitted for *Censored 2020* should be no older than April 2018.

The story has clearly defined concepts and solid, verifiable documentation. The story's claims should be supported by evidence—the more controversial the claims, the stronger the evidence necessary.

The news story has been published, either electronically or in print, in a publicly circulated newspaper, journal, magazine, newsletter, or similar publication from either a domestic or foreign source.

MAKE A TAX-DEDUCTABLE DONATION

Project Censored is supported by the Media Freedom Foundation, a 501(c)(3) nonprofit organization. We depend on tax-deductible donations to continue our work. To support our efforts on behalf of independent journalism and freedom of information, send checks to the address below or donate online at projectcensored.org. Your generous donations help us to oppose news censorship and promote media literacy.

Media Freedom Foundation
PO Box 750940
Petaluma, CA 94975
mickey@projectcensored.org
andy@projectcensored.org
Phone: (707) 241-4596

ABOUT THE EDITORS

MICKEY HUFF is director of Project Censored and the president of the Media Freedom Foundation. He has edited or co-edited ten volumes of Censored and contributed numerous chapters to these annuals since 2008. He has also co-authored essays on media and propaganda for other scholarly publications. He is professor of social science and history at Diablo Valley College, where he cochairs the History Department; he is also a lecturer in the Communications Department at California State University, East Bay, and has taught the sociology of media at Sonoma State University. Huff is executive producer and cohost of The Project Censored Show, the weekly syndicated program that originates from KPFA in Berkeley. He is a cofounding member of the Global Critical Media Literacy Project (gcml.org), sits on the advisory board for the Media Literacy and Digital Culture graduate program at Sacred Heart University, and serves on the editorial board for the journal Secrecy and Society. Huff works with the national outreach committee of Banned Books Week, the American Library Association, and the National Coalition Against Censorship, of which Project Censored is a member. He is the critical media literacy consultant for the educational Internet startup Tribeworthy.com. He is sought by media outlets from around the world for interviews on critical media literacy, propaganda, censorship issues, and contemporary historiography in the United States. He is a longtime musician and composer and lives with his family in Northern California.

ANDY LEE ROTH is the associate director of Project Censored and co-editor of eight previous editions of the Censored yearbook. He coordinates the Project's Validated Independent News program. His research, on topics ranging from ritual to broadcast news interviews to communities organizing for parklands, has been published in such journals as the International Journal of Press/Politics; Social Studies of Science; Media, Culture & Society; City & Community; and Sociological Theory. He earned a PhD in sociology at the University of California, Los Angeles, and a BA in sociology and anthropology at Haverford College. He has taught courses in sociology at Citrus College, Pomona College, Sonoma State University, the College of Marin, and Bard College, and now lives in Seattle with his sweetheart and their two wonderful cats.

For more information about the editors, to invite them to speak at your school or in your community, or to conduct interviews, please visit projectcensored.org.

ARTIST'S STATEMENT
Anson Stevens-Bollen

Murky, smoke-filled air glows red as a thousand fires creep through the rubble of a city in ruin. On patrol, a unit of war machines dominates the horizon. Guns at the ready, they tear forward with murderous intent.

The illustration I created for this year's *Censored* is an intense bit of fiction inspired by the classic novel *The War of the Worlds* by H.G. Wells, and my intention was to create a scene that accurately displays the truth of battle. The nations of the world are locked in a state of perpetual war. Ruthlessly they invade each other, ripping through smoldering cities that have only recently been mended from previous wars. These armies are commanded to sacrifice themselves and murder others, forced to take orders only made palatable by having had half their own humanity carved away in boot camp. All day, every day, people die due to these mechanized, tech-drenched, half-human soldiers. They plow forward as they consume the same resources that drive their bloodlust. This is a brutal portrait of the monster of war. It is always around, and it is always creating terror. Nobody likes to talk about it and some say it is just make-believe—but it is real, and it is real ugly.

INDEX

Balzac, Honoré de, 22
Banerjee Palmer, Maurice, 176
Banuelos, Erika, 77, 78
Barghouti, Marwan, 134
Barnum, P.T., 153
Batali, Mario, 191
BBC (television and radio network), 173, 244, 248, 251
Beard, Mary, 177
Beaujon, Andrew, 52
Belgium, 22
Beltran, Tonatiuh, 103–17
Bendib, Khalil, 23, 44, 48, 55, 64, 85, 87, 102, 118, 184
Benkler, Yochai, 94n4, 238
Berger, Thomas, 214
Bernstein, Carl, 259n3
Best Buy, 70, 71
Bezos, Jeff, 53, 54
Big Data, see data
Big Pharma, see pharmaceutical industry
Bigelow, Kathryn, 197
Bindel, Julie, 172
Bing (search engine), 262n48
Biometric Intelligence and Identification Technologies, 93
biometrics, 92–94, 106, 107, 211, 212
birth control, 186, 188, see also reproductive rights
Bishop, Rob, 66
Björk, 194
Black Lives Matter, 27, 56, 109
Black Looks: Race and Representation, 174
Blakley, Janelle, 45–47, 235
Bloomberg, 48, 89
Bluetooth, 50
Boccanfuso, Dominique, 70, 71
Bok, Sissela, 263n57
Bol Hyderabad 90.4 FM, 229
Bolivia, 61
Bols, Alex, 165
Booker, Cory, 190
Booz Allen Hamilton, 95n20
Bordell, Will, 45
Border Patrol (US), 154, see also Customs and Border Protection (US)
Boston, MA, 190
Boston Globe, 120, 123, 131, 133
Bourdain, Anthony, 103, 105, 115
BP (formerly British Petroleum), 130
Brazil, 254
Brazilian Network of Environmental Justice, 217
Breaking the Set, 11, 24
Breitbart News, 251
Brexit, 56, 244, 251
Briant, Emma L., 259n9
Britain, see United Kingdom
British Columbia, Canada, 28, 216
British National Party, 172
Brooks, Harrison, 45–47
Brooks, Richard, 173
Brown, Charlie (fictional character), 27

Brown, Jenny, 202
Brown, Michael, 64
Brown University, 144
Brown v. Board of Education, 76
Buhari, Muhammadu, 107
Buist, Steve, 233
Burke, Tarana, 189
Burkina Faso, 44
Burrows, Kenn, 48–52, 57, 58, 68–73, 82–86
Bush, George H.W., 74
Bush, George W., 11, 12
Bush Radio, 229
Business Wire, 94
Butler, Allison, 75–77
BuzzFeed, 30, 196, 251
CACI International, 95n20
California, 24, 67, 70, 79, 233, 253
California Department of Public Health, 50
California State University, East Bay, 67
Cambridge Analytica, 243, 244, 251
campaign fraud, 112, 114
Campion, Jane, 197
Campus Reform, 146
Canada, 28, 29, 51, 61, 62, 174, 214–16, 227, 233–37
Canada Border Services Agency, 174
Canada's Toxic Secret, 236
Canadian Association of Aboriginal Broadcasters, 232
Canadian Association of Journalists (CAJ), 231
Canadian Broadcasting Corporation (CBC), 51
Canadian Centre for Policy Alternatives, 234
Canadian Journalism Foundation, 236
cancer, 49–52, 156, 186
Cannes Film Festival, 196
Canterbury Christ Church University, 172, 173
Cantril, Hadley, 20, 21
capital punishment, 18
capitalism, 12, 29, 40, 150, 152, 153, 156, 157, 203, 225, 228
Card, Jean, 125
Cardiff, Wales, 220
Cardiff University, 173
Cardinal Health, 87
Carl-Klassen, Abigail, 154, 155
Carlin, John P., 60
Carlos, John, 128
Carnegie-Knight Initiative, 232
Carrasco, Tracee, 54
Catalonia, 56
Catholicism, 147
CBS (television network), 18, 19, 21, 33n10, 33n22, 48, 111, 190
celebrity gossip, 104, 107–109, 114, 192, 200, 201, 204, 205
cell phones, 48–52, 210
"PhoneGate," 51
Censored, 20th ann. ed., 223
Censored 1997, 224
Censored 1998, 224
Censored 1999, 224

Censored 2006, 225
Censored 2016, 209
Censored 2017, 209, 225
Censored 2018, 23, 145, 209
censorship, 12, 14, 23–25, 29–31, 56, 89, 123, 141,
146, 156, 157, 238, 249, 250, 254
corporate media, 29, 40, 114, 135, 223, 224,
228
historical, 21, 22, 149–52
of books, 16, 90, 91, 150, 174
of journalists, 52–54, 231
United Kingdom, 167, 169, 171, 176
Center for American Progress (CAP), 186, 187
Center for Biological Diversity, 65
Center for Community Media, 229, 230
Center for Investigative Reporting, 75, 92, 233
Center for Social Media Responsibility, 30
Center for the Study of Women in Television and
Film, 196, 197
Centers for Disease Control and Prevention (US),
86, 108, 26n40
Central Intelligence Agency (CIA), 12, 31, 45–47,
53, 95n17
Centro di Documentazione sui Conflitti Ambien-
tali (CDCA), 217
Chapman University, 145
Charles Koch Foundation (CKF), 143–45
Charlottesville, VA, 63, 121, 124, 125
"Chemical Valley," 235–37
Chertoff, Michael, 12
Chevron, 28, 216
Cheyenne River Nation, 61
Chicago, IL, 213
Chico, CA, 79
child welfare, 22, 77, 78, 87, 147, 154, 186, 187,
189, 192
child health, 50, 51, 108, 109
child labor, 147
child pornography, 70, 71, 191, 262n50
gun violence, 83, 84, 154
immigration, 105–107
China, 13, 210, 254
Chomsky, Noam, 31, 40, 224, 259n3
Chrome (web browser), 255
Chronicle of Higher Education, 171
Church Committee (US), 259n3
Cisco, 26n40
Citizens United v. Federal Election Commission, 129
Citrus College, 60
civil rights, 43, 67, 75–77, 83–86, 89–91, 93, 107,
113, 128, 187, see also human rights; see also
Constitution (US)
Civil Rights Movement, 75
Civil War (US), 27, 142, 149–52
Civilian Marksmanship Program (CMP), 83–86
C.K., Louis (Louis Székely), 190
Clarion-Ledger, 76
Clarke, Charles, 164
class, 151, 224
conflict, 121, 122
middle class, 48, 122, 202

wealthy elites, 13, 29, 119, 122–25, 129, 130,
136n2, 142–45, 203, 204, 225
male privilege, 185, 187–92, 197
wealth increase, 47, 48
working class, 121–23, 125, 126, 153, 169, 191,
201, 202
classism, 21, 120–26, 224
climate change, 57, 58, 68, 69, 98n71, 122, 131,
258
Clinton, Bill, 224
Clinton, Hillary, 11, 56
CLOUD (Clarifying Lawful Overseas Use of Data)
Act, 58–60
CNBC (television station), 251
CNET (media website), 60
CNN (television network), 56, 69, 70, 76, 103,
105, 106, 120, 123, 124, 131, 133, 251, 26n40
Co-Mo Electric Cooperative, 72
Coffee, Ratonya, 225
Cohen, Elliot D., 52–54, 77, 78
Cohen, Michael, 111–14
Cointelpro, 64
Cold War, 12, 213
Coleman, Nathaniel Adam Tobias, 170
College of Marin, 26, 43, 78, 103
College of Western Idaho, 65, 86, 89
College of William & Mary, 27
Collins, John, 26, 119–39
Colombia, 12
colonialism, 19, 61, 120, 132–35, 150, 162, 164,
169, 170, 175, 177, 212, 225, 228, 229
Columbine High School, 83, 85
Commission on Human Rights (Philippines), 44
Committee A on Academic Freedom and Tenure,
146, 148
Committee on Digital, Culture, Media and Sport
(UK Parliament), 254
Committee on Natural Resources (US House of
Representatives), 66
Committee on the Judiciary (US Senate), 263n59
Committee to Protect Journalists, 231
Commonwealth (British), 62
Communications Decency Act (US), 113
communism, 247
community organizing, see activism
Comprehensive Drug Abuse Prevention and
Control Act (US), 88
ComRes, 172
Concordia University, 230, 234, 235
Confederacy (US), 121, 145, 150, 151
Congress (US), 46, 58, 59, 66, 74, 84, 85, 88, 106,
112, 130, 190, 204, 253, 256
Congressional Review Act (CRA), 130
conservatism, 70, 105, 106, 124, 142, 143, 146,
147, 161, 171, 188, 231, 232
alt-right, 64, 125, 186
United Kingdom, 163, 164, 167, 169, 170
Conservative Monday Club (UK), 164
Conservative Party (UK), 164, 170
Constitution (US),
First Amendment, 16, 25, 89, 90, 141, 146,

Fort Lauderdale, FL, 79
Fortune, 71, 224
fossil fuels, 49, 57, 58, 135, *see also* oil and gas industry
FOSTA (Allow States and Victims to Fight Online Sex Trafficking Act) (US), 112–14
Fox News, 53, 54, 64, 81, 85, 109, 112, 120–22, 125, 131, 133, 171, 187, 188
fracking, 11
France, 22, 51, 109, 244, 251, 254
Franken, Al, 28, 190
Frechette, Julie, 28, 185–208
free market ideology, 142–44, *see also* Koch brothers
free speech, 27, 28, 52–54, 90, 113, 141, 147, 165–70, 179, *see also* Constitution (US)
    effects of terrorism, 161–63
    no-platforming, 163, 164, 171–74, 178
    safe spaces, 173–76, 178
    trigger warnings, 176–78
Free Speech TV, 158
Free Speech University Rankings (FSUR), 168
Freedom Network USA, 113
Freedom Riders, 75
Freeman, James, 54
Frontline, 109, 110, 202
Gallagher, Sean, 27, 161–83
Galton, Francis, 170
Game of Thrones, 198
Ganges River, 62
Garnet, Henry Highland, 150
Gascon, Jose Luis Martin, 44
Gates, Henry Louis, Jr., 76
Gaudet, Hazel, 20, 21, 33n22
Gaza, Israel/Palestine, 12, 148
Gee, Alistair, 80
Geek Squad, 70, 71
gender parity, 192, *see also* feminism; *see also* sexism; *see also* women
geographic information systems (GIS), 213, 215, 216
George Mason University, 144, 145
Georgia, 67
German Marshall Fund, 255
Germany, 131, 244, 251, 254
Gerwig, Greta, 197
Gesenhues, Amy, 262n48
Giants: The Global Power Elite, 28
Gibbons, Jacqueline, 103–17
Gillibrand, Kirsten, 190
Gilmour, Matt, 235
Gimlet Media, 150
Gimson, Sally, 27, 161–83
Giuliani, Rudy, 112
Global Alliance for Incinerator Alternatives (GAIA), 217
Global Engagement Center (GEC), 253, 264n80
global gag rule, 185, 186
Global Newsstream, 38
global positioning systems (GPS), 28, 213, 216
Global Reporting Centre, 232, 233

Global South, 131, 150
Global TV, 234
global warming, 57, *see also* climate change
GlobaLeaks, 211
Goddard, Gary, 191
Golden Globe Awards, 111, 191, 192
Goldfield, Eleanor, 27, 141, 142, 155–58
Goldsmiths, University of London, 175, 177
Goodlatte, Bob, 106
Google, 24, 25, 30, 95n117, 131, 154, 209, 210, 246, 248, 249, 251, 254, 255, 262n48, 262n50
GotNews, 263n64
Gould, Rand, 89, 90
GQ (magazine), 128
Grammy Awards, 111
Gramsci, Antonio, 203
Granados, Maria, 103–17
Grant, Trevor, 235
Grassroots Leadership, 154
Greece, 82, 244
Greene, Robyn, 59
Greer, Germaine, 172–74
Grover's Mill, NJ, 19
Guardian, 43–45, 47, 78–81, 88, 90, 91, 164, 174, 177, 251
Guatemala, 109, 232
Guess, Andrew, 18
GuildHE (UK education organization), 165
Gulf (oil company), 214
Guliani, Neema Singh, 60
Gullah peoples, 152
gun violence, 27, 84, 85, 91, 92, 153, 154, 157, 246, 247
    gun control, 18, 83–86, 104, 154, 157
Gurbuz, Izzy, 177
Gust, Onni, 177
Gyimah, Sam, 179
Gyldensted, Cathrine, 69
Ha, Thu-Huong, 90
Haidt, Jonathan, 178
Hain, Alyssa, 81, 82
Haiti, 105, 106
Hale, Courtney, 89–91
Halifax International Security Forum, 249
Hamilton, Canada, 233
Hamilton, Christina, 103–17
Hamilton 68 Dashboard, 12, 255, 265n94
Hamilton Spectator, 233
Handy, Nettye, 152
Hanrahan, John, 53
Harris, Eric, 83
Harsløf, Ivan, 224
Harvard University, 68, 92
hashtivism, 28, 104, 194, 206
Hatch, Orrin, 60
Hatewatch, 63
Head Start (US federal program), 187
healthcare, 14, 67, 122, 186, 213
    spending, 81, 82
Healthcare Finance, 82
Hechinger Report, 75, 76

112–14
sex trafficking, 22, 112–14
sexism, 20, 21, 147, 149–52, 161, 162, 168, 185,
192, see also film industry
#TimesUp, 185, 192, 193, 198, 199,
204–206
sexual harassment and assault, 28, 34n28, 77, 112,
113, 125, 187–90, 201–206, see also #MeToo;
see also #TimesUp
abuser justifications, 193, 194, 198–200, 203
anti-harassment plan, 191, 192
economics and consent, 193–96, 205
government officials, 67, 187, 190, 192, 193
Shafir, Gershon, 134
Shah, Raj, 105
Shehadeh, Raja, 134
Shell (oil company), 214
Shiva, Vandana, 58
Shorrock, Tim, 46, 47, 95n20
Showing Up for Racial Justice, 109
Siddiquee, Imran, 200
Silicon Valley, CA, 209, 210
Simmons, Jeff, 63–65
Simmons, Russell, 190
Simon, Paul, 85
Sisi, Abdel Fattah el-, 44
Skidmore, Mark, 73–75
Slate (media website), 18, 20, 91
Slaughter, Jane, 201, 202
slavery, 22, 27, 109, 169, 212
American history, 149–52
slave rebellions, 150, 151
Slipman, Sue, 164
Smith, Brad, 60
Smith, Evan, 164
Smith, L. Joseph, 58–60
Smith, Tommie, 128
Snapchat, 59
Snopes, 24, 255
Snow, Isabelle (Izzy), 78–81, 103–17
Snowden, Edward, 53, 209, 211
"snowflakes," 161, 168, 176
Social Democratic Party (SDP) (UK), 164
social media, 18, 30, 52–54, 59, 179, 209, 210,
236, 243, see also Internet
academia, 146–48
bans, 52–54
fact-checking, 253–55
fake accounts, 250, 251
influence on elections, 245, 246, 249, 251,
252, 254
Information Warfare (IW), 250–52, 262n52
trolls, 12, 30, 248, 251
Social Sciences and Humanities Research
Council, 234
socialism, 122
Society of Professional Journalists, 24, 34n35
Socolow, Michael J., 19–21
Solomon, Norman, 55
Sonntag, Patti, 234, 238
Sonoma State University, 67, 225

Sosa, Anabel, 89–91
South (US), 142
South Africa, 162, 163, 211, 229, 254
South Korea, 254
Southern Poverty Law Center (SPLC), 63, 75, 76
Southernmost Homeless Assistance League, 79
Southwestern Border Sheriffs' Coalition (SBSC),
93
Spacey, Kevin, 190
Spagnolo, J., 27, 141, 142, 152–55
Spain, 244
Spanish–American War, 84
Spayd, Liz, 134
Speakeasy (London School of Economics organi-
zation), 176
Speech, Privacy, and Technology Project, 93
Spiked, 162, 167, 168
Sports Illustrated, 128
Sputnik (media website and radio network), 56,
249
Sri Lanka, 44
St. George's House, 175
St. Petersburg, Russia, 251
Standing Rock Nation, 61
Stanley, Jason, 171
Stanton, Russ, 233
Stead, W.T., 22, 34n28
Stein, Jill, 11
Stevens-Bollen, Anson, 17
Stewart, Breanna, 191
Stored Communications Act, 59
Students Not Suspects, 167
Sunday Times, 177
Superfund (US federal program), 156
Supreme Court (US), 204
Surface, Bethany, 48–52, 82–86
surveillance, 11, 89–91, see also intelligence ap-
paratus (US)
anti-surveillance activism, 211, 212, 219
biometric identification, 92–94, 106, 107,
211, 212
digital, 28, 45, 46, 58–60, 70, 71, 95n17,
210–13
university emails, 163
SurveyMonkey, 262n48
Sutherland Springs, TX, 85, 246
Swaine, Jon, 90
Sweden, 254
Sweeney, David, 190
Syracuse University, 63, 144
Syria, 13, 82
Tab (University College London newspaper), 170
Taibbi, Matt, 56
Tallinn Manual Process, 256
Tampa Bay, FL, 92
Tampa Bay Times, 92
Tanasescu, Mihnea, 61, 62
Tapper, Jake, 12
Tarbell, Ida, 149, 150
Tatchell, Peter, 172, 173
Taylor, Keeanga-Yamahtta, 170

Te Urewera Act (New Zealand), 62
Tea Party, 122
Telegraph, 170
teleSUR, 13, 88
television (TV), 40, 95n17, 103, 111, 114, 141, 142,
    189, 196–99, 204, 205, 225, 233, 234, 236,
    238
terrorism, 63–65, 161–63, 166, 167, 172, 253
Texas, 67, 90, 154, 246
Texas Department of Family and Protective
    Services, 154
Thatcher, Margaret, 165
Thomas, Clarence, 203, 204
Tiede, Hans-Joerg, 27, 141, 142, 146–49
Times (London), 167
Times Higher Education, 170
#TimesUp movement, 28, 185, 191–94, 202–205
Title X (US federal program), 186
Today (television show), 190
Tories, *see* Conservative Party (UK)
Toronto, Canada, 174
Toronto Star, 234
torture, 11, 64
Tractica, 93
Tranchina, Nicole, 225
TransCanada, 216
transgender people, 113, 162, 172–74, 187, *see also*
    LGBTQ+ people
trauma, 152, 153, 155, 177, 178
Tribal Digital Village initiative, 72
Trillium, 109
Trotsky, Leon, 163, 164
Trump, Donald, 11–13, 16, 23, 25, 27, 31, 44, 48,
    56, 63, 64, 68, 70, 72, 88, 94, 121, 122, 135,
    171, 184, 187, 188, 206
    NFL response, 127
    policy, 55, 105, 129, 131, 134
    relationship with the media, 12, 104, 105,
        120, 123, 124, 141, 251
    scandals, 26, 55, 104–107, 111–14, 125
    sexual harassment allegations, 190, 192, 193
    war on women, 185, 186
Trust Project, 255
"truth decay," *see* fake news
Truthdig, 54, 55
Truthout, 76, 83
Tucker, Ky, 65, 66
Turner, Brock, 199
Turner, Camilla, 170
Twitter, 30, 56, 104–106, 148, 187, 246, 251, 254,
    255
Uganda, 77
Ukraine, 252
UltraViolet (feminist organization), 188
Uncivil, 27, 141, 142, 149–52
UNICEF (United Nations Children's Fund), 77
Union of Jewish Students (UK), 164
unions, 211, 216, 231, *see also* labor rights
    student unions, 28, 161–64, 168, 172, 173,
        175–77
    union busting, 165

Unist'ot'en peoples, 28, 216
United Airlines, 109, 110
United Kingdom (UK), 22, 28, 33n7, 62, 69,
    161–83, 244, 251, 254
United States Postal Service (USPS), 89, 90
University College London (UCL), 166, 170
University of Alberta, 215
University of Arizona, 144
University of British Columbia (UBC), 232, 234,
    235, 237
University of California, Berkeley, 27, 133
University of California, Davis, 230
University of California, San Francisco (UCSF), 81
University of Cambridge, 169, 177
University of Edinburgh, 177
University of Essex, 259n9
University of Hyderabad, 229
University of Illinois, 148
University of Kentucky, 144
University of Manchester, 172, 177
University of Massachusetts Amherst, 75
University of Michigan, 30
University of Nottingham, 177
University of Oxford, 162, 168, 169, 177
University of Regina, 29, 45, 227, 234, 236
University of Southern California (USC), 233
University of the Western Cape (UWC), 229
University of Utah, 144
University of Vermont, 49, 54, 70, 89
University of Virginia, 27
UnKoch My Campus, 27, 141–45
UPS (United Parcel Service), 210
Urban Poor Consortium (UPC), 219
US Indigenous Data Sovereignty Network, 214
U.S. News & World Report, 82
USAWatchdog, 73
USA PATRIOT Act, 12
USA Today, 62, 81
Ut, Nick, 262n50
Utah, 66
Utah Test and Training Range, 66
V for Vendetta, 157
Validated Independent News (VIN), 37–41, 227,
    228, 232, 252, 253
Vallance-Jones, Fred, 231
Van Boekhout, Kelly, 67, 68
van Pelt, Lucy (fictional character), 27
Vanstone, Ellen, 198, 199
Vardaman, James K., 76
Vault 7, 45, 46
Veles, Macedonia, 251
Venezuela, 13, 14
Verizon, 210
veterans, 127
Vice (media website, magazine, and television
    network), 13
Vietnam War, 262n50
Vizetelly, Henry, 22
Voice of Detroit, 90
Volkswagen, 51
von Trier, Lars, 194

Vox, 13, 104
Wake Forest University, 144
Wall Street, 218
Wall Street Journal, 52, 54, 86, 111, 120, 131
Walter Cronkite School of Journalism and Mass
  Communication, 232
Wang, Peter, 84
war, 11–14, 27, 65, 66, 83–86, 149–52, 212, 225,
  see also veterans; *see also* weapons
War of the Worlds (book), 17, 19, 21, 32, 34n25,
  34n27
"War of the Worlds" (radio program), 18–20,
  30, 32
Warren, Rossalyn, 252
Warzel, Charlie, 30, 31
Washington (state), 66
Washington, DC, 11, 12, 76, 86, 132, 184, 185, 202,
  203, 254
Washington-Baltimore News Guild, 53, 231
Washington Post, 13, 24, 25, 27, 47, 52–54, 59, 62,
  71, 76, 77, 81, 82, 85, 86, 104, 120, 122, 123,
  128, 129, 131, 133, 134, 190, 210, 231, 232, 251
Washingtonian, 52–54
waste management, 57, 81, 82
WBUR (radio station), 190
wealth inequality, *see* class
Weave News, 26, 120
Webb, Whitney, 53
Webster, Stormi, 107, 109
Weinberger, Sharon, 63
Weinstein, Harvey, 28, 188, 194, 195
Weinstein Company, 188
Welles, Orson, 19–21, 33n10
Wells, H.G., 17, 19, 21, 33n8, 34n27
weapons, 12, 13, 47, 56–58, 66, 74, 83–86, 91, 92,
  153, 154, 212, 246, 247, 251
Wertmüller, Lina, 197
Wessler, Nathan, 93
West Bank, Israel/Palestine, 14
West Palm Beach, FL, 79
West Virginia, 87
Western Carolina University, 144
Wet'suwet'en First Nation, 216
Whanganui River, 61, 62
White House, 23, 103–107, 141
White House Correspondents' Dinner, 103
white supremacists, 63–65, 121, 124, 125, 145
Whole Story (media website), 68
Wi-Fi, 48, 50, 52
WikiLeaks, 45–47, 95n17, 261n46
Wikipedia, 248, 252
Wilders, Geert, 174
Wiles, Tay, 66
Williams, Rob, 48–52, 54–56, 70, 71, 89–91
Williams, Serena, 108
Williams, Zoe, 174
Windows (operating system), 95n17
Winfrey, Oprah, 191
Winter, Jana, 63
wireless technology, 48–52, 72
  and children, 50, 51

Wisconsin, 61
Wittgenstein, Ludwig, 25
Wolff, Michael, 23
Wolff, Michelle, 103
women, 108, 125, 173, 185, 188, 189, 203, 204
  health, 49, 50, 185–87
  power of storytelling, 153, 196–98
  rights, *see* feminism
  violence against, 172, 177, 187, 190, 199,
    206, *see also* sexual harassment and as-
    sault; *see also* #MeToo movement
  work, 28, 127, 149, 151, 186, 195, 196,
    200–202, 205
Women, Infants, and Children (WIC) (US federal
  program), 187
Women's March, 123, 185, 204
Women's National Basketball Association, 191
Wong, Katie, 103–17
Woolley, Samuel C., 246
Worcester State University, 230
World Beyond War, 83–85
World Justice Project (WJP), 43–45
World Rainforest Movement, 217
World War I, 212
World War II, 13
World Wide Web Consortium (W3C), 255
WUSF (radio station), 92
Wyden, Ron, 113
xenophobia, 185, 203
Xi Jinping, 254
Yale University, 18, 43, 68, 69, 171
Yamuna River, 62
Yandex (search engine), 248
Yang, Amber, 57, 58, 68–73
Yanukovych, Viktor, 252
Yellin, Jared, 75–77
Yelp (reviews website), 113
Yemen, 156
YES! Magazine, 61, 62
young people, 47, 51, 76, 83–86, 166, 189, 191,
  194, 198, 199, *see also* child welfare; *see also*
  education; *see also* schools
YouTube, 261n40, 262n50
Zinke, Ryan, 104
Zionism, 132, 133, 164
Zola, Émile, 22
Zucker, Kyle, 43–45, 103–17
Zuckerberg, Mark, 263n59

PROJECT CENSORED THE MOVIE
ENDING THE REIGN OF JUNK FOOD NEWS

AVAILABLE AT VIMEO, ITUNES, GOOGLE PLAY, AND
AMAZON PRIME VIDEO, STREAMING OR DOWNLOAD.
ALSO AVAILABLE FOR PURCHASE IN DVD FORMAT!
SEE PROJECTCENSOREDTHEMOVIE.COM FOR DETAILS.

Determined to break the grip of Junk Food News on the American public, two California fathers uncover the true agenda of the corporate media while they investigate the importance of a free and independent press.

This award-winning documentary, six years in the making, takes an in-depth look at what is wrong with the news media in the US and what we can do about it. The film highlights the work of forty-year veteran media democracy organization Project Censored and their commitment to providing solutions through media literacy and critical thinking education while celebrating the best in underreported, independent journalism.

Project Censored: The Movie, made by former PC Sonoma State University student Doug Hecker and longtime Project supporter Christopher Oscar, features original interviews and montages (edited by Mike Fischer) about the Project and media censorship with Noam Chomsky, Howard Zinn, Daniel Ellsberg, Michael Parenti, Oliver Stone, Cynthia McKinney, Nora Barrows-Friedman, Peter Kuznick, Khalil Bendib, Abby Martin, Project-affiliated faculty and students, as well as Project founder Carl Jensen, former director and president of the Media Freedom Foundation Peter Phillips, current director Mickey Huff, and associate director Andy Lee Roth. Plus much, much more!